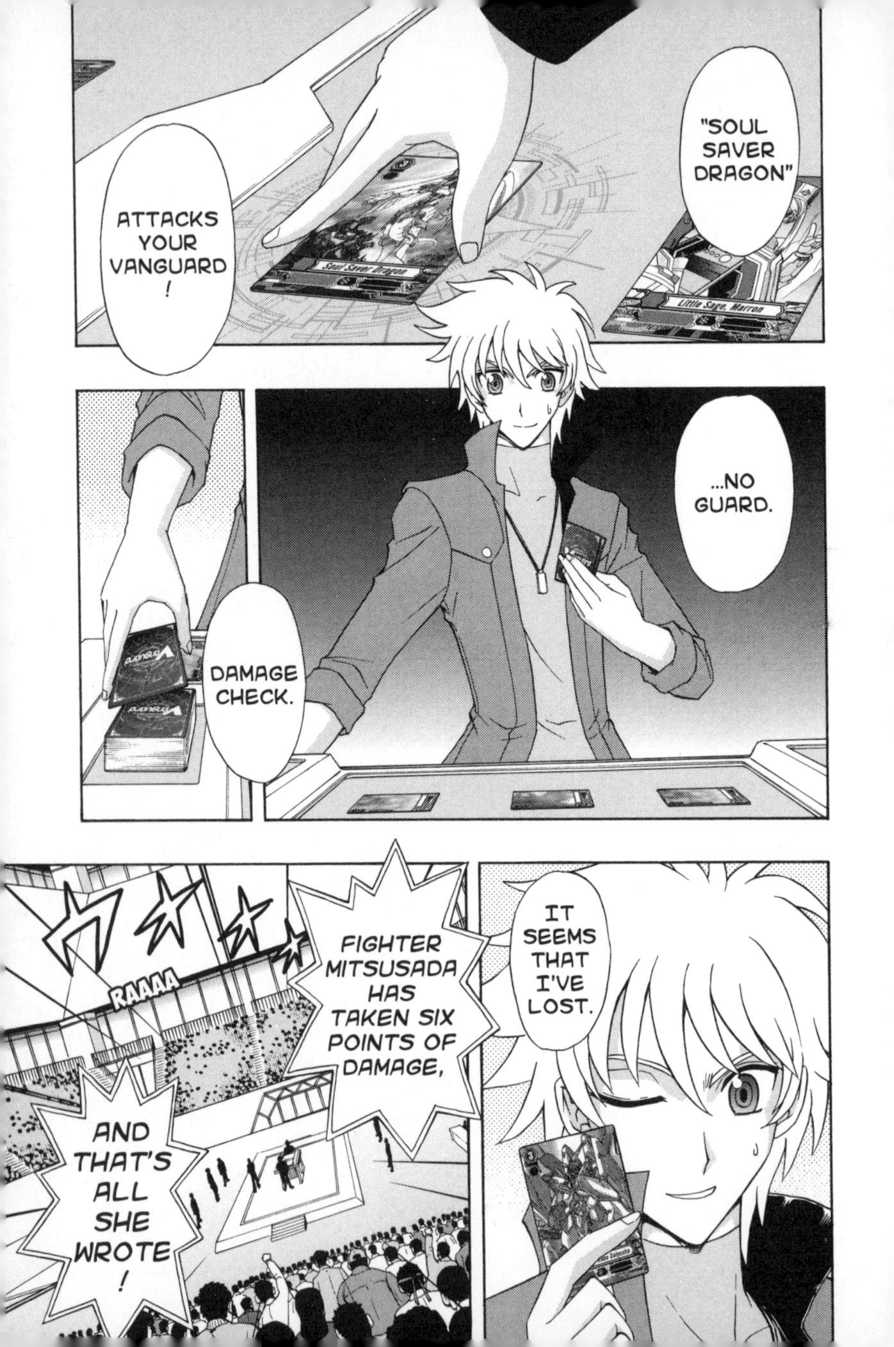
"SOUL SAVER DRAGON"
Soul Saver Dragon
Little Sage, Marron
ATTACKS YOUR VANGUARD!
...NO GUARD.
DAMAGE CHECK.
IT SEEMS THAT I'VE LOST.
RAAAA
FIGHTER MITSUSADA HAS TAKEN SIX POINTS OF DAMAGE,
AND THAT'S ALL SHE WROTE!

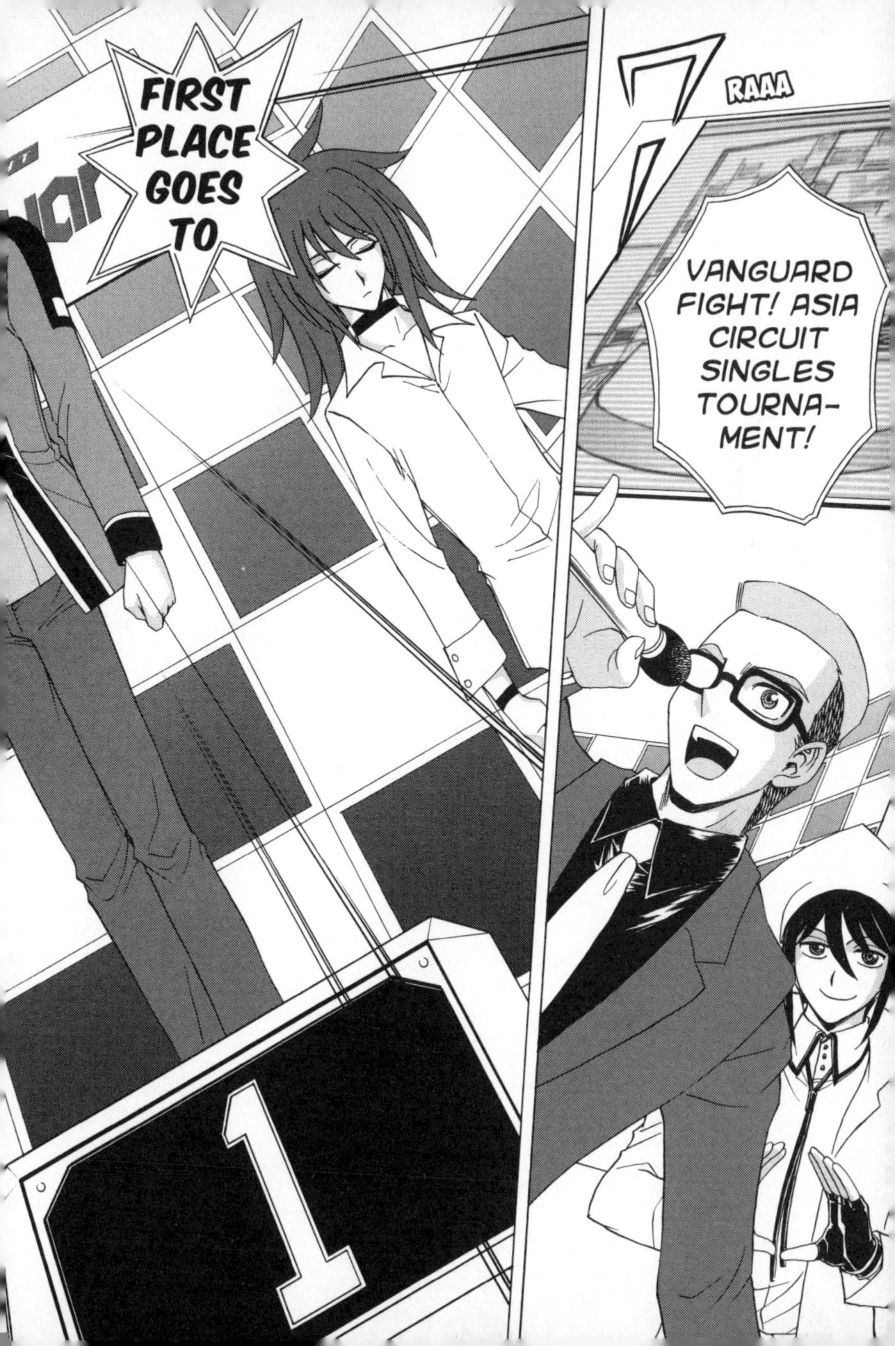
RAAA
VANGUARD FIGHT! ASIA CIRCUIT SINGLES TOURNA-MENT!
FIRST PLACE GOES TO

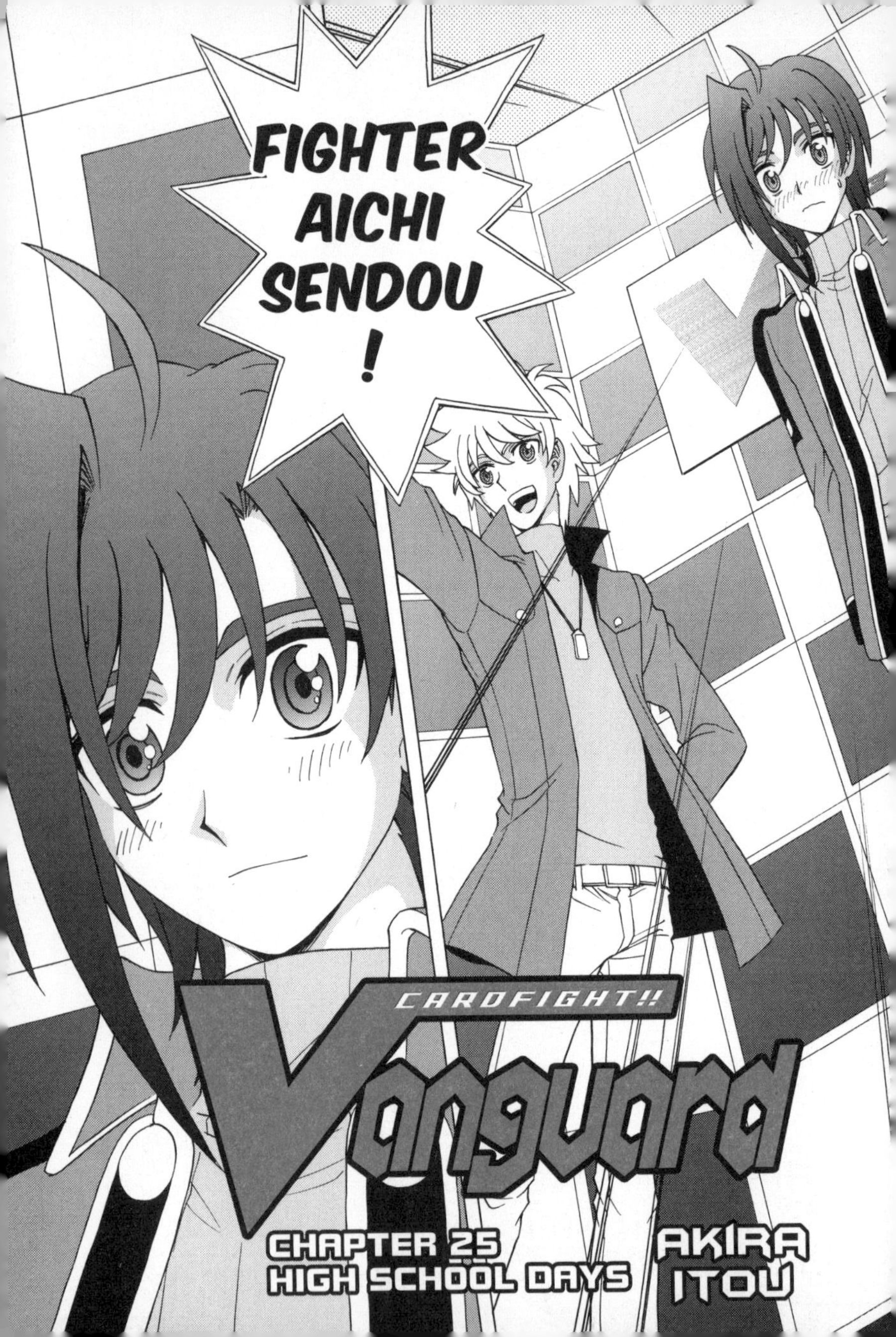
FIGHTER AICHI SENDOU !
CARDFIGHT!! Vanguard
CHAPTER 25
HIGH SCHOOL DAYS
AKIRA ITOU

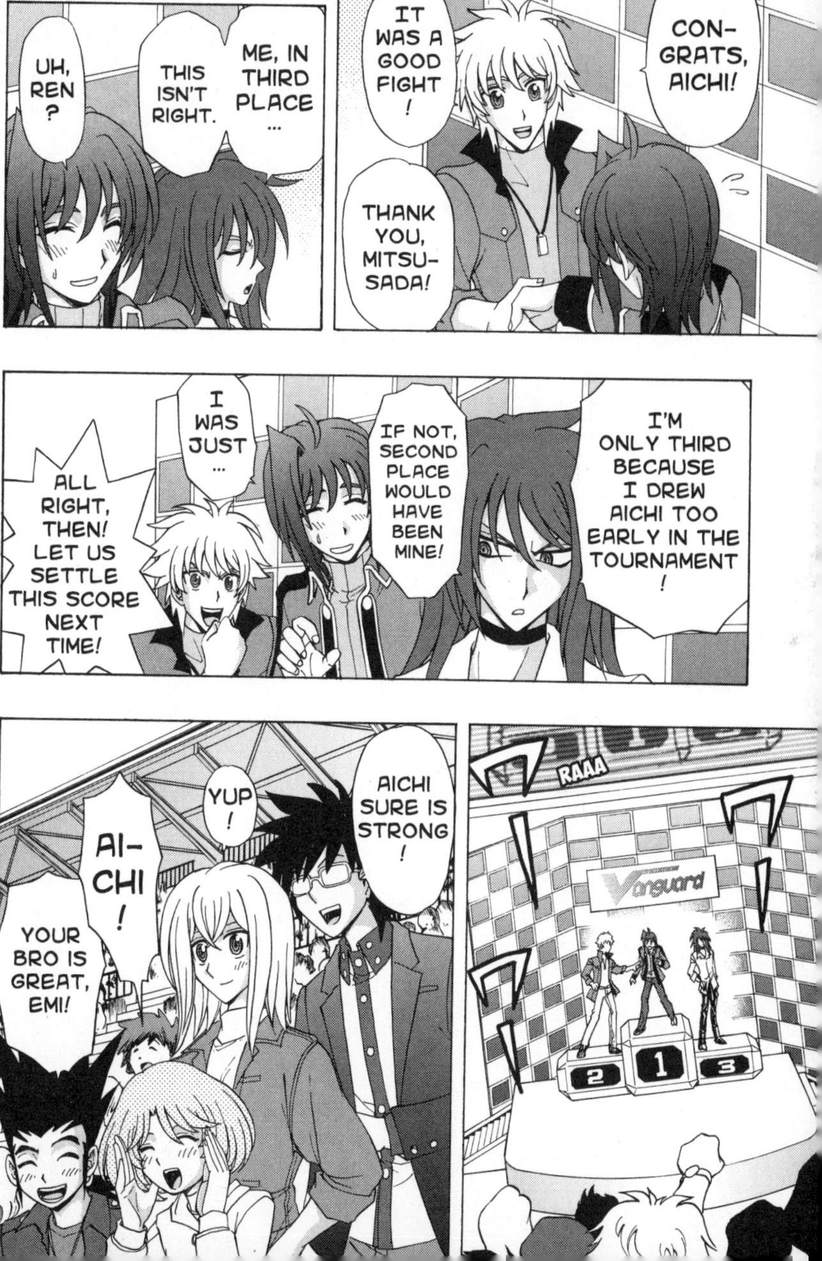
CON-GRATS, AICHI!
IT WAS A GOOD FIGHT!
THANK YOU, MITSU-SADA!
ME, IN THIRD PLACE...
THIS ISN'T RIGHT.
UH, REN?
I'M ONLY THIRD BECAUSE I DREW AICHI TOO EARLY IN THE TOURNAMENT!
IF NOT, SECOND PLACE WOULD HAVE BEEN MINE!
I WAS JUST...
ALL RIGHT, THEN! LET US SETTLE THIS SCORE NEXT TIME!
RAAA
Vanguard
2
1
3
AICHI SURE IS STRONG!
YUP!
AI-CHI!
YOUR BRO IS GREAT, EMI!

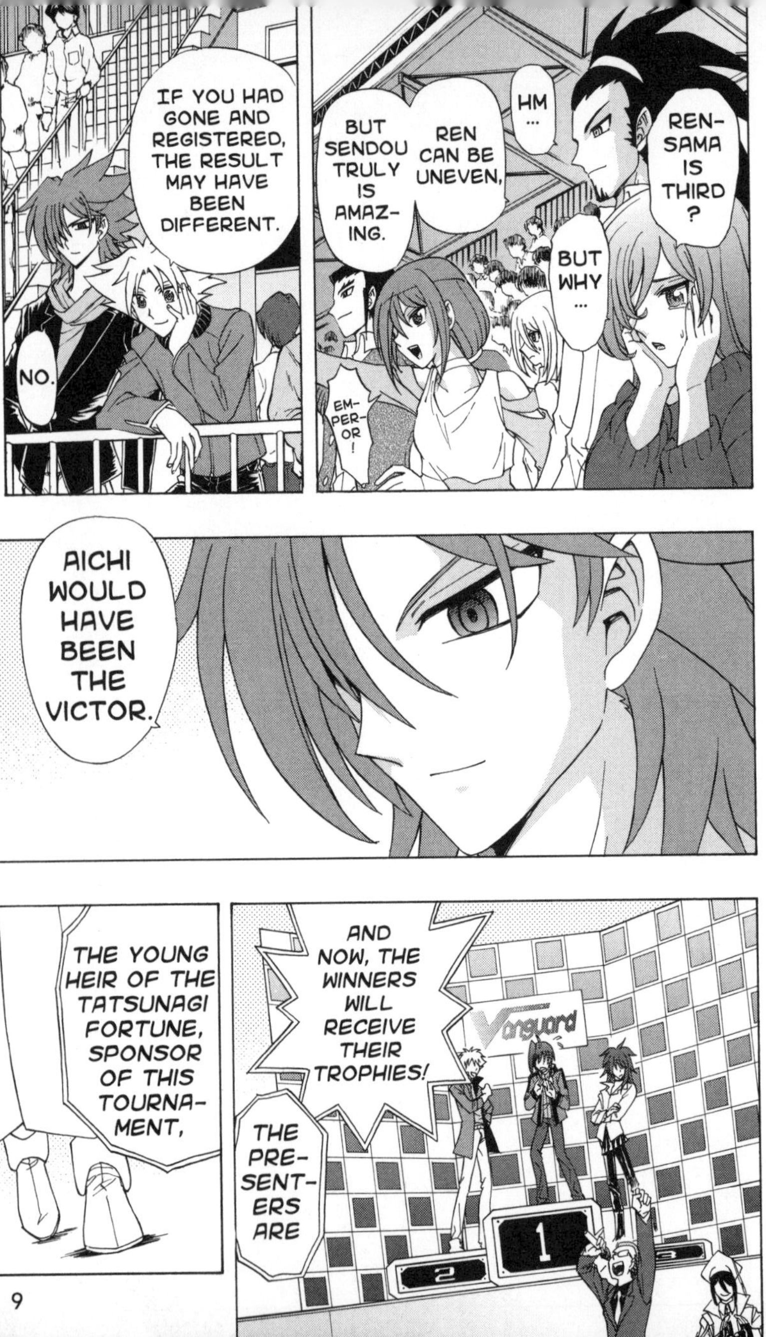
REN-SAMA IS THIRD?
HM...
BUT WHY...
REN CAN BE UNEVEN,
BUT SENDOU TRULY IS AMAZ-ING.
EMPER-OR!
IF YOU HAD GONE AND REGISTERED, THE RESULT MAY HAVE BEEN DIFFERENT.
NO.
AICHI WOULD HAVE BEEN THE VICTOR.
AND NOW, THE WINNERS WILL RECEIVE THEIR TROPHIES!
Vanguard
THE PRE-SENT-ERS ARE
1
2
3
THE YOUNG HEIR OF THE TATSUNAGI FORTUNE, SPONSOR OF THIS TOURNA-MENT,

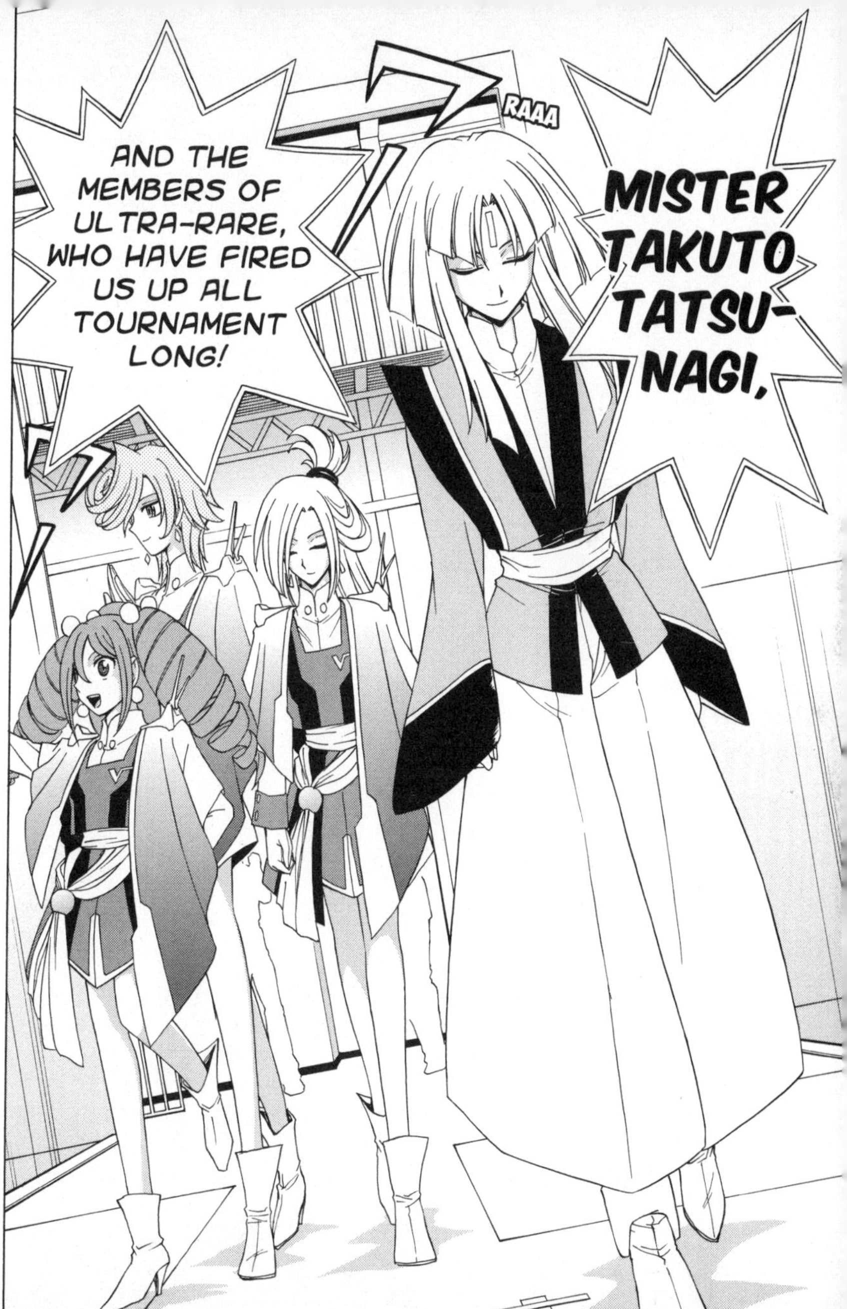
MISTER TAKUTO TATSU-NAGI,
RAAA
AND THE MEMBERS OF ULTRA-RARE, WHO HAVE FIRED US UP ALL TOURNAMENT LONG!

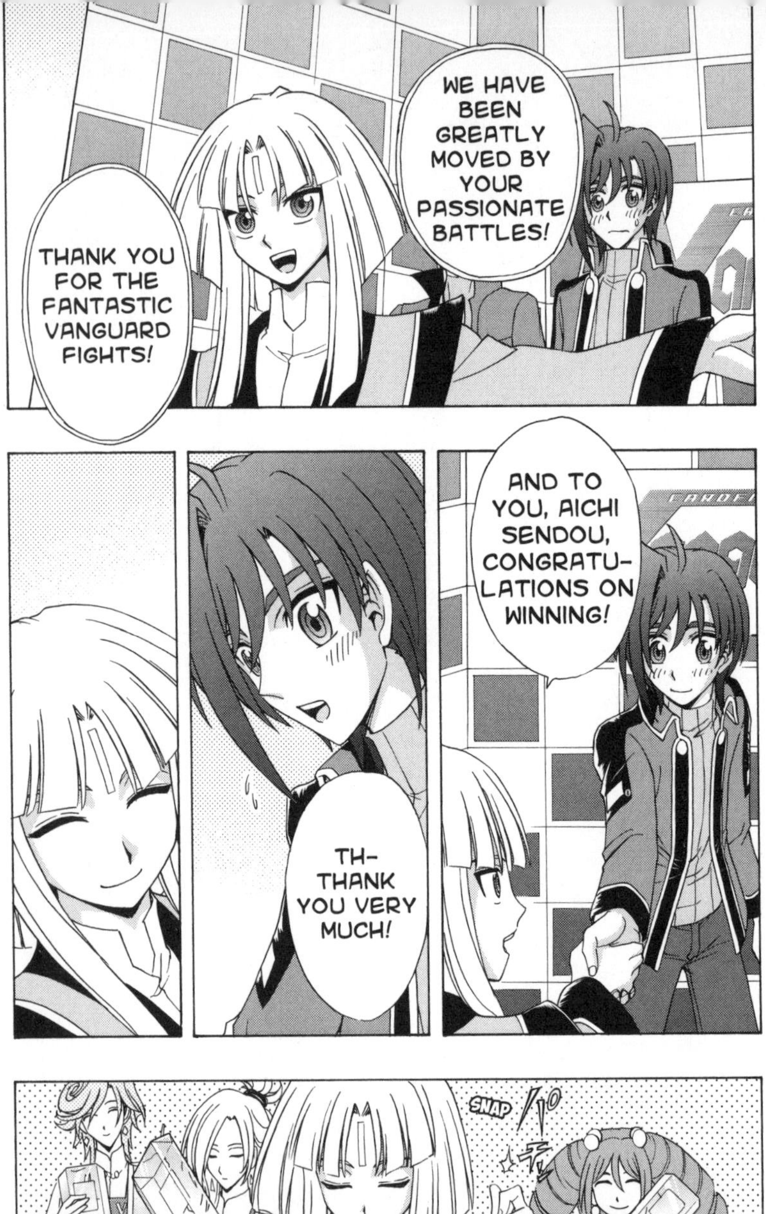
WE HAVE BEEN GREATLY MOVED BY YOUR PASSIONATE BATTLES!
THANK YOU FOR THE FANTASTIC VANGUARD FIGHTS!
AND TO YOU, AICHI SENDOU, CONGRATU-LATIONS ON WINNING!
TH-THANK YOU VERY MUCH!
SNAP

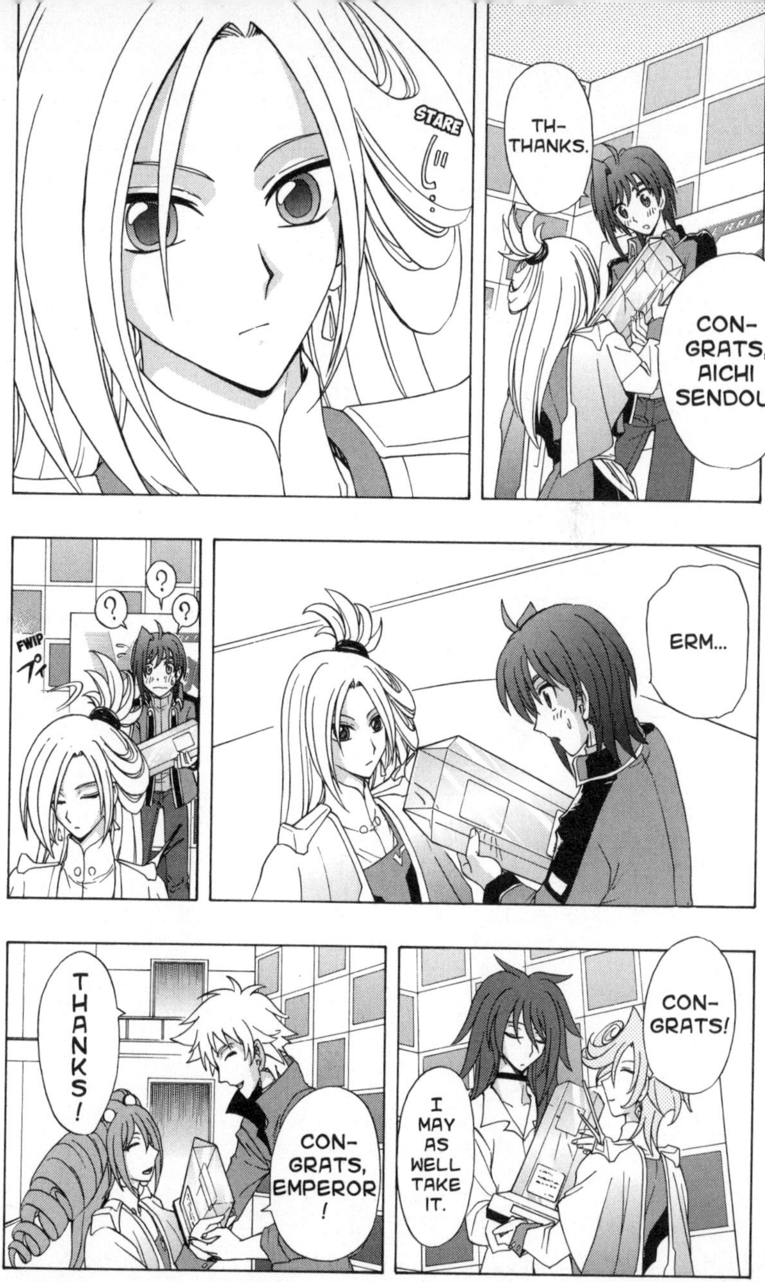
CON-GRATS, AICHI SENDOU.
TH-THANKS.
STARE
じー
ERM...
?
?
?
FWIP
プイ
CON-GRATS!
I MAY AS WELL TAKE IT.
CON-GRATS, EMPEROR!
THANKS!

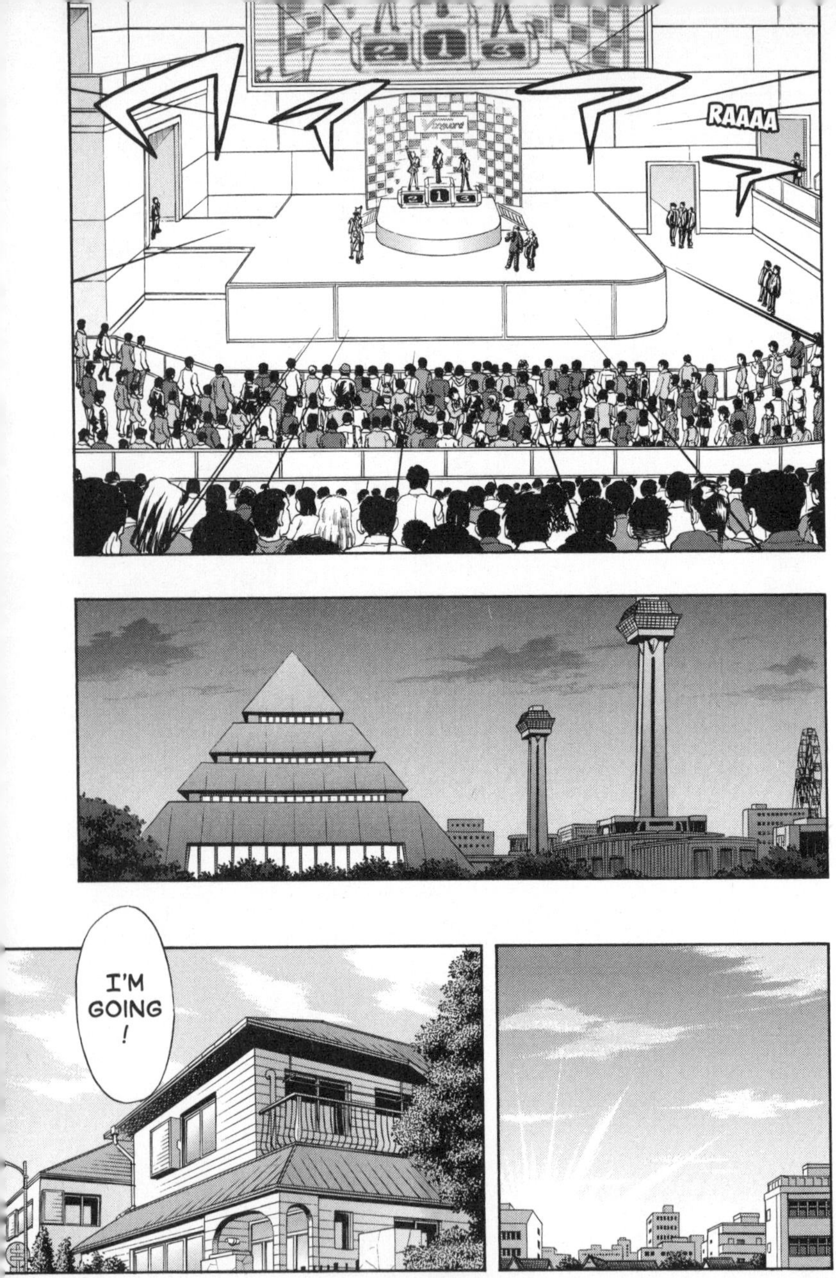
RAAAA
I'M GOING !

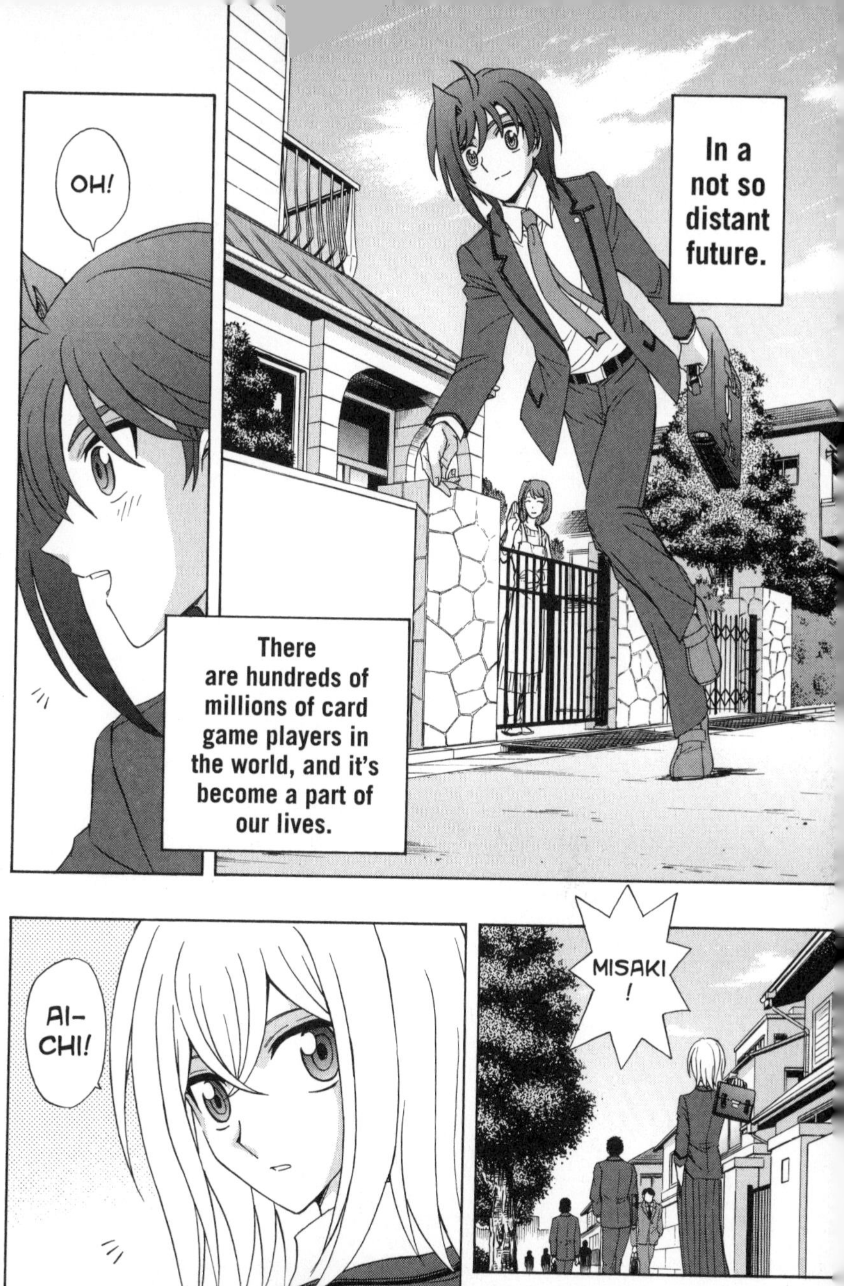
In a not so distant future.
There are hundreds of millions of card game players in the world, and it's become a part of our lives.
OH!
MISAKI!
AI-CHI!

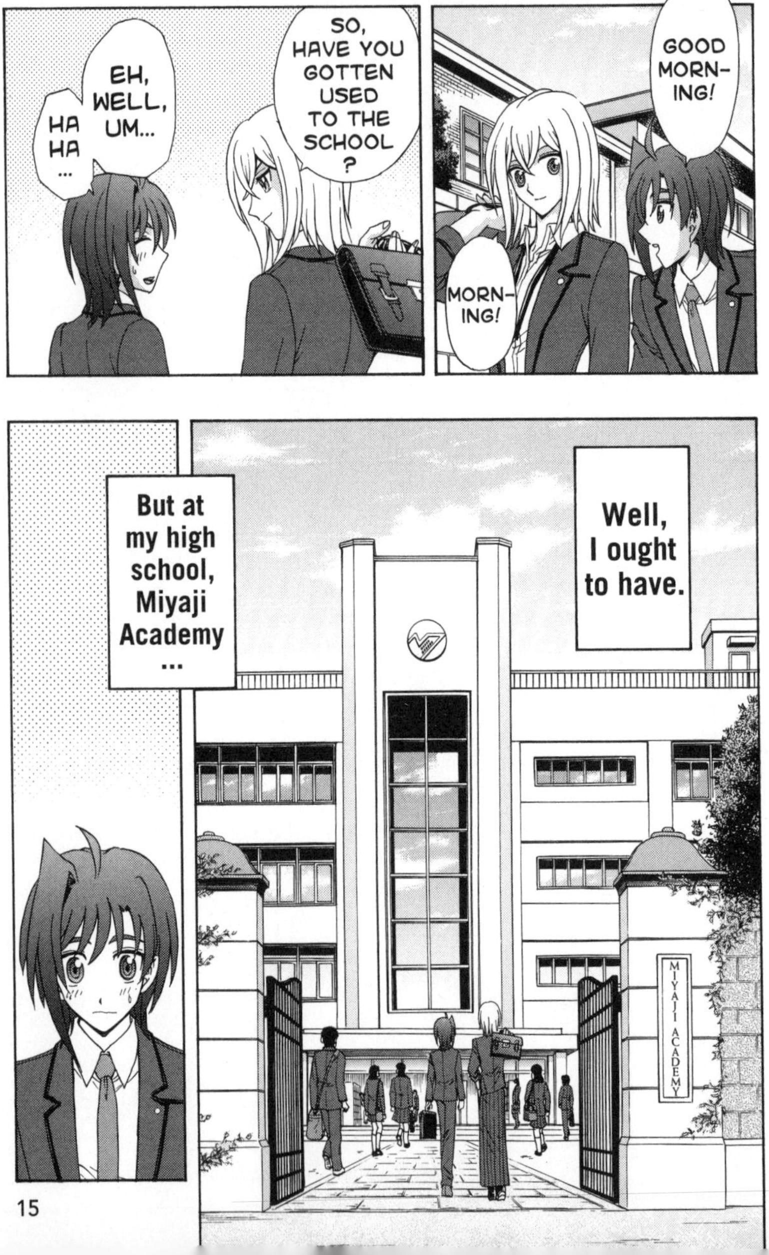
GOOD MORN-ING!
MORN-ING!
SO, HAVE YOU GOTTEN USED TO THE SCHOOL ?
EH, WELL, UM...
HA HA ...
Well, I ought to have.
MIYAJI ACADEMY
But at my high school, Miyaji Academy ...

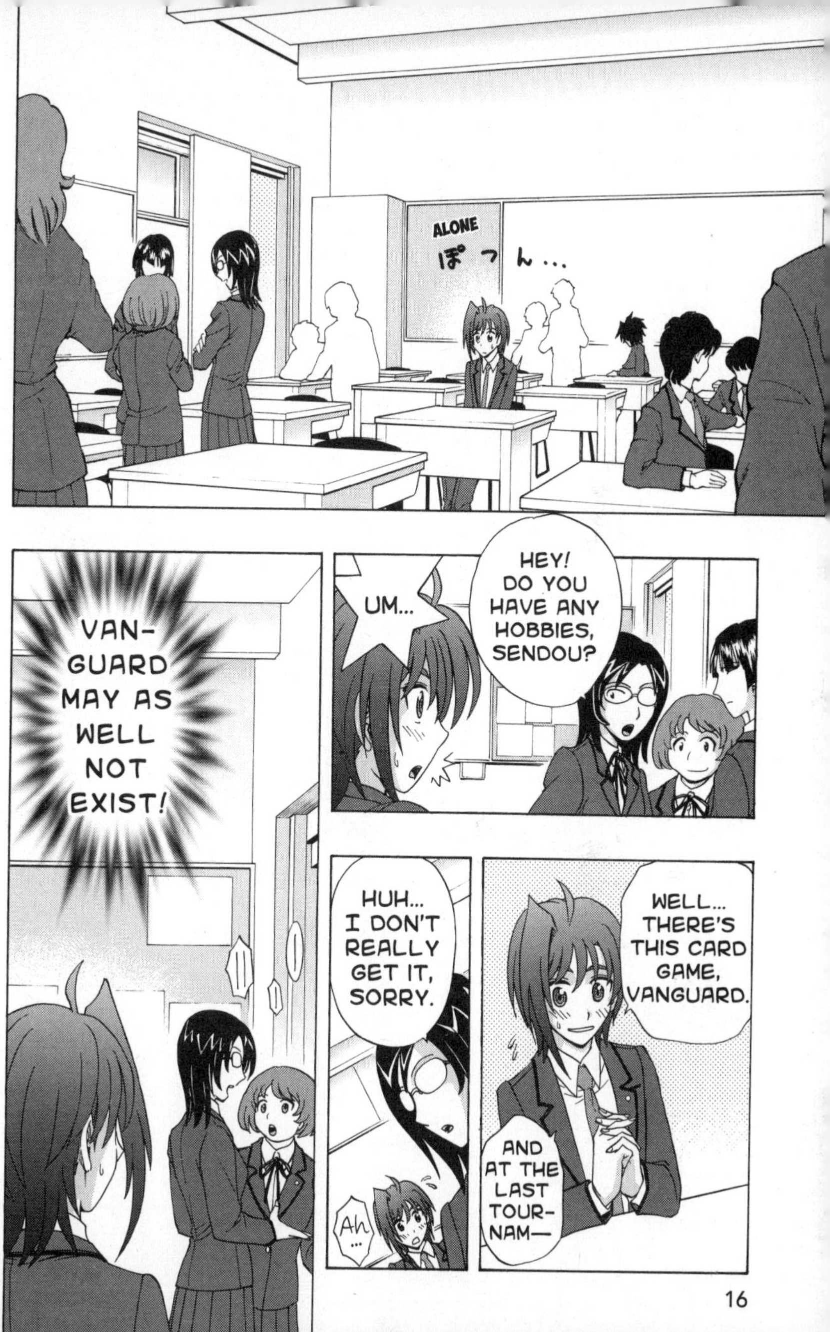
ALONE
ぽつん…
HEY! DO YOU HAVE ANY HOBBIES, SENDOU?
UM...
WELL... THERE'S THIS CARD GAME, VANGUARD.
AND AT THE LAST TOUR-NAM—
HUH... I DON'T REALLY GET IT, SORRY.
Ah...
VAN-GUARD MAY AS WELL NOT EXIST!

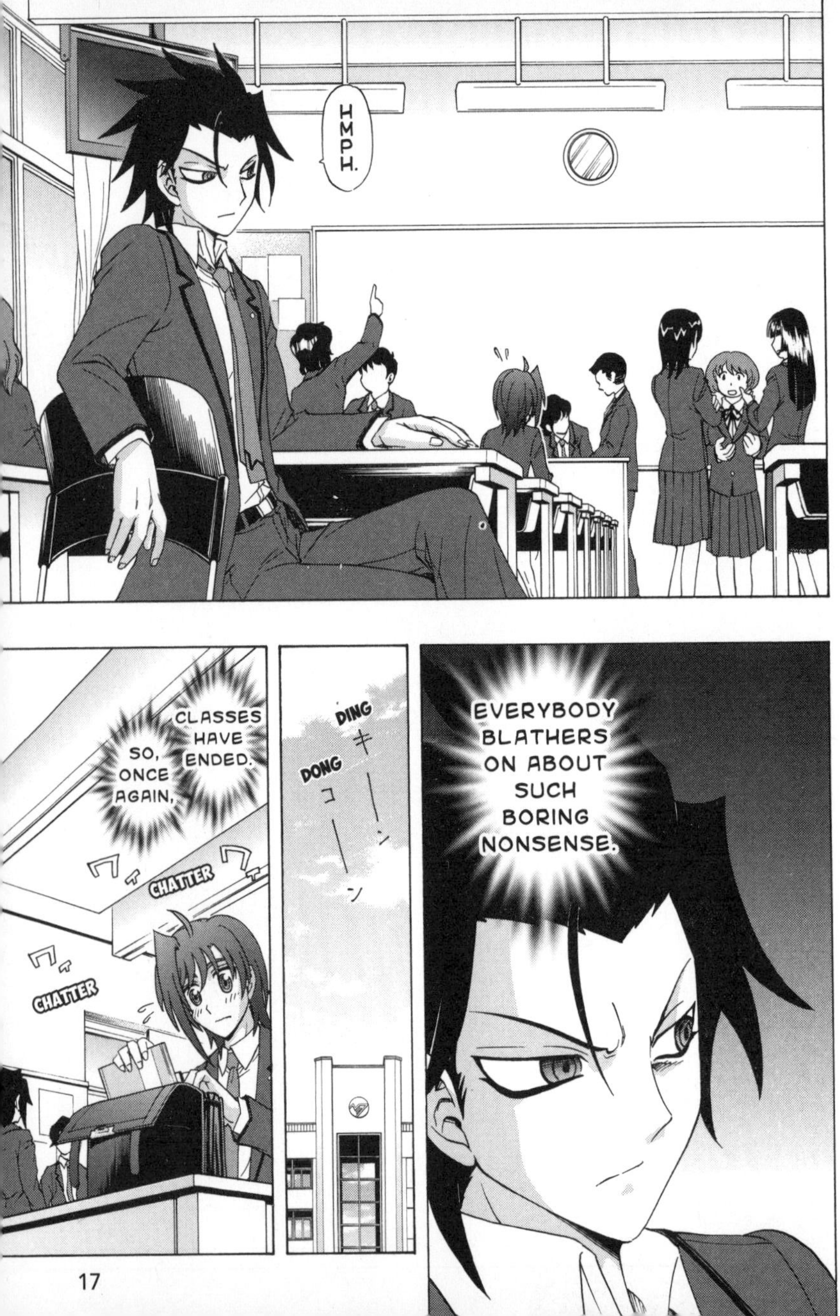
HMPH.
EVERYBODY BLATHERS ON ABOUT SUCH BORING NONSENSE.
DING
DONG
SO, ONCE AGAIN,
CLASSES HAVE ENDED.
CHATTER
CHATTER

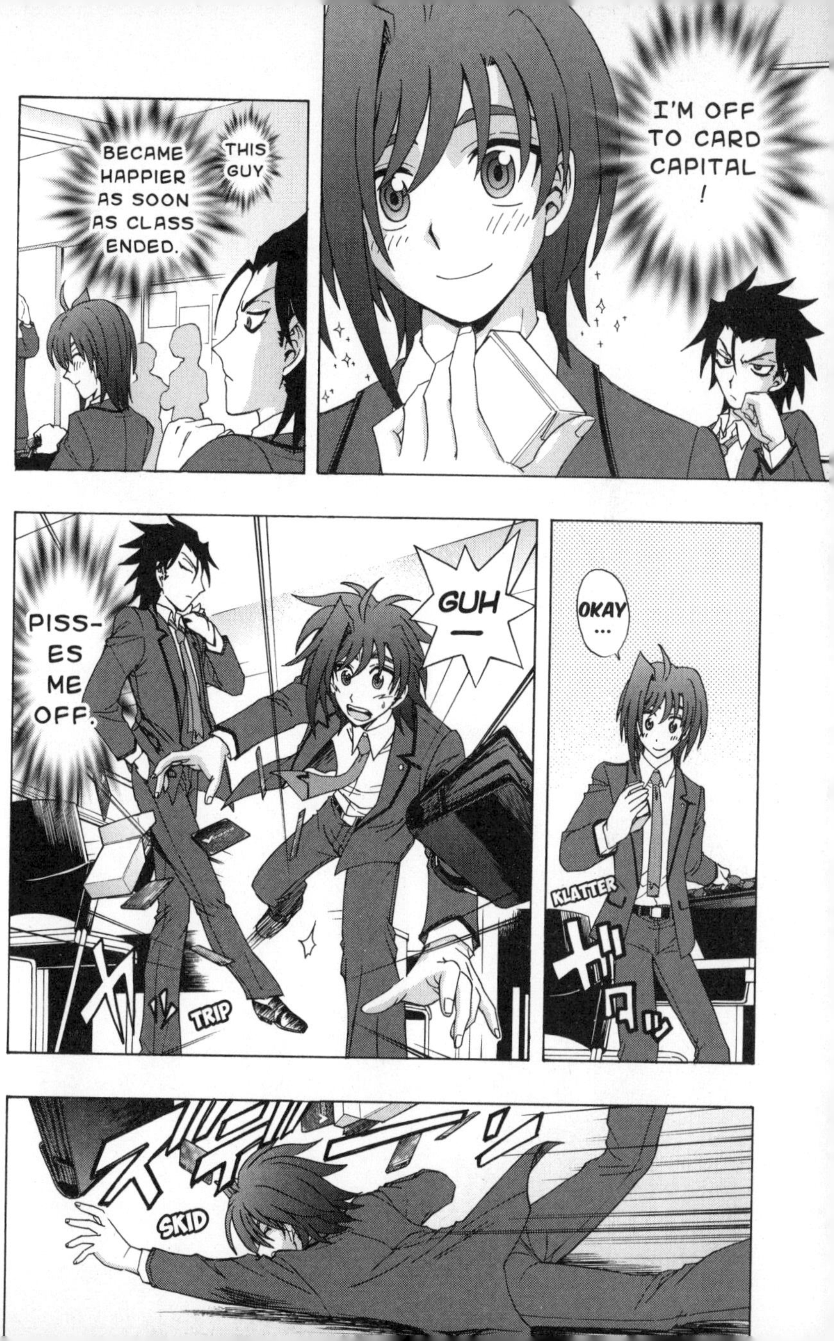

I'M OFF TO CARD CAPITAL !
THIS GUY
BECAME HAPPIER AS SOON AS CLASS ENDED.
OKAY ...
KLATTER
GUH —
PISS-ES ME OFF.
TRIP
SKID

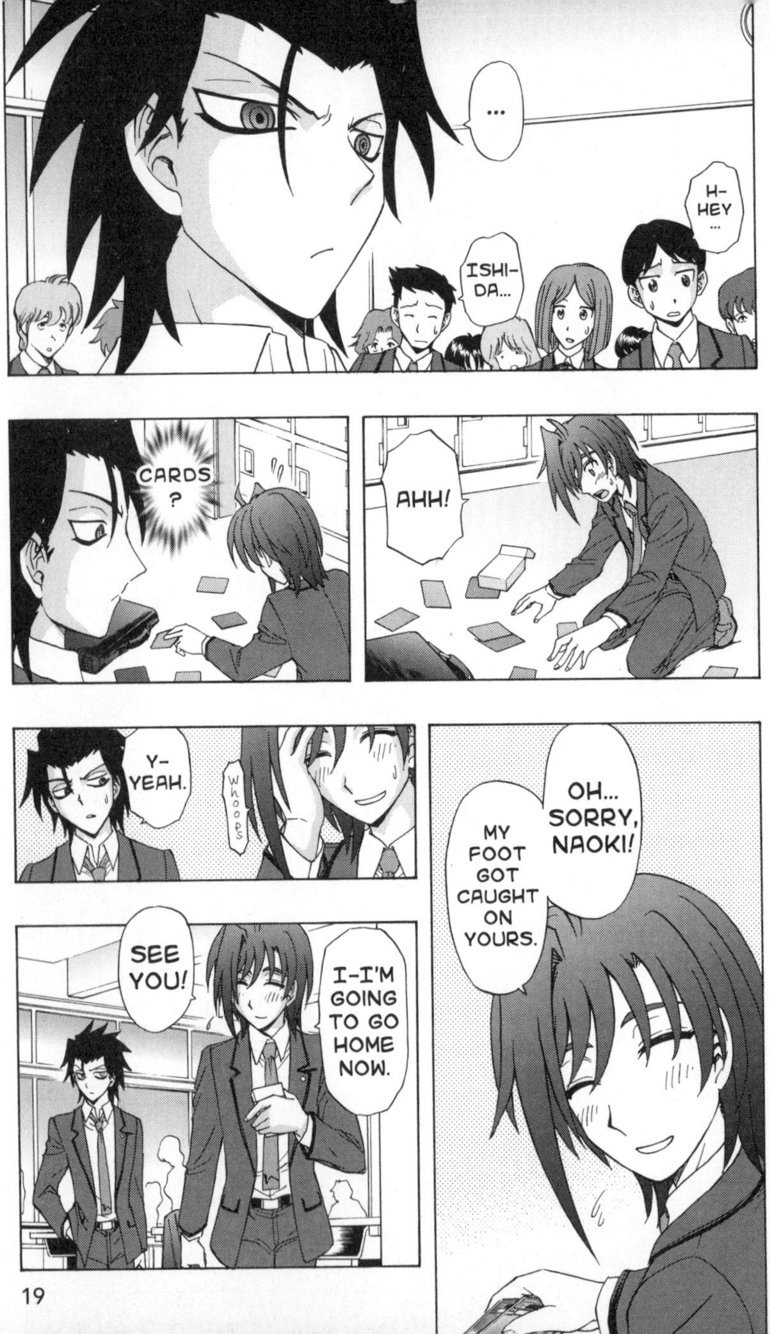
...
H-HEY...
ISHI-DA...
AHH!
CARDS?
OH... SORRY, NAOKI!
MY FOOT GOT CAUGHT ON YOURS.
whoops
Y-YEAH.
I-I'M GOING TO GO HOME NOW.
SEE YOU!

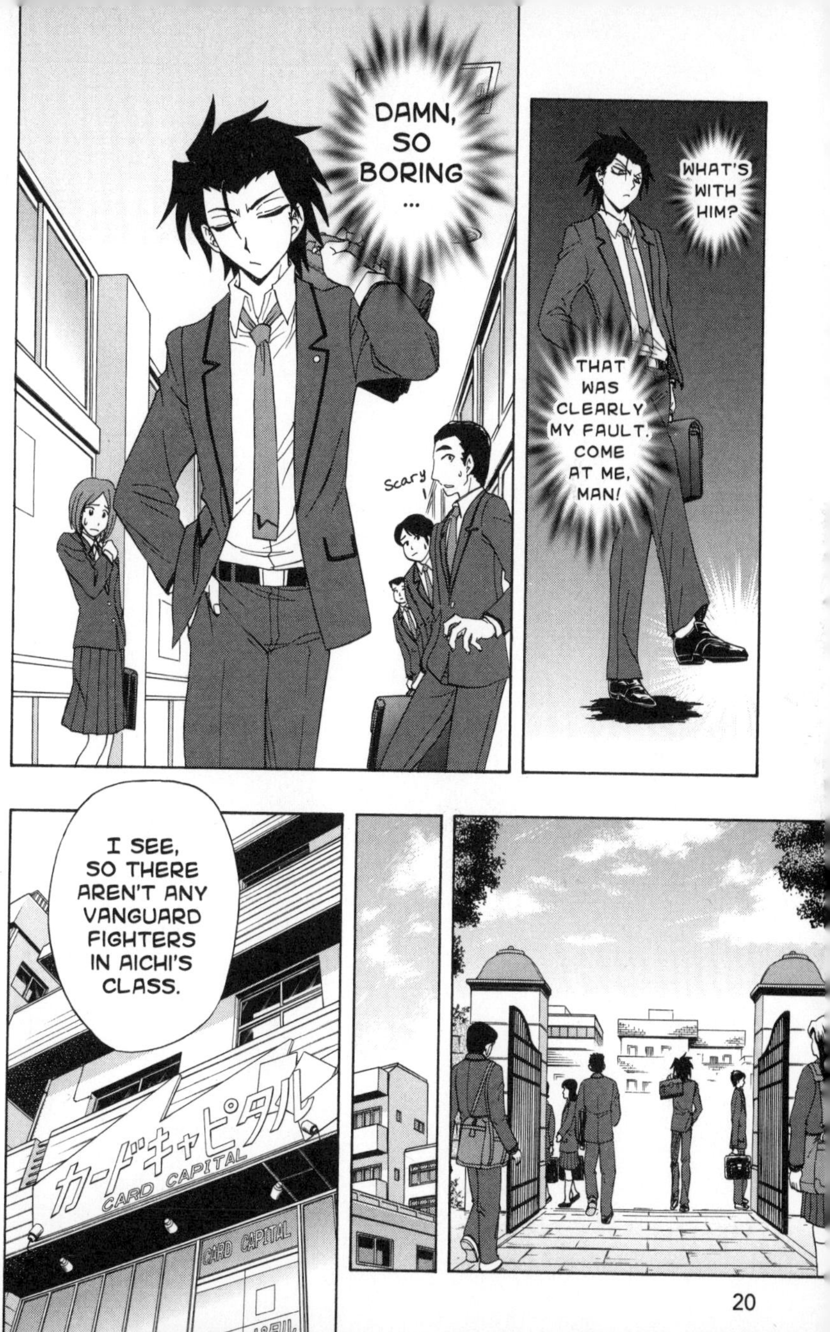
WHAT'S WITH HIM?
THAT WAS CLEARLY MY FAULT. COME AT ME, MAN!
DAMN, SO BORING ...
Scary
I SEE, SO THERE AREN'T ANY VANGUARD FIGHTERS IN AICHI'S CLASS.
カードキャピタル
CARD CAPITAL
CARD CAPITAL

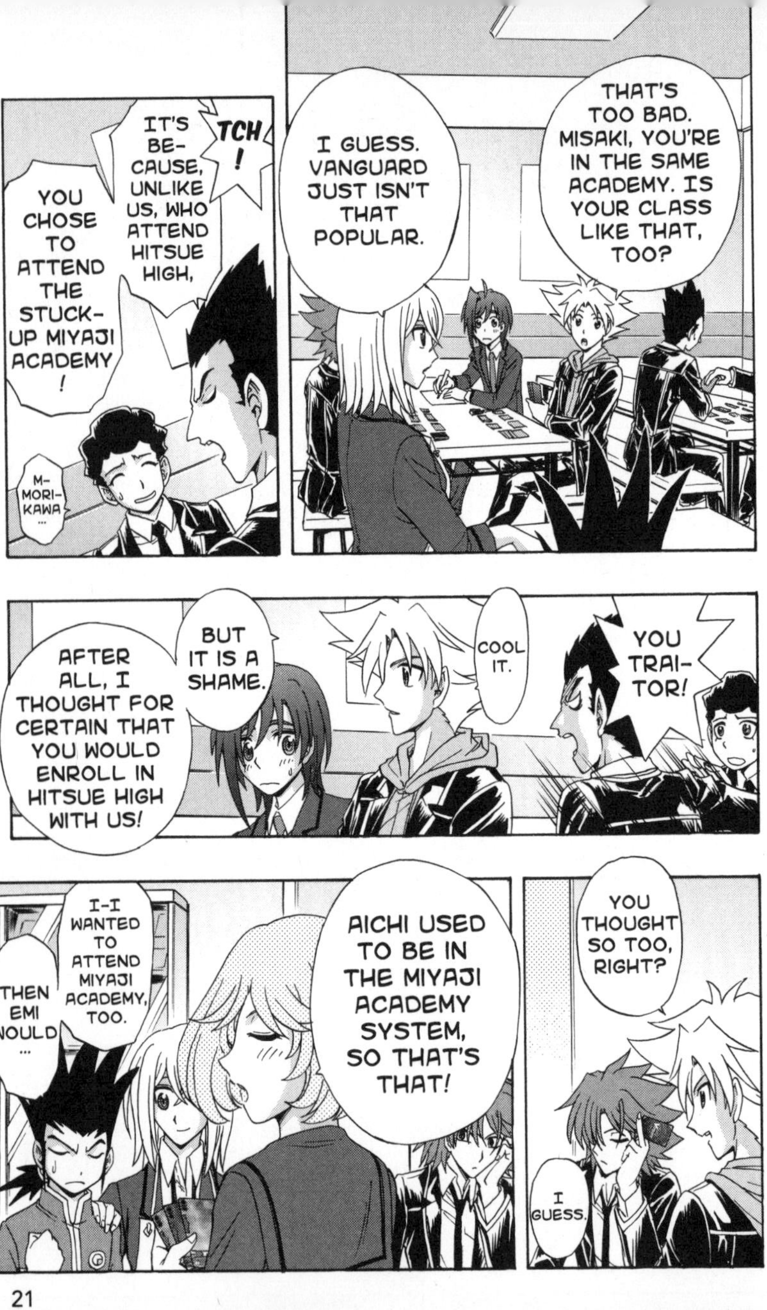
THAT'S TOO BAD. MISAKI, YOU'RE IN THE SAME ACADEMY. IS YOUR CLASS LIKE THAT, TOO?
I GUESS. VANGUARD JUST ISN'T THAT POPULAR.
TCH!
IT'S BE-CAUSE, UNLIKE US, WHO ATTEND HITSUE HIGH,
YOU CHOSE TO ATTEND THE STUCK-UP MIYAJI ACADEMY!
M-MORI-KAWA...
YOU TRAI-TOR!
COOL IT.
BUT IT IS A SHAME.
AFTER ALL, I THOUGHT FOR CERTAIN THAT YOU WOULD ENROLL IN HITSUE HIGH WITH US!
YOU THOUGHT SO TOO, RIGHT?
I GUESS.
AICHI USED TO BE IN THE MIYAJI ACADEMY SYSTEM, SO THAT'S THAT!
I-I WANTED TO ATTEND MIYAJI ACADEMY, TOO.
THEN EMI WOULD...

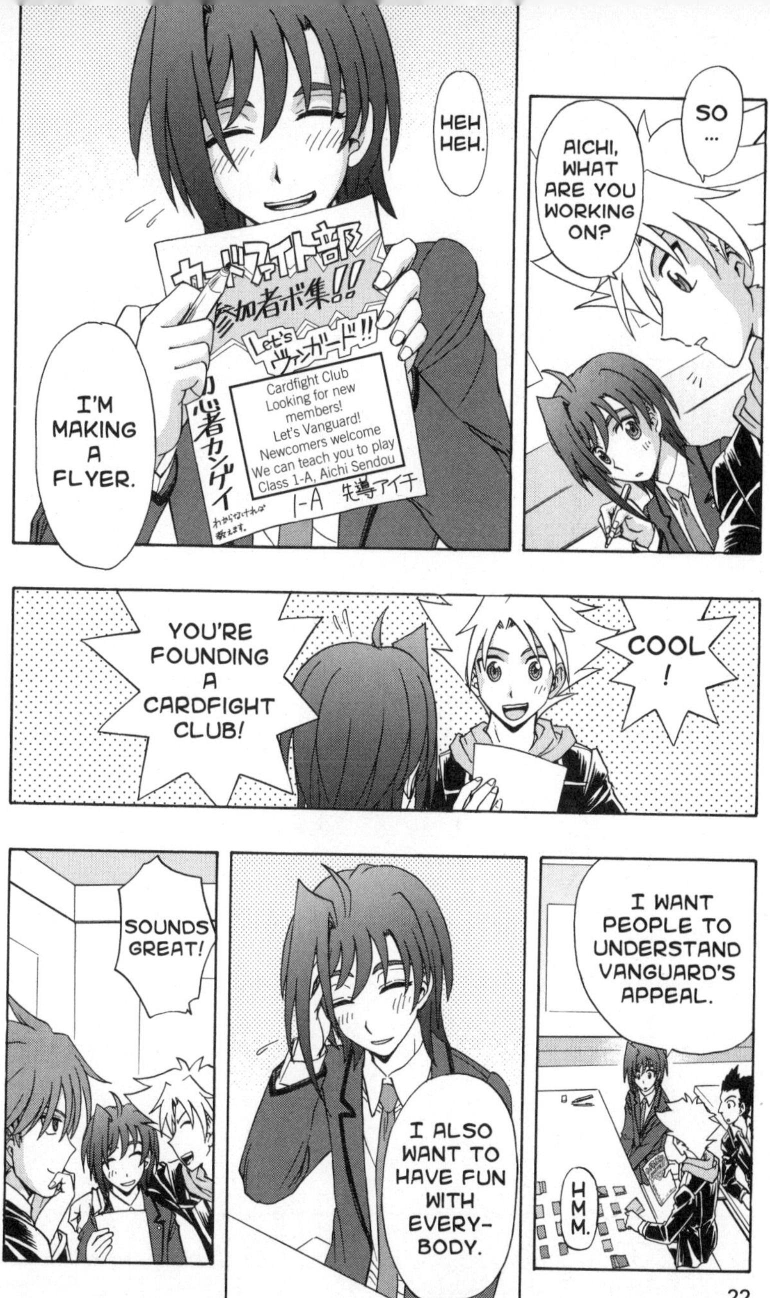
SO ...
AICHI, WHAT ARE YOU WORKING ON?
HEH HEH.
カードファイト部
参加者ボ集!!
Let's ヴァンガード!!
初心者カンゲイ
わからなければ教えます。
1-A 先導アイチ
Cardfight Club
Looking for new members!
Let's Vanguard!
Newcomers welcome
We can teach you to play
Class 1-A, Aichi Sendou
I'M MAKING A FLYER.
COOL!
YOU'RE FOUNDING A CARDFIGHT CLUB!
I WANT PEOPLE TO UNDERSTAND VANGUARD'S APPEAL.
HMM.
I ALSO WANT TO HAVE FUN WITH EVERY-BODY.
SOUNDS GREAT!

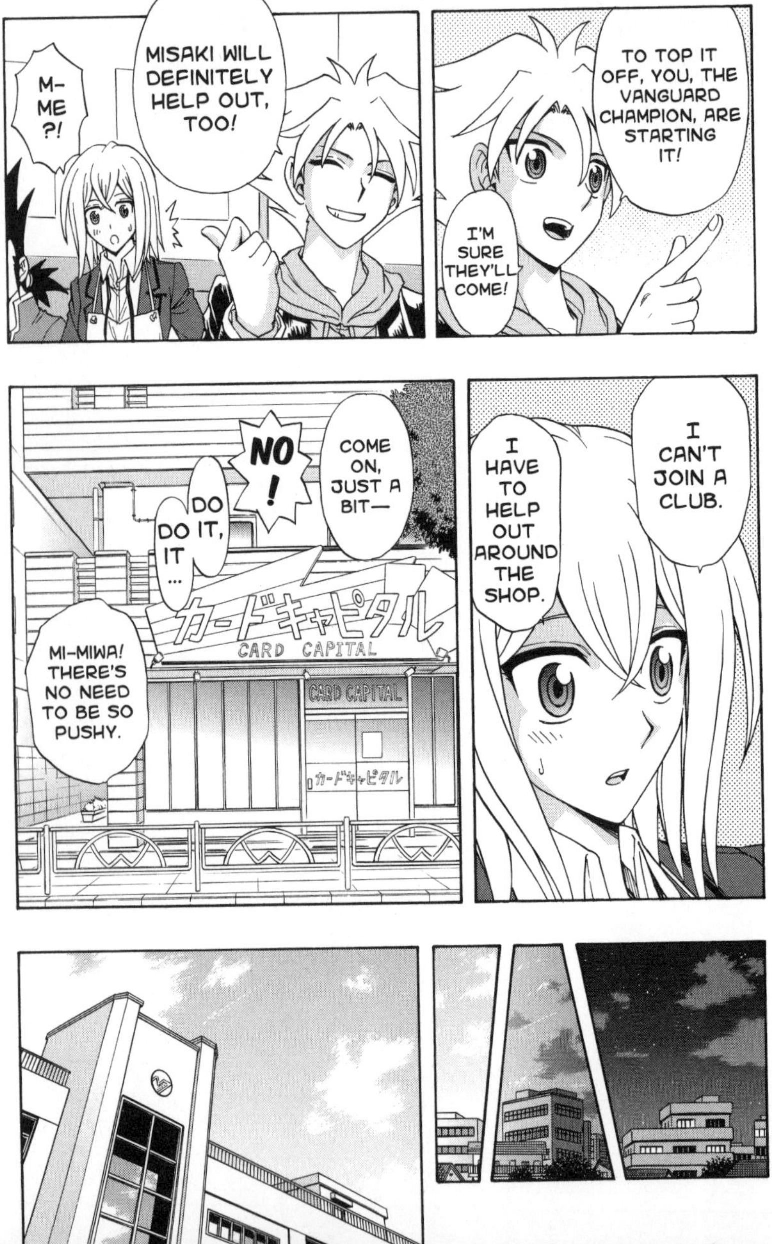
TO TOP IT OFF, YOU, THE VANGUARD CHAMPION, ARE STARTING IT!
I'M SURE THEY'LL COME!
MISAKI WILL DEFINITELY HELP OUT, TOO!
M-ME?!
I CAN'T JOIN A CLUB.
I HAVE TO HELP OUT AROUND THE SHOP.
COME ON, JUST A BIT—
NO!
DO IT,
DO IT ...
カードキャピタル
CARD CAPITAL
CARD CAPITAL
カードキャピタル
MI-MIWA! THERE'S NO NEED TO BE SO PUSHY.

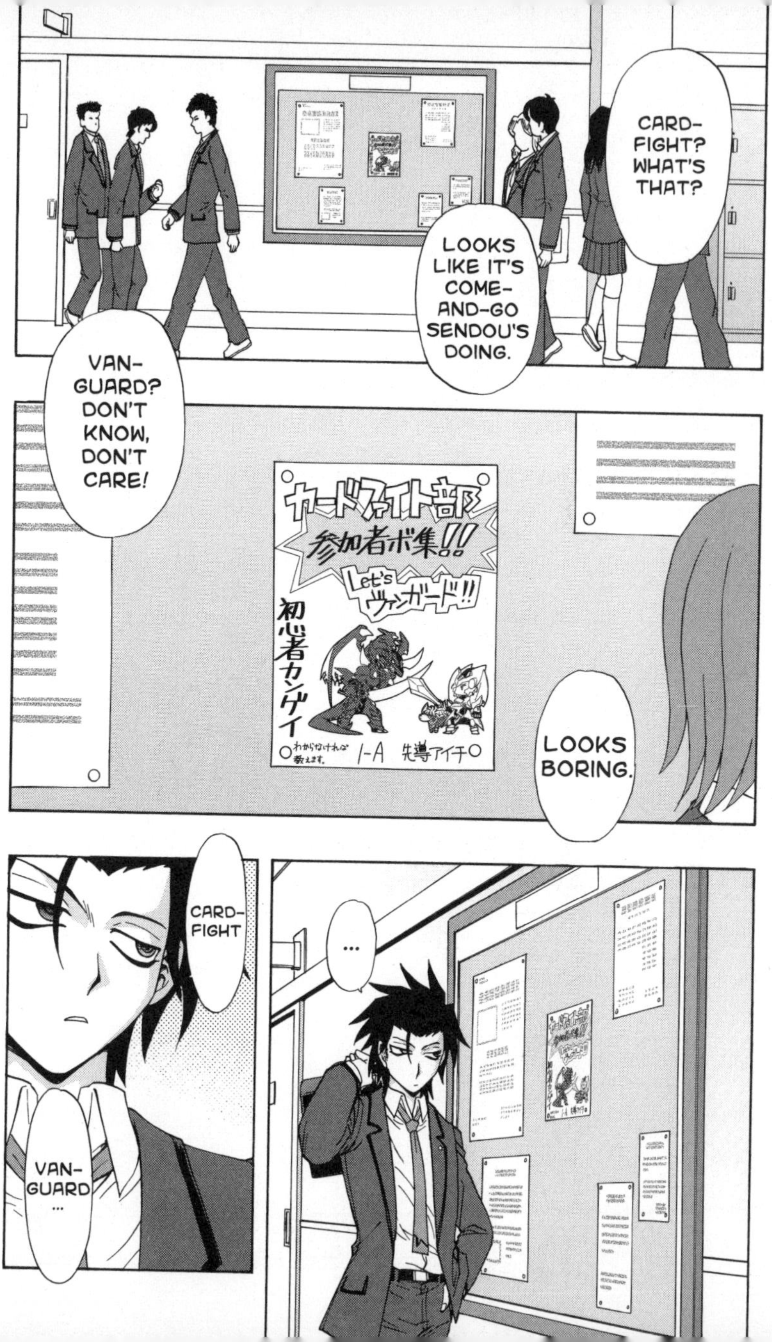
CARD-FIGHT? WHAT'S THAT?
LOOKS LIKE IT'S COME-AND-GO SENDOU'S DOING.
VAN-GUARD? DON'T KNOW, DON'T CARE!
カードファイト部
参加者ボ集!!
Let's ヴァンガード!!
初心者カンゲイ
わからなければ教えます。
1-A 先導アイチ
LOOKS BORING.
...
CARD-FIGHT
VAN-GUARD ...

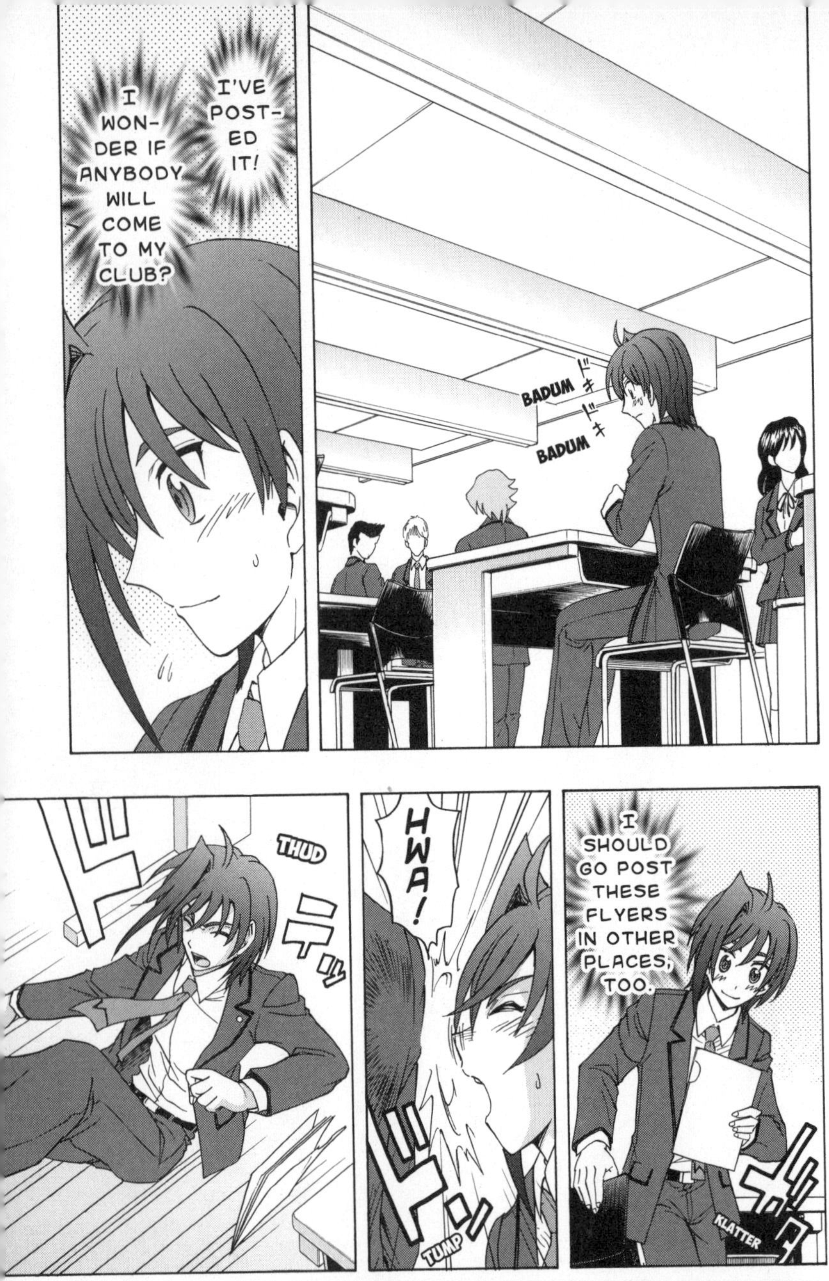
BADUM
BADUM
I'VE POST-ED IT!
I WONDER IF ANYBODY WILL COME TO MY CLUB?
I SHOULD GO POST THESE FLYERS IN OTHER PLACES, TOO.
KLATTER
HWA!
TUMP
THUD

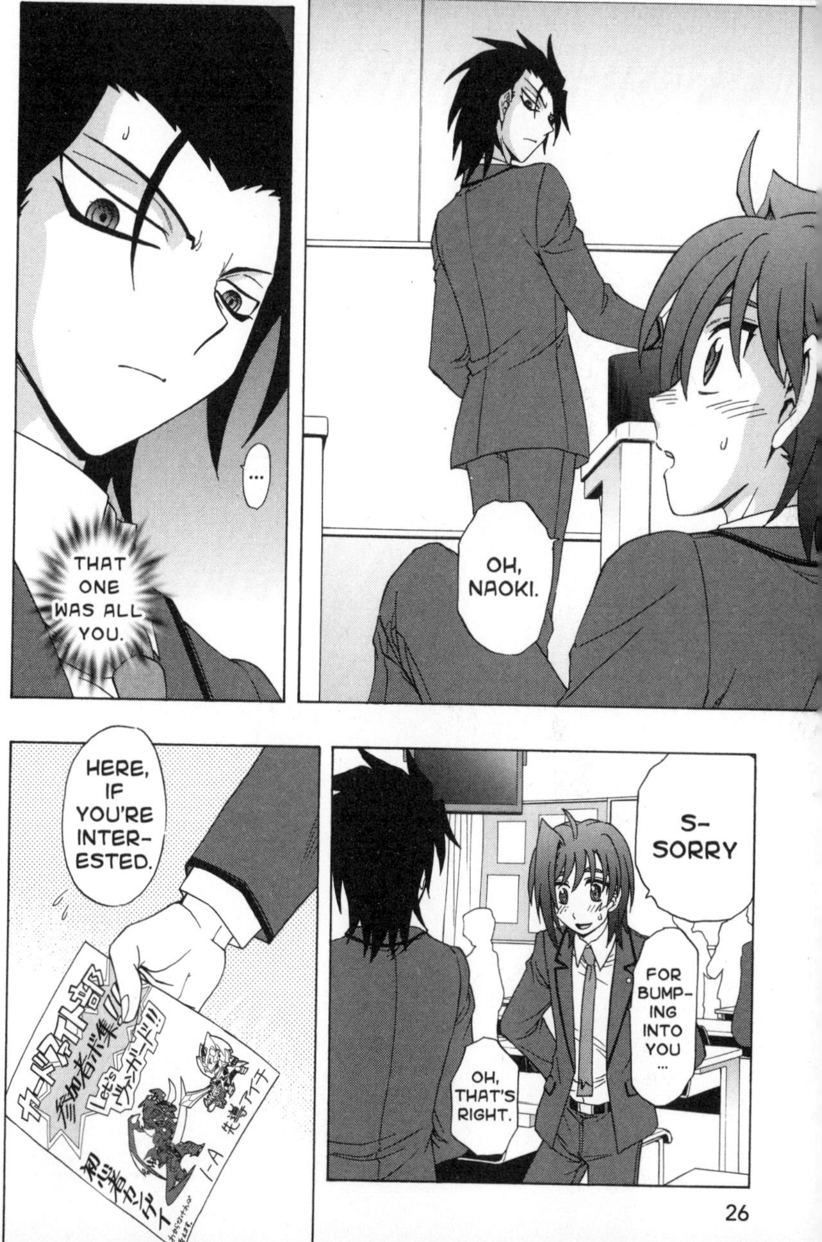
OH, NAOKI.
...
THAT ONE WAS ALL YOU.
S-SORRY
FOR BUMPING INTO YOU ...
OH, THAT'S RIGHT.
HERE, IF YOU'RE INTER-ESTED.
Let's
1-A 先導アイチ

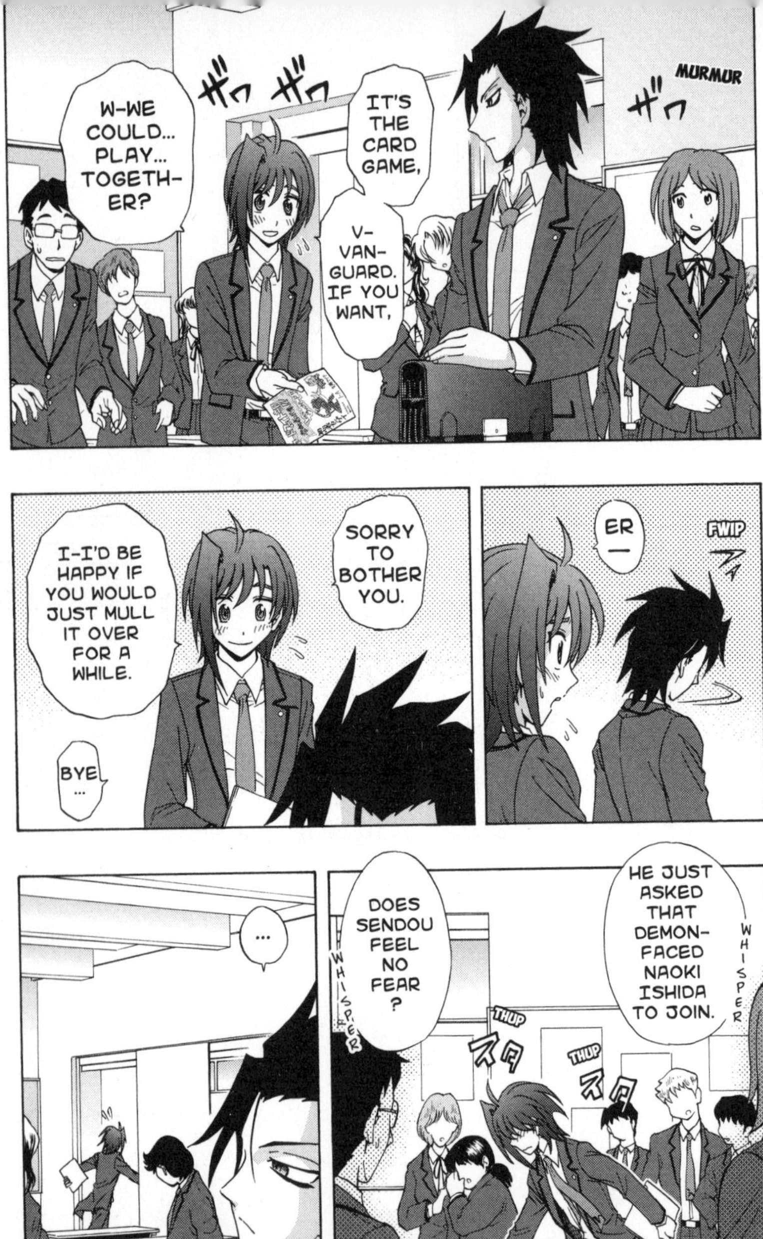
MURMUR
ザワ
IT'S THE CARD GAME,
V-VANGUARD. IF YOU WANT,
ザワ ザワ
W-WE COULD... PLAY... TOGETH-ER?
FWIP
ER —
SORRY TO BOTHER YOU.
I-I'D BE HAPPY IF YOU WOULD JUST MULL IT OVER FOR A WHILE.
BYE ...
HE JUST ASKED THAT DEMON-FACED NAOKI ISHIDA TO JOIN.
WHISPER
DOES SENDOU FEEL NO FEAR?
WHISPER
THUP
スタ
THUP
スタ
...

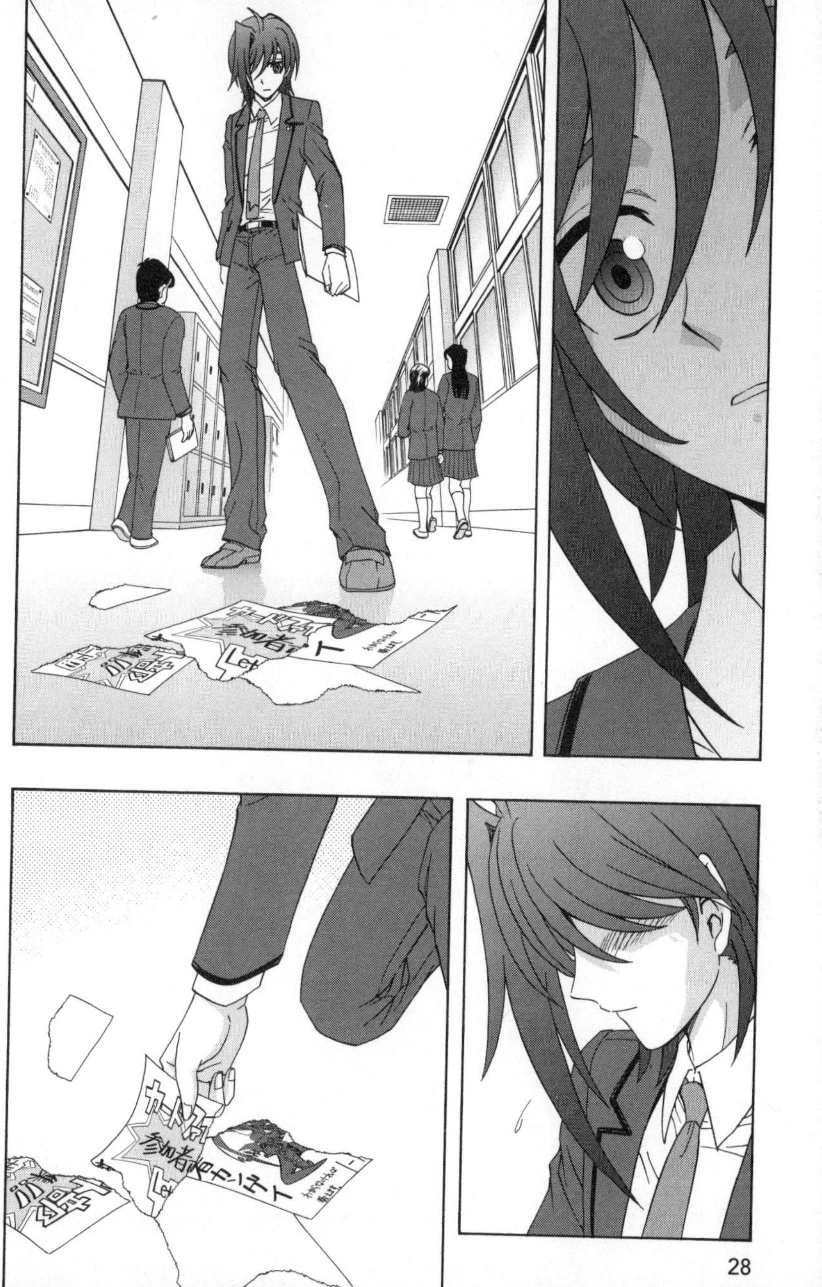
参加者

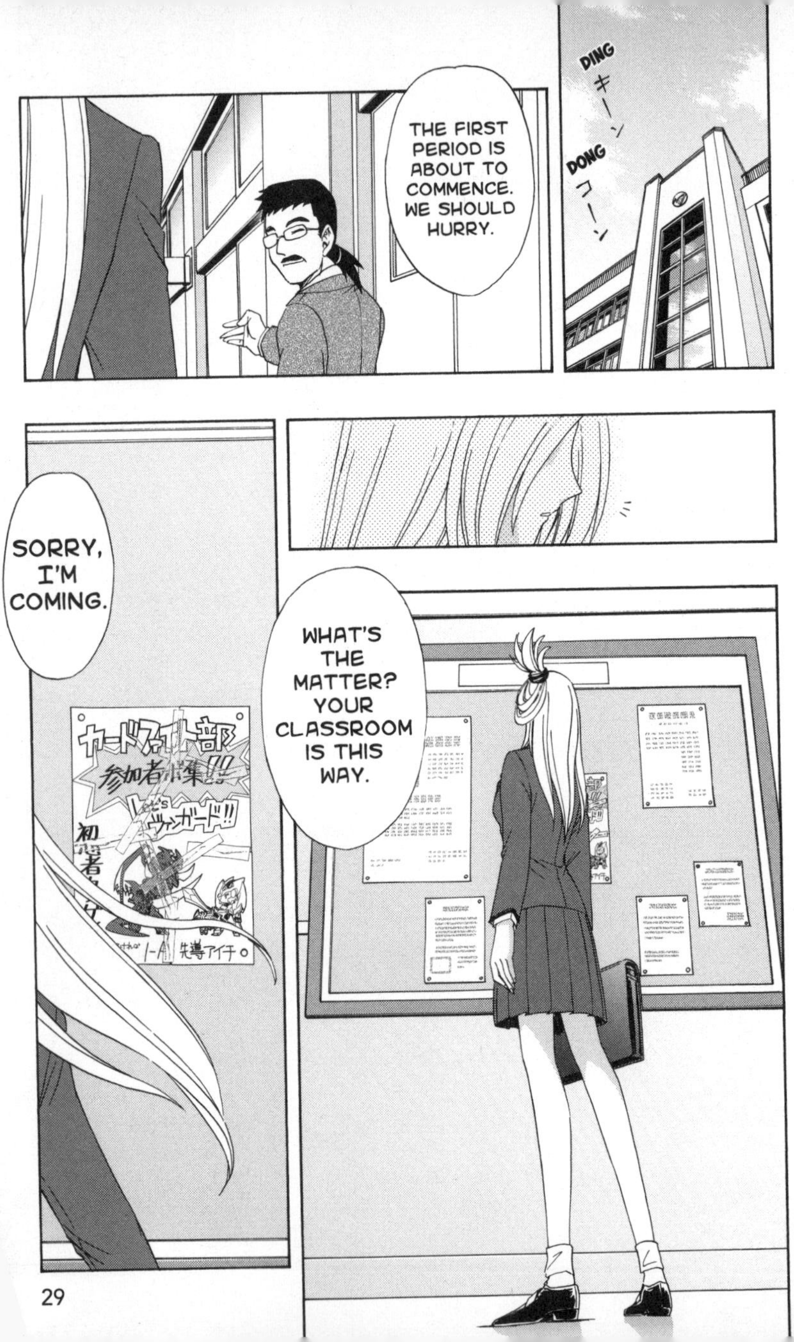
DING
キーン
DONG
コーン
THE FIRST PERIOD IS ABOUT TO COMMENCE. WE SHOULD HURRY.
WHAT'S THE MATTER? YOUR CLASSROOM IS THIS WAY.
SORRY, I'M COMING.
カードファイト部
参加者募集!!
Let's ヴァンガード!!
1-A 先導アイチ

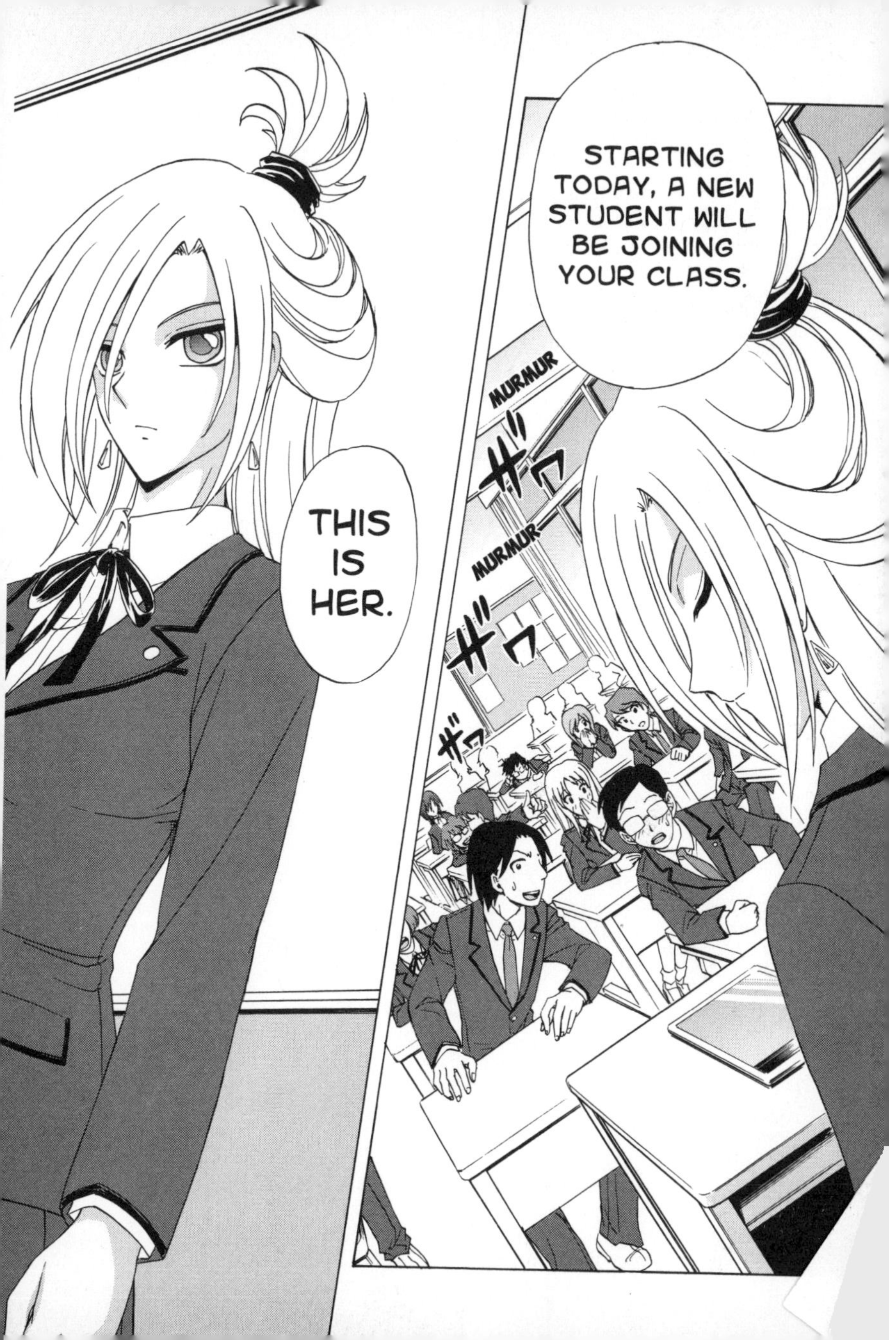
STARTING TODAY, A NEW STUDENT WILL BE JOINING YOUR CLASS.
MURMUR
ザワ
MURMUR
ザワ
ザワ
THIS IS HER.

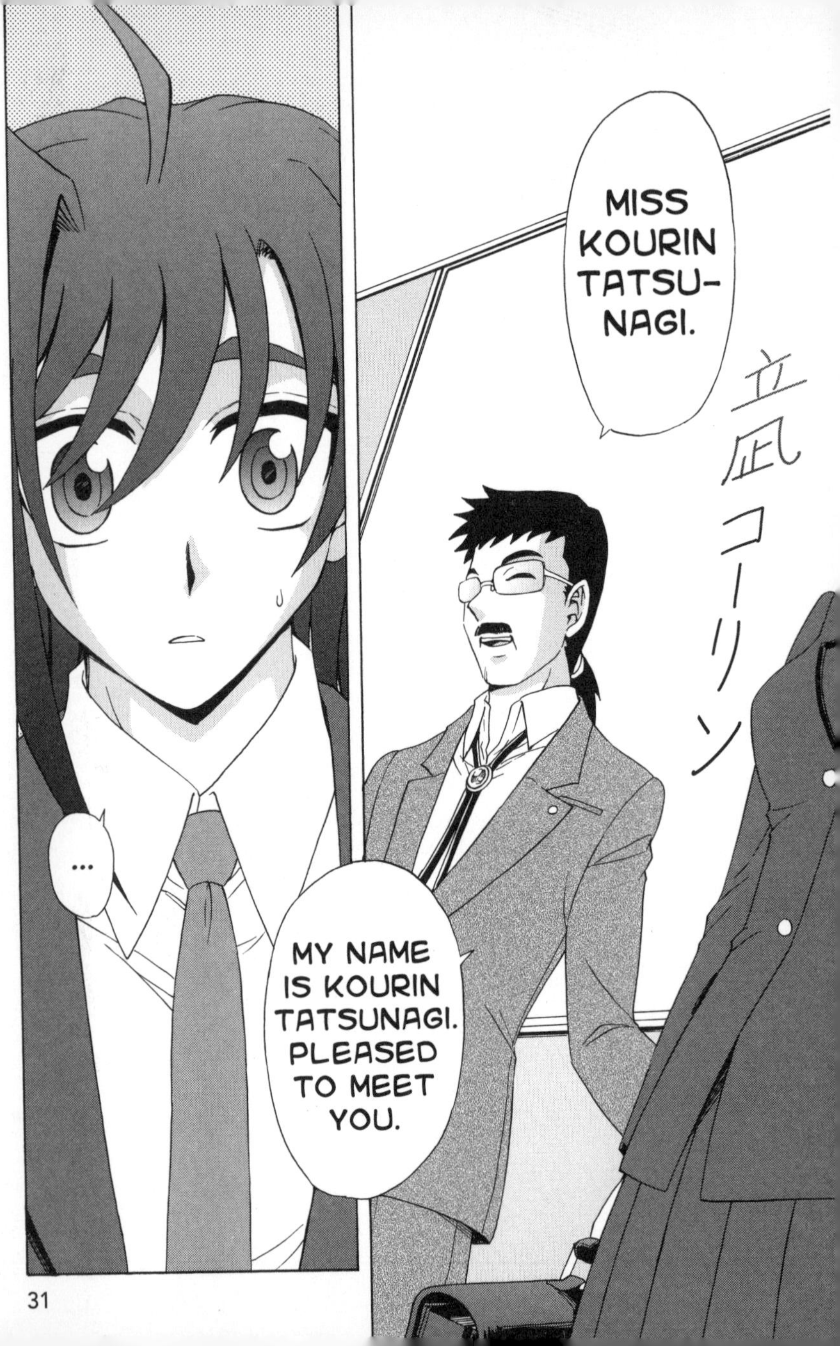
MISS KOURIN TATSU-NAGI.
立凪コーリン
...
MY NAME IS KOURIN TATSUNAGI. PLEASED TO MEET YOU.

BONUS! CARDFIGHT!! Vanguard NEVER-BEFORE-SEEN IMAGE BOARDS

We're releasing Mr. Itou's hand-drawn image boards, drawn specifically for this comic! Please enjoy the sketches of these settings, not shown in the main part of the manga!

Naoki has a bright older brother who's in college. It seems that Naoki is constantly under pressure from him.

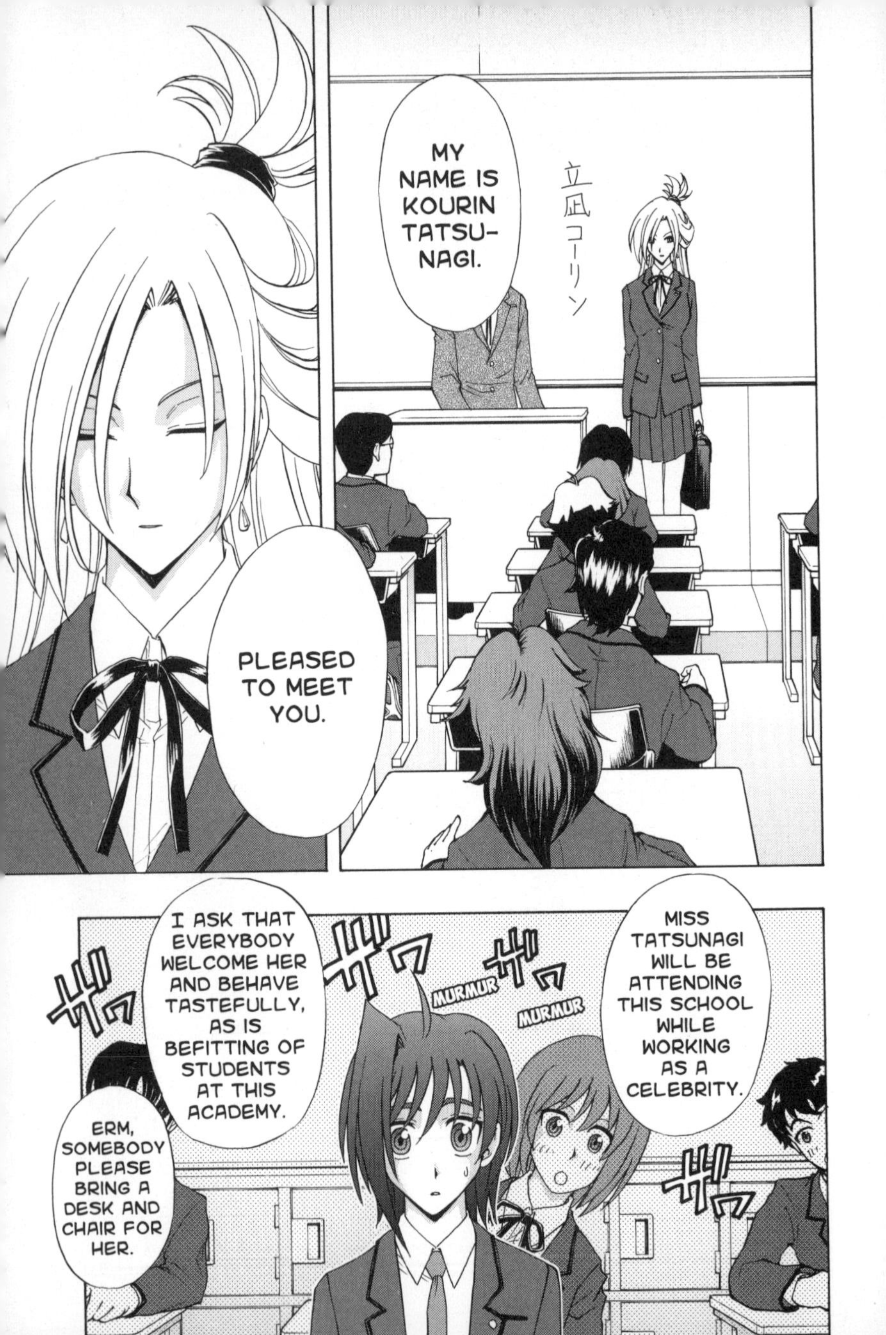
MY NAME IS KOURIN TATSU-NAGI.
立凪コーリン
PLEASED TO MEET YOU.
MISS TATSUNAGI WILL BE ATTENDING THIS SCHOOL WHILE WORKING AS A CELEBRITY.
MURMUR
MURMUR
I ASK THAT EVERYBODY WELCOME HER AND BEHAVE TASTEFULLY, AS IS BEFITTING OF STUDENTS AT THIS ACADEMY.
ERM, SOMEBODY PLEASE BRING A DESK AND CHAIR FOR HER.

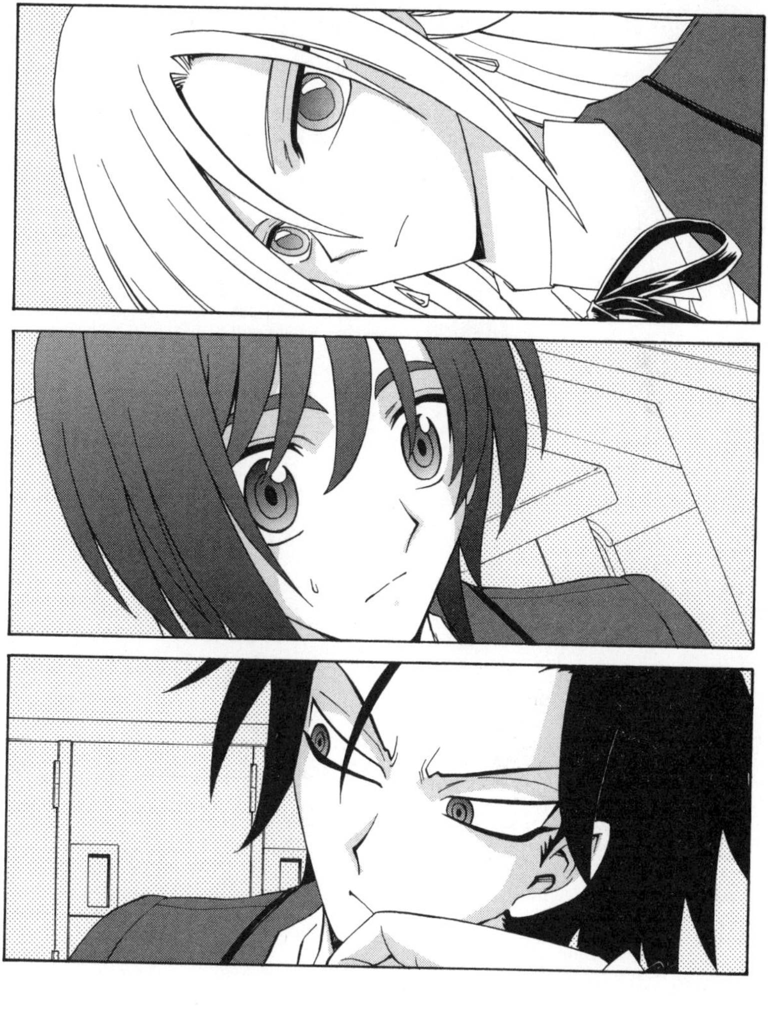

#026 AN IDOL JOINS?!

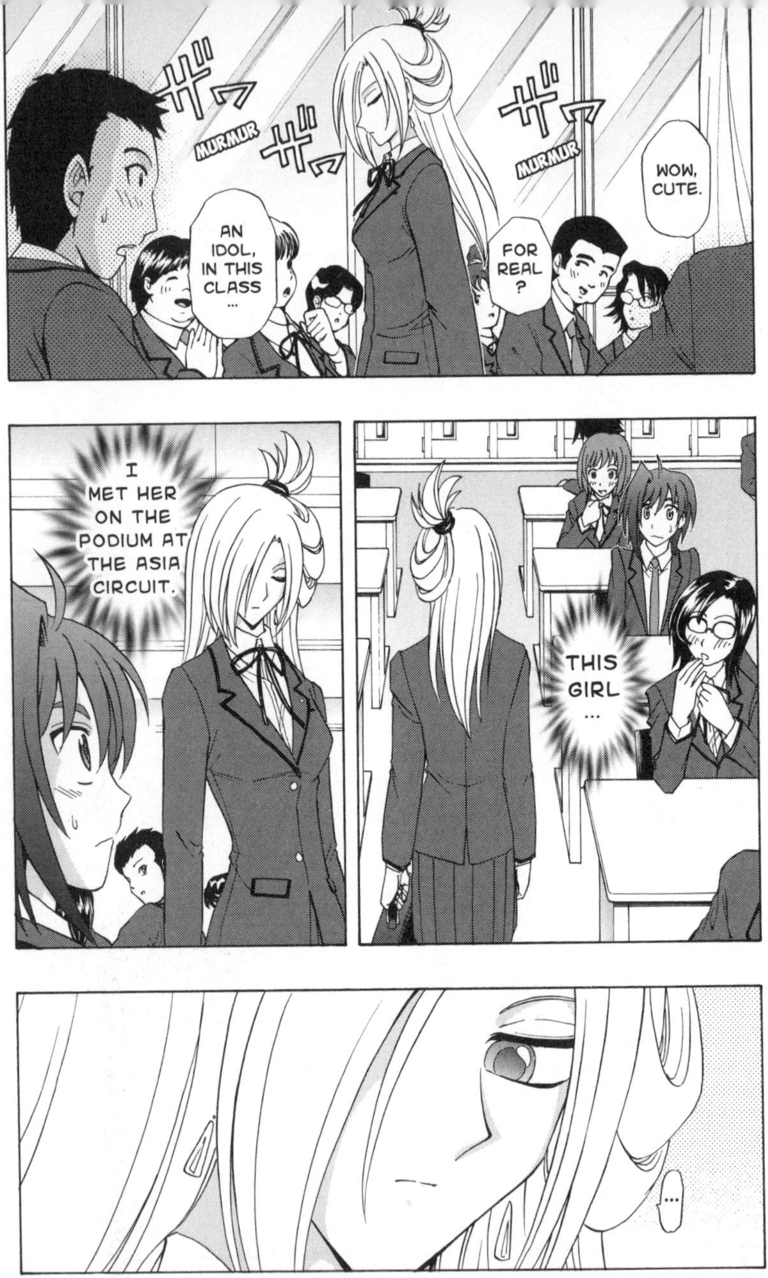
WOW, CUTE.
ザワ ザワ
MURMUR
FOR REAL?
AN IDOL, IN THIS CLASS ...
ザワ ザワ
MURMUR
THIS GIRL ...
I MET HER ON THE PODIUM AT THE ASIA CIRCUIT.
...

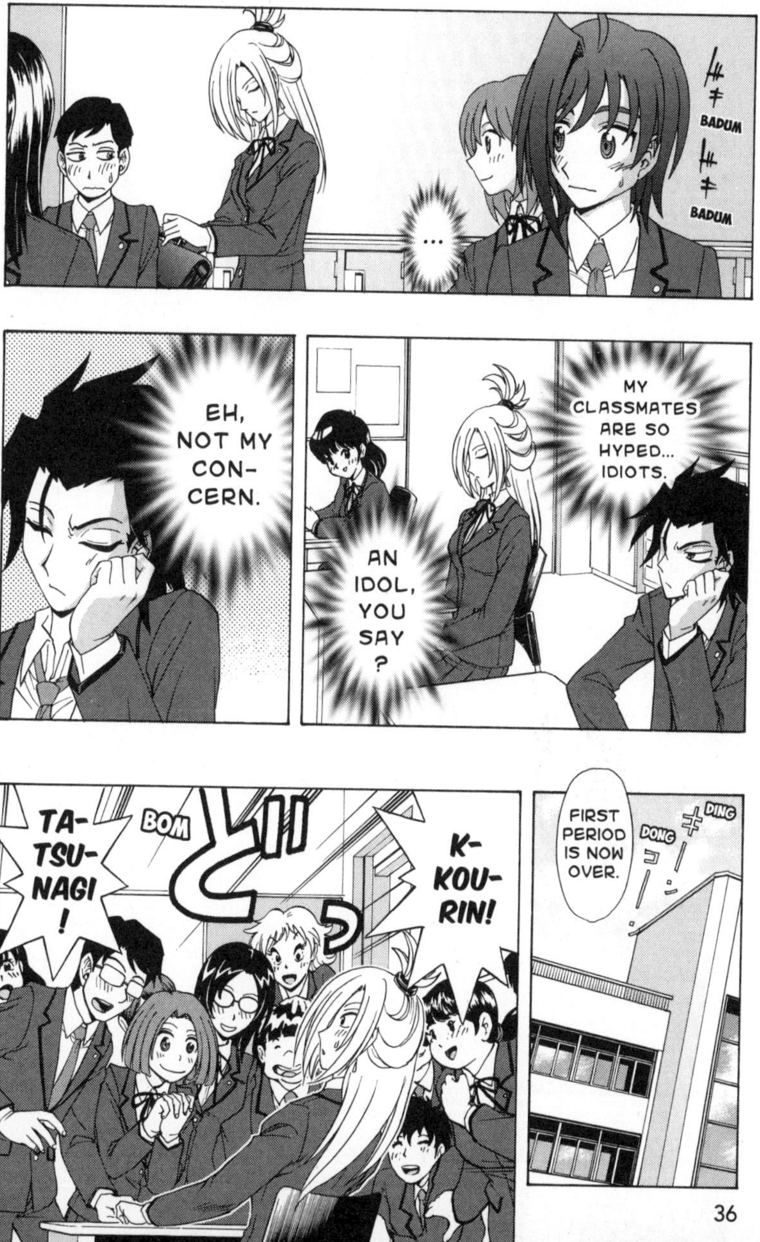
BADUM
BADUM
...
MY CLASSMATES ARE SO HYPED... IDIOTS.
AN IDOL, YOU SAY?
EH, NOT MY CON-CERN.
DING
DONG
FIRST PERIOD IS NOW OVER.
K-KOU-RIN!
BOM
TA-TSU-NAGI!

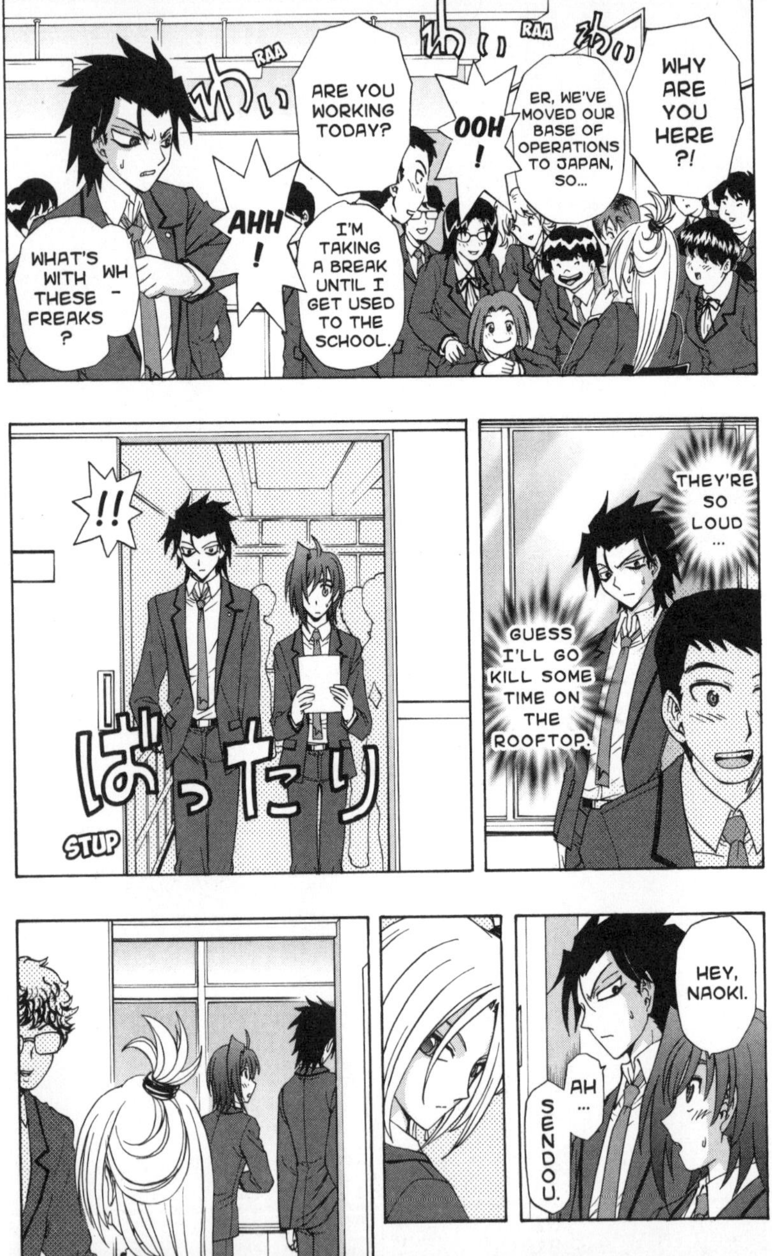
WHY ARE YOU HERE?!
ER, WE'VE MOVED OUR BASE OF OPERATIONS TO JAPAN, SO...
RAA
OOH!
RAA
ARE YOU WORKING TODAY?
AHH!
I'M TAKING A BREAK UNTIL I GET USED TO THE SCHOOL.
WH-
WHAT'S WITH THESE FREAKS?
THEY'RE SO LOUD...
GUESS I'LL GO KILL SOME TIME ON THE ROOFTOP.
!!
ぱったり
STUP
HEY, NAOKI.
AH...
SENDOU.

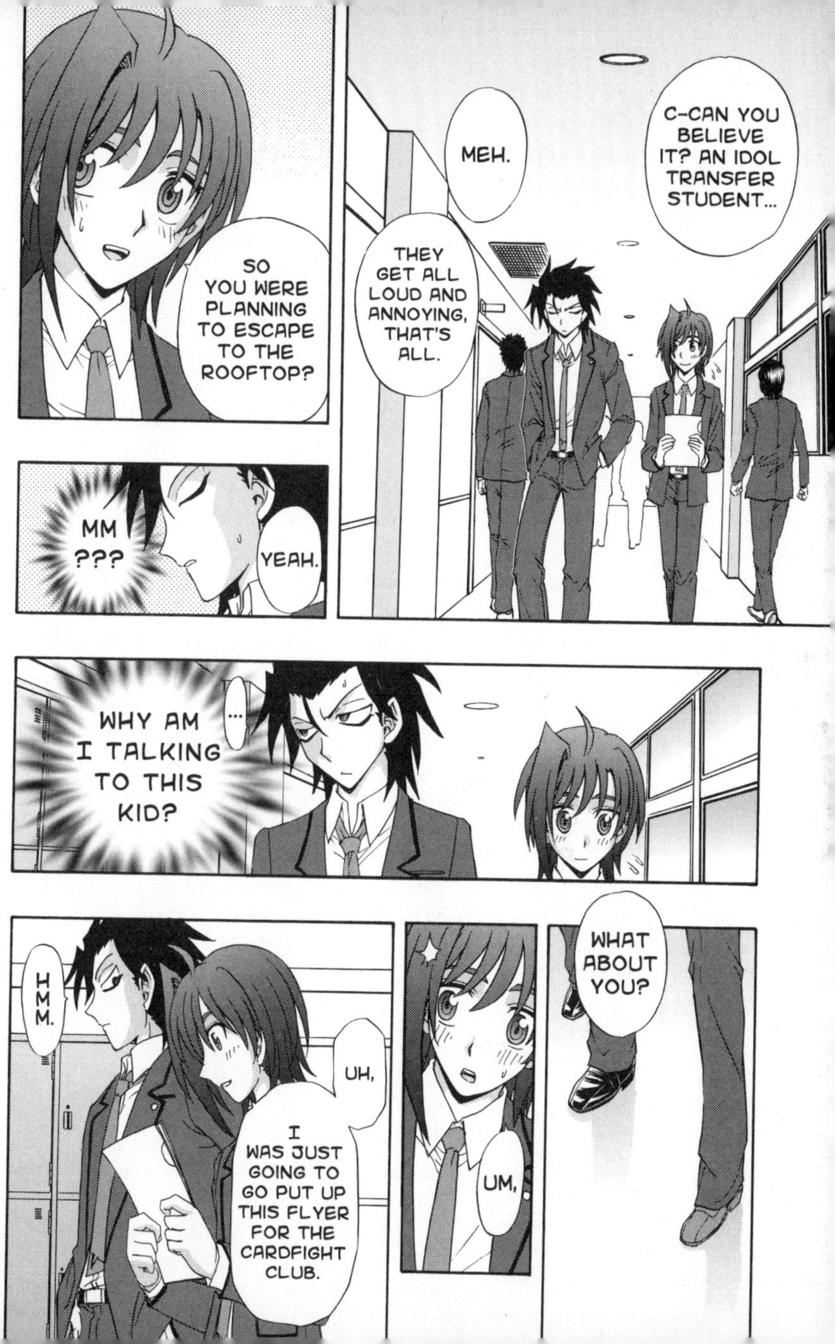
C-CAN YOU BELIEVE IT? AN IDOL TRANSFER STUDENT...
MEH.
THEY GET ALL LOUD AND ANNOYING, THAT'S ALL.
SO YOU WERE PLANNING TO ESCAPE TO THE ROOFTOP?
YEAH.
MM ???
...
WHY AM I TALKING TO THIS KID?
WHAT ABOUT YOU?
UM,
UH,
I WAS JUST GOING TO GO PUT UP THIS FLYER FOR THE CARDFIGHT CLUB.
HMM.

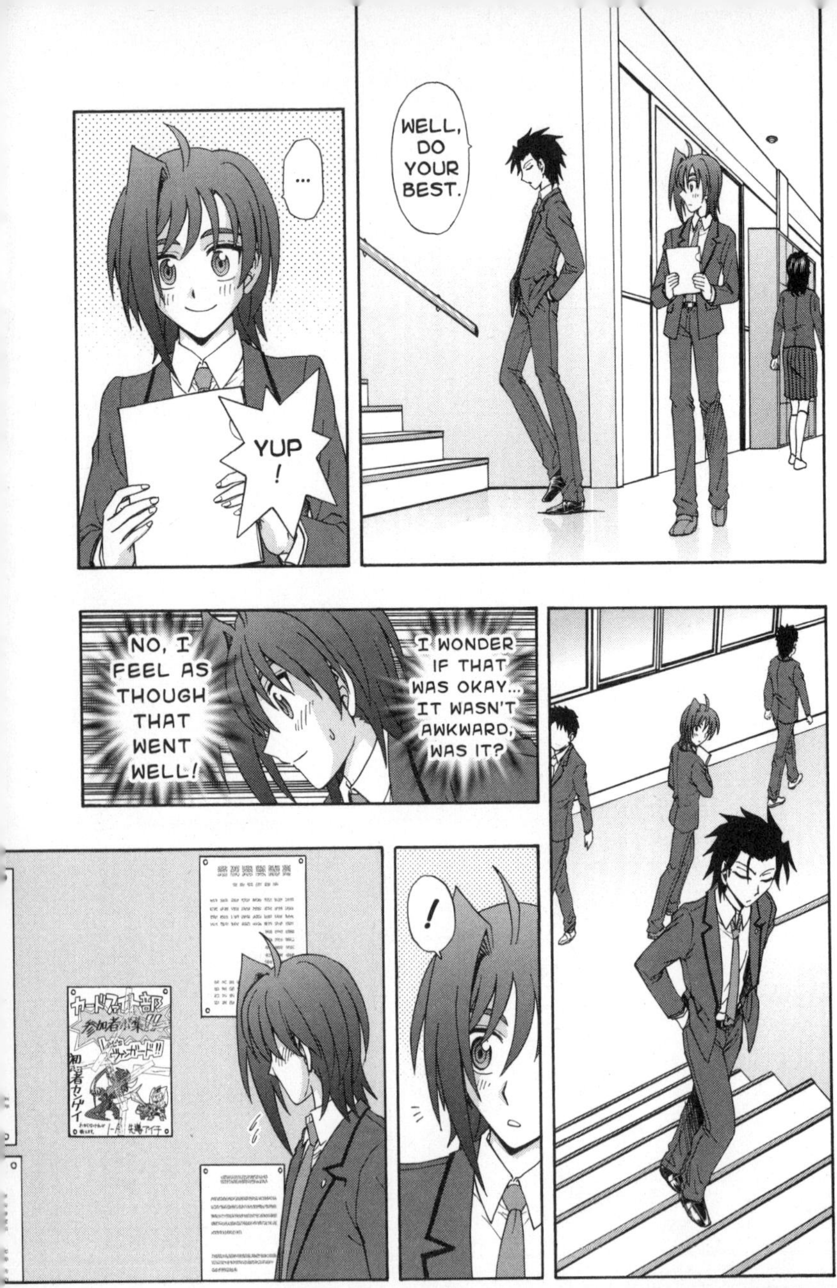
WELL, DO YOUR BEST.
...
YUP!
I WONDER IF THAT WAS OKAY... IT WASN'T AWKWARD, WAS IT?
NO, I FEEL AS THOUGH THAT WENT WELL!
!

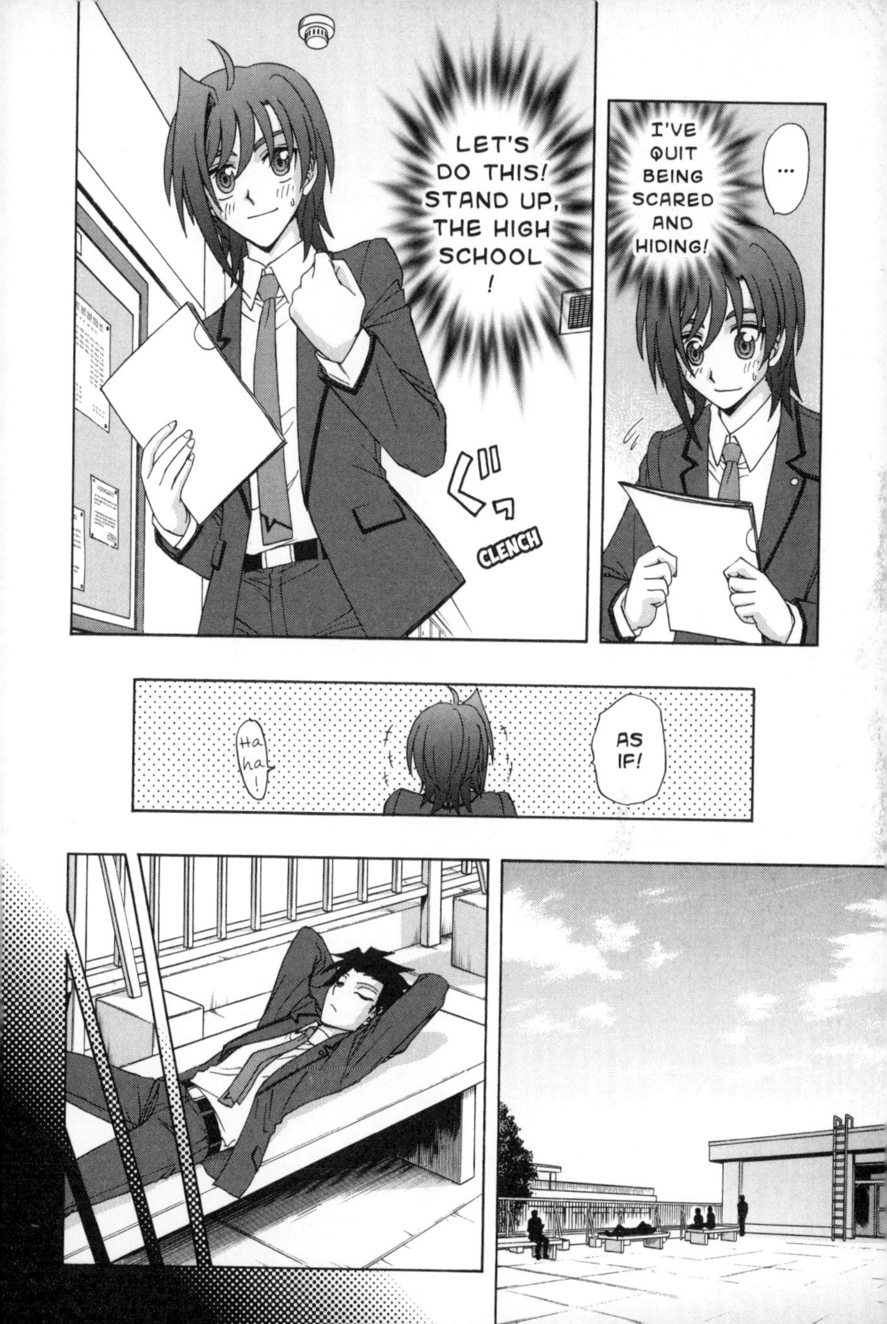
...
I'VE QUIT BEING SCARED AND HIDING!
LET'S DO THIS! STAND UP, THE HIGH SCHOOL!
CLENCH
AS IF!
Ha ha!

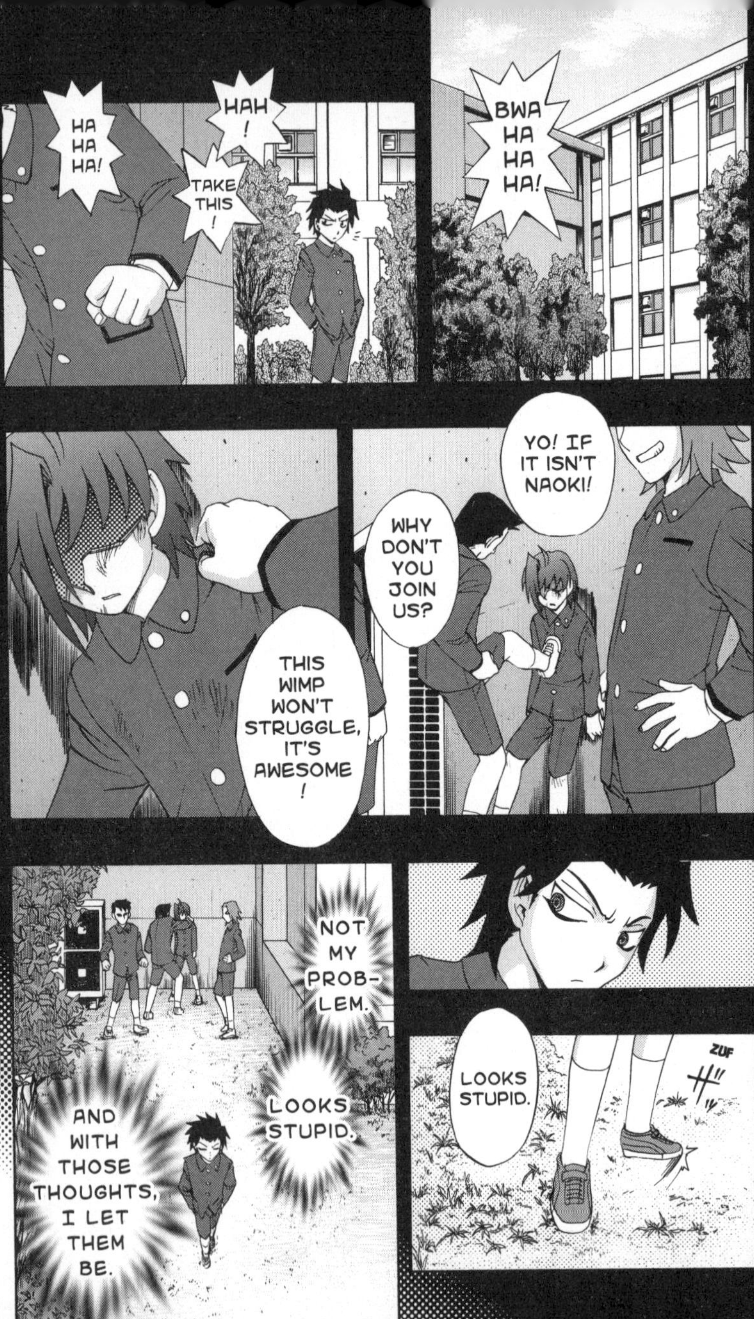
BWA HA HA HA!
HAH!
HA HA HA!
TAKE THIS!
YO! IF IT ISN'T NAOKI!
WHY DON'T YOU JOIN US?
THIS WIMP WON'T STRUGGLE, IT'S AWESOME!
ZUF
LOOKS STUPID.
NOT MY PROB-LEM.
LOOKS STUPID.
AND WITH THOSE THOUGHTS, I LET THEM BE.

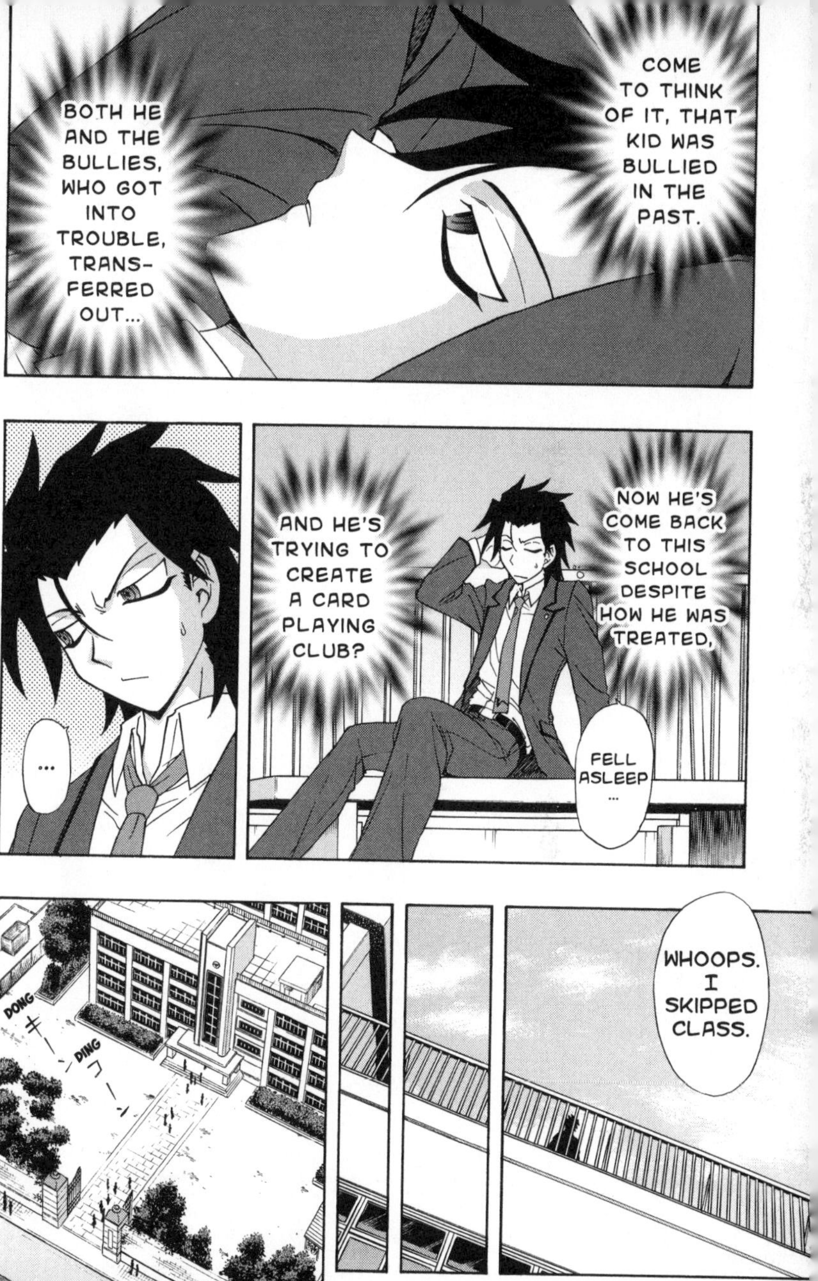
COME TO THINK OF IT, THAT KID WAS BULLIED IN THE PAST.
BOTH HE AND THE BULLIES, WHO GOT INTO TROUBLE, TRANS-FERRED OUT...
NOW HE'S COME BACK TO THIS SCHOOL DESPITE HOW HE WAS TREATED,
AND HE'S TRYING TO CREATE A CARD PLAYING CLUB?
FELL ASLEEP ...
...
WHOOPS. I SKIPPED CLASS.
DONG
DING

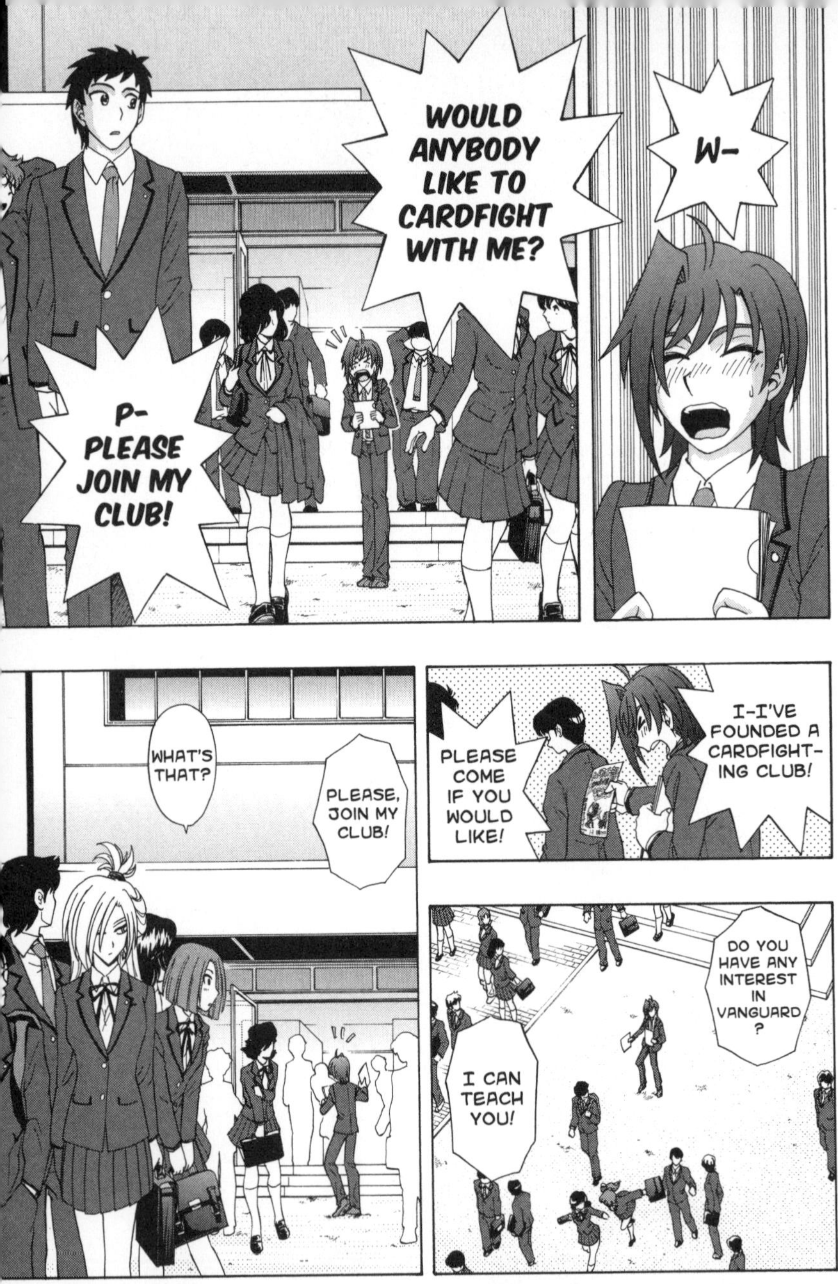
W-
WOULD ANYBODY LIKE TO CARDFIGHT WITH ME?
P- PLEASE JOIN MY CLUB!
I-I'VE FOUNDED A CARDFIGHTING CLUB!
PLEASE COME IF YOU WOULD LIKE!
DO YOU HAVE ANY INTEREST IN VANGUARD?
I CAN TEACH YOU!
PLEASE, JOIN MY CLUB!
WHAT'S THAT?

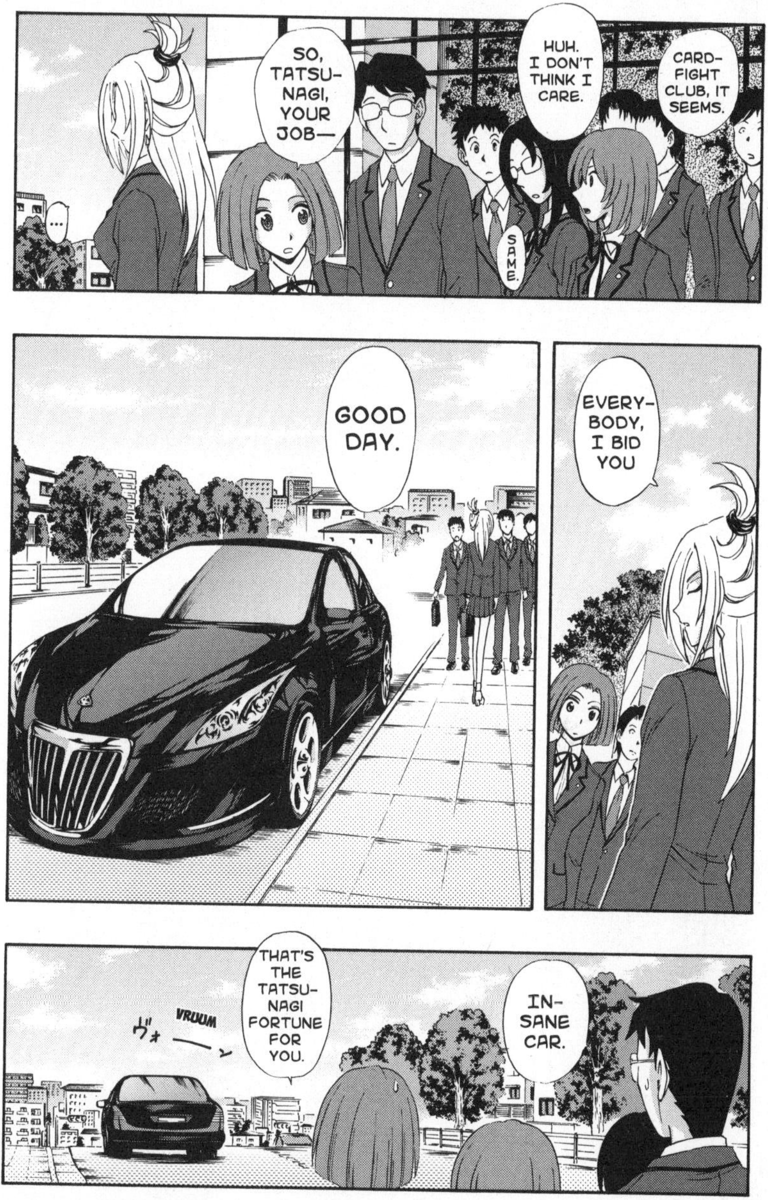
CARD-FIGHT CLUB, IT SEEMS.
HUH. I DON'T THINK I CARE.
SAME.
SO, TATSU-NAGI, YOUR JOB—
...
EVERY-BODY, I BID YOU
GOOD DAY.
IN-SANE CAR.
THAT'S THE TATSU-NAGI FORTUNE FOR YOU.
VRUUM
ヴォーン

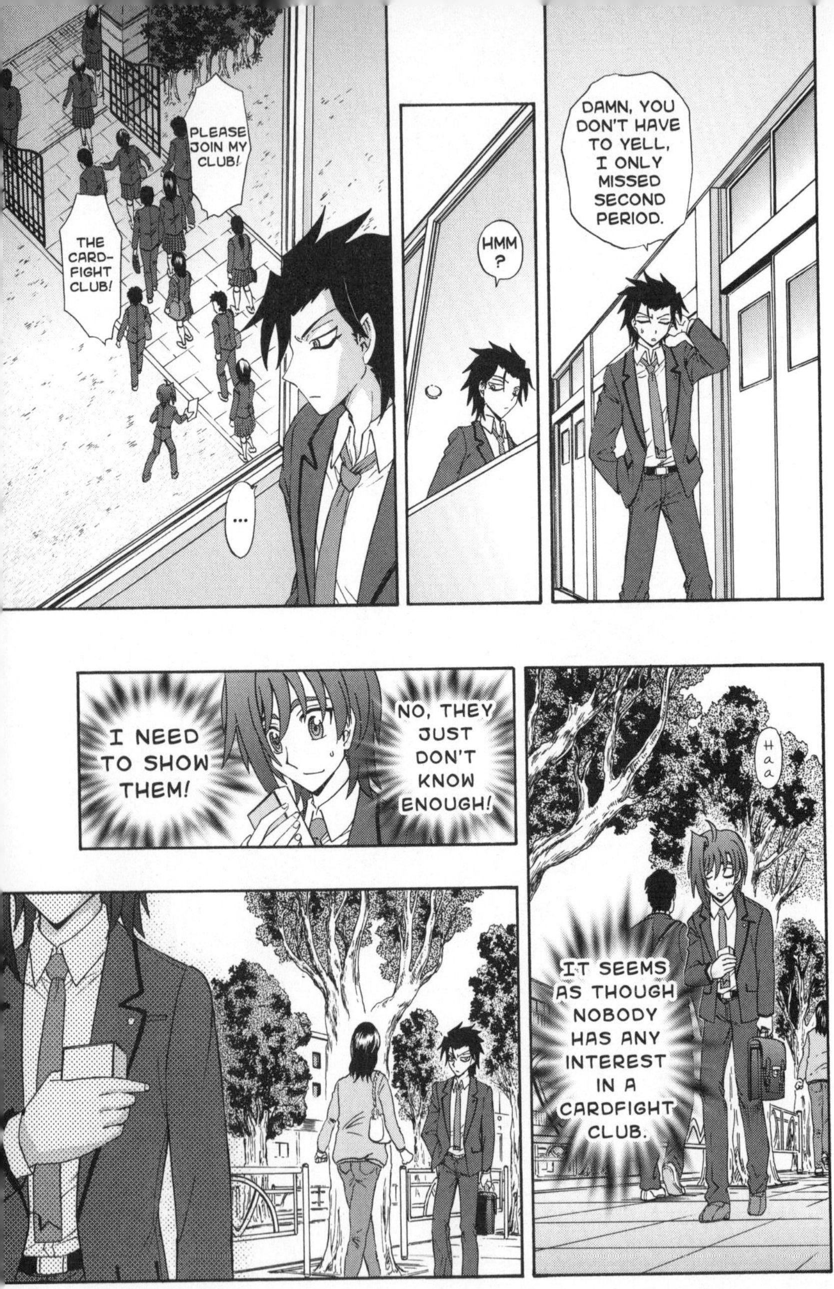

DAMN, YOU DON'T HAVE TO YELL, I ONLY MISSED SECOND PERIOD.
HMM ?
PLEASE JOIN MY CLUB!
THE CARD-FIGHT CLUB!
...
Haa
IT SEEMS AS THOUGH NOBODY HAS ANY INTEREST IN A CARDFIGHT CLUB.
NO, THEY JUST DON'T KNOW ENOUGH!
I NEED TO SHOW THEM!

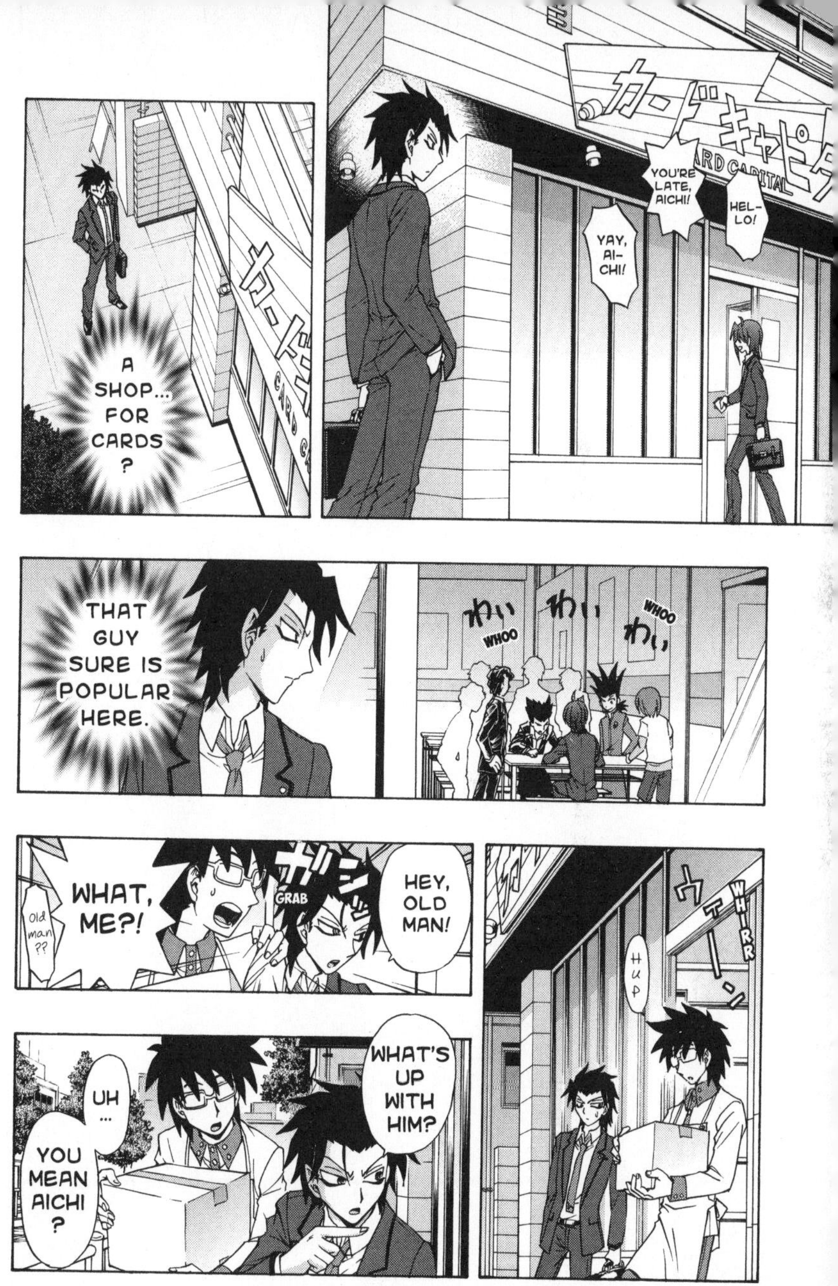
CARD CAPITAL
HEL-LO!
YOU'RE LATE, AICHI!
YAY, AI-CHI!
A SHOP... FOR CARDS?
わい
WHOO
わい
わい
WHOO
THAT GUY SURE IS POPULAR HERE.
WHIRR
HUP
HEY, OLD MAN!
GRAB
WHAT, ME?!
Old man??
WHAT'S UP WITH HIM?
UH... YOU MEAN AICHI?

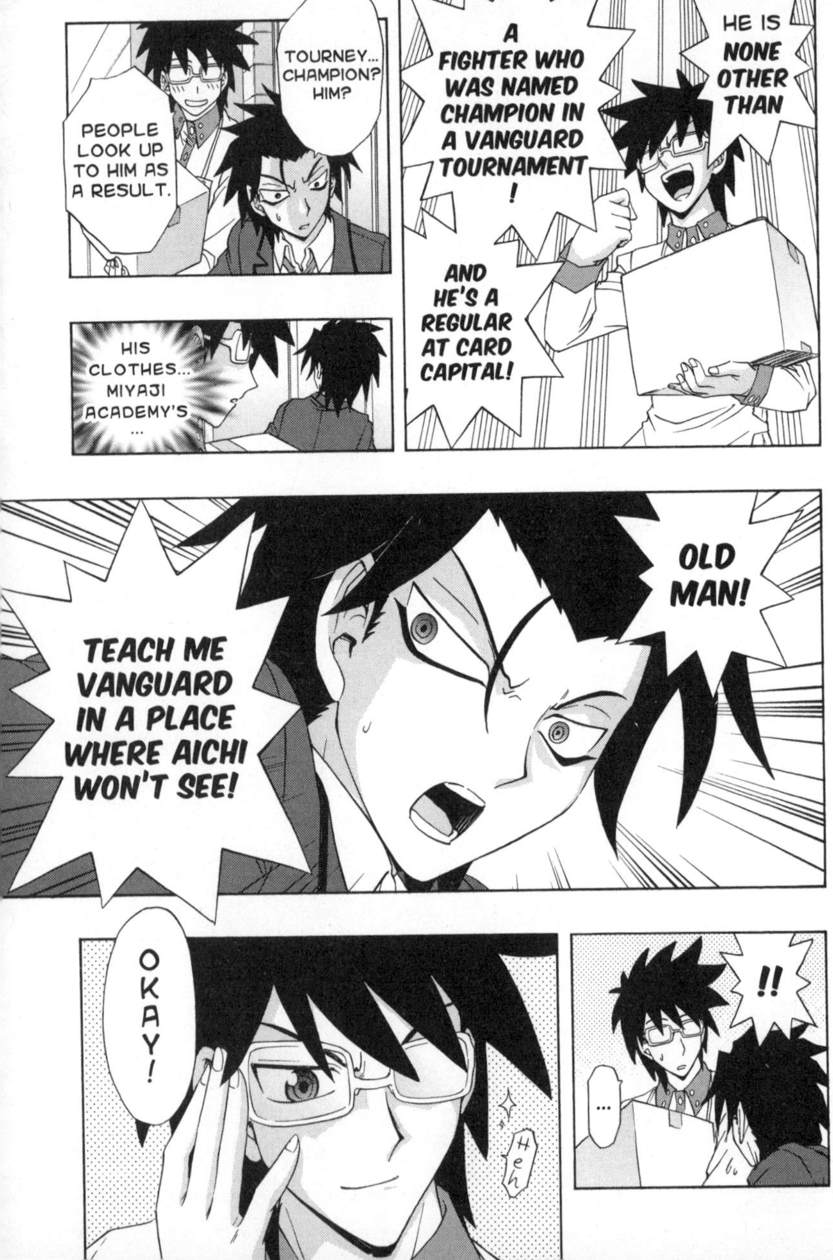

HE IS NONE OTHER THAN
A FIGHTER WHO WAS NAMED CHAMPION IN A VANGUARD TOURNAMENT!
AND HE'S A REGULAR AT CARD CAPITAL!
TOURNEY... CHAMPION? HIM?
PEOPLE LOOK UP TO HIM AS A RESULT.
HIS CLOTHES... MIYAJI ACADEMY'S ...
OLD MAN!
TEACH ME VANGUARD IN A PLACE WHERE AICHI WON'T SEE!
!!
...
OKAY!
Heh

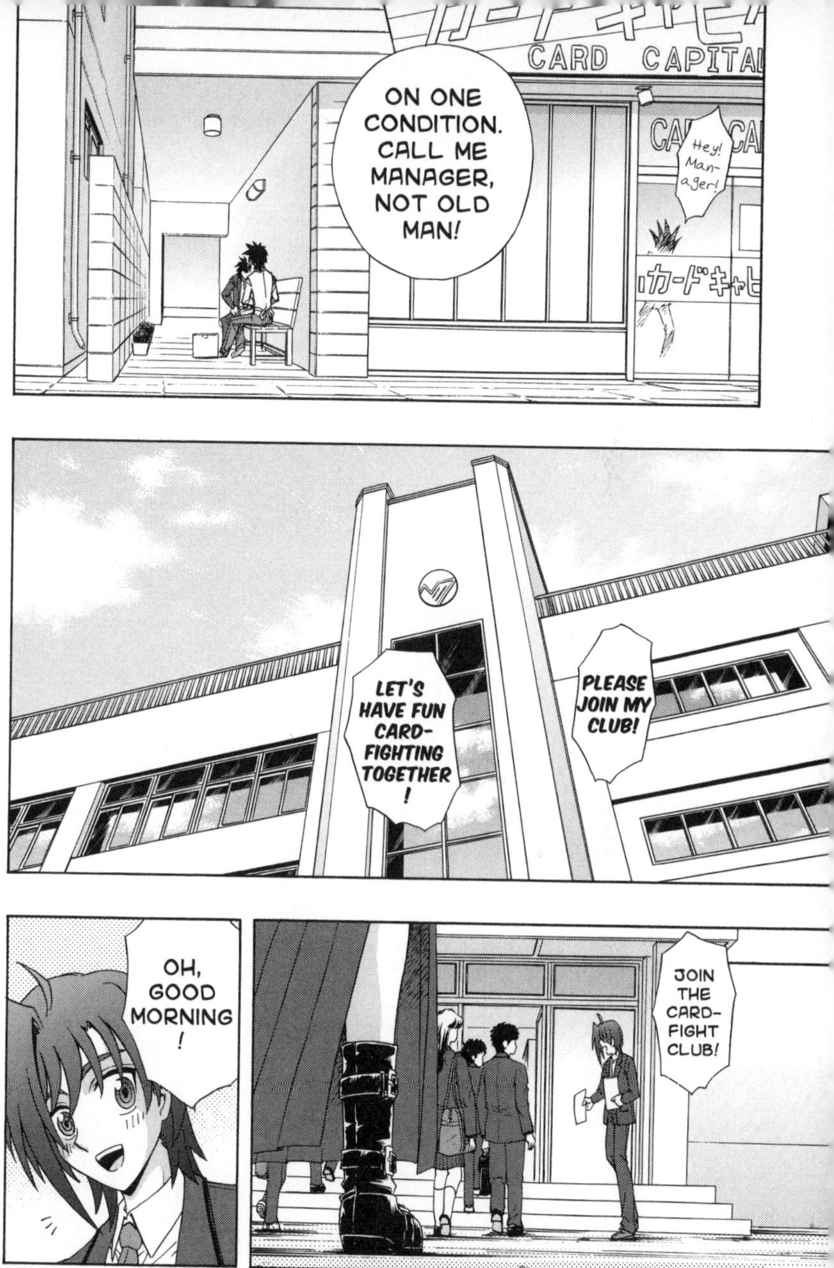
CARD CAPITAL
Hey! Manager!
ON ONE CONDITION. CALL ME MANAGER, NOT OLD MAN!
PLEASE JOIN MY CLUB!
LET'S HAVE FUN CARD-FIGHTING TOGETHER!
JOIN THE CARD-FIGHT CLUB!
OH, GOOD MORNING!

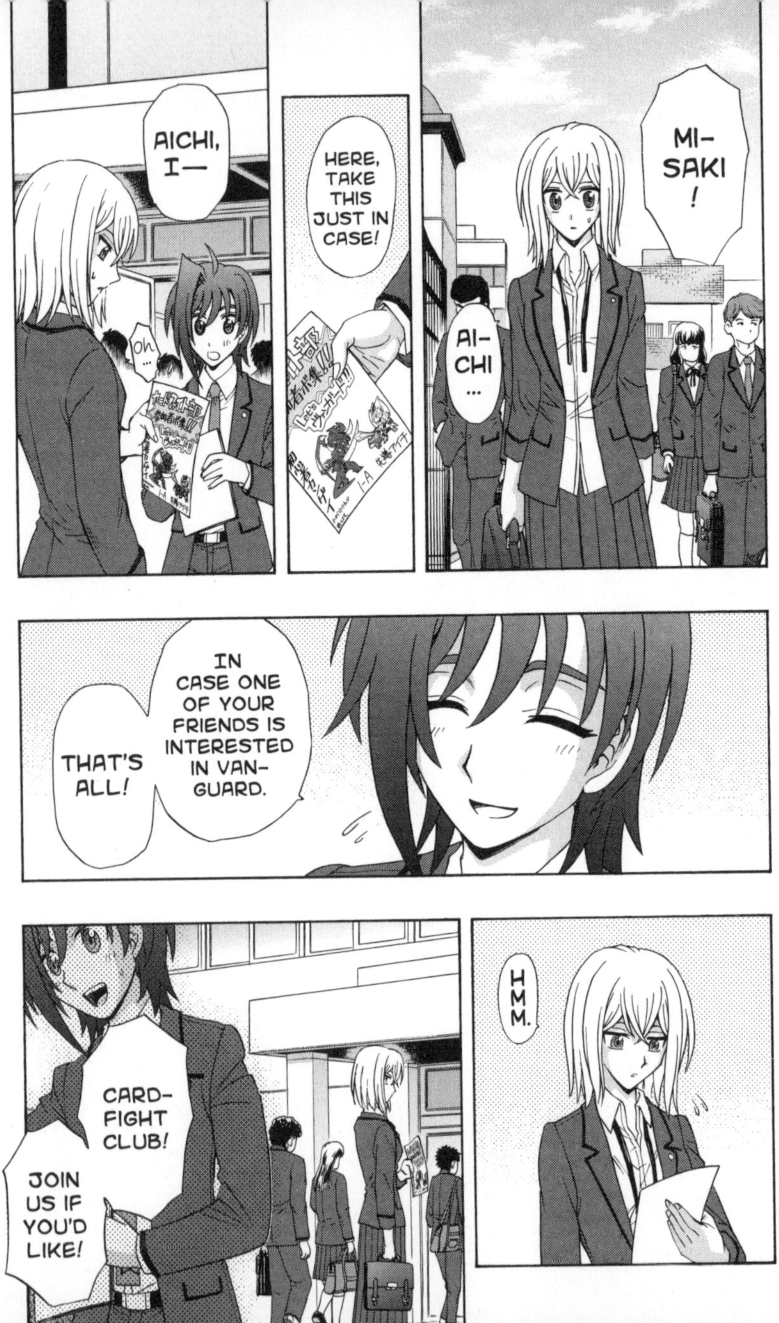

MI-SAKI!
AI-CHI...
HERE, TAKE THIS JUST IN CASE!
AICHI, I—
Oh...
IN CASE ONE OF YOUR FRIENDS IS INTERESTED IN VAN-GUARD.
THAT'S ALL!
HMM.
CARD-FIGHT CLUB!
JOIN US IF YOU'D LIKE!

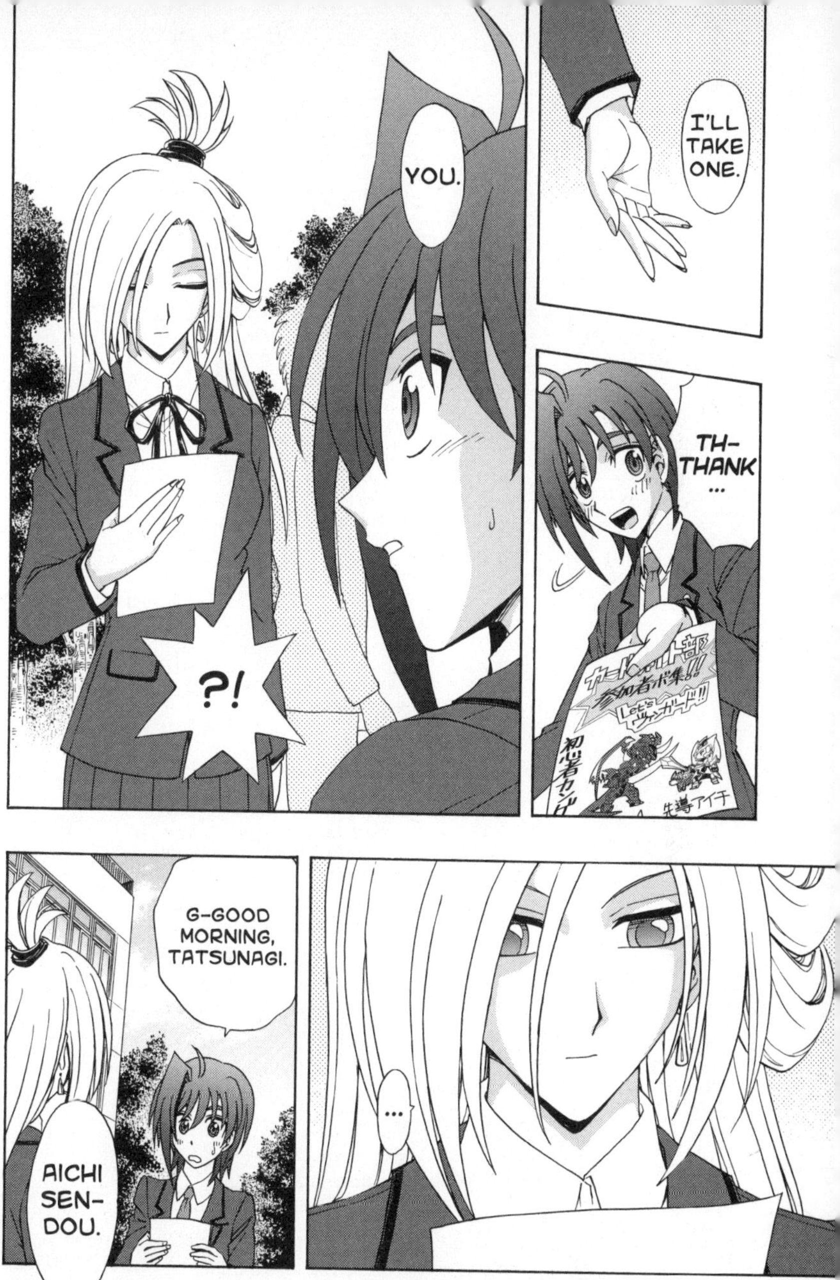
I'LL TAKE ONE.
TH- THANK ...
YOU.
?!
...
G-GOOD MORNING, TATSUNAGI.
AICHI SEN- DOU.

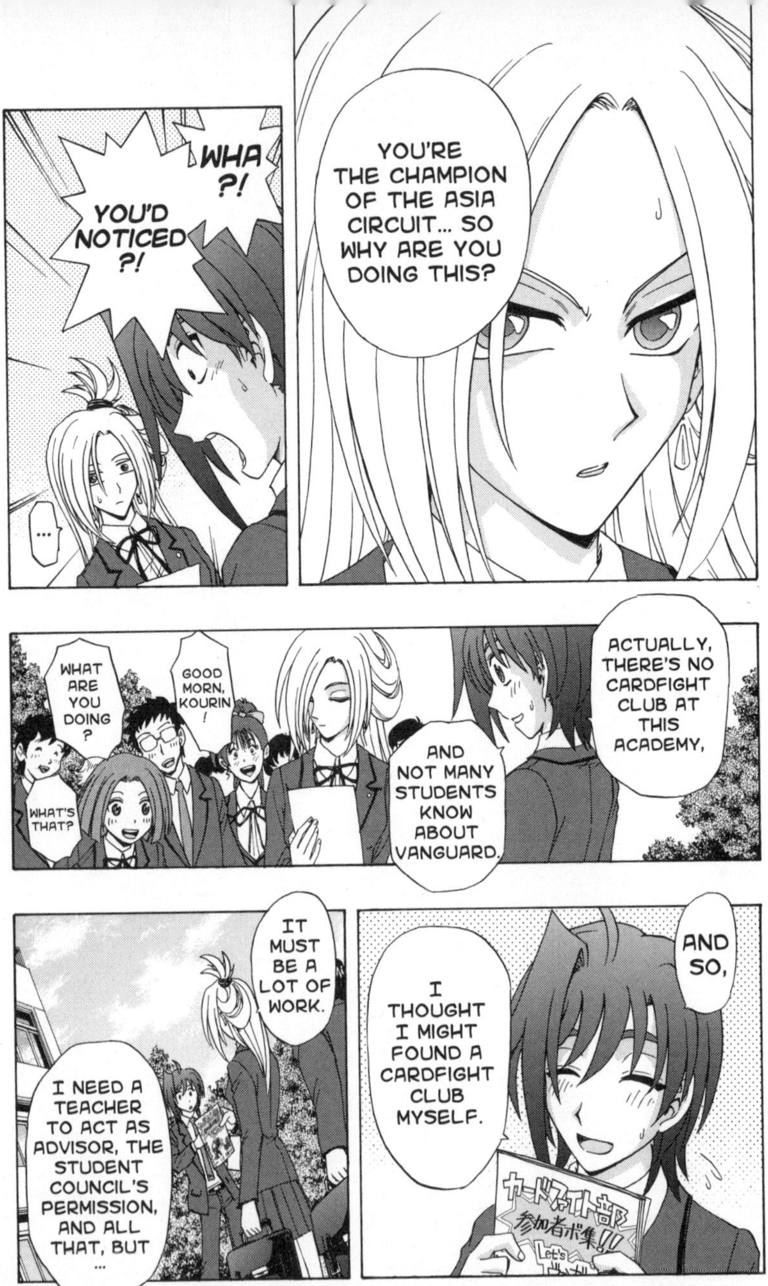
YOU'RE THE CHAMPION OF THE ASIA CIRCUIT... SO WHY ARE YOU DOING THIS?
WHA ?!
YOU'D NOTICED ?!
...
ACTUALLY, THERE'S NO CARDFIGHT CLUB AT THIS ACADEMY,
AND NOT MANY STUDENTS KNOW ABOUT VANGUARD.
GOOD MORN, KOURIN!
WHAT ARE YOU DOING?
WHAT'S THAT?
AND SO,
I THOUGHT I MIGHT FOUND A CARDFIGHT CLUB MYSELF.
カードファイト部
Let's
IT MUST BE A LOT OF WORK.
I NEED A TEACHER TO ACT AS ADVISOR, THE STUDENT COUNCIL'S PERMISSION, AND ALL THAT, BUT ...

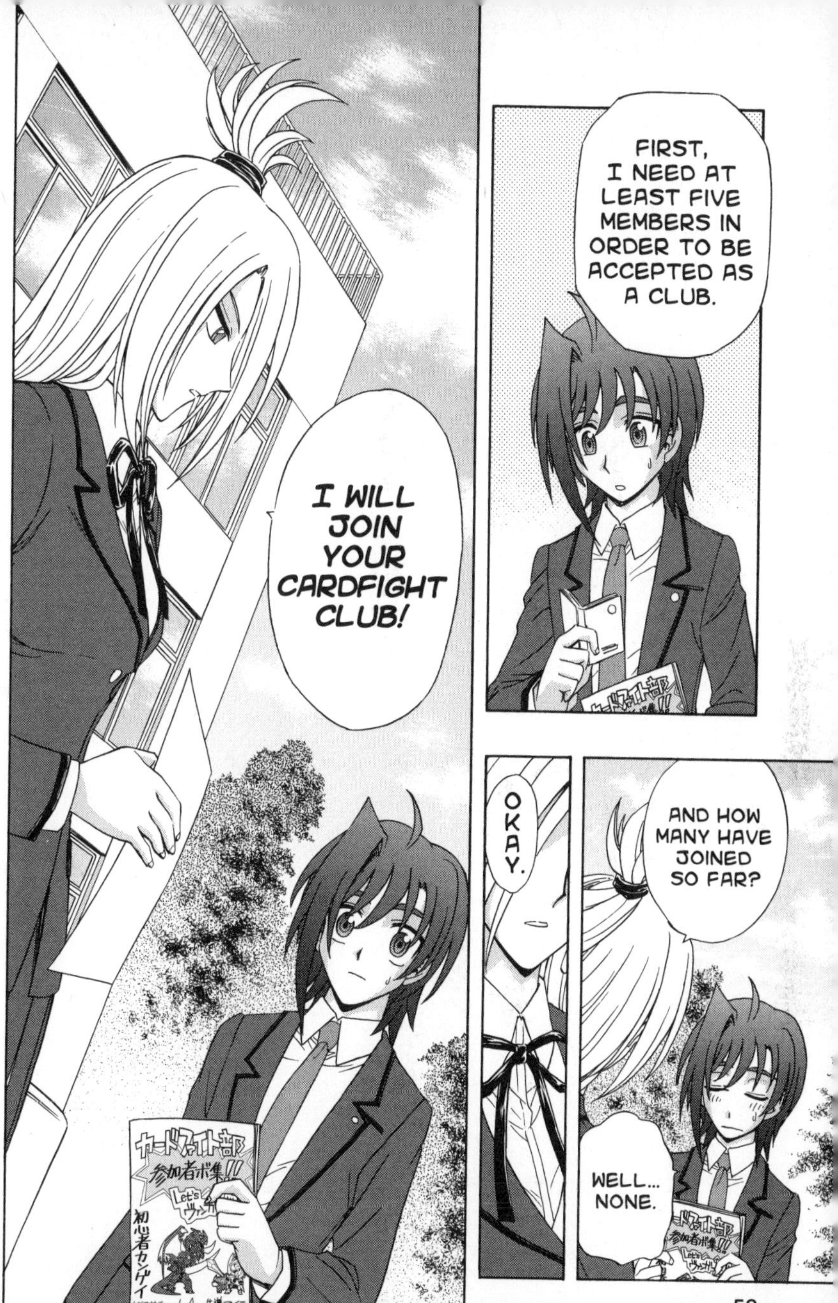
FIRST, I NEED AT LEAST FIVE MEMBERS IN ORDER TO BE ACCEPTED AS A CLUB.
AND HOW MANY HAVE JOINED SO FAR?
WELL... NONE.
OKAY.
I WILL JOIN YOUR CARDFIGHT CLUB!
カードファイト部
参加者ボ集!!
初心者カンゲイ
1-A 先導アイチ

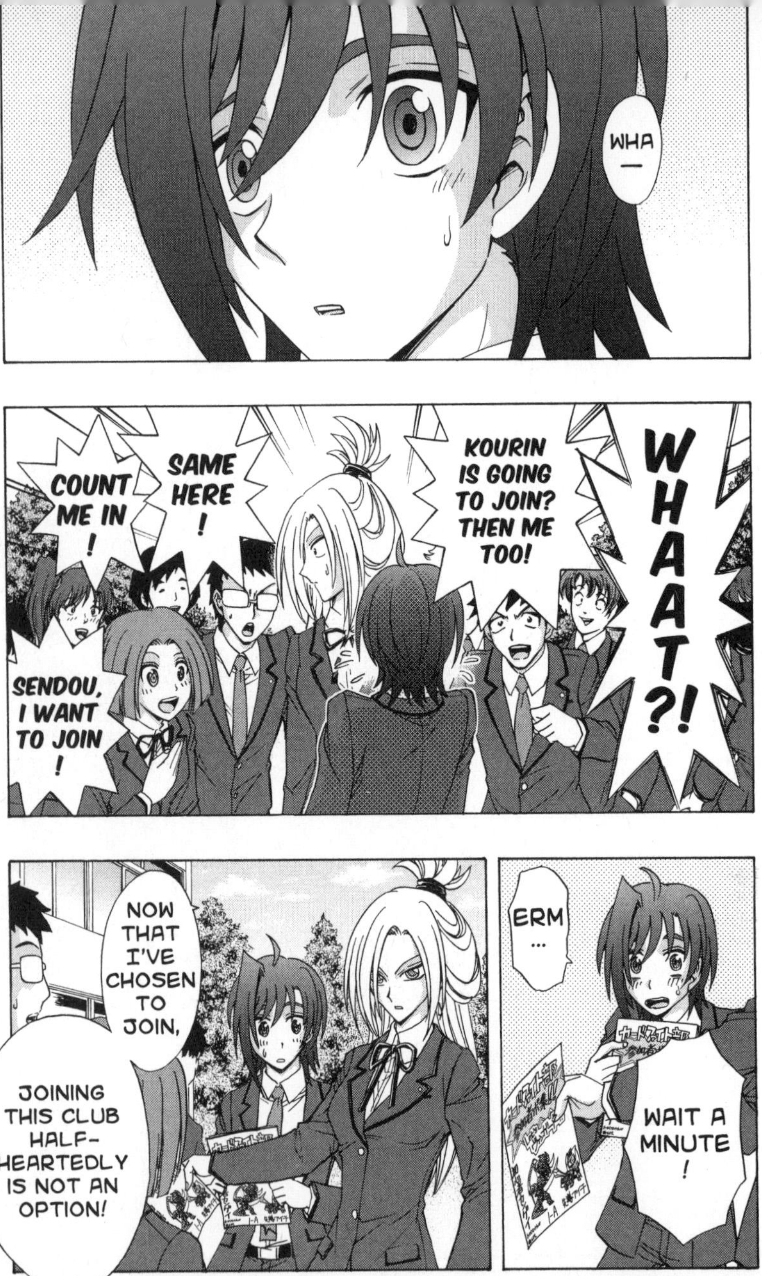
WHA—
WHAAT?!
KOURIN IS GOING TO JOIN? THEN ME TOO!
SAME HERE!
COUNT ME IN!
SENDOU, I WANT TO JOIN!
ERM...
WAIT A MINUTE!
NOW THAT I'VE CHOSEN TO JOIN,
JOINING THIS CLUB HALF-HEARTEDLY IS NOT AN OPTION!

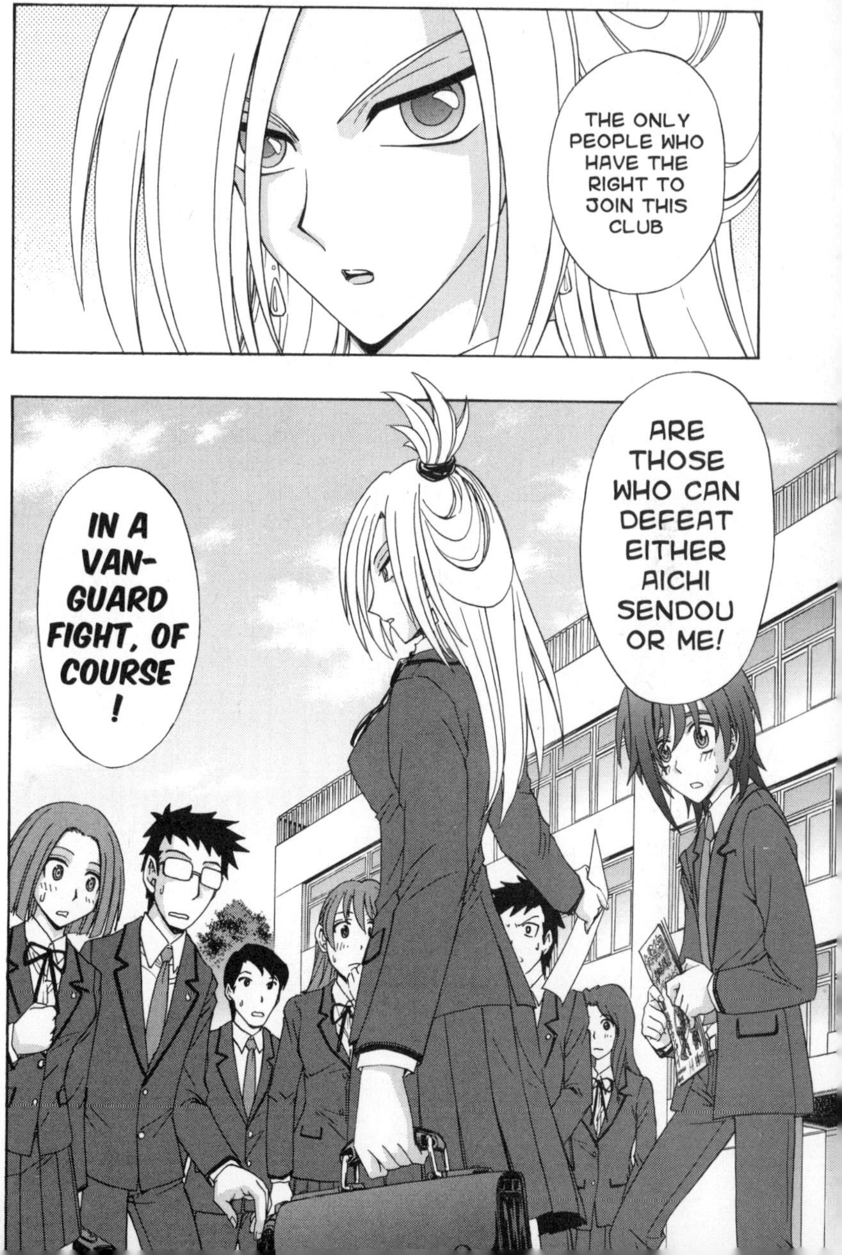
THE ONLY PEOPLE WHO HAVE THE RIGHT TO JOIN THIS CLUB
ARE THOSE WHO CAN DEFEAT EITHER AICHI SENDOU OR ME!
IN A VAN-GUARD FIGHT, OF COURSE!

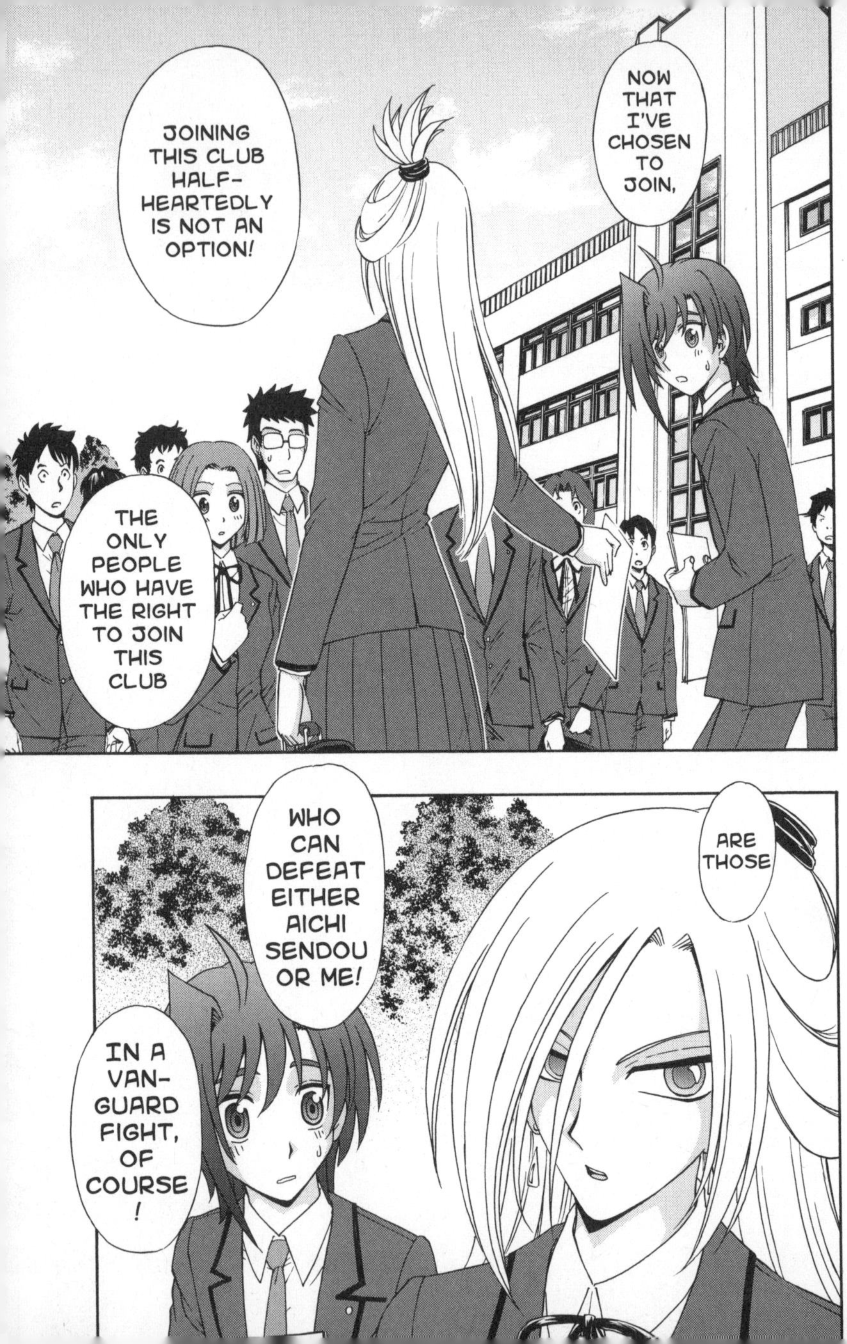
NOW THAT I'VE CHOSEN TO JOIN,
JOINING THIS CLUB HALF-HEARTEDLY IS NOT AN OPTION!
THE ONLY PEOPLE WHO HAVE THE RIGHT TO JOIN THIS CLUB
ARE THOSE
WHO CAN DEFEAT EITHER AICHI SENDOU OR ME!
IN A VAN-GUARD FIGHT, OF COURSE!

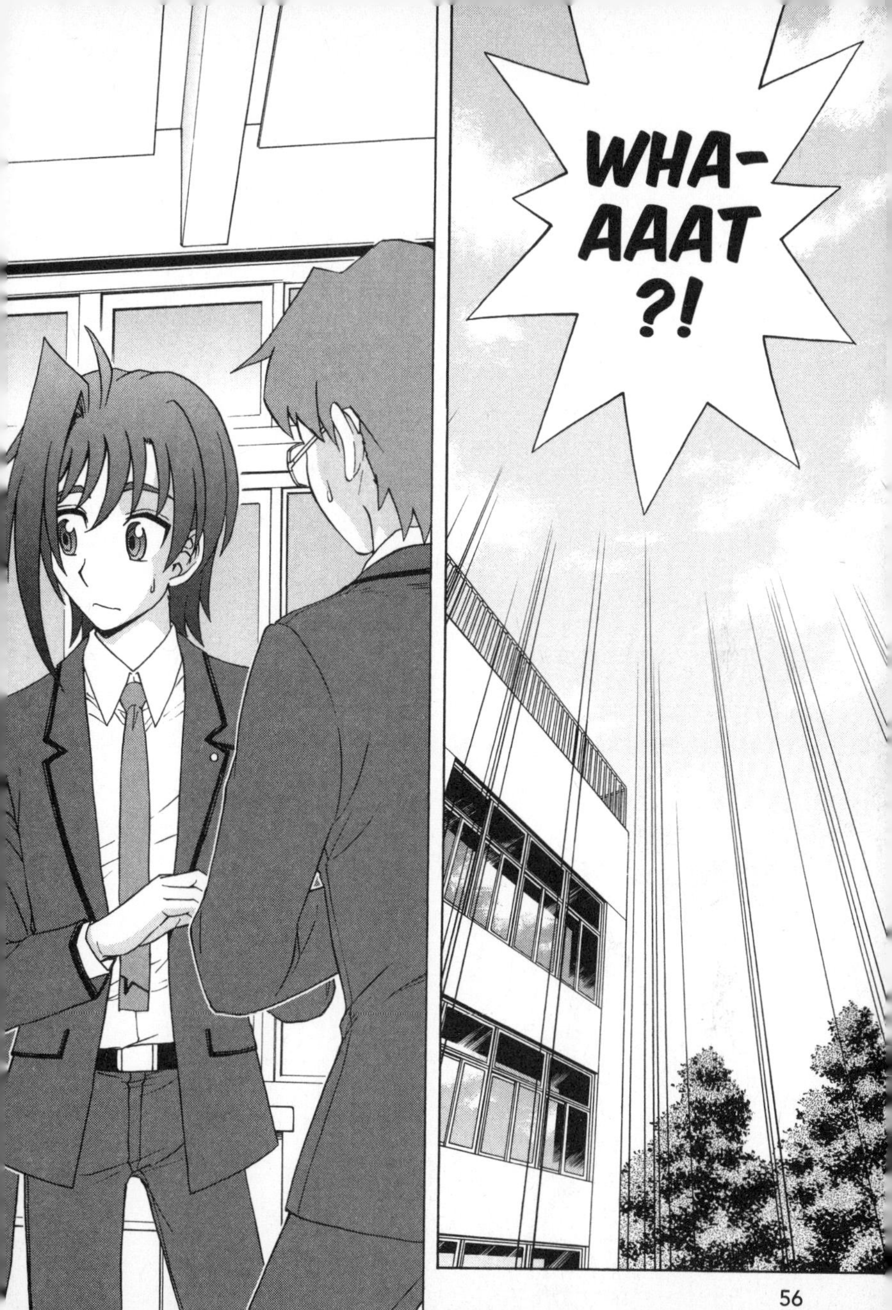
WHA-AAAT?!

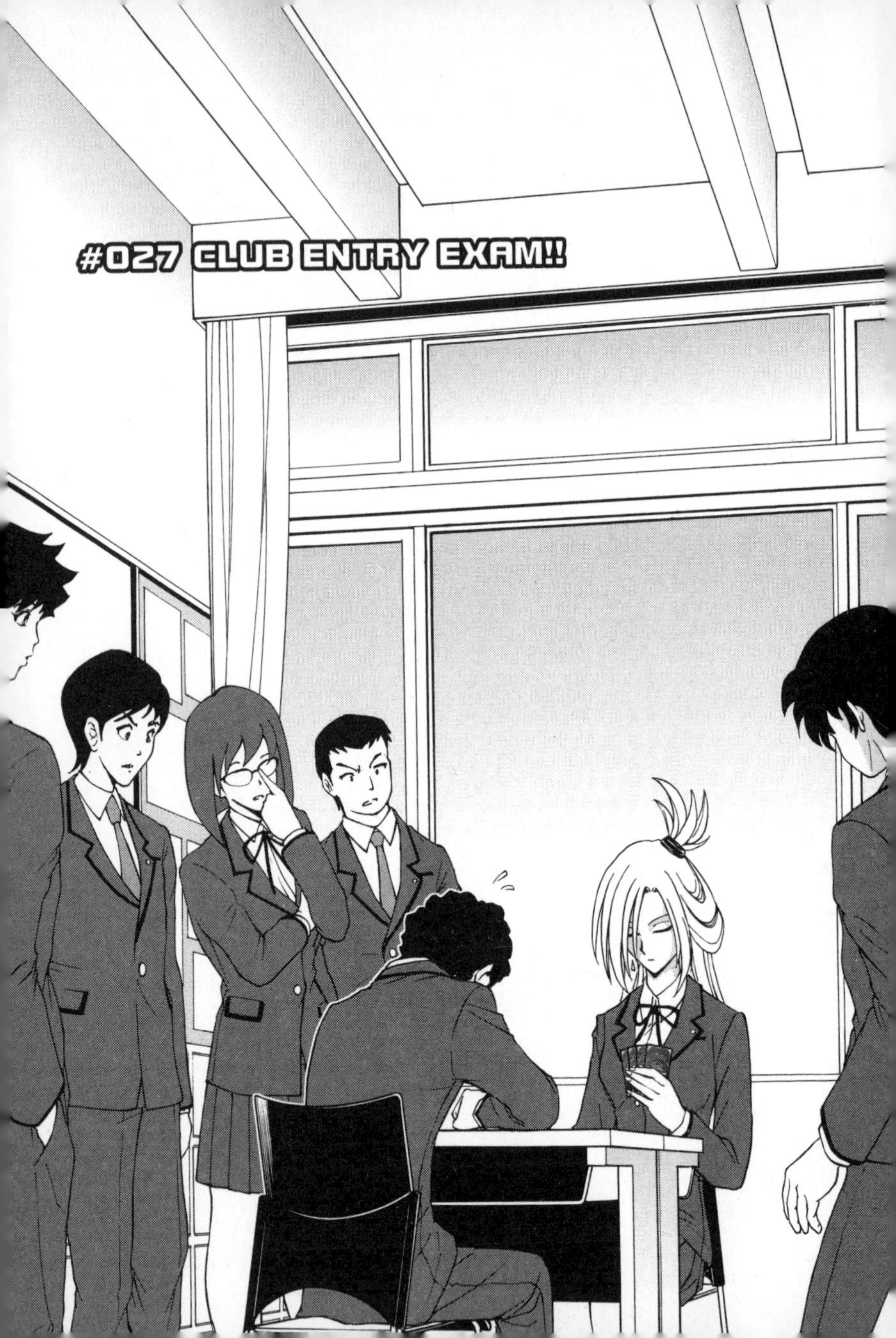
#027 CLUB ENTRY EXAM!!

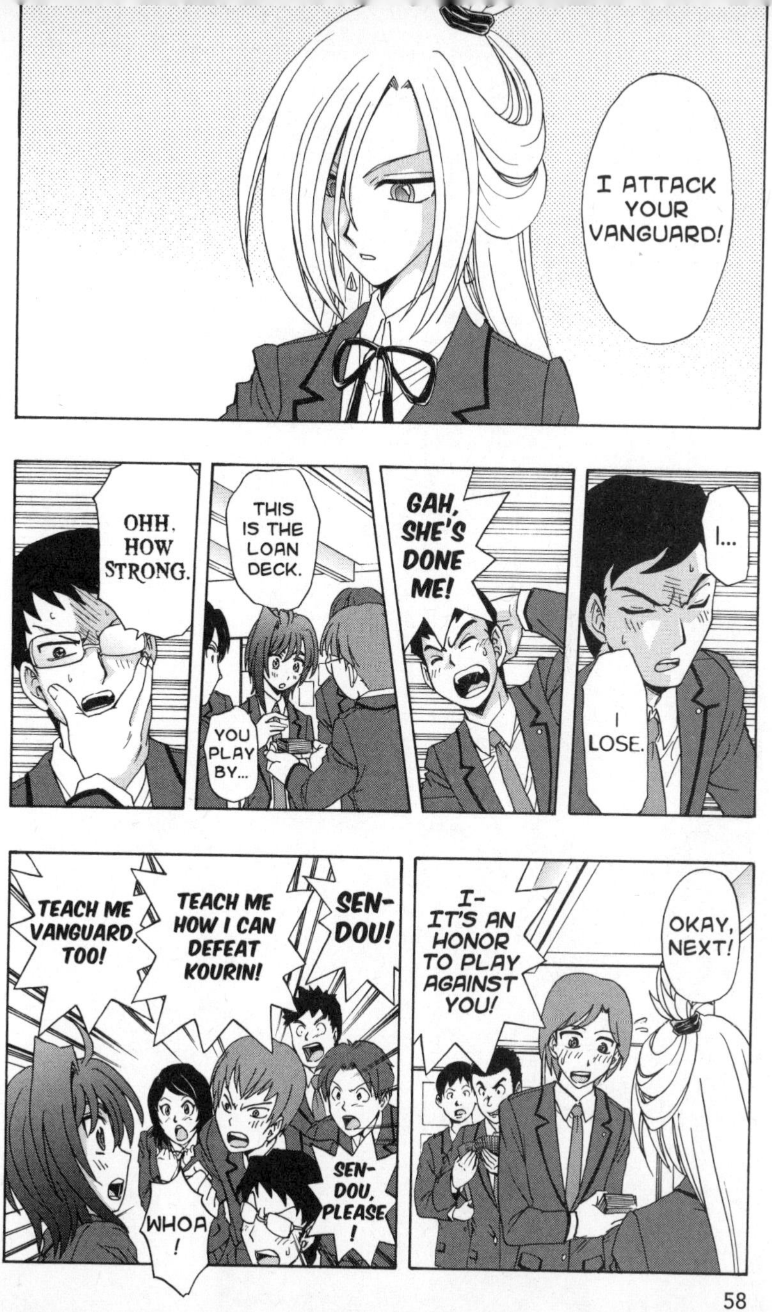
I ATTACK YOUR VANGUARD!
I...
I LOSE.
GAH, SHE'S DONE ME!
THIS IS THE LOAN DECK.
YOU PLAY BY...
OHH. HOW STRONG.
OKAY, NEXT!
I- IT'S AN HONOR TO PLAY AGAINST YOU!
SEN-DOU!
TEACH ME HOW I CAN DEFEAT KOURIN!
TEACH ME VANGUARD, TOO!
SEN-DOU, PLEASE!
WHOA!

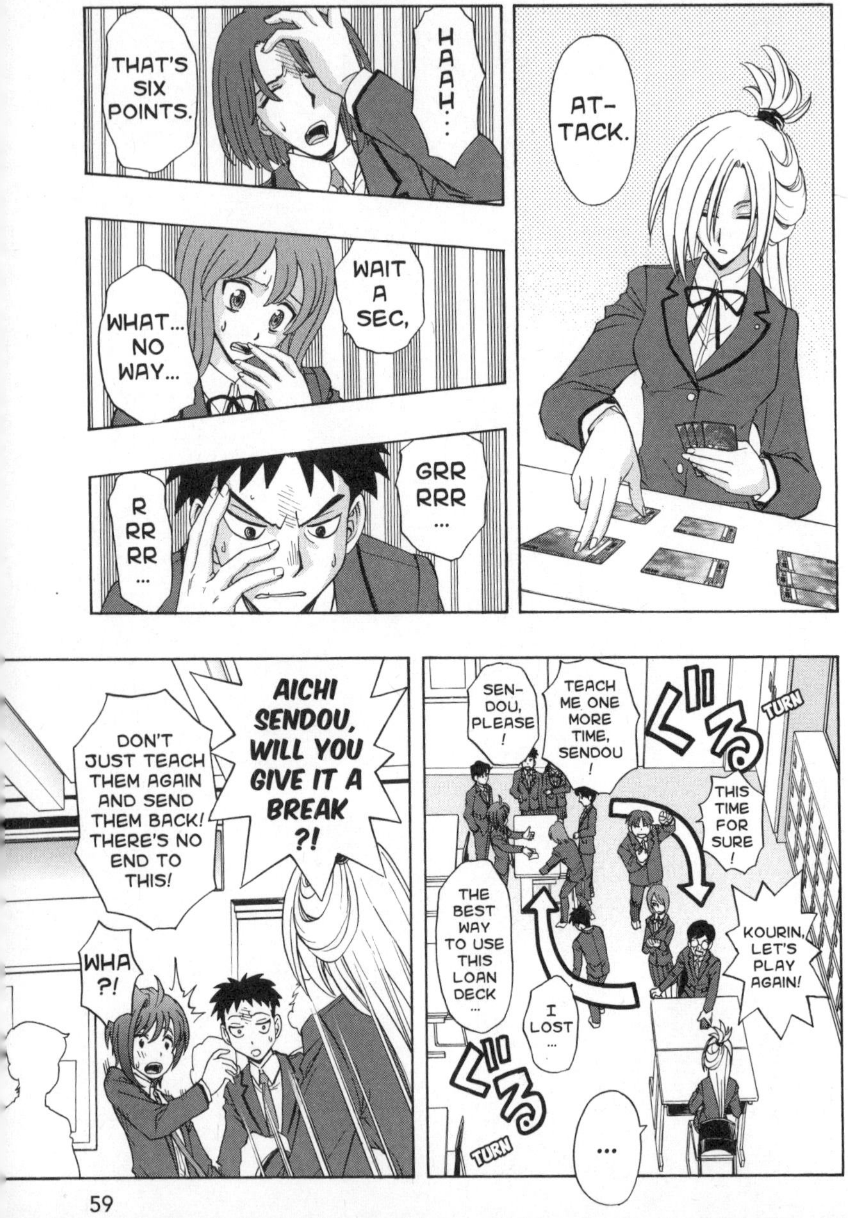
AT-TACK.
HAAH...
THAT'S SIX POINTS.
WAIT A SEC,
WHAT... NO WAY...
GRR RRR ...
R RR RR ...
TURN
TEACH ME ONE MORE TIME, SENDOU!
SEN-DOU, PLEASE!
THIS TIME FOR SURE!
KOURIN, LET'S PLAY AGAIN!
THE BEST WAY TO USE THIS LOAN DECK ...
I LOST ...
TURN
...
AICHI SENDOU, WILL YOU GIVE IT A BREAK?!
DON'T JUST TEACH THEM AGAIN AND SEND THEM BACK! THERE'S NO END TO THIS!
WHA?!

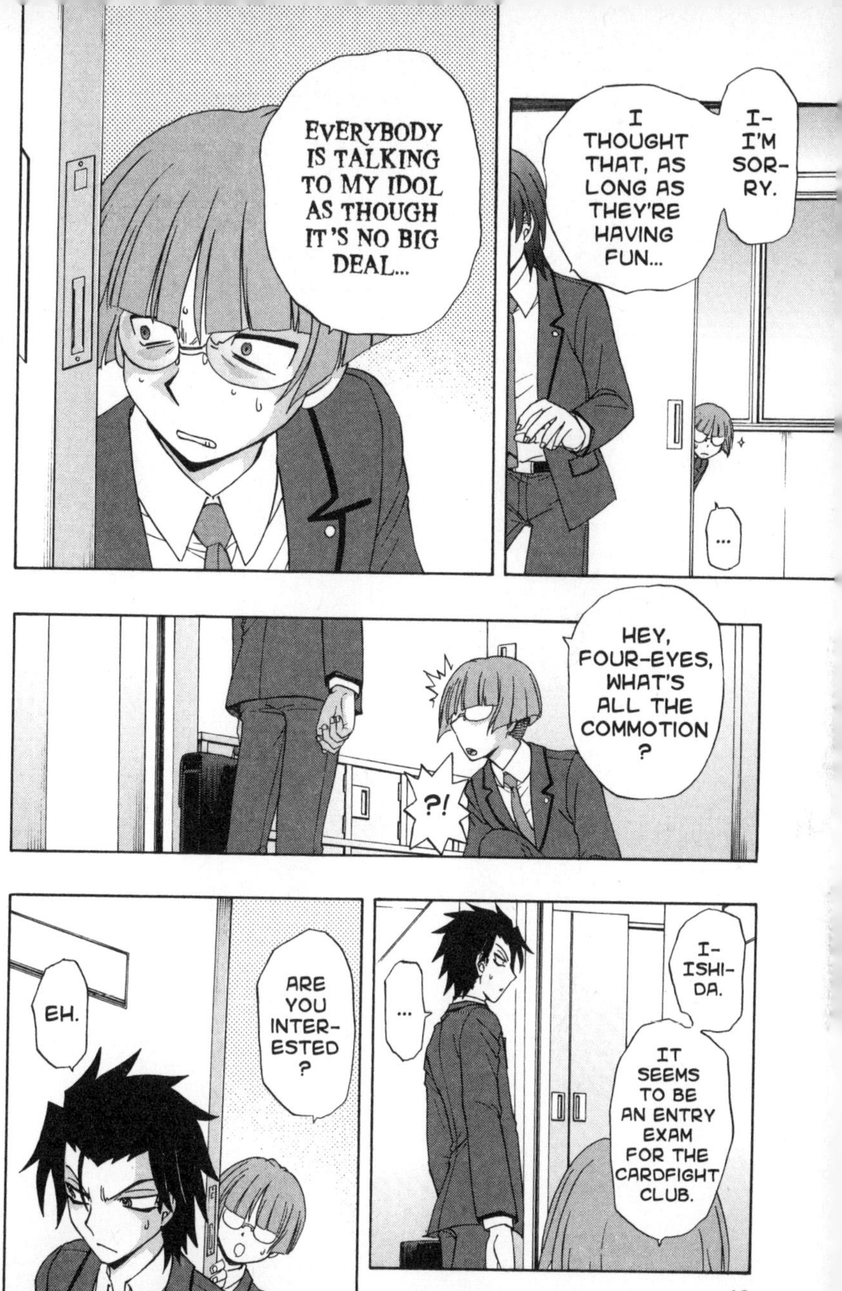
I- I'M SORRY.
I THOUGHT THAT, AS LONG AS THEY'RE HAVING FUN...
...
EVERYBODY IS TALKING TO MY IDOL AS THOUGH IT'S NO BIG DEAL...
HEY, FOUR-EYES, WHAT'S ALL THE COMMOTION?
?!
I- ISHIDA.
IT SEEMS TO BE AN ENTRY EXAM FOR THE CARDFIGHT CLUB.
...
ARE YOU INTERESTED?
EH.

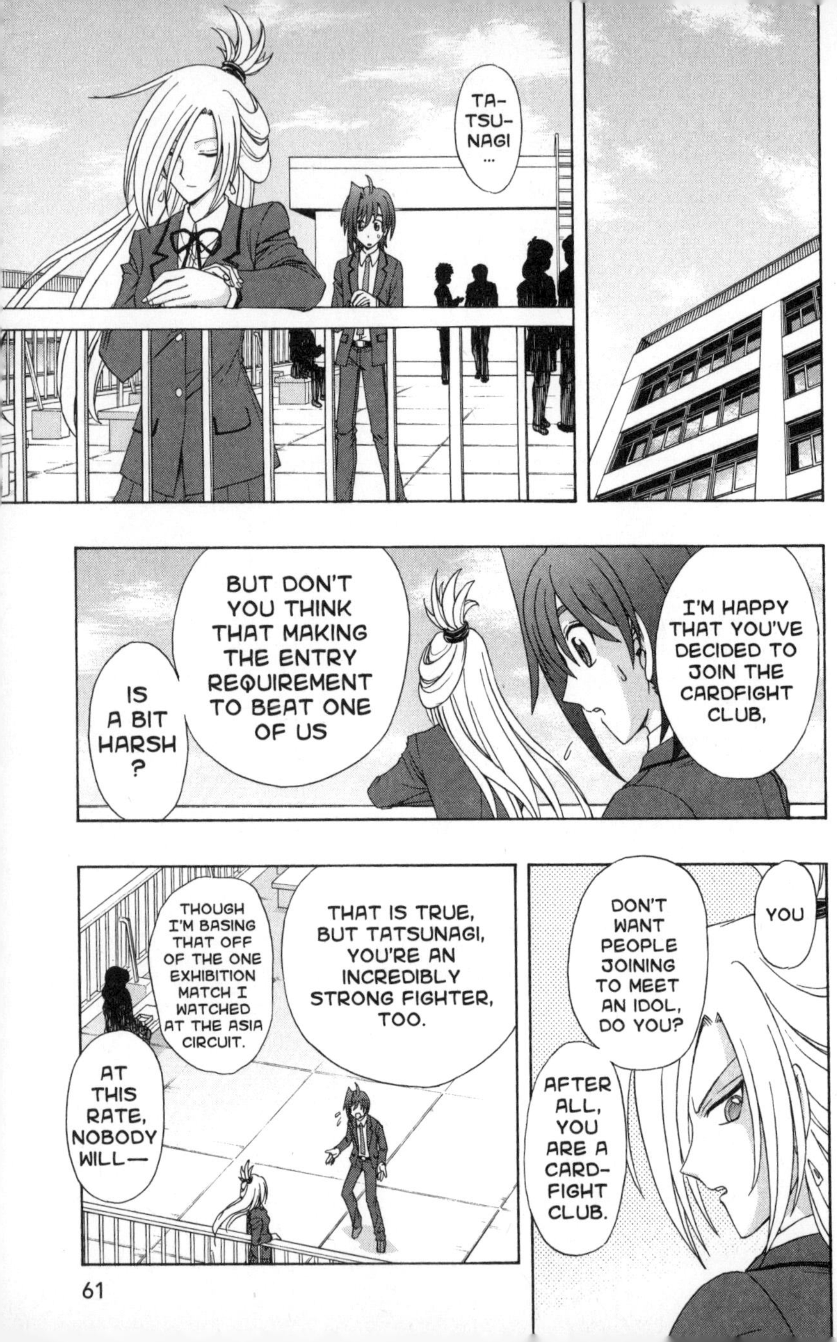
TA-TSU-NAGI ...
I'M HAPPY THAT YOU'VE DECIDED TO JOIN THE CARDFIGHT CLUB,
BUT DON'T YOU THINK THAT MAKING THE ENTRY REQUIREMENT TO BEAT ONE OF US
IS A BIT HARSH ?
YOU
DON'T WANT PEOPLE JOINING TO MEET AN IDOL, DO YOU?
AFTER ALL, YOU ARE A CARD-FIGHT CLUB.
THAT IS TRUE, BUT TATSUNAGI, YOU'RE AN INCREDIBLY STRONG FIGHTER, TOO.
THOUGH I'M BASING THAT OFF OF THE ONE EXHIBITION MATCH I WATCHED AT THE ASIA CIRCUIT.
AT THIS RATE, NOBODY WILL—

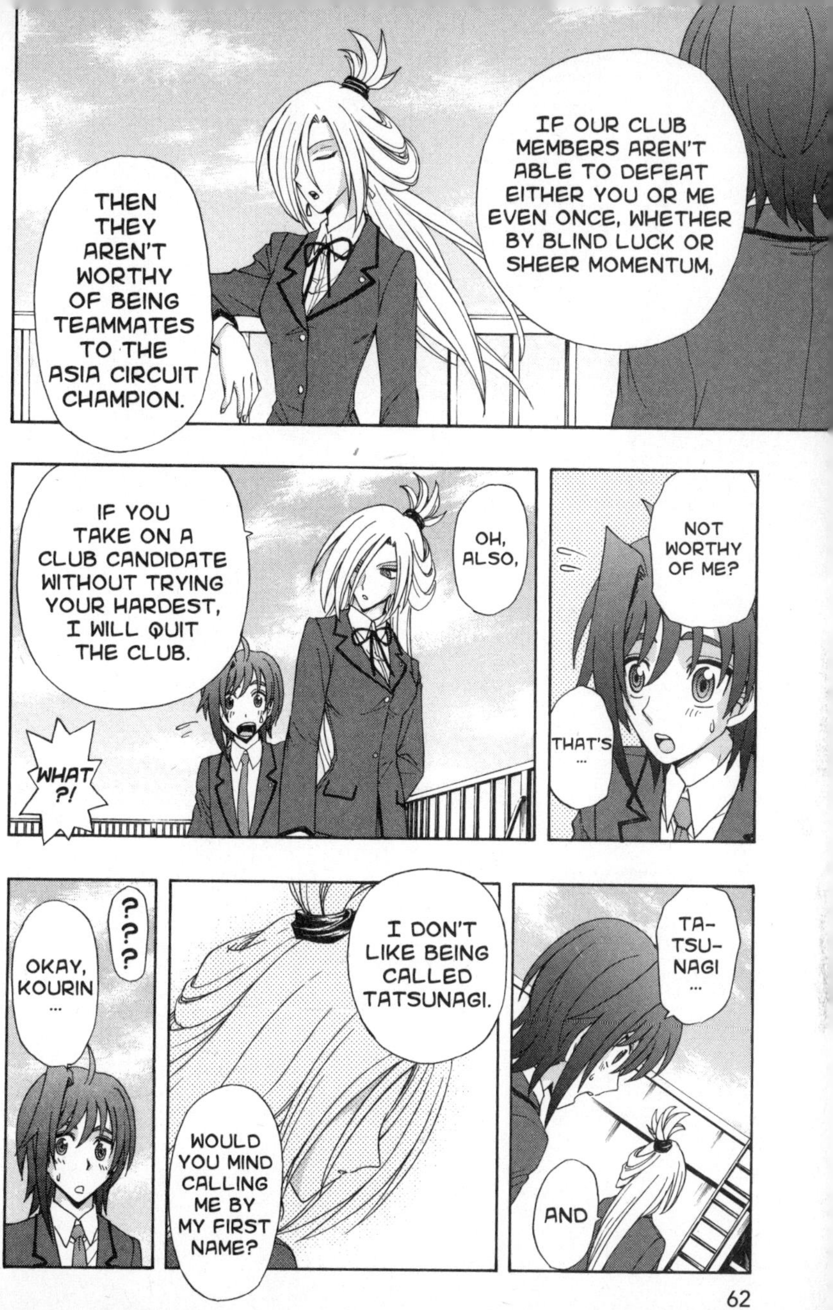
IF OUR CLUB MEMBERS AREN'T ABLE TO DEFEAT EITHER YOU OR ME EVEN ONCE, WHETHER BY BLIND LUCK OR SHEER MOMENTUM,
THEN THEY AREN'T WORTHY OF BEING TEAMMATES TO THE ASIA CIRCUIT CHAMPION.
NOT WORTHY OF ME?
THAT'S ...
OH, ALSO,
IF YOU TAKE ON A CLUB CANDIDATE WITHOUT TRYING YOUR HARDEST, I WILL QUIT THE CLUB.
WHAT ?!
TA-TSU-NAGI ...
AND
I DON'T LIKE BEING CALLED TATSUNAGI.
WOULD YOU MIND CALLING ME BY MY FIRST NAME?
???
OKAY, KOURIN ...

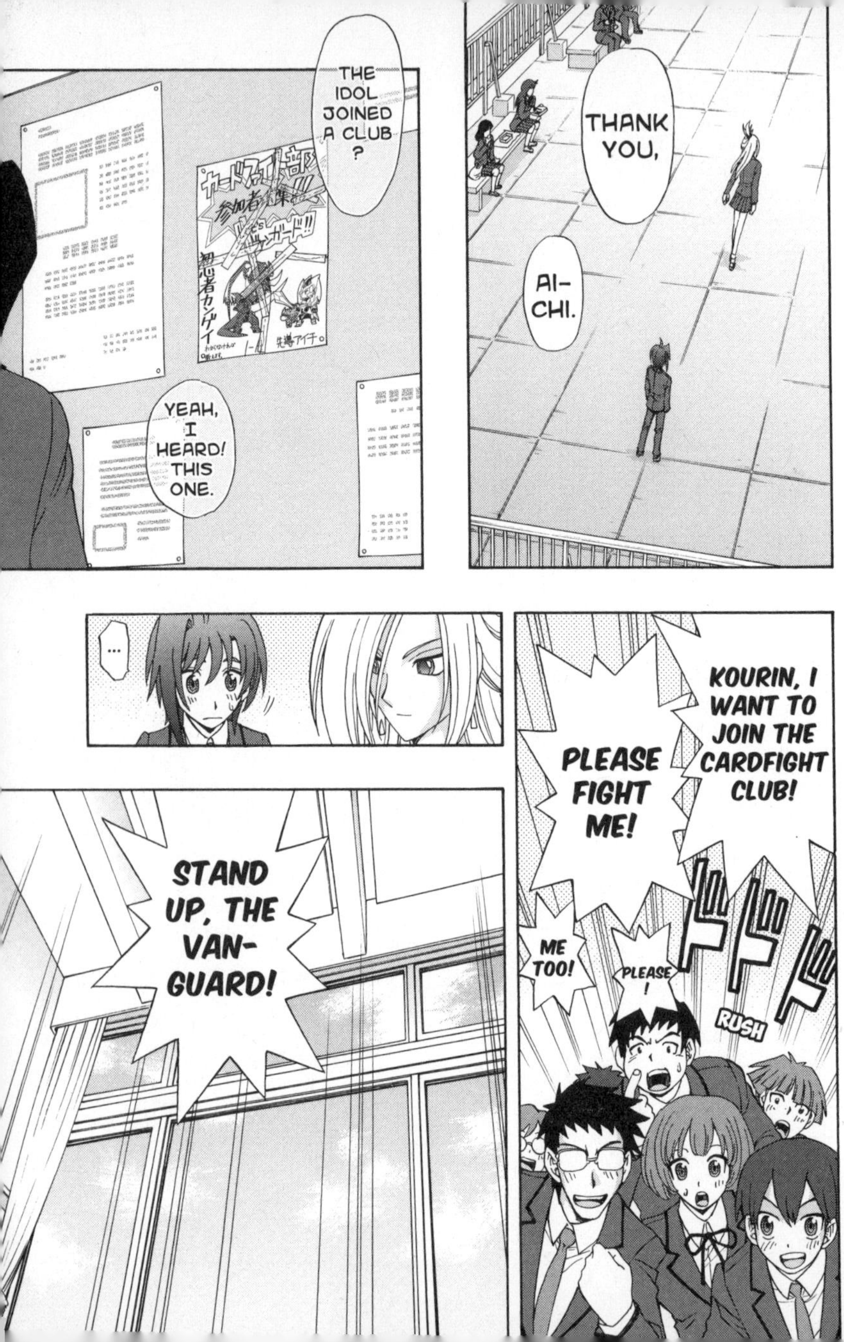
THANK YOU,
AI-CHI.
THE IDOL JOINED A CLUB?
YEAH, I HEARD! THIS ONE.
KOURIN, I WANT TO JOIN THE CARDFIGHT CLUB!
PLEASE FIGHT ME!
RUSH
PLEASE!
ME TOO!
...
STAND UP, THE VAN-GUARD!

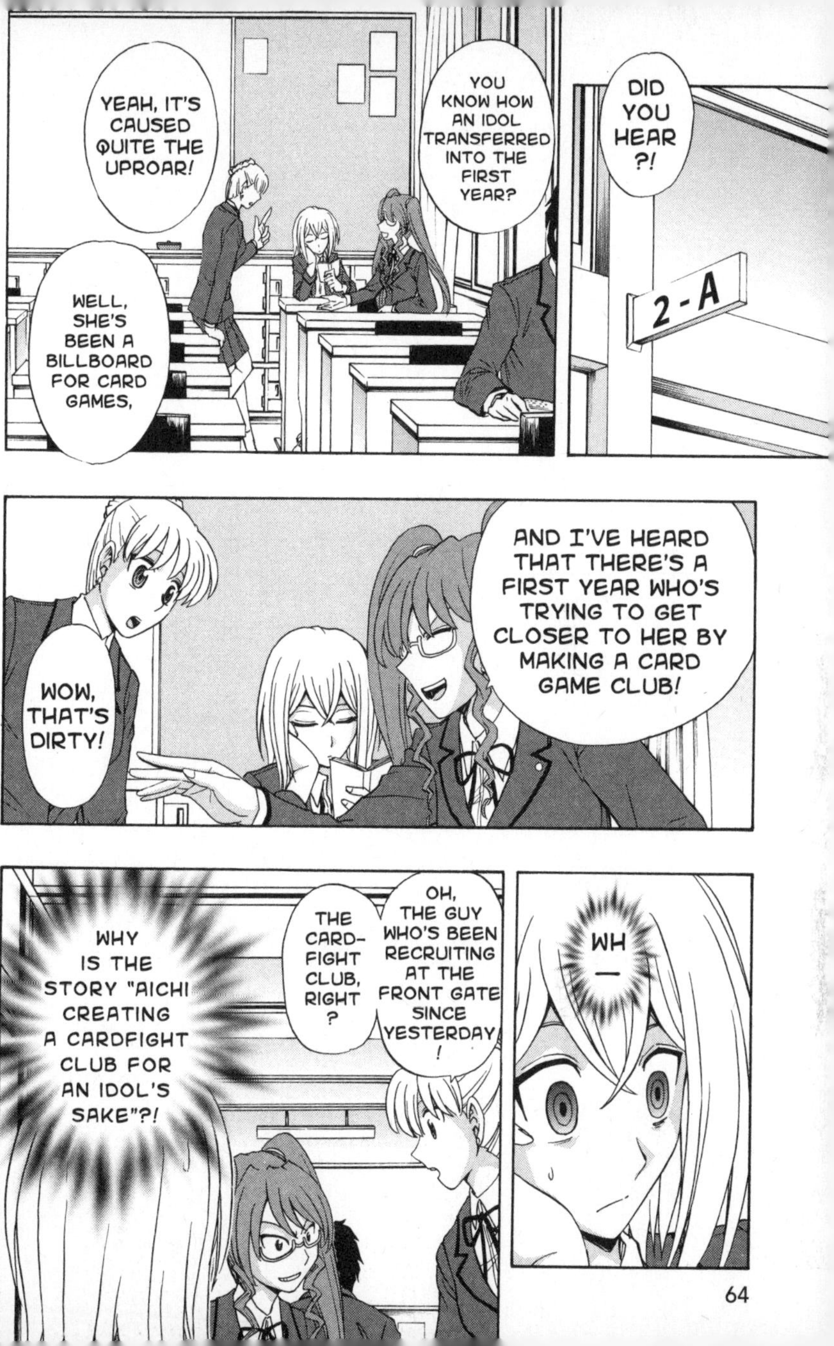
DID YOU HEAR?!
YOU KNOW HOW AN IDOL TRANSFERRED INTO THE FIRST YEAR?
YEAH, IT'S CAUSED QUITE THE UPROAR!
WELL, SHE'S BEEN A BILLBOARD FOR CARD GAMES,
2-A
AND I'VE HEARD THAT THERE'S A FIRST YEAR WHO'S TRYING TO GET CLOSER TO HER BY MAKING A CARD GAME CLUB!
WOW, THAT'S DIRTY!
WH—
OH, THE GUY WHO'S BEEN RECRUITING AT THE FRONT GATE SINCE YESTERDAY!
THE CARD-FIGHT CLUB, RIGHT?
WHY IS THE STORY "AICHI CREATING A CARDFIGHT CLUB FOR AN IDOL'S SAKE"?!

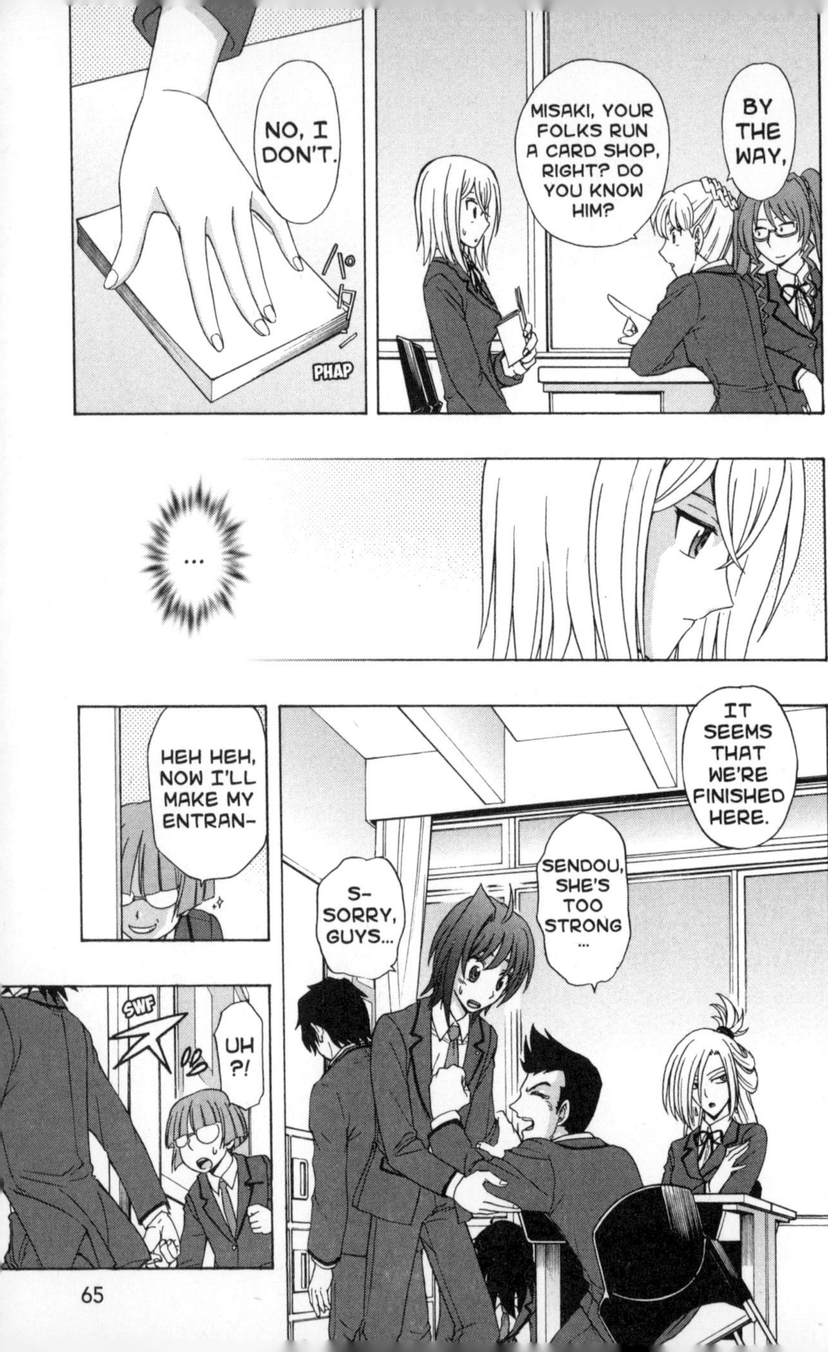
BY THE WAY,
MISAKI, YOUR FOLKS RUN A CARD SHOP, RIGHT? DO YOU KNOW HIM?
NO, I DON'T.
PHAP
...
IT SEEMS THAT WE'RE FINISHED HERE.
SENDOU, SHE'S TOO STRONG ...
S-SORRY, GUYS...
HEH HEH, NOW I'LL MAKE MY ENTRAN-
SWF
UH ?!

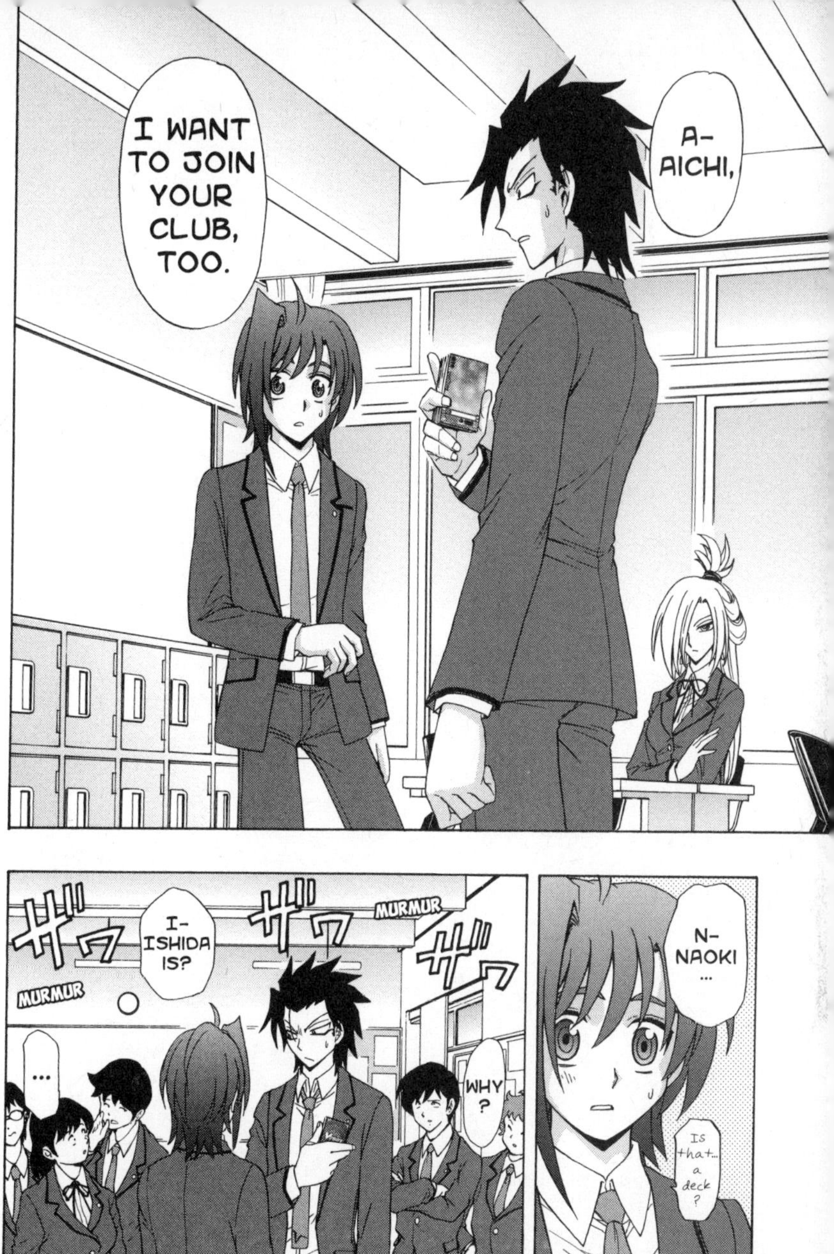
A-AICHI,
I WANT TO JOIN YOUR CLUB, TOO.
N-NAOKI...
Is that... a deck?
ザワ
MURMUR
ザワ
I-ISHIDA IS?
ザワ
MURMUR
WHY?
...

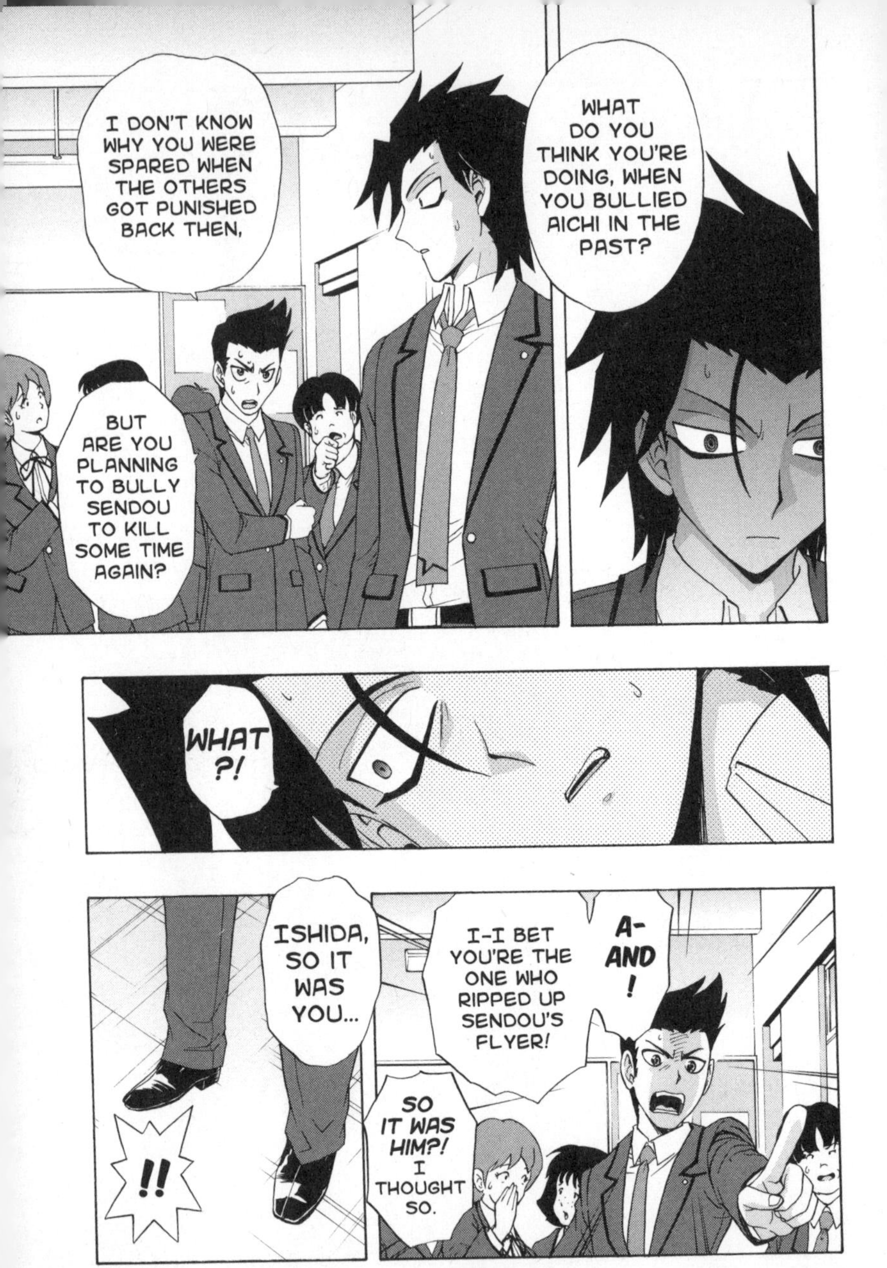
WHAT DO YOU THINK YOU'RE DOING, WHEN YOU BULLIED AICHI IN THE PAST?
I DON'T KNOW WHY YOU WERE SPARED WHEN THE OTHERS GOT PUNISHED BACK THEN,
BUT ARE YOU PLANNING TO BULLY SENDOU TO KILL SOME TIME AGAIN?
WHAT ?!
A-AND !
I-I BET YOU'RE THE ONE WHO RIPPED UP SENDOU'S FLYER!
SO IT WAS HIM?! I THOUGHT SO.
ISHIDA, SO IT WAS YOU...
!!

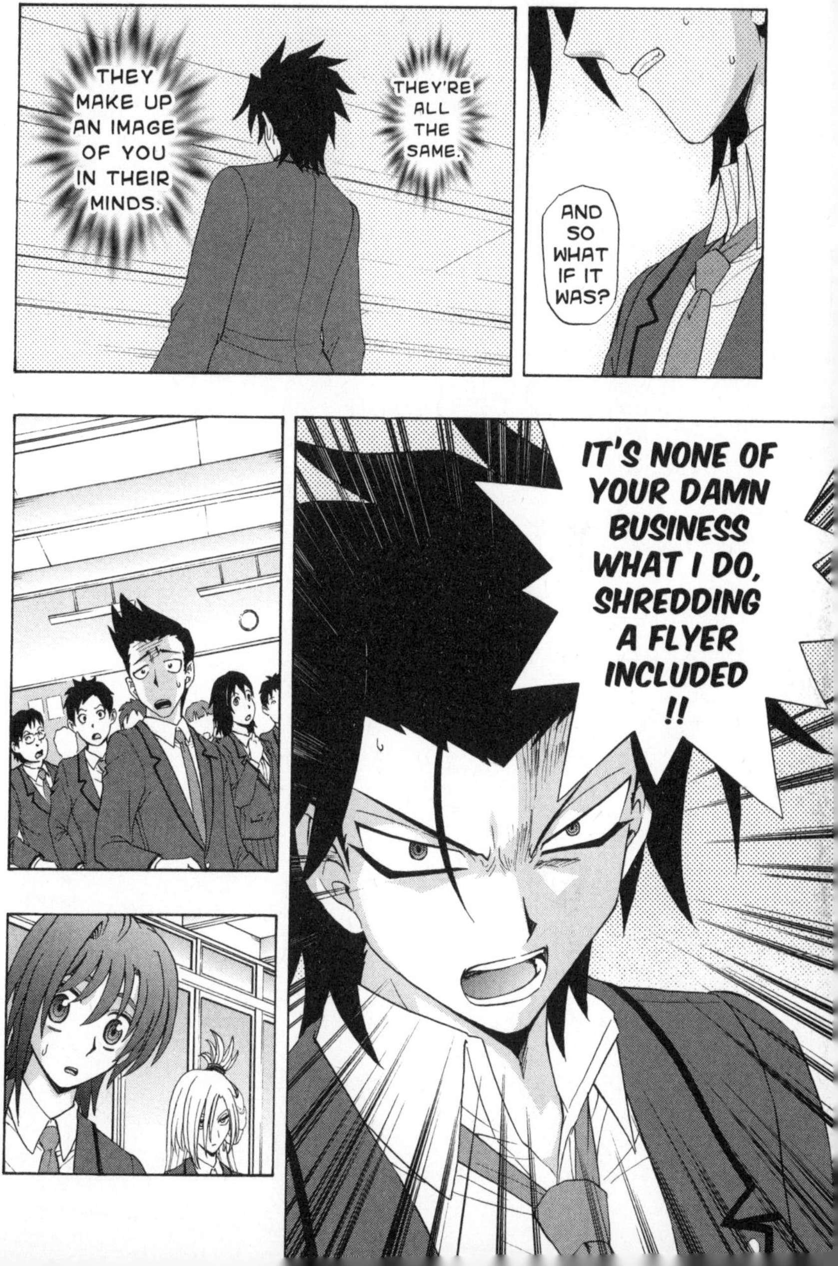
AND SO WHAT IF IT WAS?
THEY'RE ALL THE SAME.
THEY MAKE UP AN IMAGE OF YOU IN THEIR MINDS.
IT'S NONE OF YOUR DAMN BUSINESS WHAT I DO, SHREDDING A FLYER INCLUDED!!

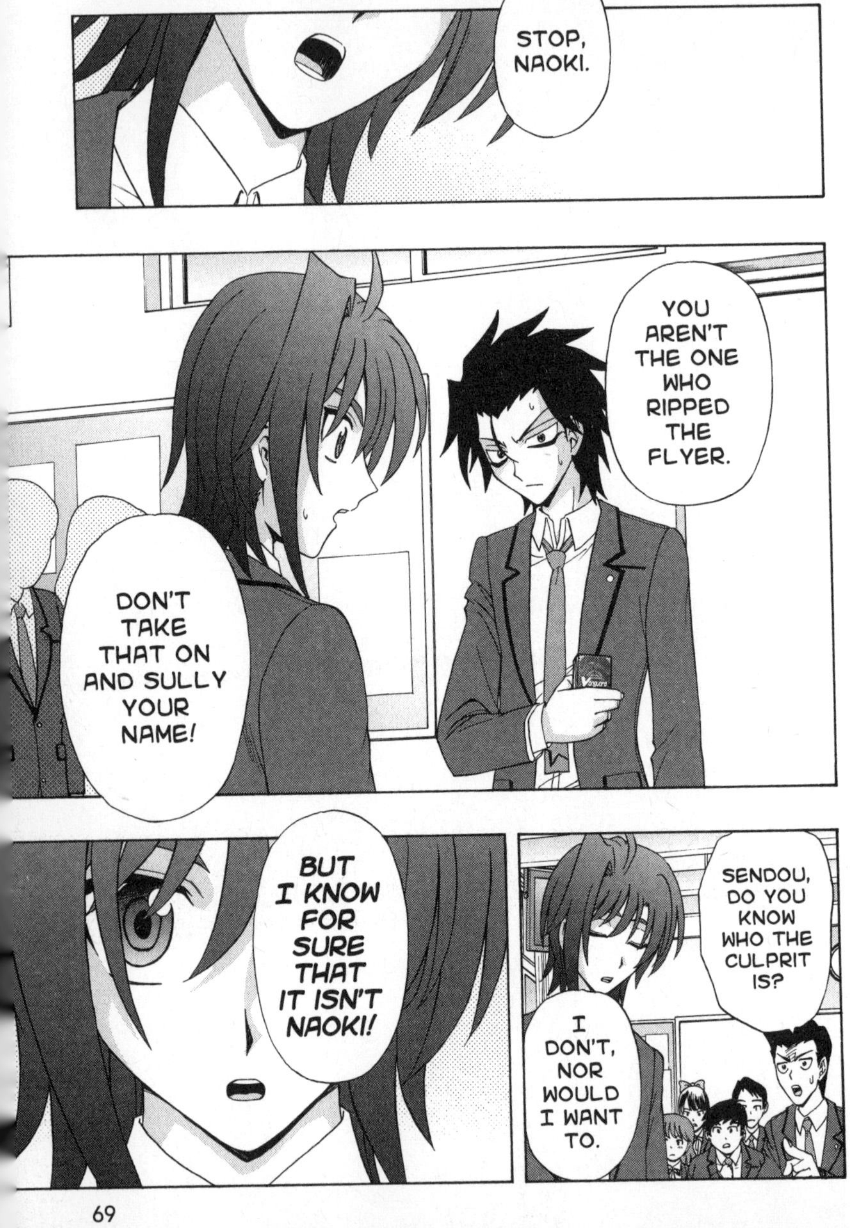
STOP, NAOKI.
YOU AREN'T THE ONE WHO RIPPED THE FLYER.
DON'T TAKE THAT ON AND SULLY YOUR NAME!
SENDOU, DO YOU KNOW WHO THE CULPRIT IS?
I DON'T, NOR WOULD I WANT TO.
BUT I KNOW FOR SURE THAT IT ISN'T NAOKI!

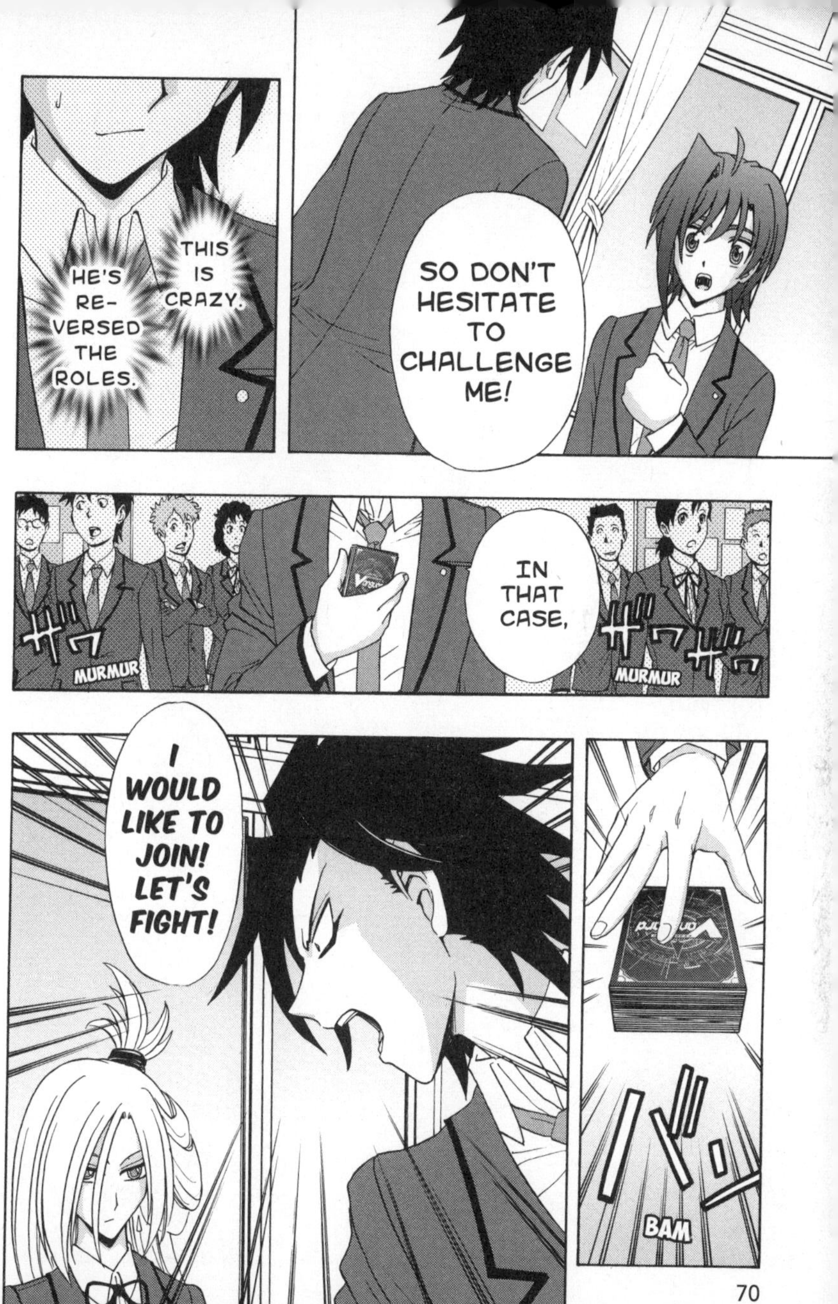
SO DON'T HESITATE TO CHALLENGE ME!
THIS IS CRAZY.
HE'S RE-VERSED THE ROLES.
IN THAT CASE,
MURMUR
MURMUR
BAM
I WOULD LIKE TO JOIN! LET'S FIGHT!

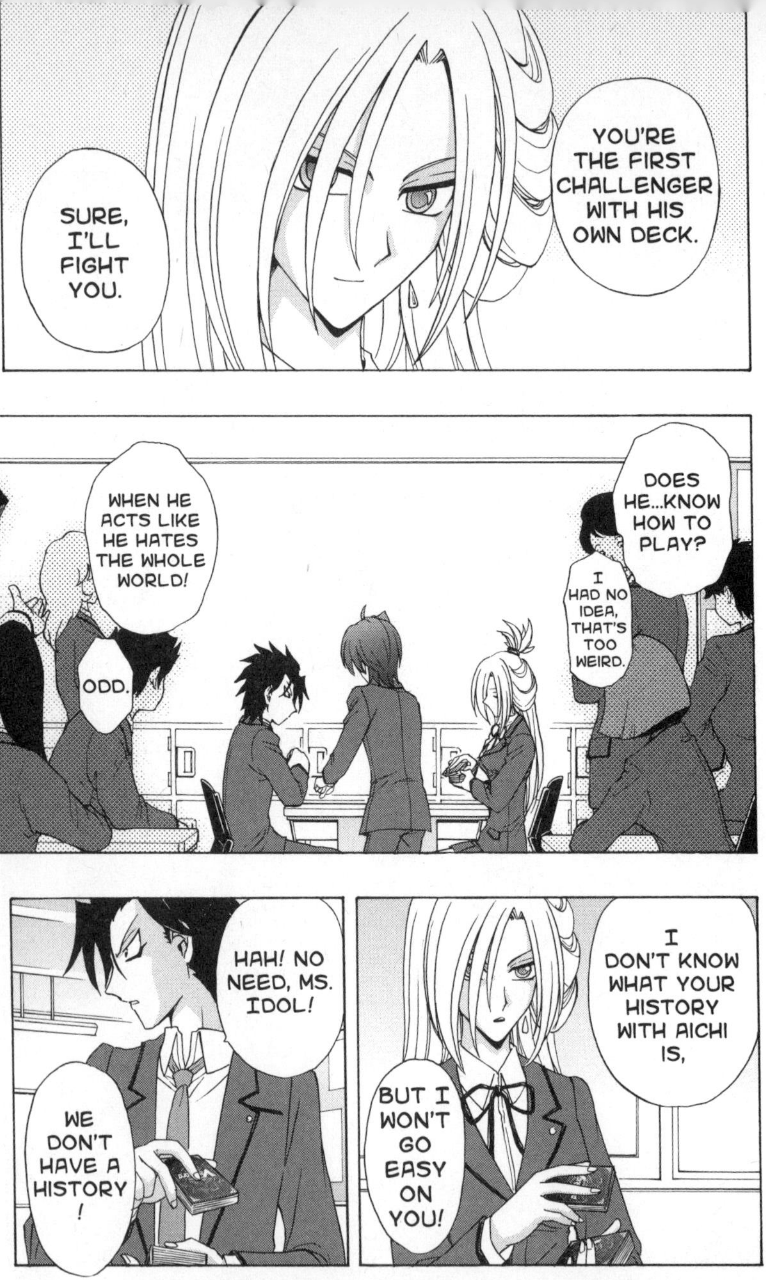
YOU'RE THE FIRST CHALLENGER WITH HIS OWN DECK.
SURE, I'LL FIGHT YOU.
DOES HE...KNOW HOW TO PLAY?
I HAD NO IDEA, THAT'S TOO WEIRD.
WHEN HE ACTS LIKE HE HATES THE WHOLE WORLD!
ODD.
I DON'T KNOW WHAT YOUR HISTORY WITH AICHI IS,
BUT I WON'T GO EASY ON YOU!
HAH! NO NEED, MS. IDOL!
WE DON'T HAVE A HISTORY!

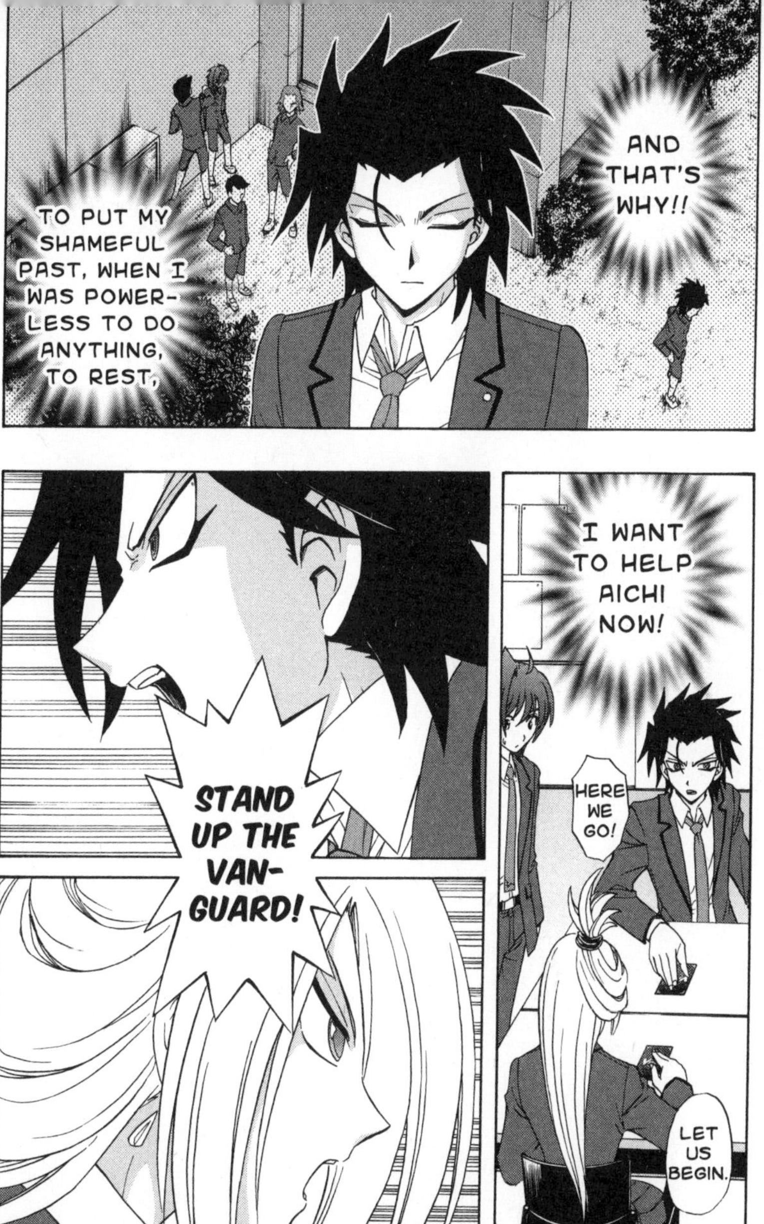
AND THAT'S WHY!!
TO PUT MY SHAMEFUL PAST, WHEN I WAS POWER-LESS TO DO ANYTHING, TO REST,
I WANT TO HELP AICHI NOW!
HERE WE GO!
LET US BEGIN.
STAND UP THE VAN-GUARD!

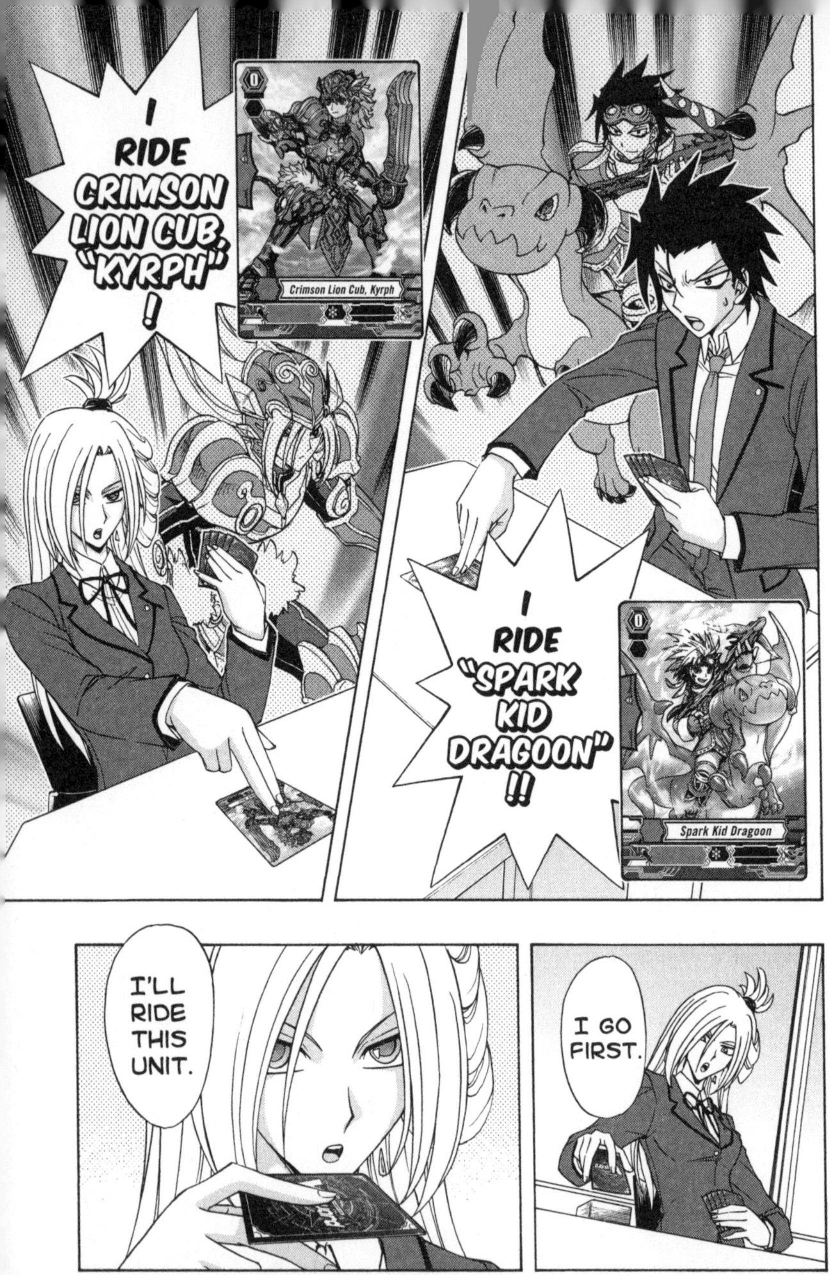
I RIDE "SPARK KID DRAGOON"!!
Spark Kid Dragoon
I RIDE CRIMSON LION CUB, "KYRPH"!
Crimson Lion Cub, Kyrph
I GO FIRST.
I'LL RIDE THIS UNIT.

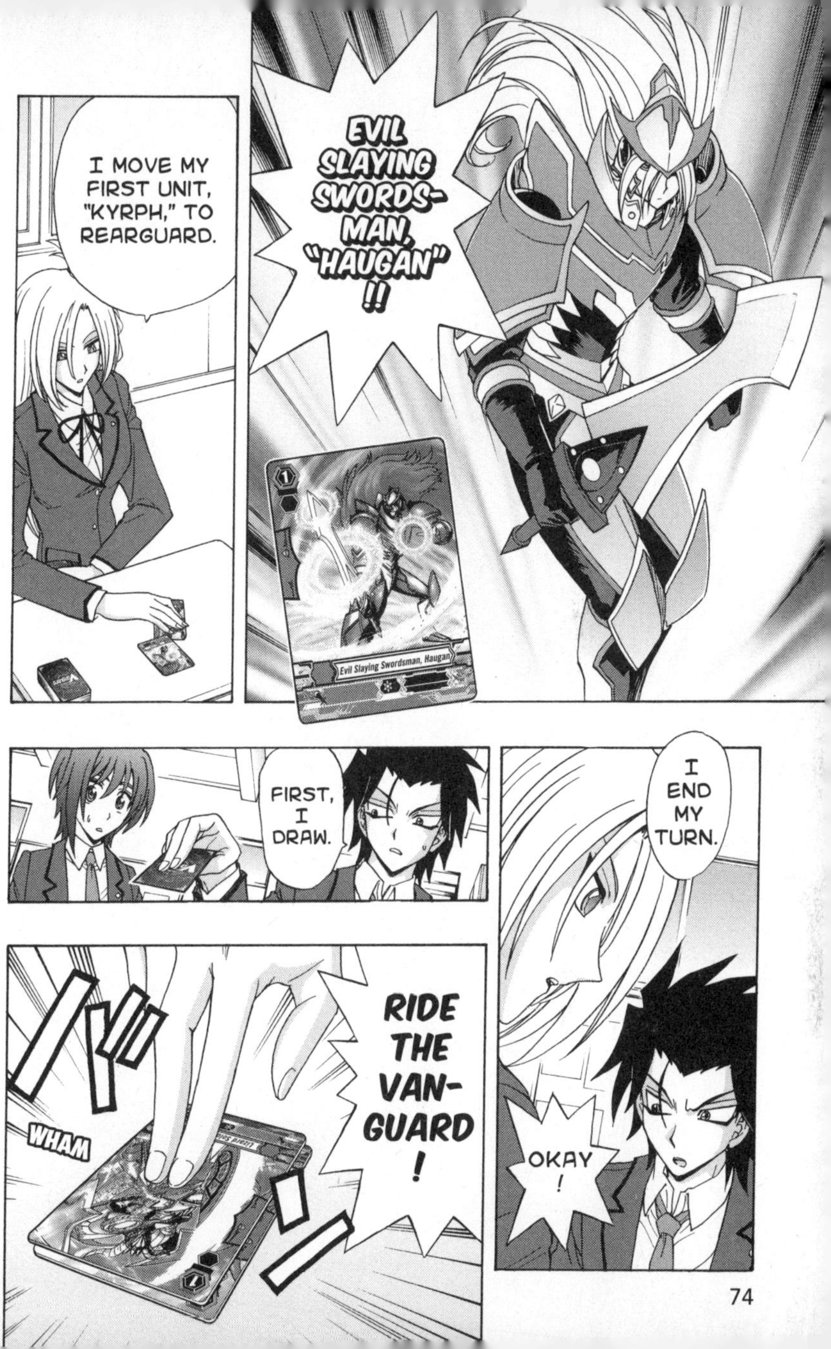
EVIL SLAYING SWORDS-MAN, "HAUGAN" !!
Evil Slaying Swordsman, Haugan
I MOVE MY FIRST UNIT, "KYRPH," TO REARGUARD.
I END MY TURN.
OKAY!
FIRST, I DRAW.
WHAM
RIDE THE VAN-GUARD!

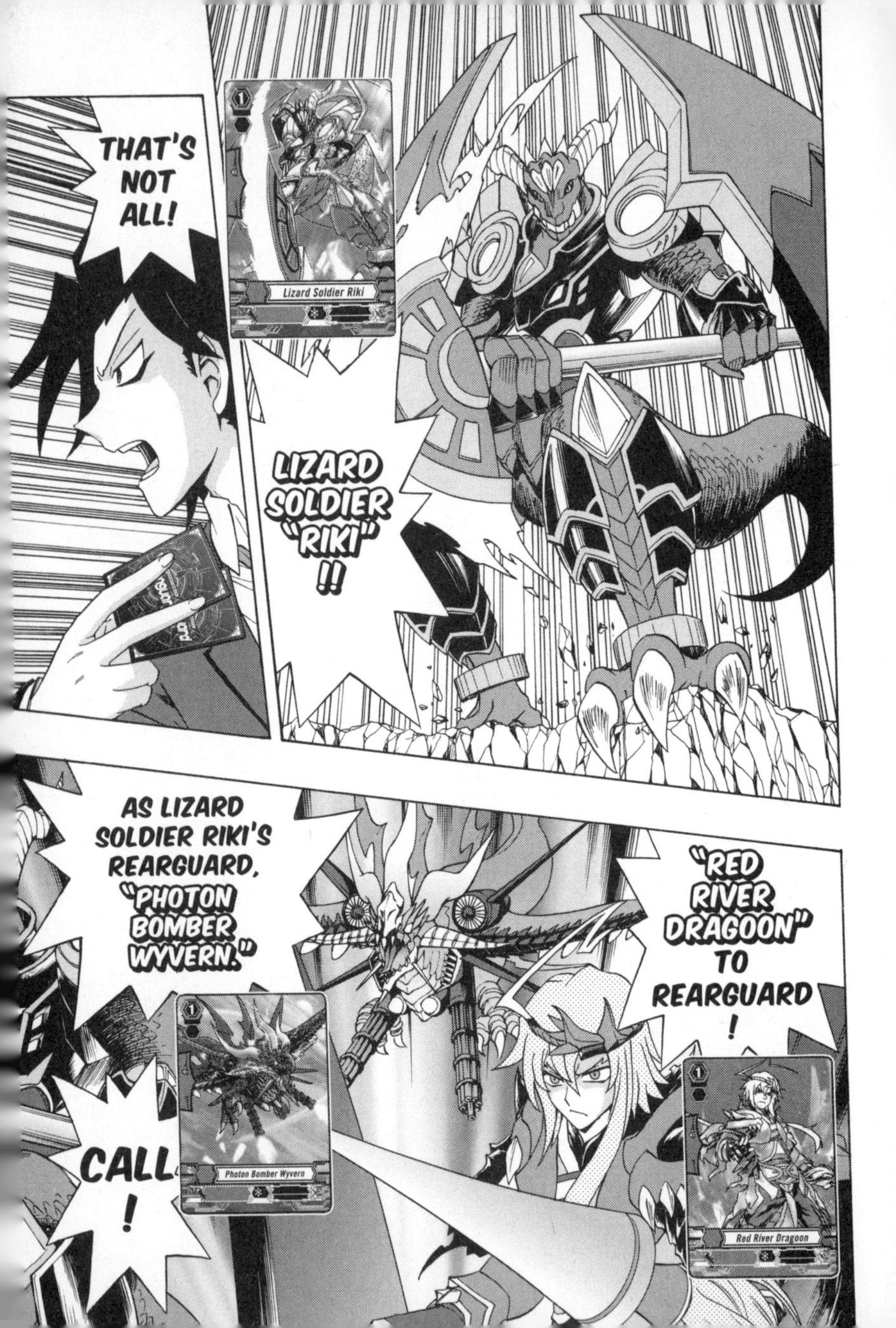
Lizard Soldier Riki
LIZARD SOLDIER "RIKI" !!
THAT'S NOT ALL!
"RED RIVER DRAGOON" TO REARGUARD !
Red River Dragoon
AS LIZARD SOLDIER RIKI'S REARGUARD, "PHOTON BOMBER WYVERN."
Photon Bomber Wyvern
CALL !

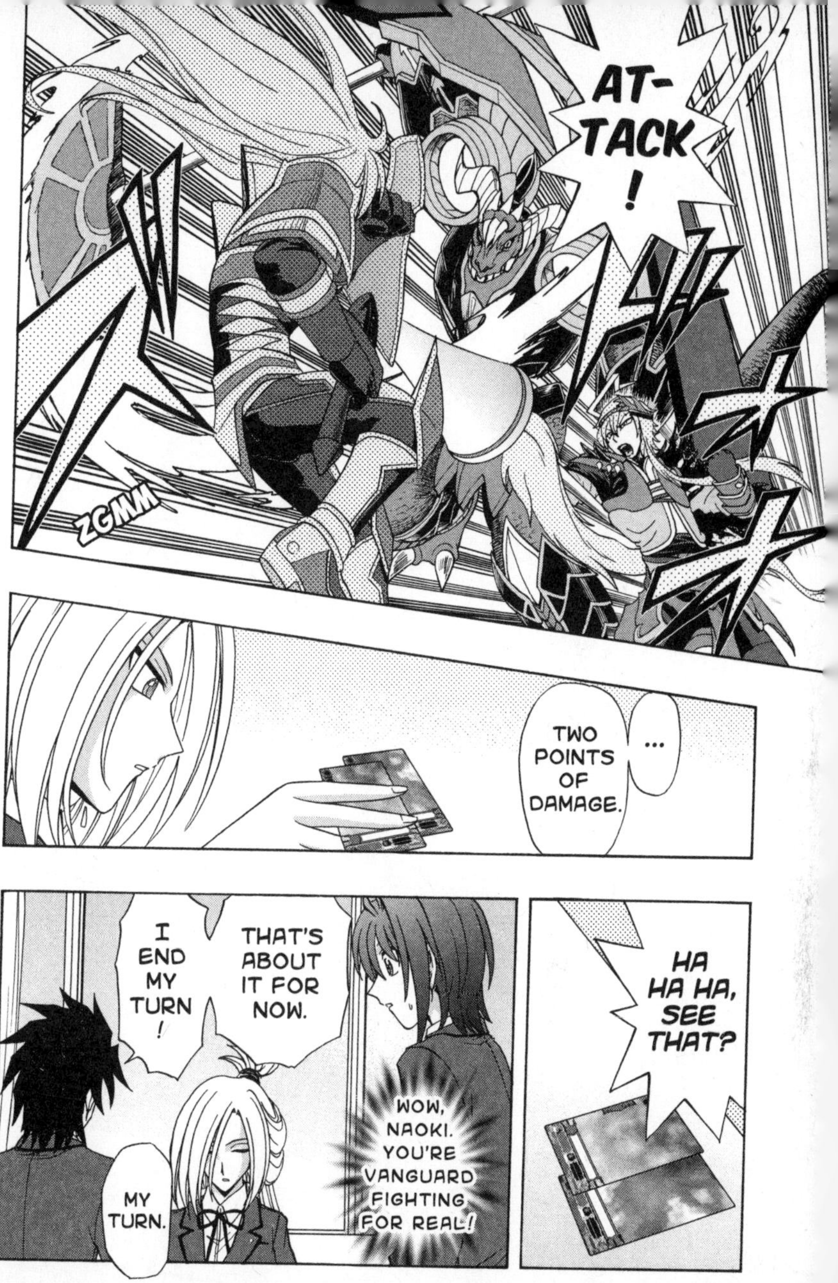
AT-TACK!
ZGMM
...
TWO POINTS OF DAMAGE.
HA HA HA, SEE THAT?
THAT'S ABOUT IT FOR NOW.
I END MY TURN!
WOW, NAOKI. YOU'RE VANGUARD FIGHTING FOR REAL!
MY TURN.

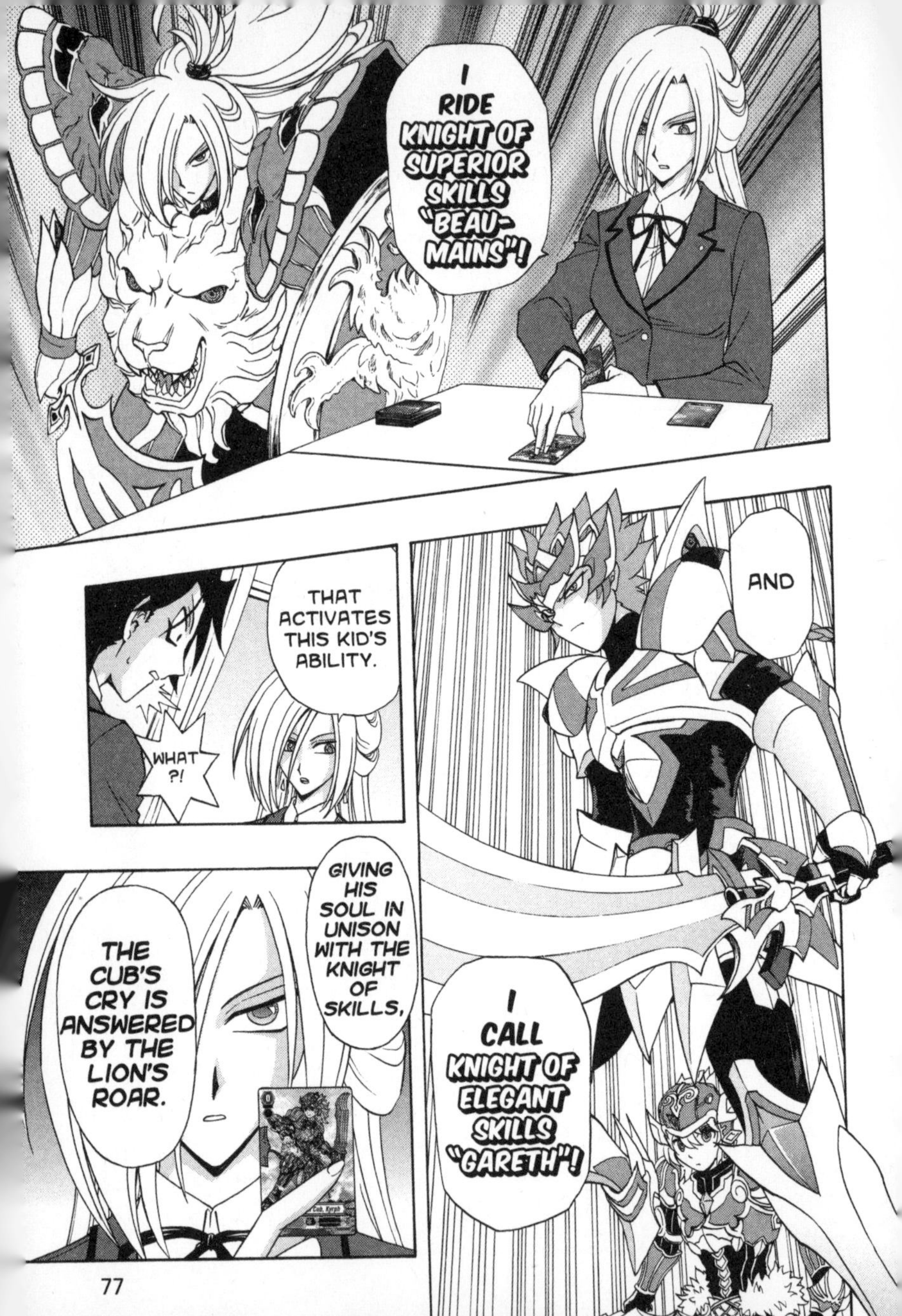
I RIDE KNIGHT OF SUPERIOR SKILLS "BEAU-MAINS"!
AND
I CALL KNIGHT OF ELEGANT SKILLS "GARETH"!
THAT ACTIVATES THIS KID'S ABILITY.
WHAT ?!
GIVING HIS SOUL IN UNISON WITH THE KNIGHT OF SKILLS,
THE CUB'S CRY IS ANSWERED BY THE LION'S ROAR.

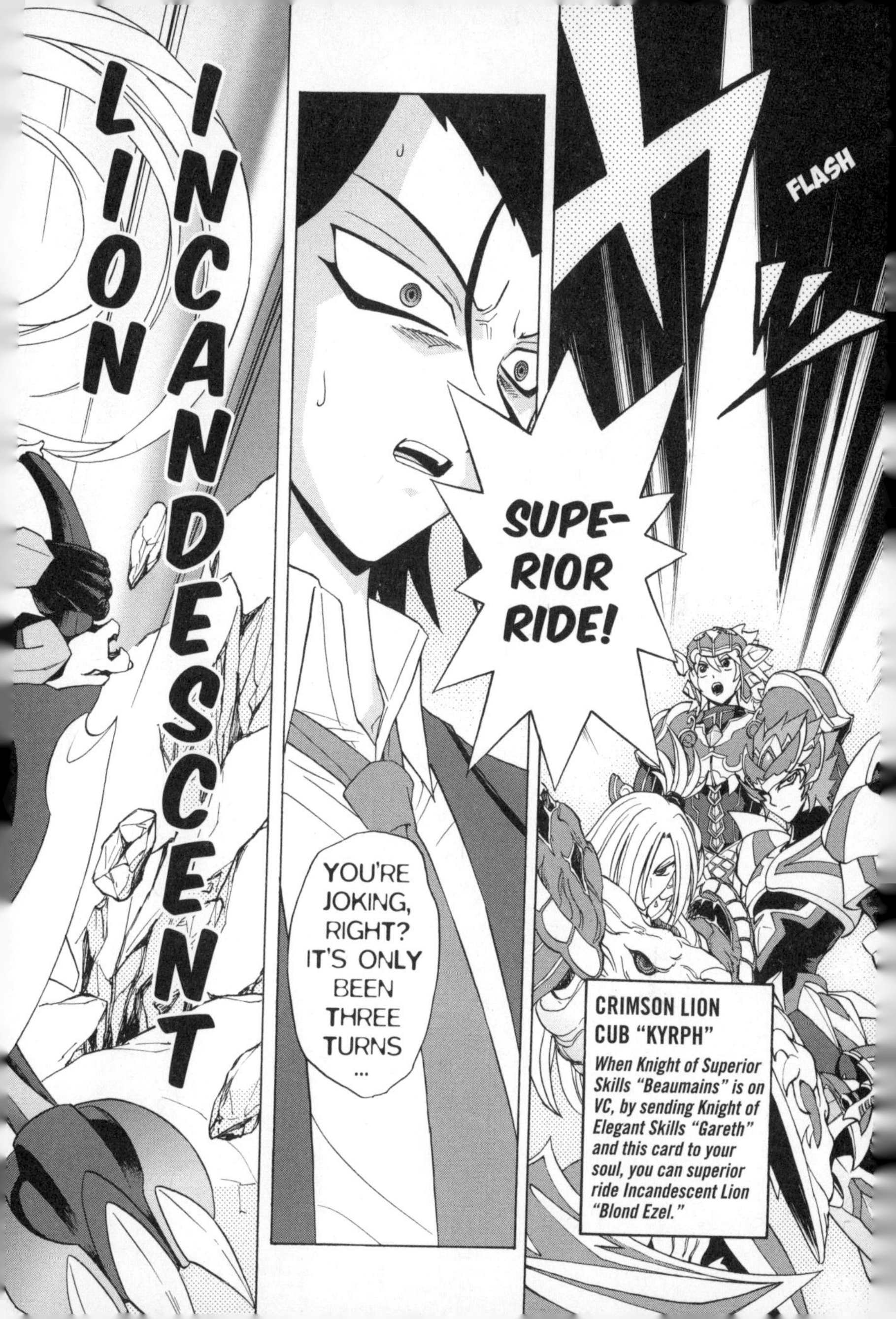
FLASH
SUPE-RIOR RIDE!
CRIMSON LION CUB "KYRPH"
When Knight of Superior Skills "Beaumains" is on VC, by sending Knight of Elegant Skills "Gareth" and this card to your soul, you can superior ride Incandescent Lion "Blond Ezel."
YOU'RE JOKING, RIGHT? IT'S ONLY BEEN THREE TURNS ...
INCANDESCENT LION

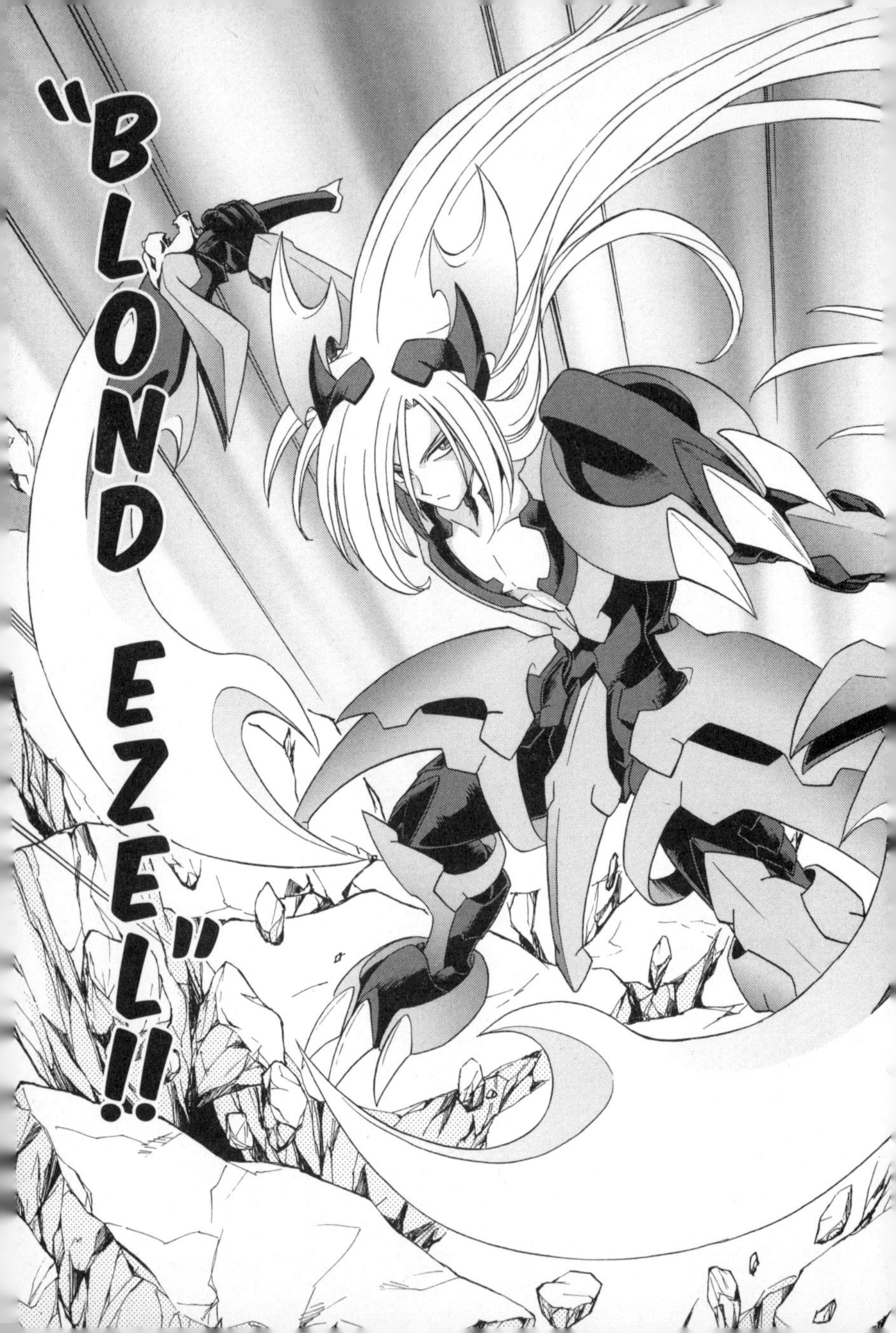
"BLOND EZELL"!!

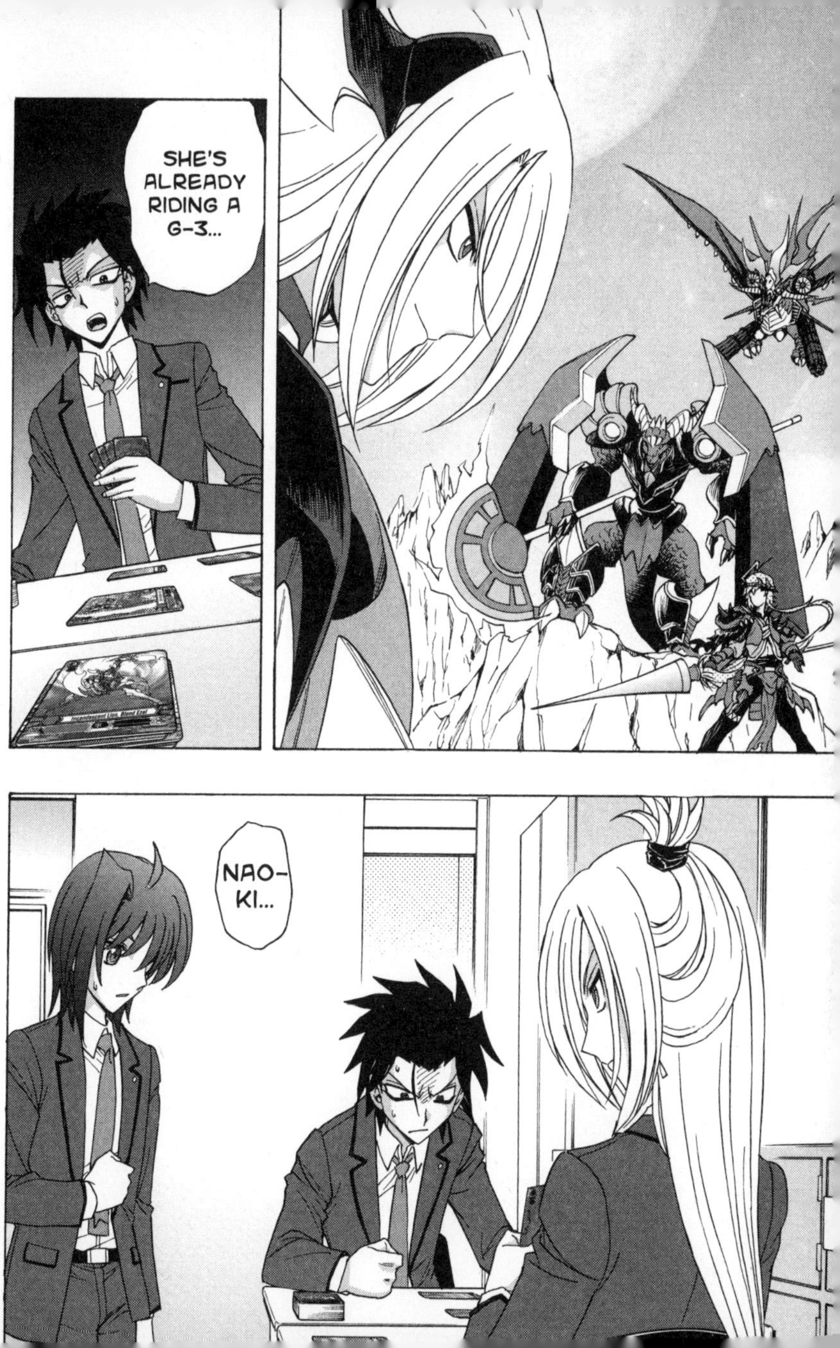
SHE'S ALREADY RIDING A G-3...
NAO-KI...

CARDFIGHT!!
Vanguard

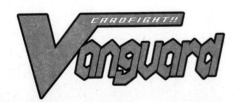

BONUS! CARDFIGHT!! Vanguard NEVER-BEFORE-SEEN IMAGE BOARDS

Shingo has a brother in grade school. Shingo's stiff ways stem from his desire to be a proper role model...

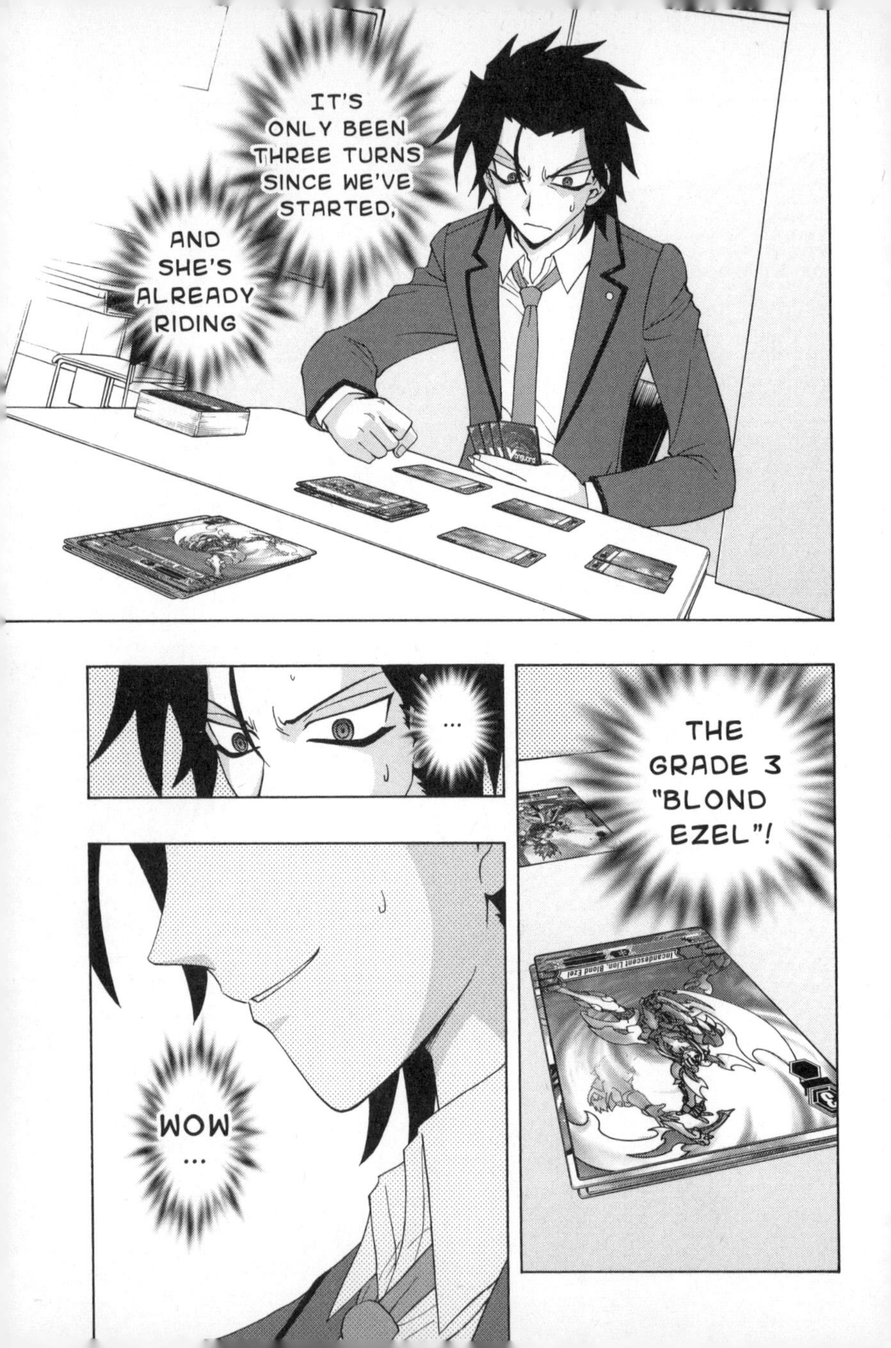
IT'S ONLY BEEN THREE TURNS SINCE WE'VE STARTED,
AND SHE'S ALREADY RIDING
THE GRADE 3 "BLOND EZEL"!
Incandescent Lion, Blond Ezel
...
WOW ...

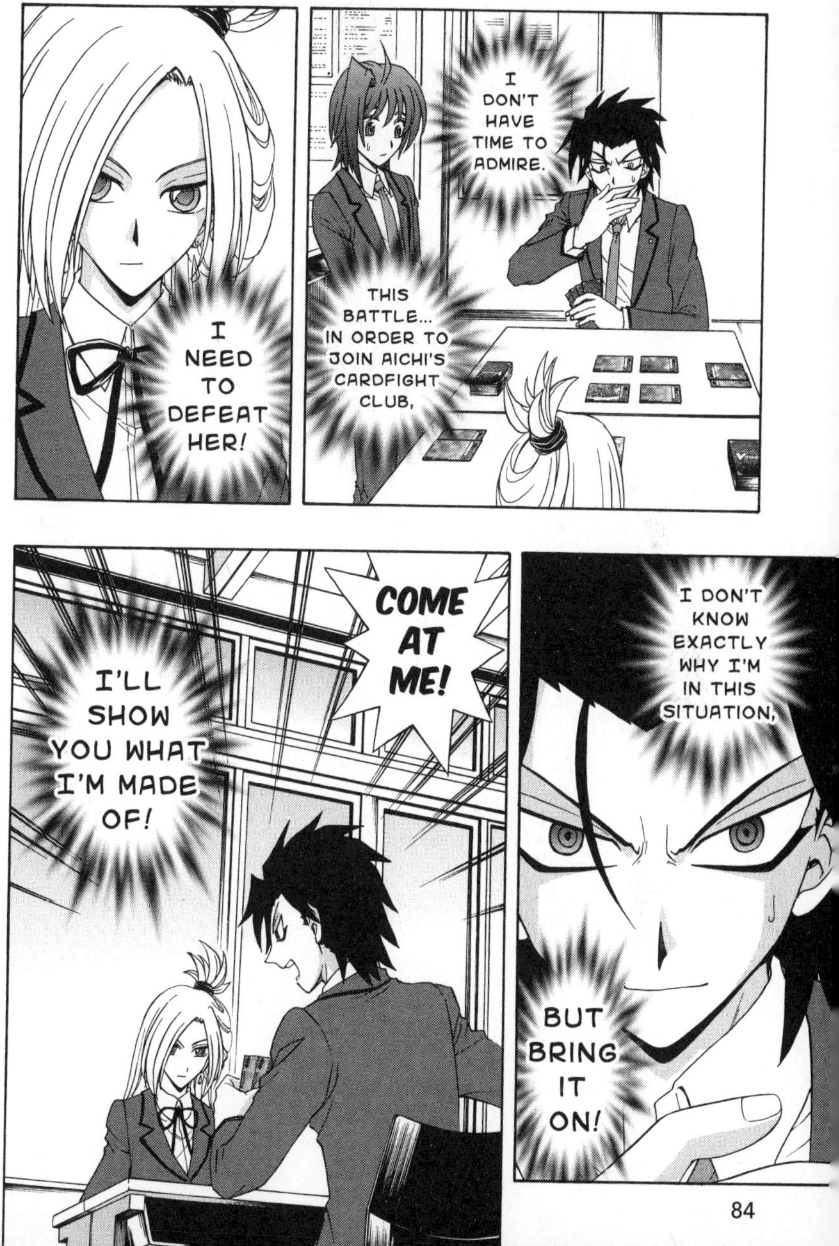
I DON'T HAVE TIME TO ADMIRE.
THIS BATTLE... IN ORDER TO JOIN AICHI'S CARDFIGHT CLUB,
I NEED TO DEFEAT HER!
I DON'T KNOW EXACTLY WHY I'M IN THIS SITUATION,
BUT BRING IT ON!
COME AT ME!
I'LL SHOW YOU WHAT I'M MADE OF!

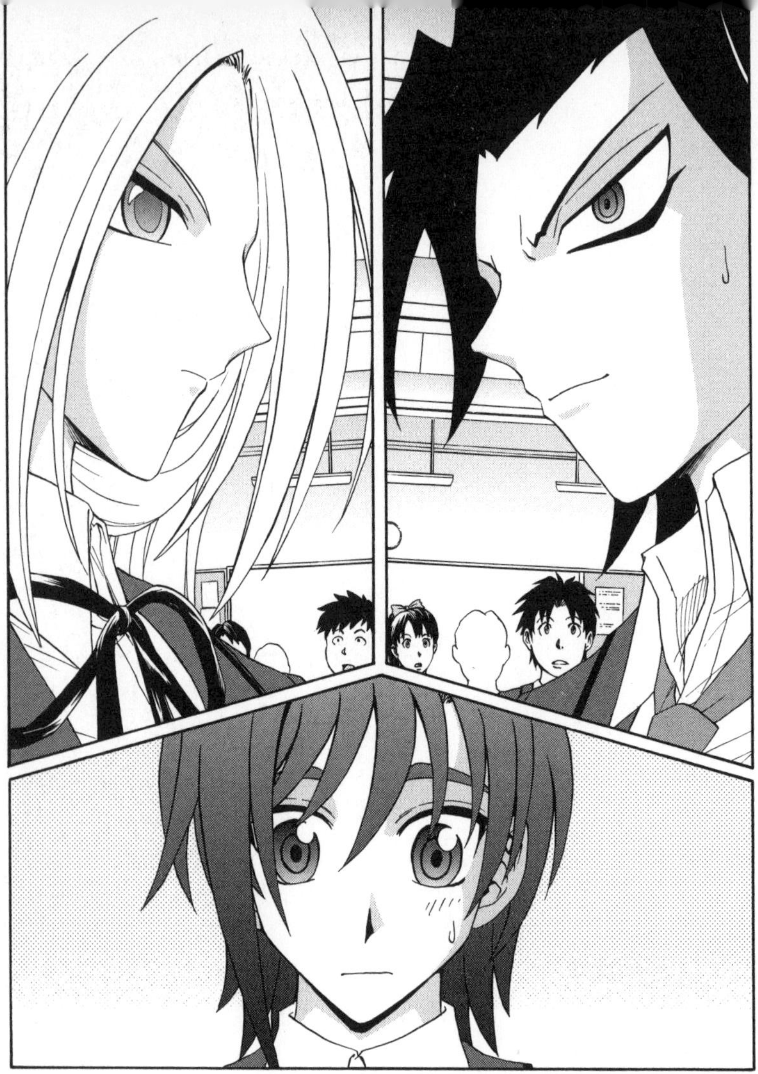

#028 A NEW BUDDY

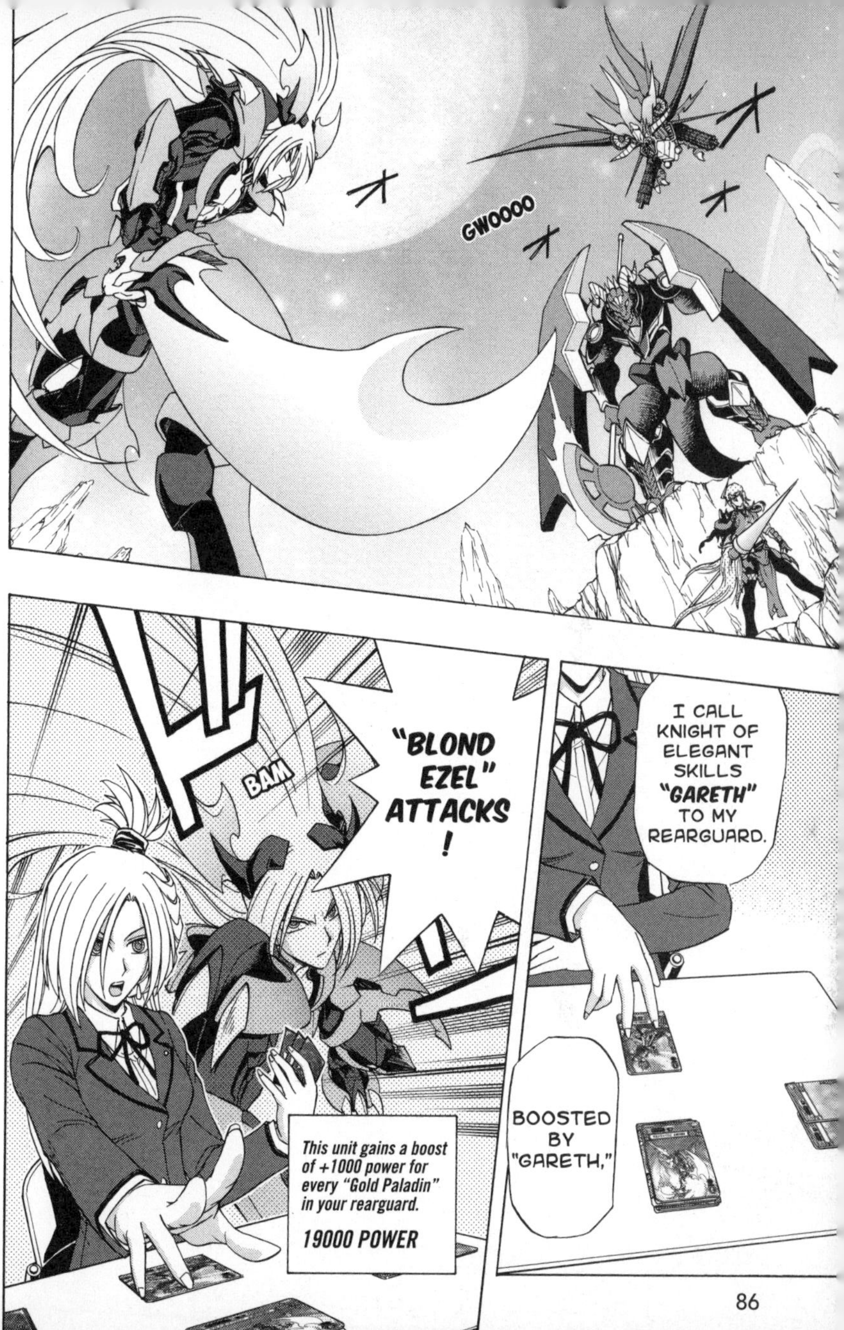
GWOOOO
I CALL KNIGHT OF ELEGANT SKILLS "GARETH" TO MY REARGUARD.
BOOSTED BY "GARETH,"
"BLOND EZEL" ATTACKS !
BAM
This unit gains a boost of +1000 power for every "Gold Paladin" in your rearguard.
19000 POWER

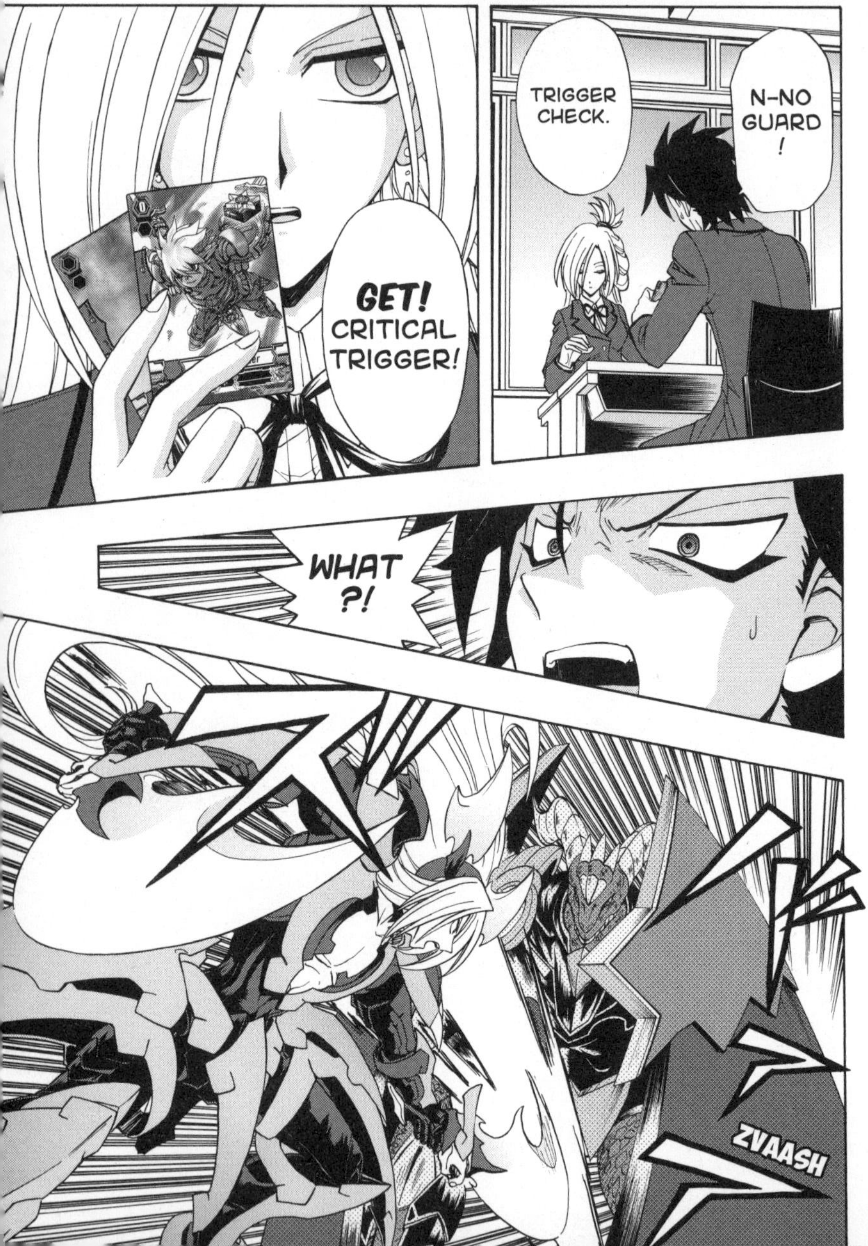
N-NO GUARD!
TRIGGER CHECK.
GET! CRITICAL TRIGGER!
WHAT?!
ZVAASH

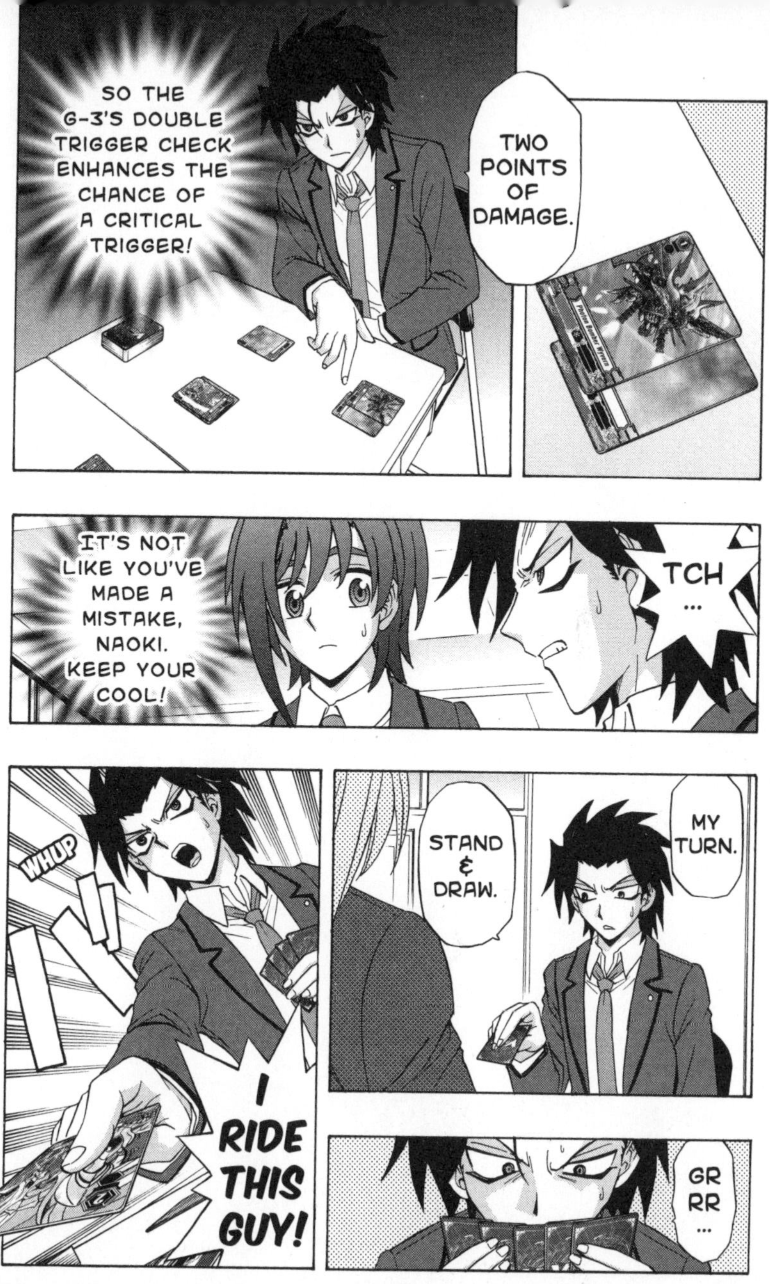
TWO POINTS OF DAMAGE.
SO THE G-3'S DOUBLE TRIGGER CHECK ENHANCES THE CHANCE OF A CRITICAL TRIGGER!
TCH ...
IT'S NOT LIKE YOU'VE MADE A MISTAKE, NAOKI. KEEP YOUR COOL!
MY TURN.
STAND & DRAW.
GR RR ...
WHUP
I RIDE THIS GUY!

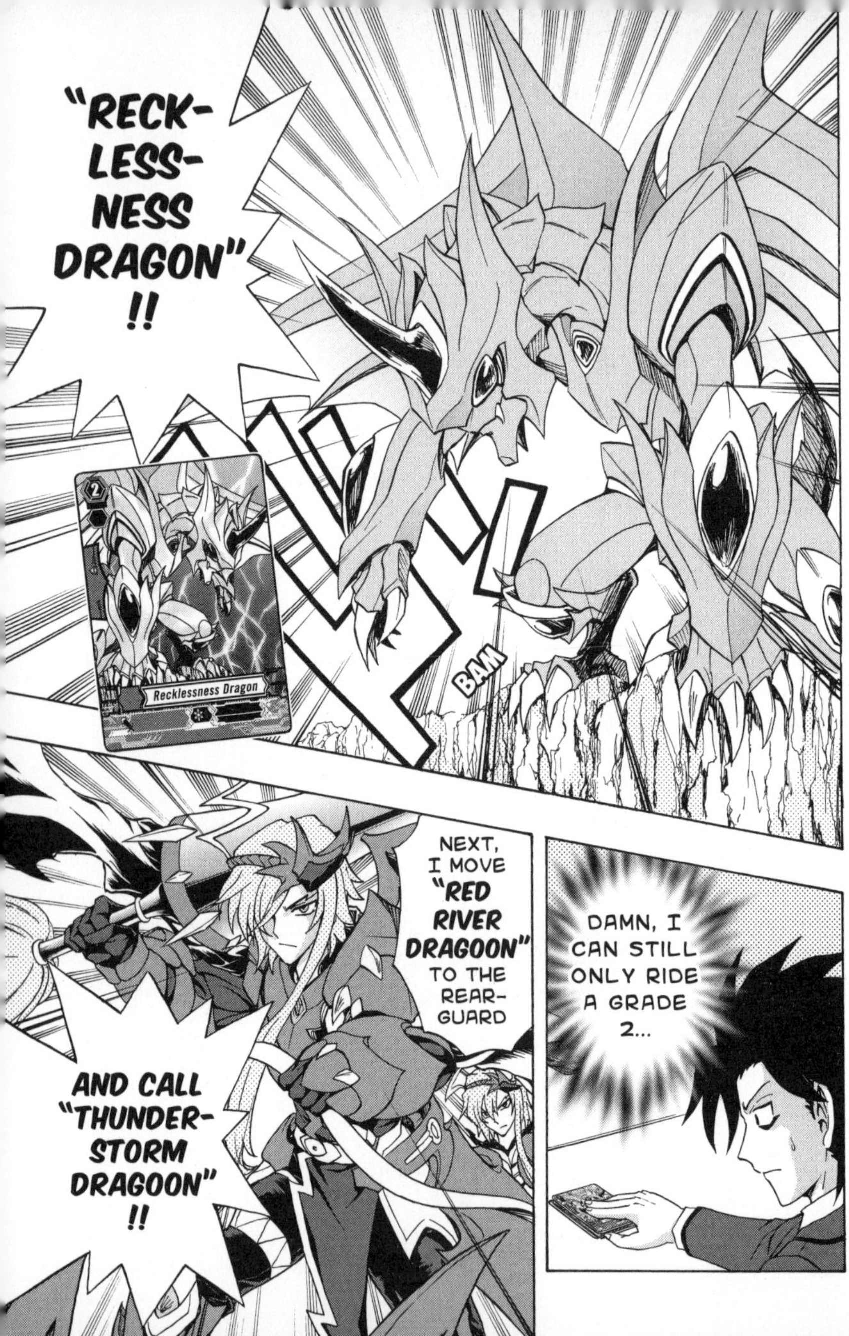
"RECK-LESS-NESS DRAGON"!!
Recklessness Dragon
BAM
DAMN, I CAN STILL ONLY RIDE A GRADE 2...
NEXT, I MOVE "RED RIVER DRAGOON" TO THE REAR-GUARD
AND CALL "THUNDER-STORM DRAGOON"!!

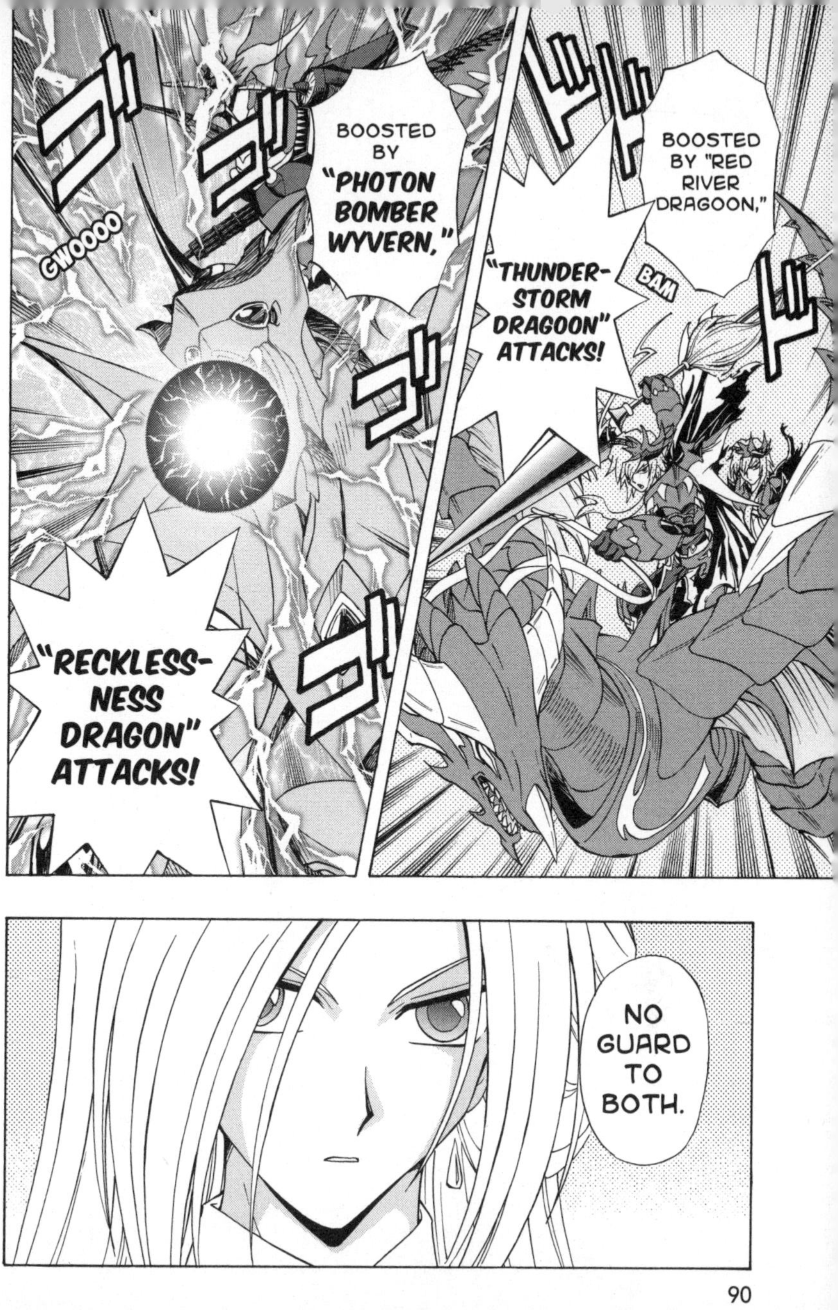
BOOSTED BY "RED RIVER DRAGOON,"
"THUNDER-STORM DRAGOON" ATTACKS!
BAM
BOOSTED BY "PHOTON BOMBER WYVERN,"
GWOOOO
"RECKLESS-NESS DRAGOON" ATTACKS!
NO GUARD TO BOTH.

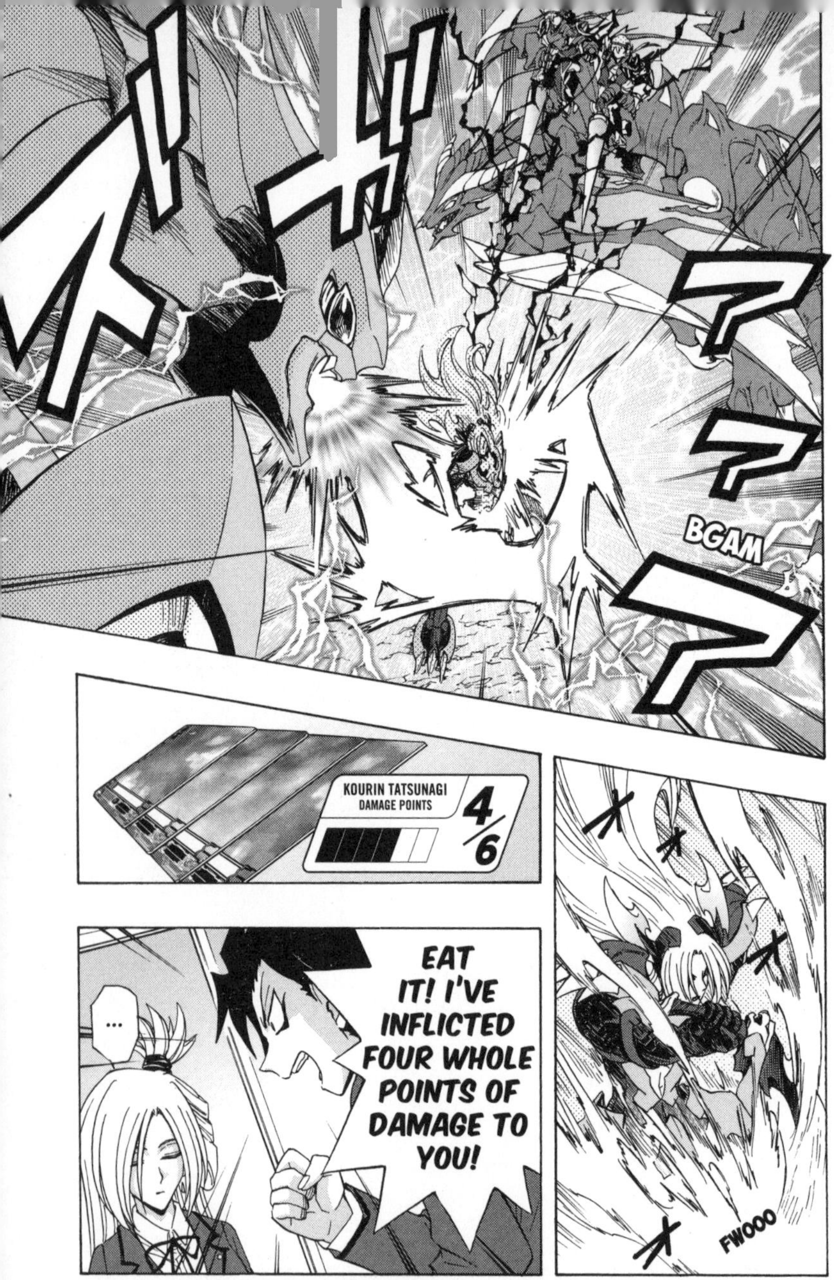
BGAM
FWOOO
KOURIN TATSUNAGI
DAMAGE POINTS
4/6
EAT IT! I'VE INFLICTED FOUR WHOLE POINTS OF DAMAGE TO YOU!
...

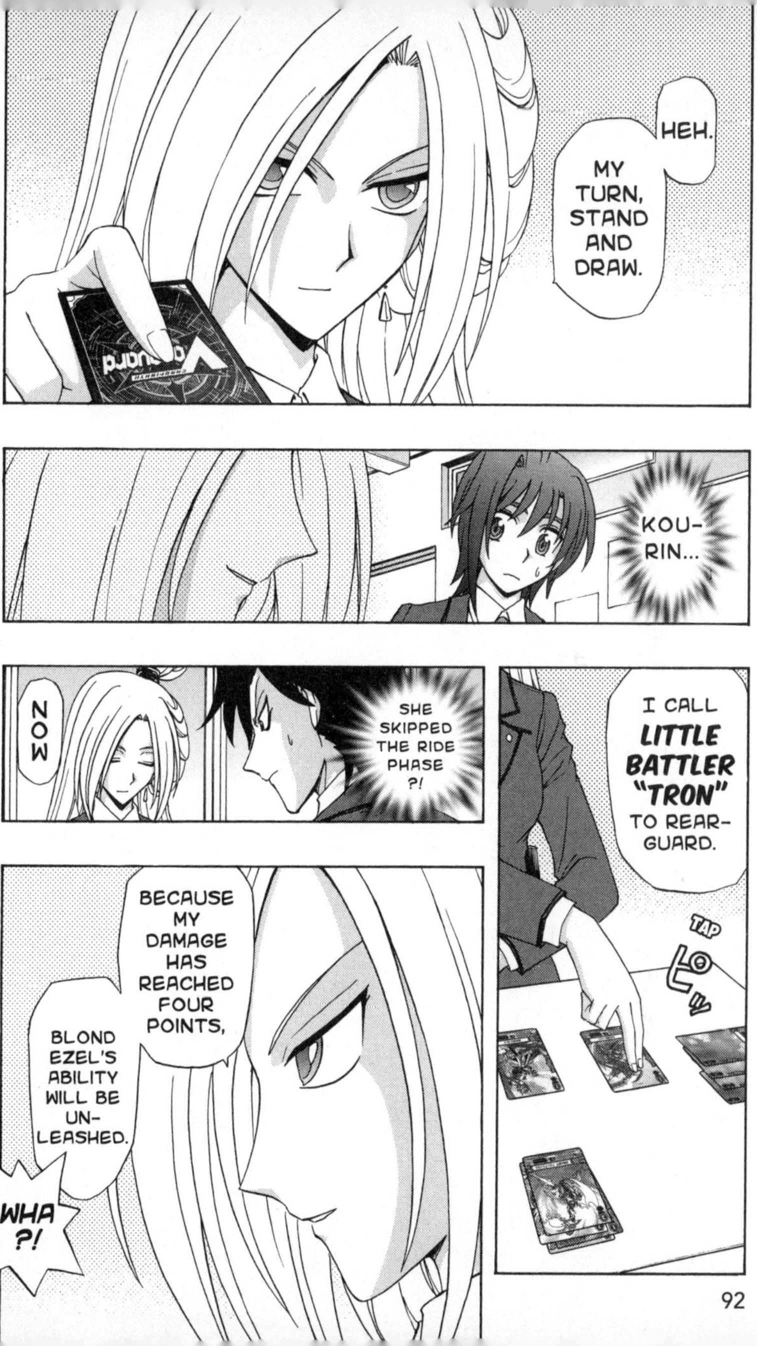
HEH.
MY TURN, STAND AND DRAW.
KOU-RIN...
I CALL LITTLE BATTLER "TRON" TO REAR-GUARD.
TAP
SHE SKIPPED THE RIDE PHASE ?!
NOW
BECAUSE MY DAMAGE HAS REACHED FOUR POINTS,
BLOND EZEL'S ABILITY WILL BE UN-LEASHED.
WHA ?!

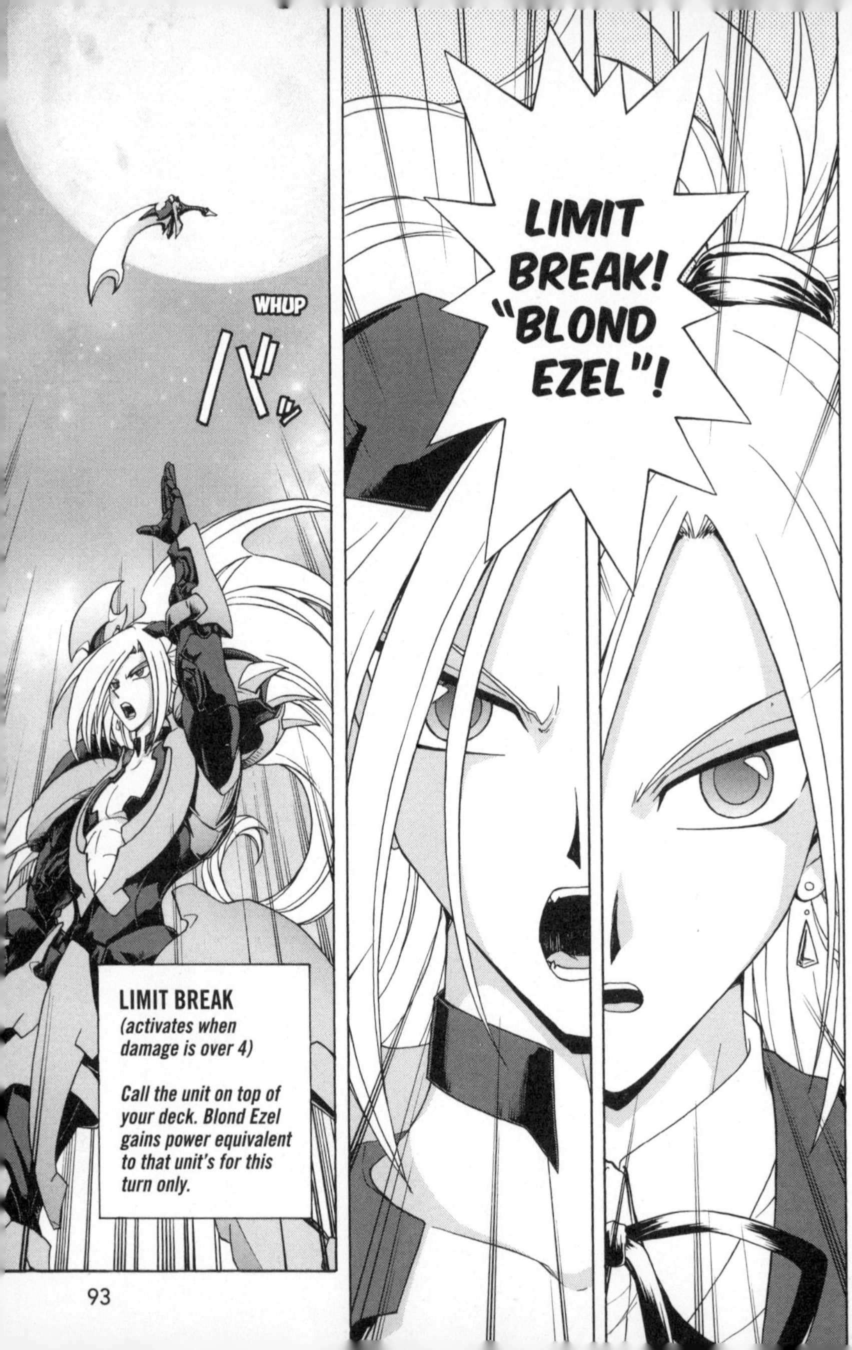
LIMIT BREAK! "BLOND EZEL"!
WHUP
バッ
LIMIT BREAK
(activates when damage is over 4)
Call the unit on top of your deck. Blond Ezel gains power equivalent to that unit's for this turn only.

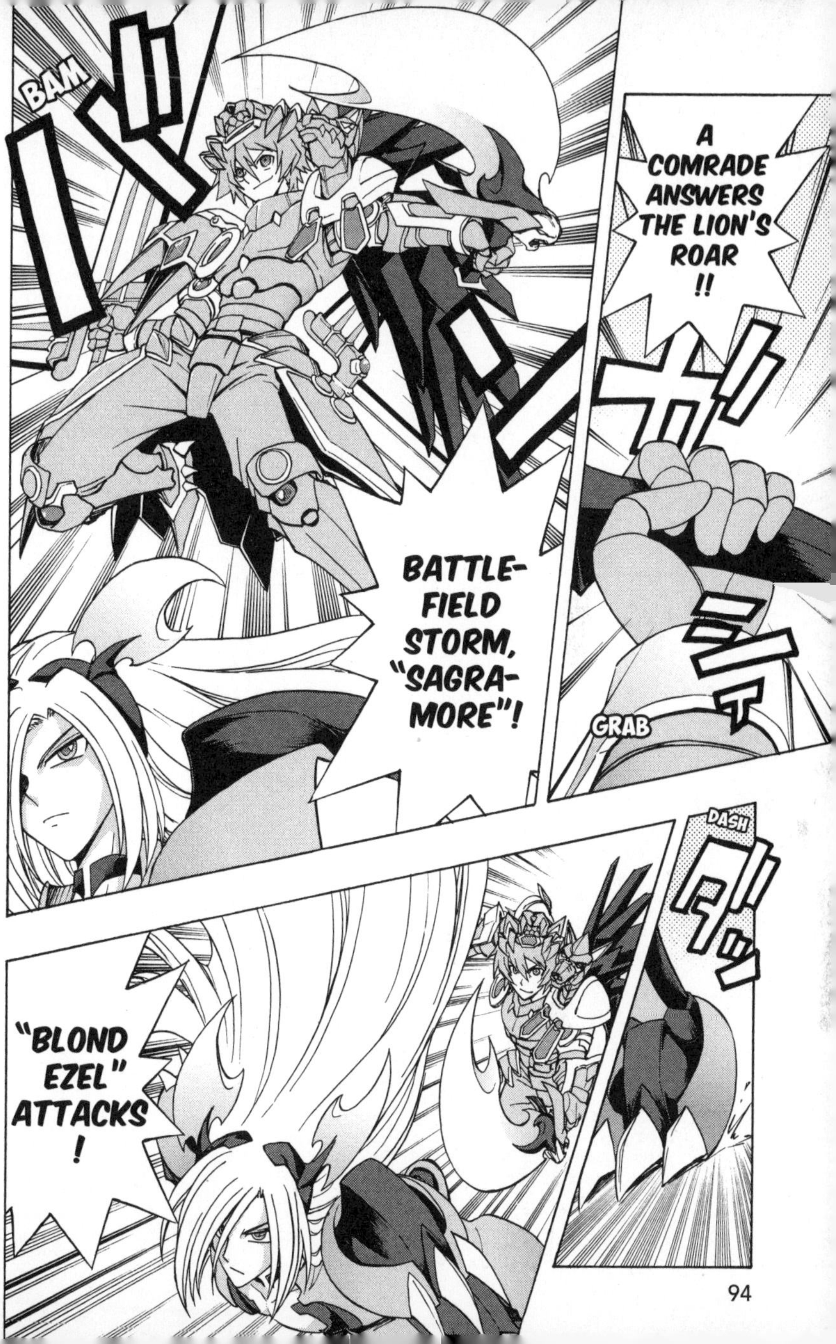
A COMRADE ANSWERS THE LION'S ROAR !!
GRAB
BAM
BATTLE-FIELD STORM, "SAGRA-MORE"!
DASH
"BLOND EZEL" ATTACKS !

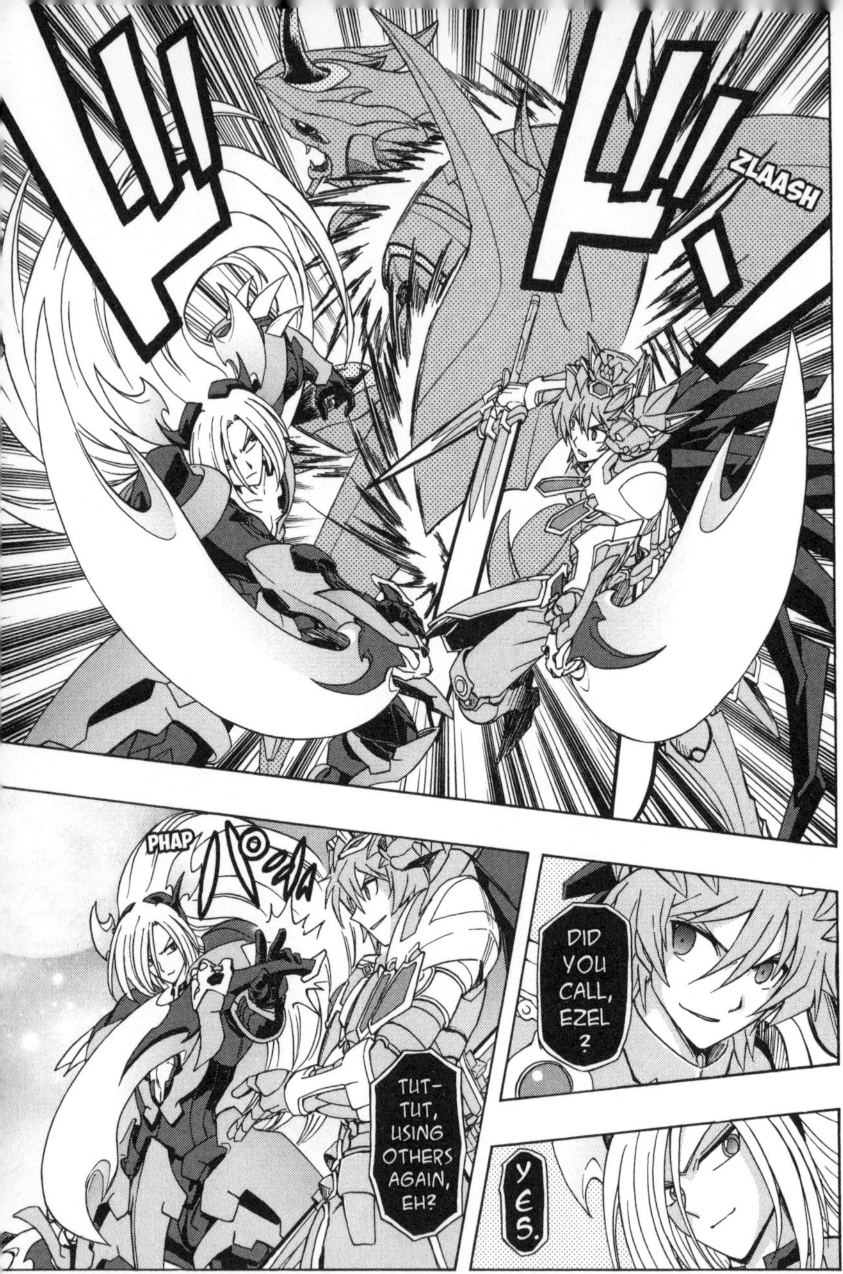
ZLAASH
DID YOU CALL, EZEL?
YES.
PHAP
TUT-TUT, USING OTHERS AGAIN, EH?

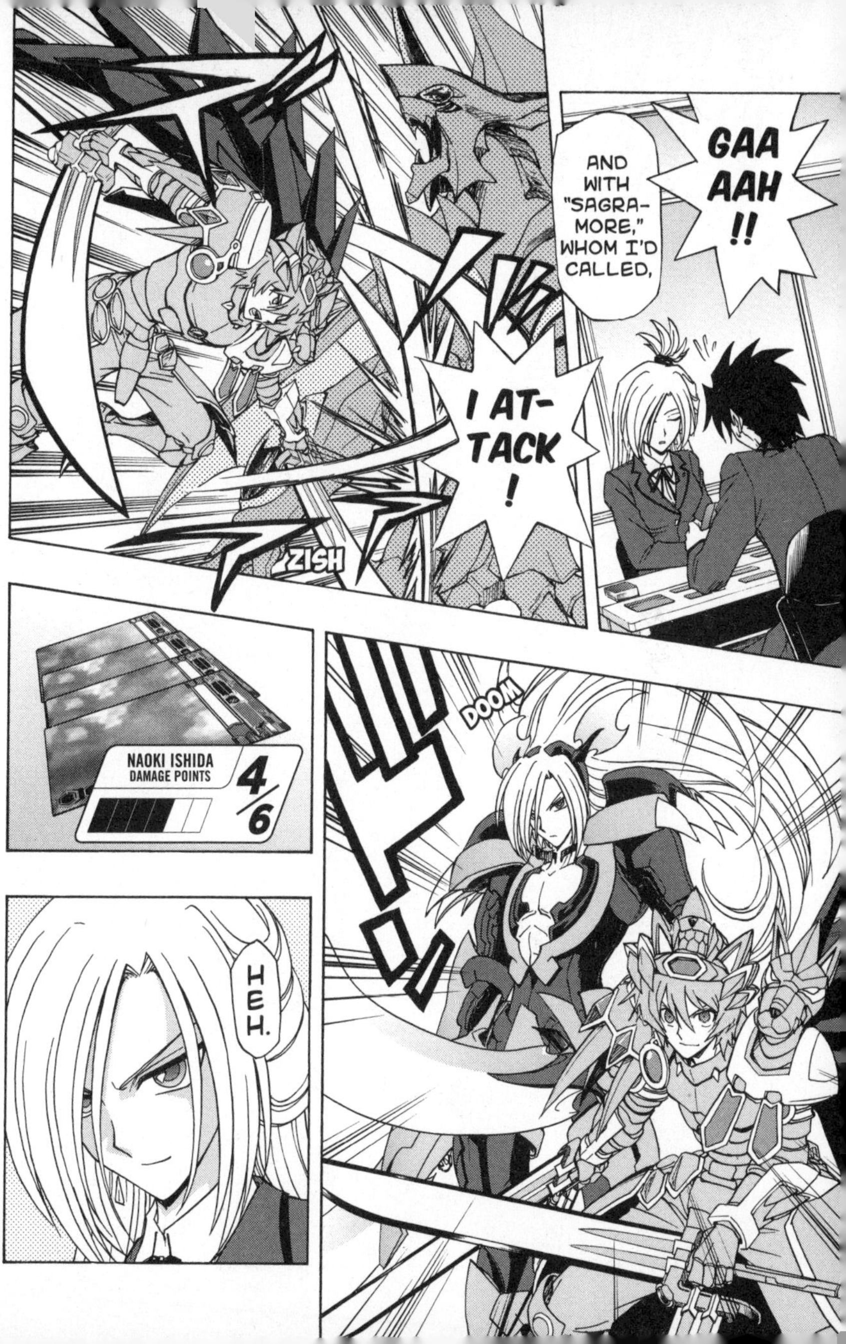
GAA AAH !!
AND WITH "SAGRA-MORE," WHOM I'D CALLED,
I AT-TACK !
ZISH
DOOM
NAOKI ISHIDA
DAMAGE POINTS
4/6
HEH.

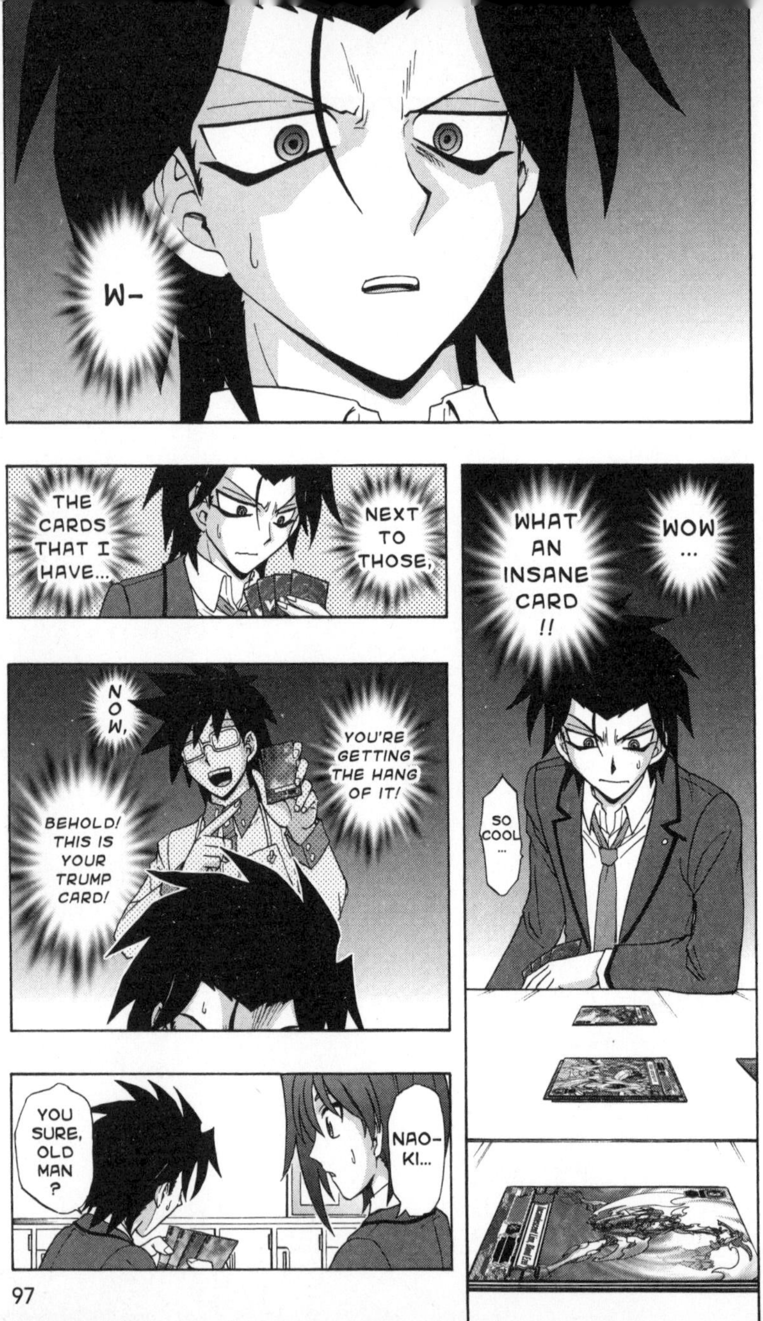
W-
WOW...
WHAT AN INSANE CARD!!
SO COOL...
NEXT TO THOSE,
THE CARDS THAT I HAVE...
YOU'RE GETTING THE HANG OF IT!
NOW,
BEHOLD! THIS IS YOUR TRUMP CARD!
NAO-KI...
YOU SURE, OLD MAN?

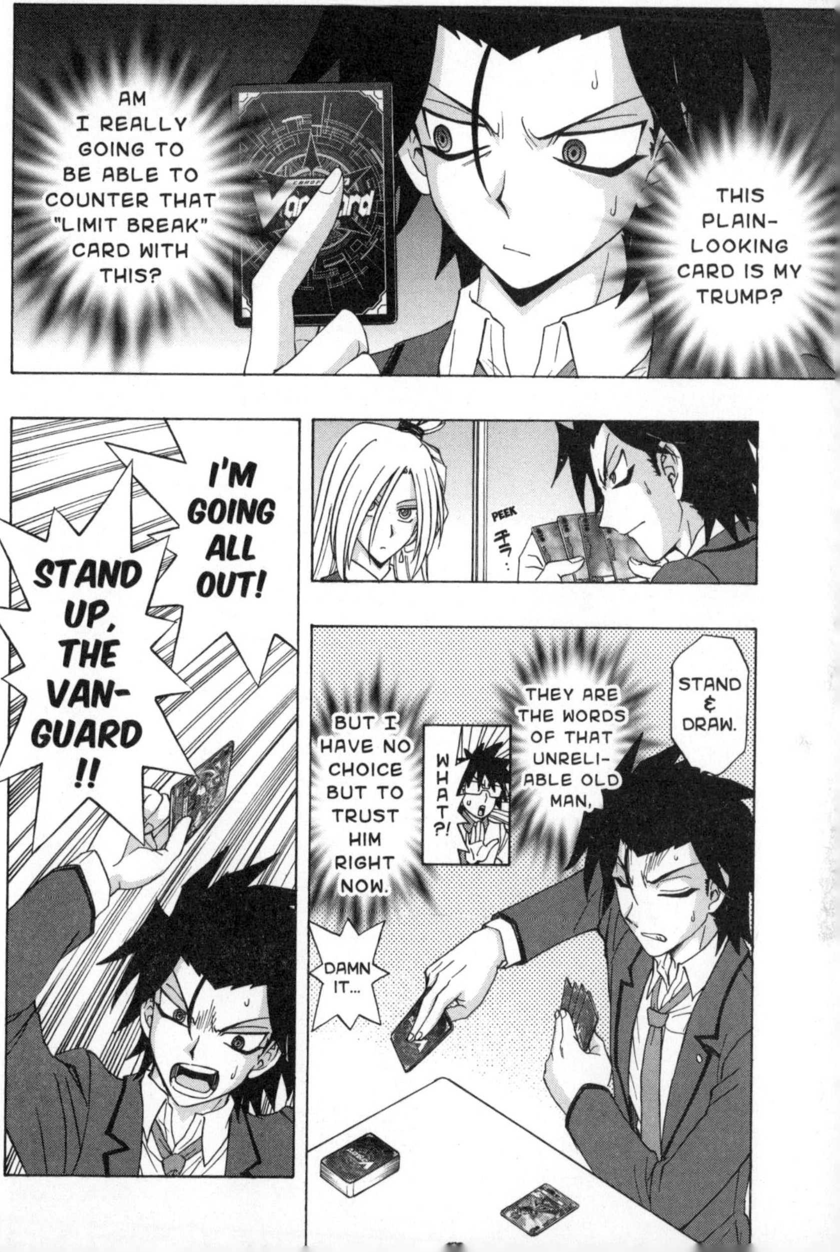
THIS PLAIN-LOOKING CARD IS MY TRUMP?
AM I REALLY GOING TO BE ABLE TO COUNTER THAT "LIMIT BREAK" CARD WITH THIS?
PEEK
チラ…
STAND & DRAW.
THEY ARE THE WORDS OF THAT UNRELIABLE OLD MAN,
WHAT?!
BUT I HAVE NO CHOICE BUT TO TRUST HIM RIGHT NOW.
DAMN IT...
I'M GOING ALL OUT!
STAND UP, THE VAN-GUARD!!

FLASH

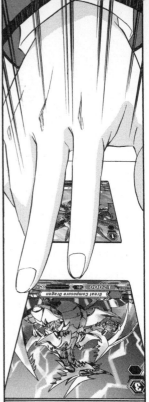

Great Composure Dragon

12000

GRAASH

FWUM

WHAM

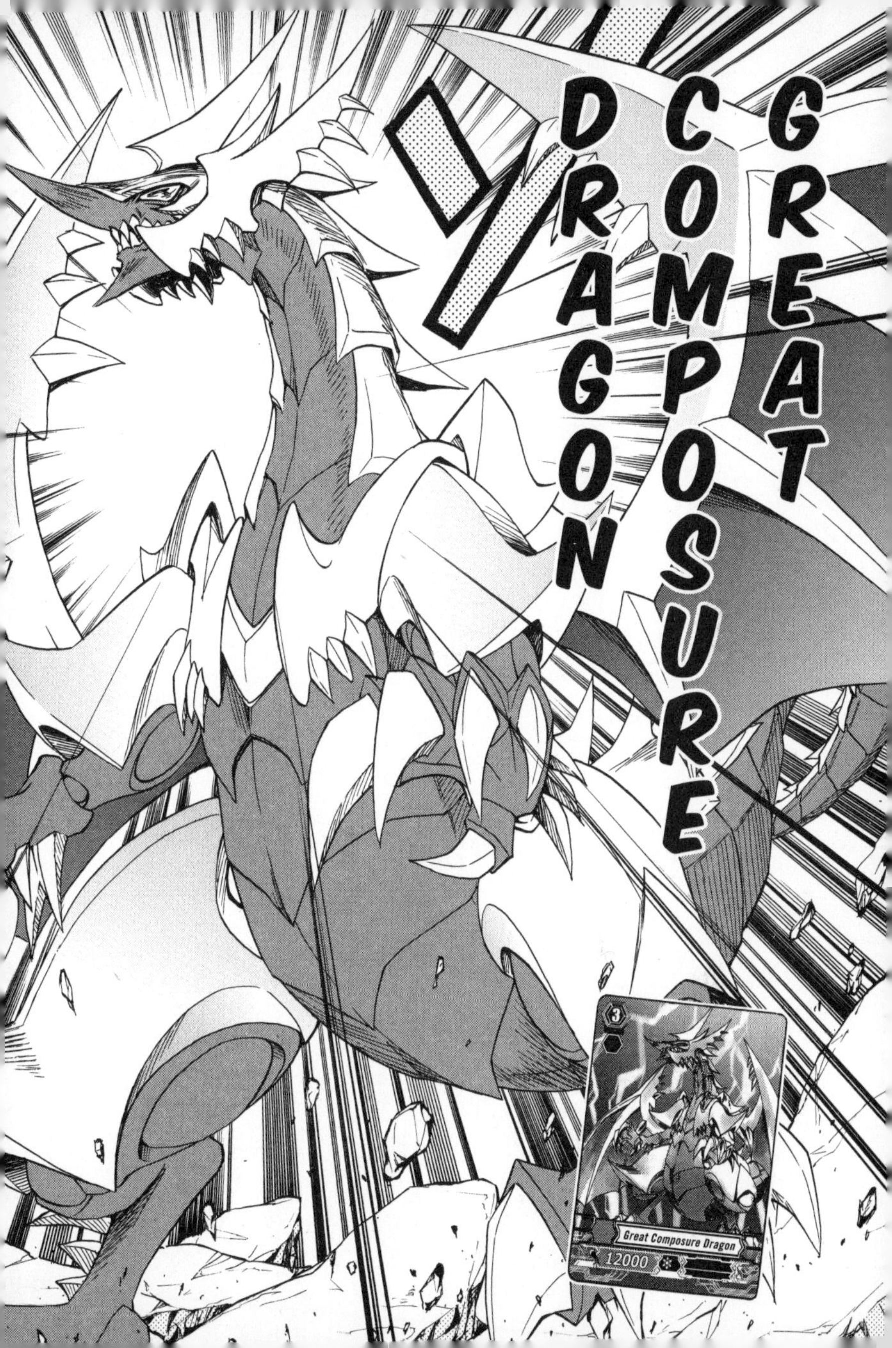

GREAT COMPOSURE DRAGON
Great Composure Dragon
12000

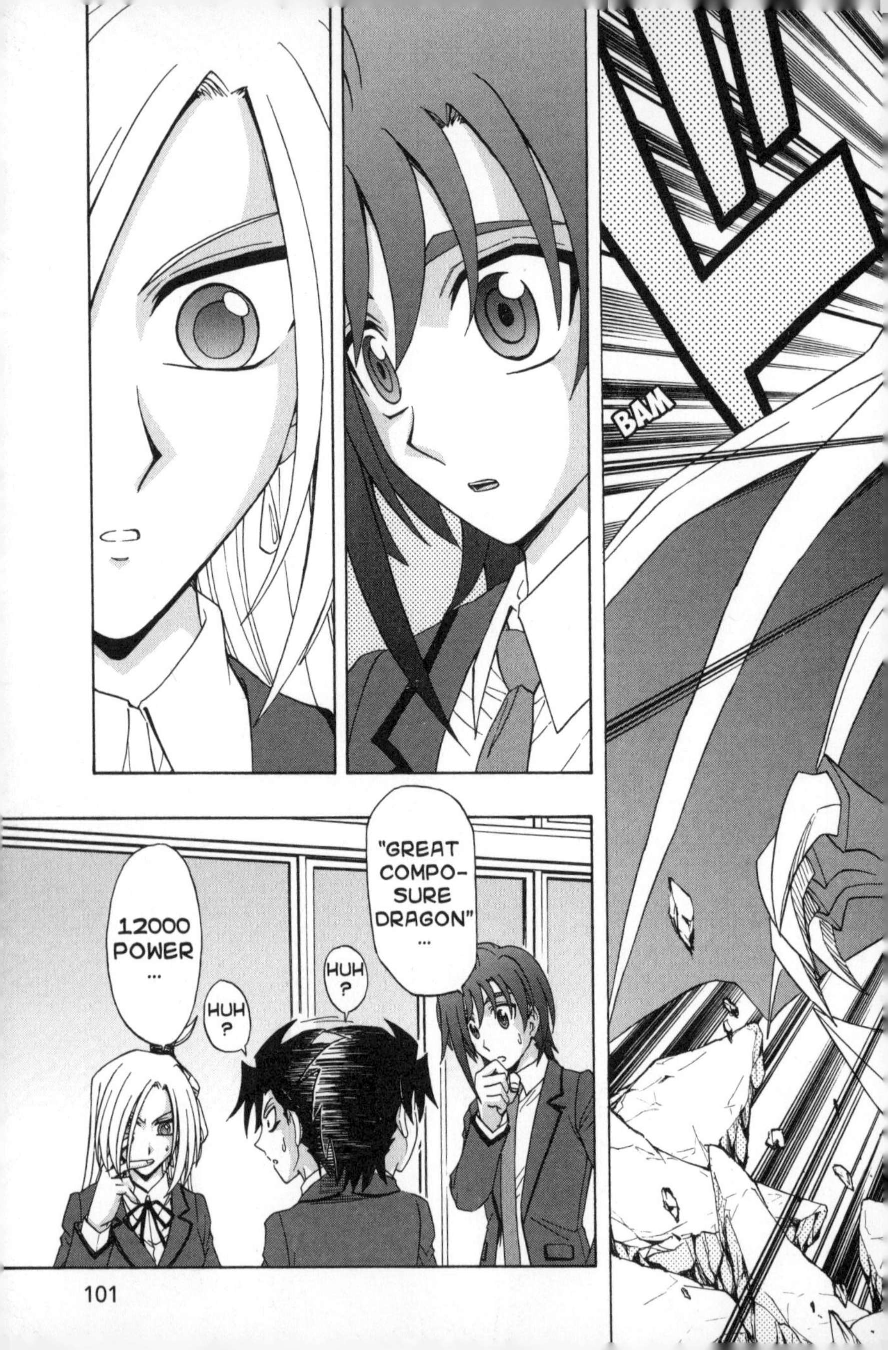
BAM
"GREAT COMPO-SURE DRAGON" ...
HUH?
HUH?
12000 POWER ...

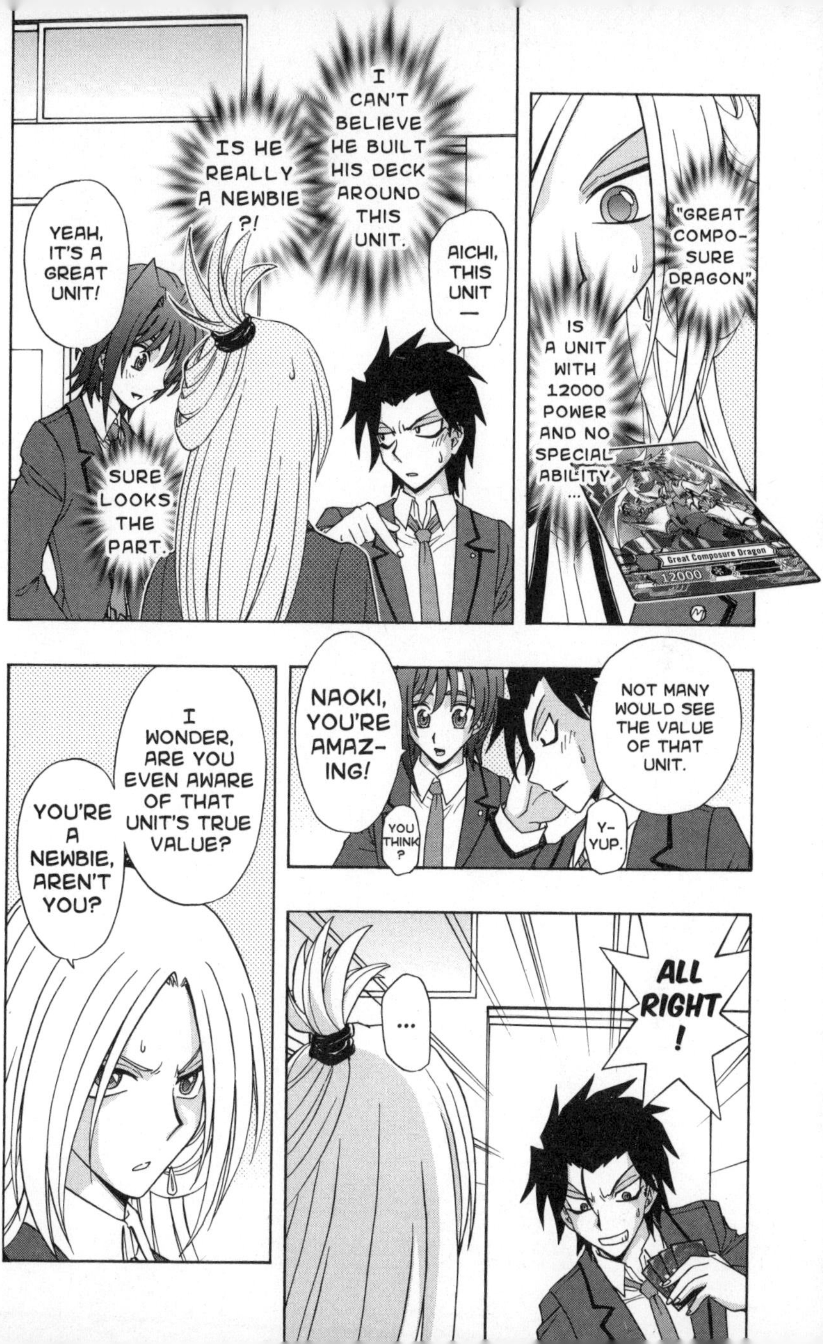
"GREAT COMPOSURE DRAGON"
IS A UNIT WITH 12000 POWER AND NO SPECIAL ABILITY...
Great Composure Dragon
12000
AICHI, THIS UNIT—
I CAN'T BELIEVE HE BUILT HIS DECK AROUND THIS UNIT.
IS HE REALLY A NEWBIE?!
YEAH, IT'S A GREAT UNIT!
SURE LOOKS THE PART.
NOT MANY WOULD SEE THE VALUE OF THAT UNIT.
NAOKI, YOU'RE AMAZING!
Y-YUP.
YOU THINK?
ALL RIGHT!
...
I WONDER, ARE YOU EVEN AWARE OF THAT UNIT'S TRUE VALUE?
YOU'RE A NEWBIE, AREN'T YOU?

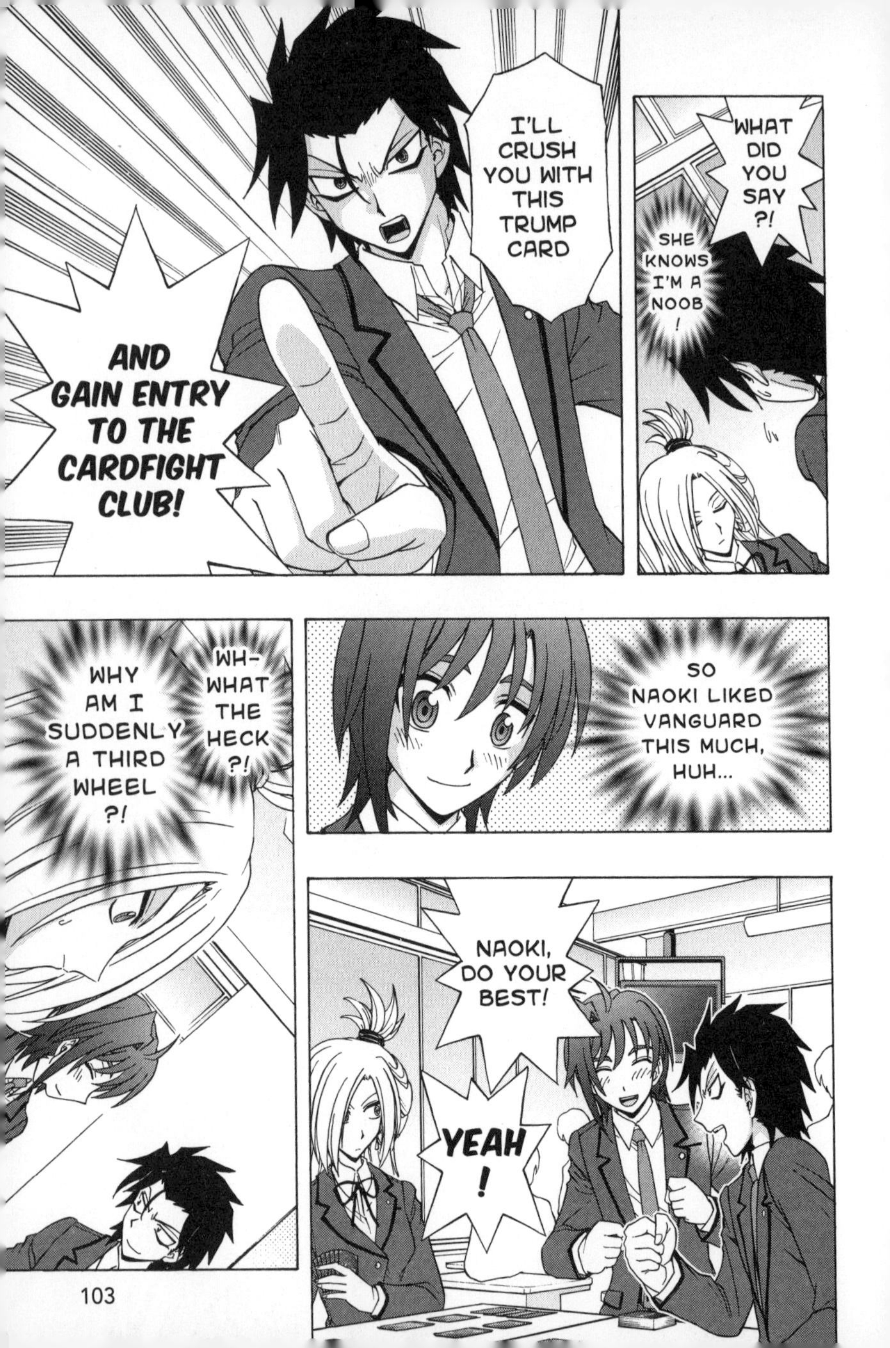
WHAT DID YOU SAY ?!
SHE KNOWS I'M A NOOB !
I'LL CRUSH YOU WITH THIS TRUMP CARD
AND GAIN ENTRY TO THE CARDFIGHT CLUB!
SO NAOKI LIKED VANGUARD THIS MUCH, HUH...
NAOKI, DO YOUR BEST!
YEAH !
WH- WHAT THE HECK ?!
WHY AM I SUDDENLY A THIRD WHEEL ?!

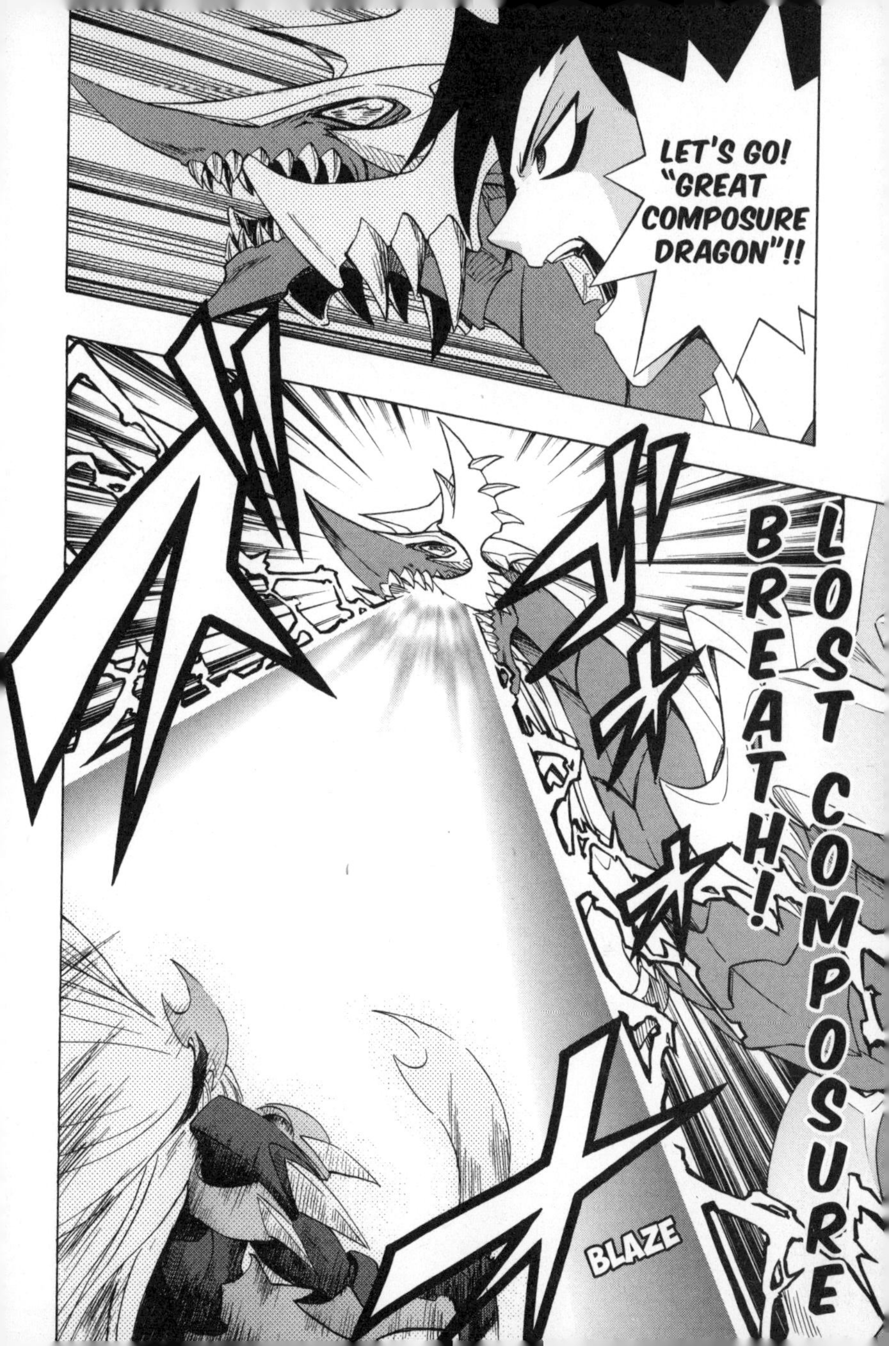
LET'S GO! "GREAT COMPOSURE DRAGON"!!
LOST COMPOSURE BREATH!
BLAZE

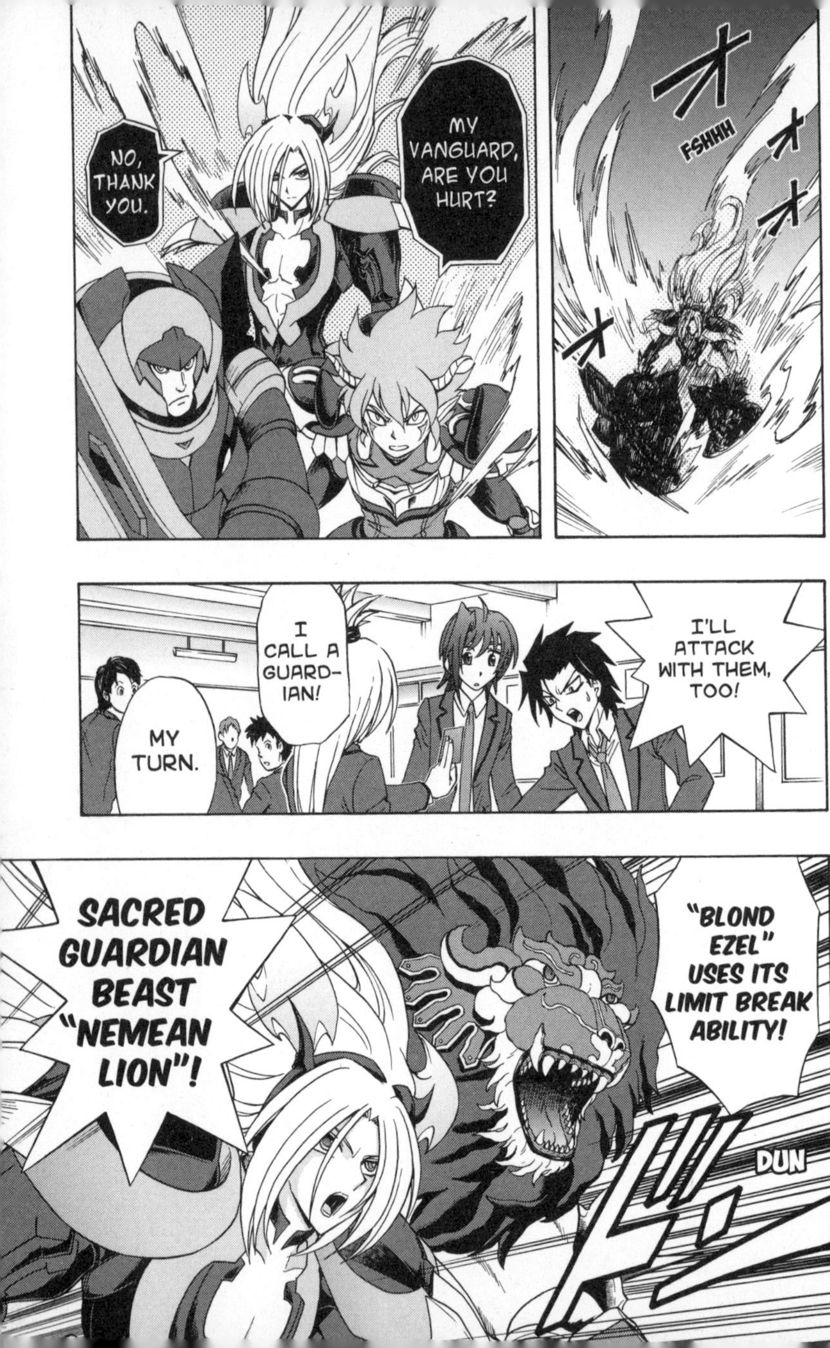
FSHHH
MY VANGUARD, ARE YOU HURT?
NO, THANK YOU.
I'LL ATTACK WITH THEM, TOO!
I CALL A GUARDIAN!
MY TURN.
"BLOND EZEL" USES ITS LIMIT BREAK ABILITY!
SACRED GUARDIAN BEAST "NEMEAN LION"!
DUN

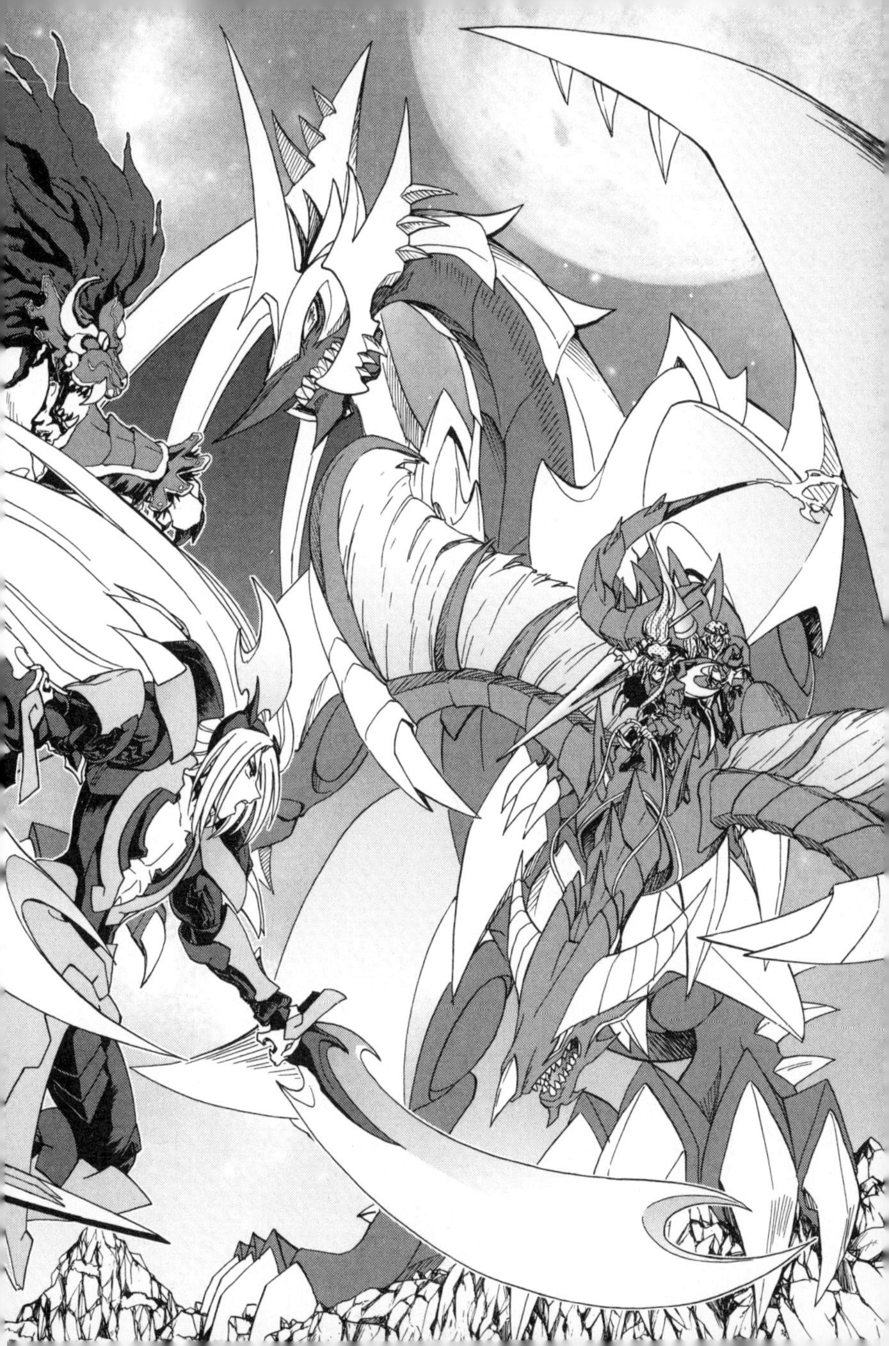

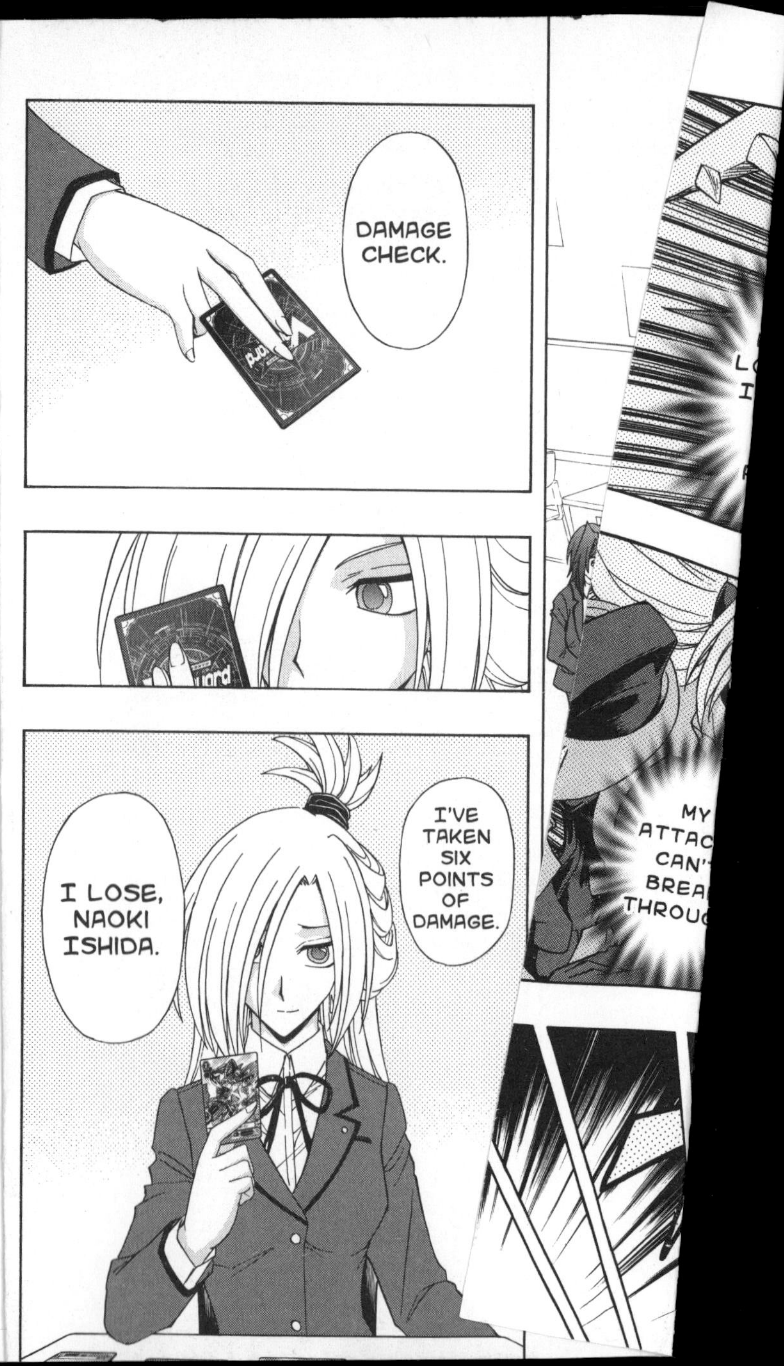
DAMAGE CHECK.
I'VE TAKEN SIX POINTS OF DAMAGE.
I LOSE, NAOKI ISHIDA.

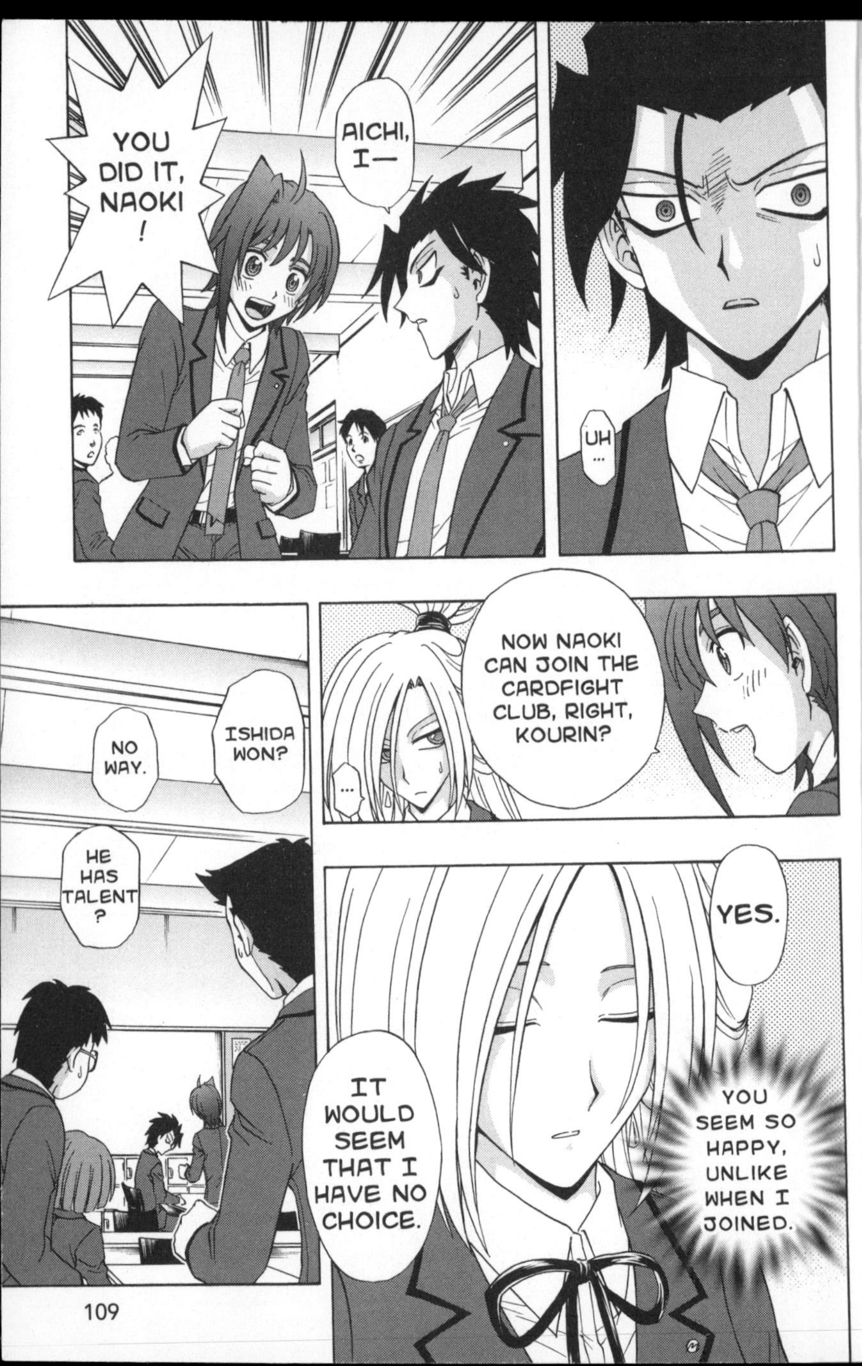
UH ...
YOU DID IT, NAOKI!
AICHI, I—
NOW NAOKI CAN JOIN THE CARDFIGHT CLUB, RIGHT, KOURIN?
...
YES.
IT WOULD SEEM THAT I HAVE NO CHOICE.
YOU SEEM SO HAPPY, UNLIKE WHEN I JOINED.
ISHIDA WON?
NO WAY.
HE HAS TALENT?

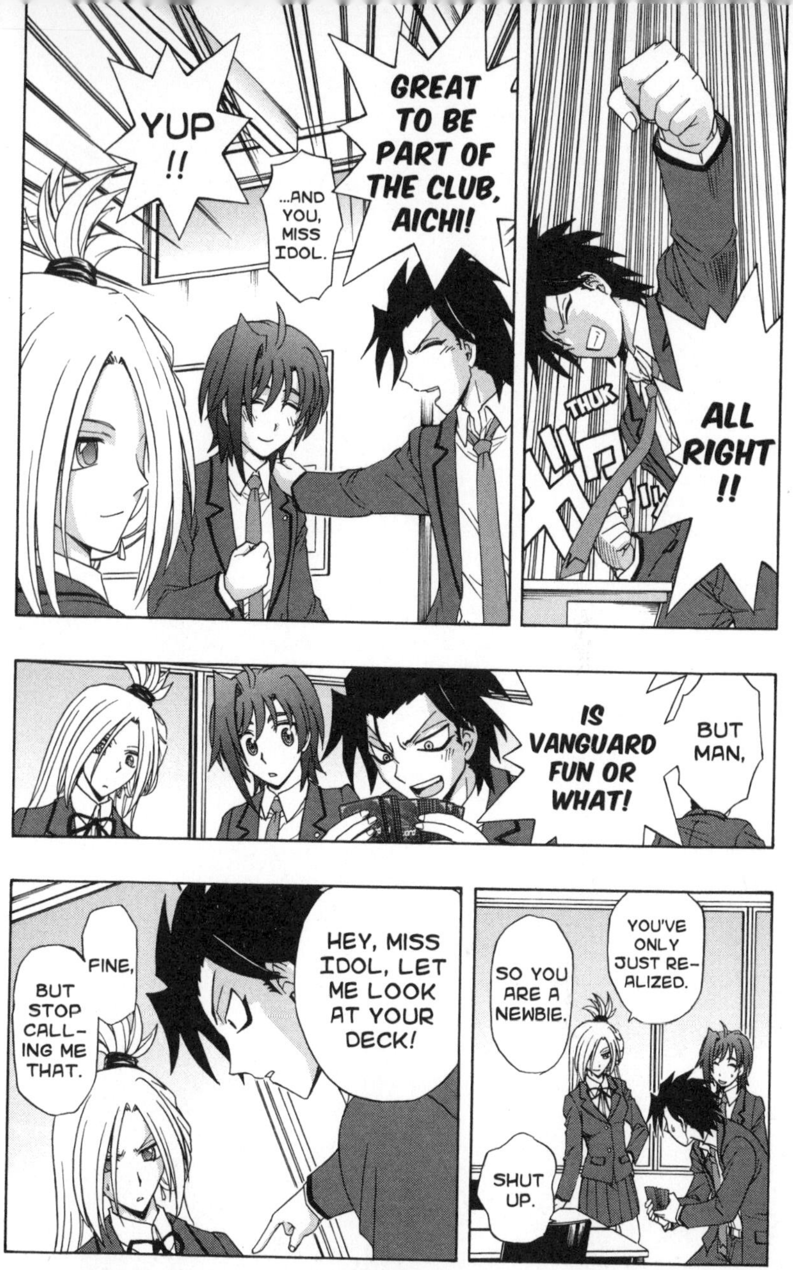
ALL RIGHT !!
THUK
GREAT TO BE PART OF THE CLUB, AICHI!
YUP !!
...AND YOU, MISS IDOL.
BUT MAN,
IS VANGUARD FUN OR WHAT!
YOU'VE ONLY JUST RE-ALIZED.
SO YOU ARE A NEWBIE.
SHUT UP.
HEY, MISS IDOL, LET ME LOOK AT YOUR DECK!
FINE,
BUT STOP CALLING ME THAT.

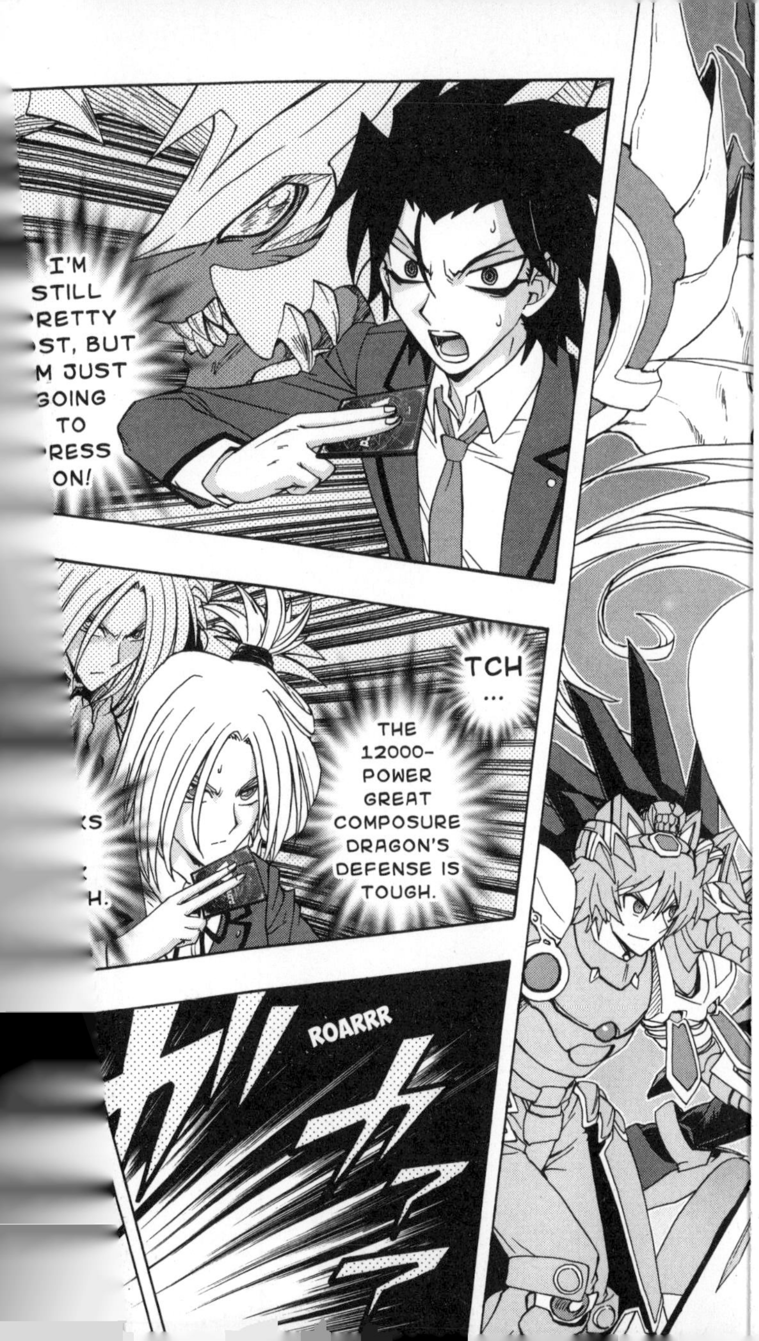
I'M STILL RETTY ST, BUT M JUST GOING TO RESS ON!
TCH ...
THE 12000-POWER GREAT COMPOSURE DRAGON'S DEFENSE IS TOUGH.
ROARRR

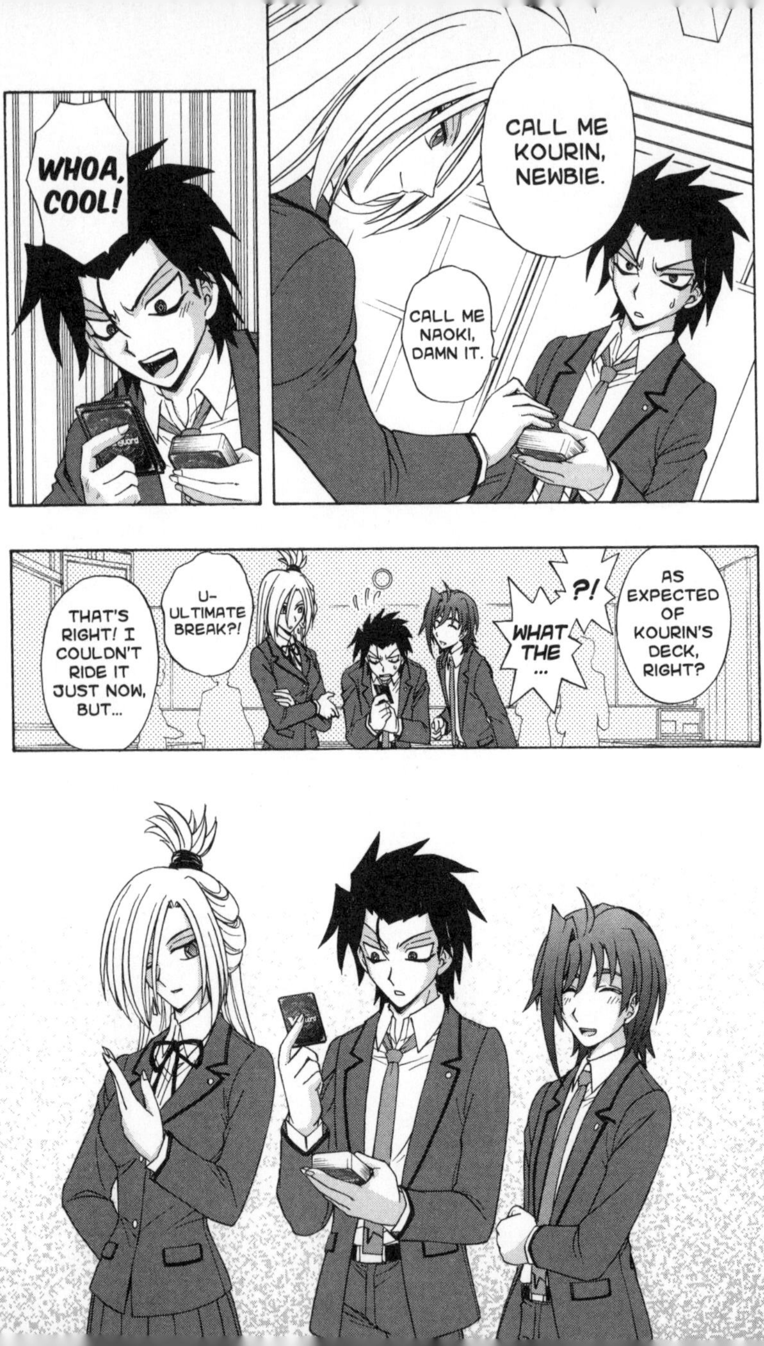
CALL ME KOURIN, NEWBIE.
CALL ME NAOKI, DAMN IT.
WHOA, COOL!
AS EXPECTED OF KOURIN'S DECK, RIGHT?
?!
WHAT THE ...
U-ULTIMATE BREAK?!
THAT'S RIGHT! I COULDN'T RIDE IT JUST NOW, BUT...

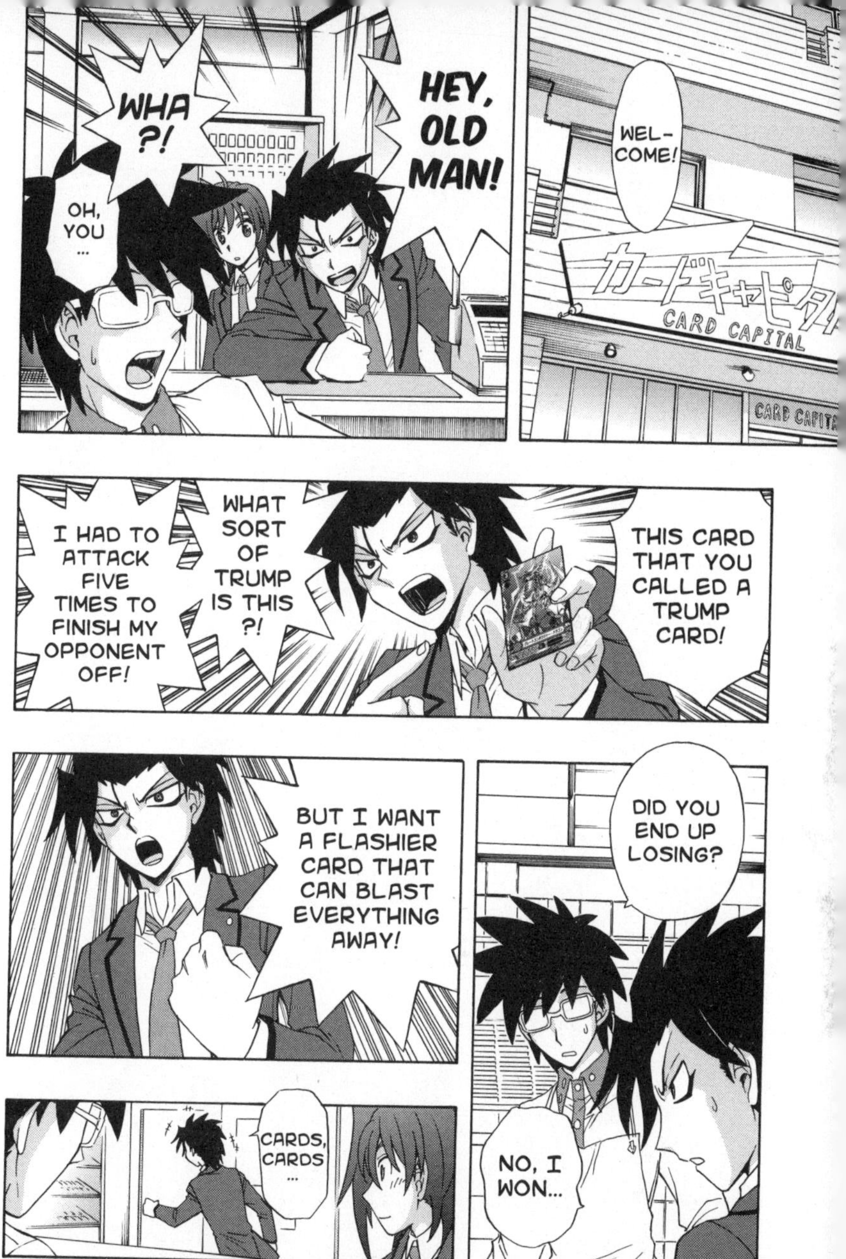
WEL-
COME!
カードキャピタ
CARD CAPITAL
CARD CAPITA
HEY, OLD MAN!
WHA ?!
OH, YOU ...
THIS CARD THAT YOU CALLED A TRUMP CARD!
WHAT SORT OF TRUMP IS THIS ?!
I HAD TO ATTACK FIVE TIMES TO FINISH MY OPPONENT OFF!
DID YOU END UP LOSING?
NO, I WON...
BUT I WANT A FLASHIER CARD THAT CAN BLAST EVERYTHING AWAY!
CARDS, CARDS ...

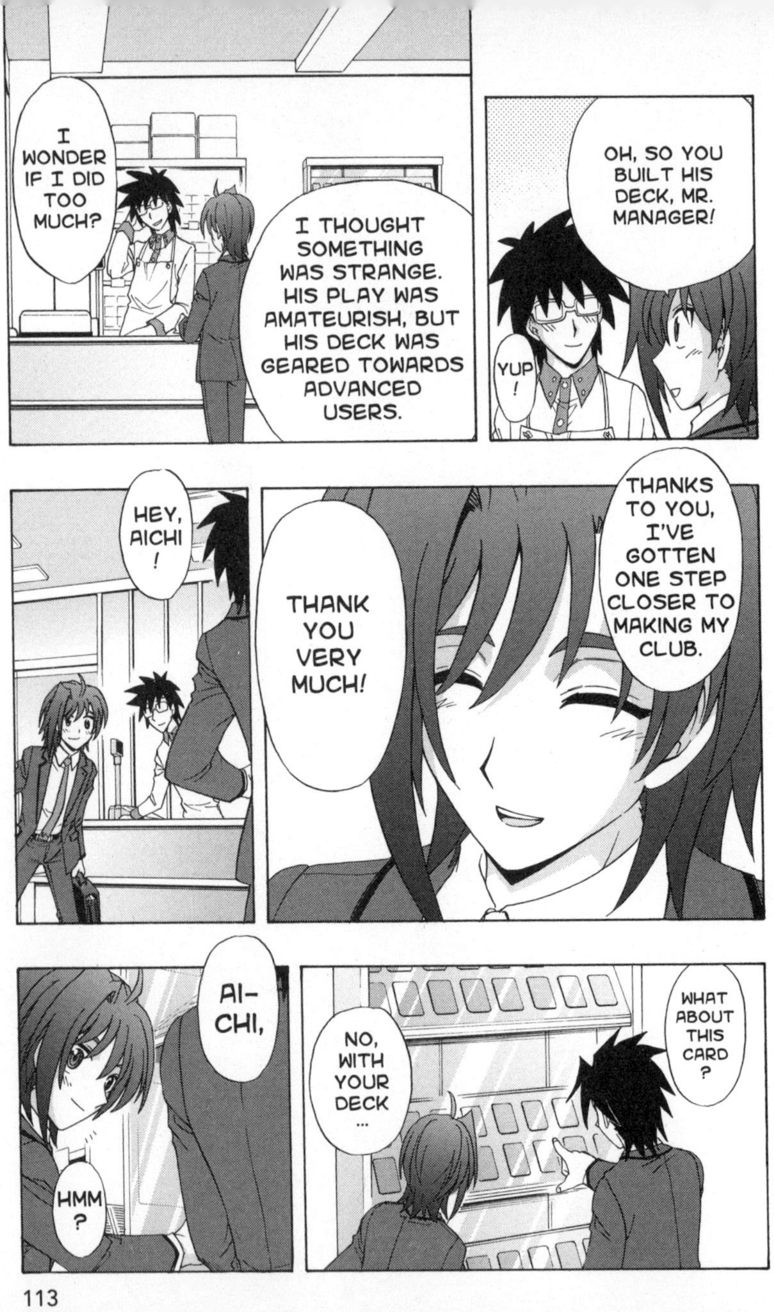
OH, SO YOU BUILT HIS DECK, MR. MANAGER!
YUP!
I THOUGHT SOMETHING WAS STRANGE. HIS PLAY WAS AMATEURISH, BUT HIS DECK WAS GEARED TOWARDS ADVANCED USERS.
I WONDER IF I DID TOO MUCH?
THANKS TO YOU, I'VE GOTTEN ONE STEP CLOSER TO MAKING MY CLUB.
THANK YOU VERY MUCH!
HEY, AICHI!
WHAT ABOUT THIS CARD?
NO, WITH YOUR DECK...
AI-CHI,
HMM?

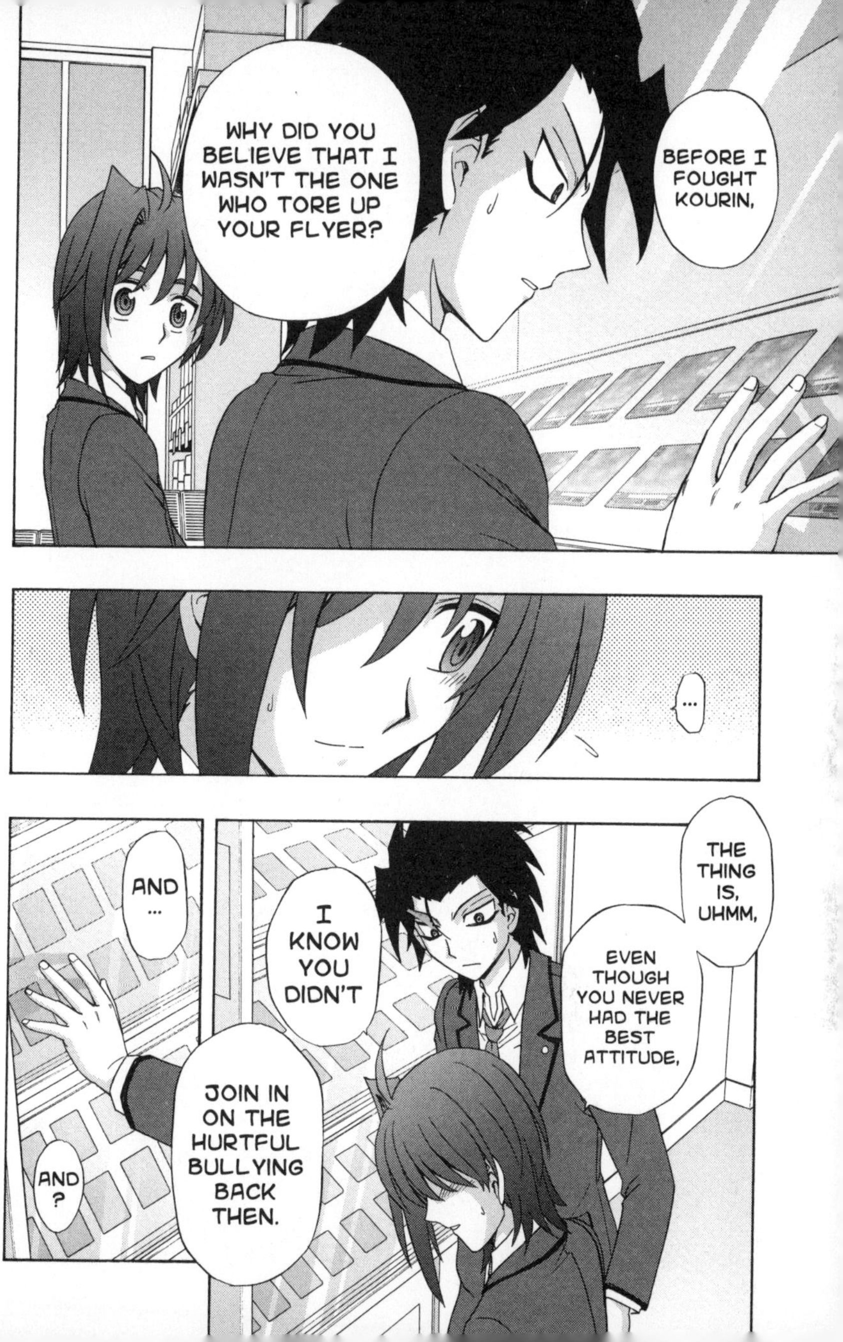
BEFORE I FOUGHT KOURIN,
WHY DID YOU BELIEVE THAT I WASN'T THE ONE WHO TORE UP YOUR FLYER?
...
THE THING IS, UHMM,
EVEN THOUGH YOU NEVER HAD THE BEST ATTITUDE,
I KNOW YOU DIDN'T
JOIN IN ON THE HURTFUL BULLYING BACK THEN.
AND ...
AND ?

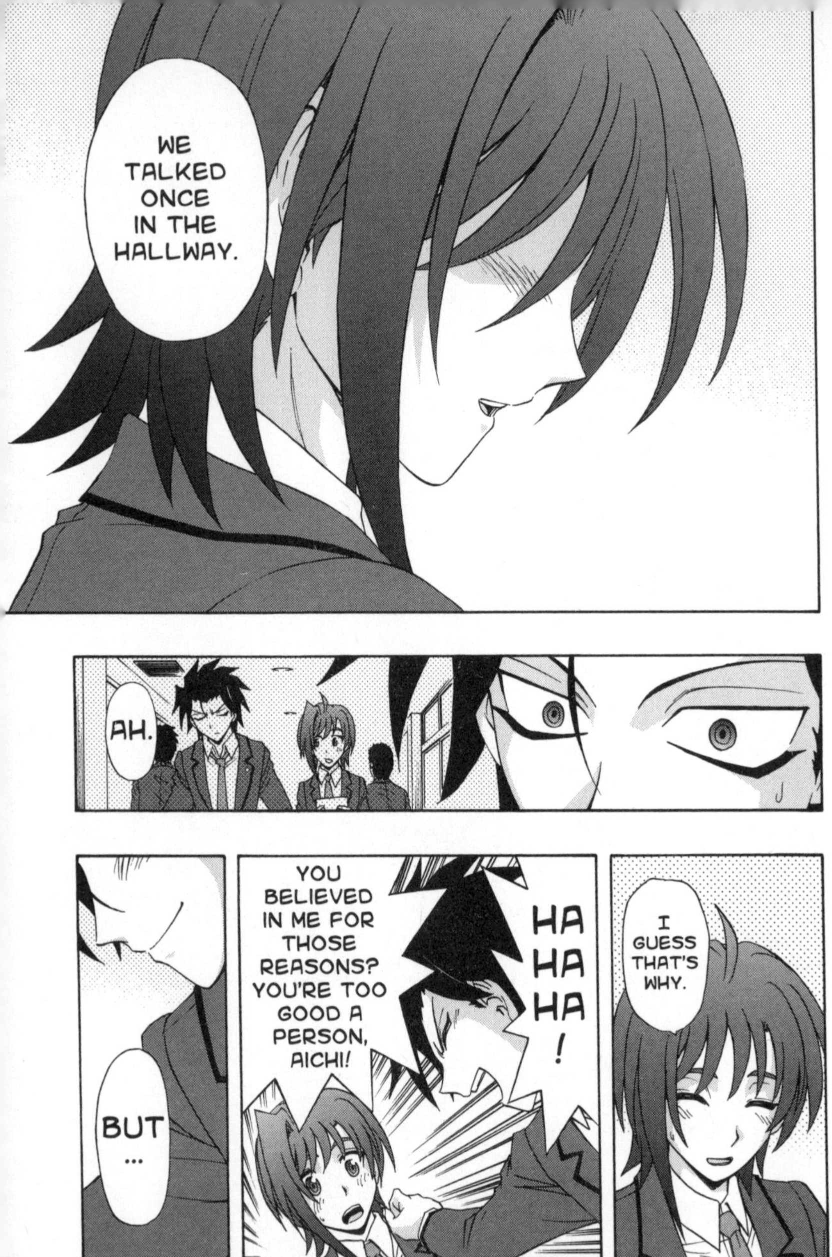
WE TALKED ONCE IN THE HALLWAY.
AH.
I GUESS THAT'S WHY.
HA HA HA!
YOU BELIEVED IN ME FOR THOSE REASONS? YOU'RE TOO GOOD A PERSON, AICHI!
BUT ...

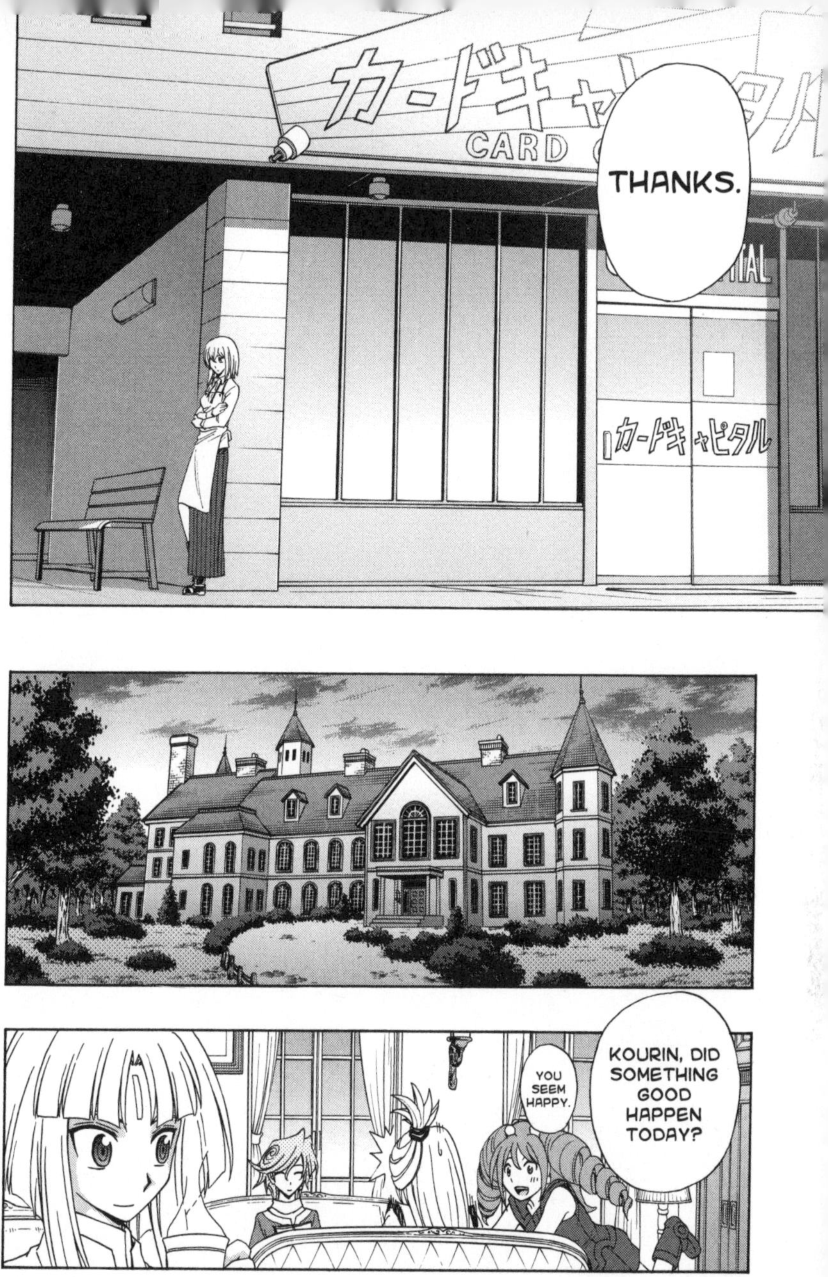
CARD
THANKS.
カードキャピタル
KOURIN, DID SOMETHING GOOD HAPPEN TODAY?
YOU SEEM HAPPY.

CARDFIGHT!!
Vanguard

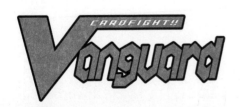

BONUS! CARDFIGHT!! Vanguard

NEVER-BEFORE-SEEN IMAGE BOARDS

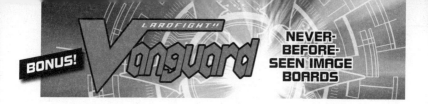

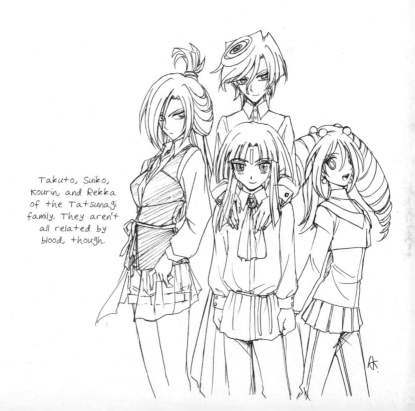

Takuto, Suiko, Kourin, and Rekka of the Tatsunagi family. They aren't all related by blood, though.

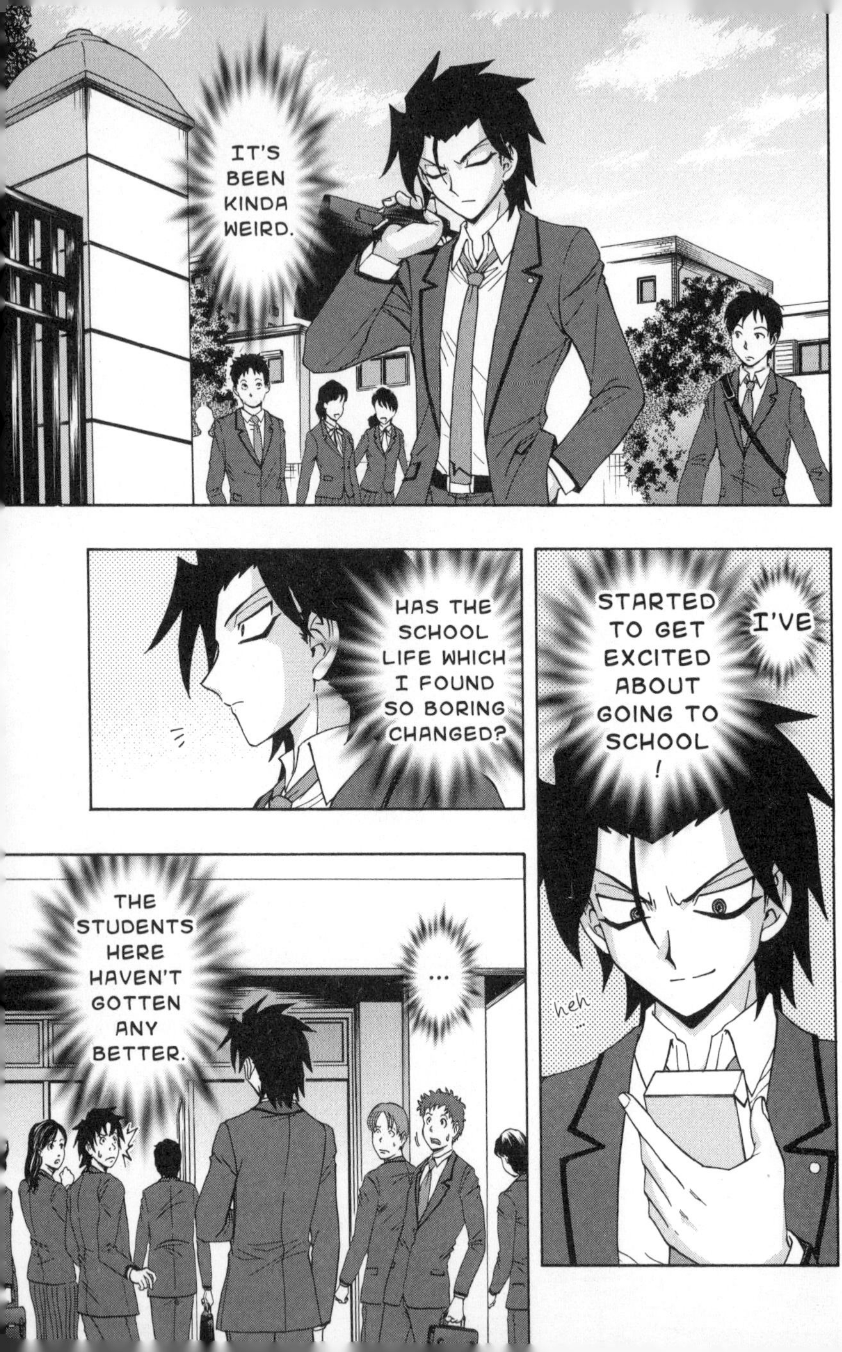
IT'S BEEN KINDA WEIRD.
I'VE
STARTED TO GET EXCITED ABOUT GOING TO SCHOOL!
heh...
HAS THE SCHOOL LIFE WHICH I FOUND SO BORING CHANGED?
...
THE STUDENTS HERE HAVEN'T GOTTEN ANY BETTER.

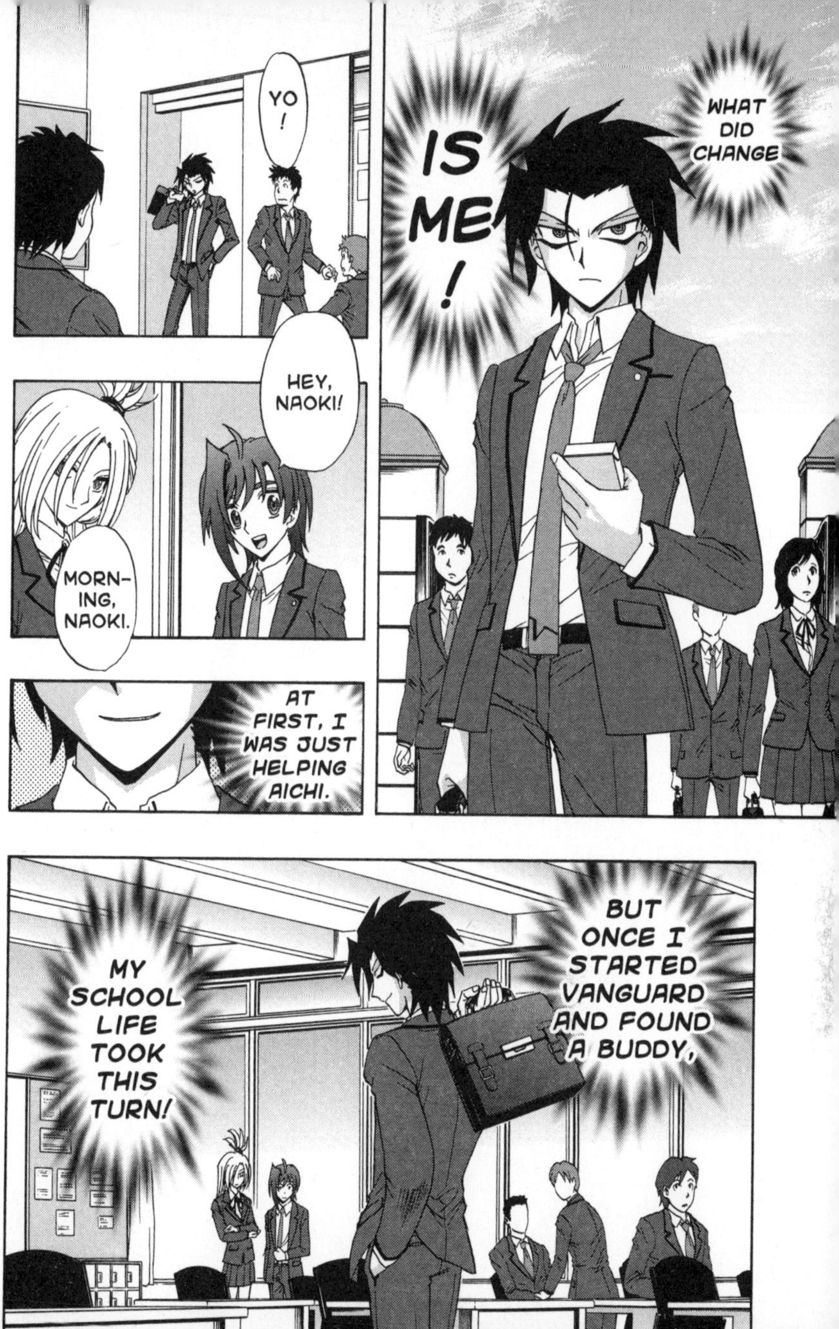
WHAT DID CHANGE
IS ME!
YO!
HEY, NAOKI!
MORNING, NAOKI.
AT FIRST, I WAS JUST HELPING AICHI.
BUT ONCE I STARTED VANGUARD AND FOUND A BUDDY,
MY SCHOOL LIFE TOOK THIS TURN!

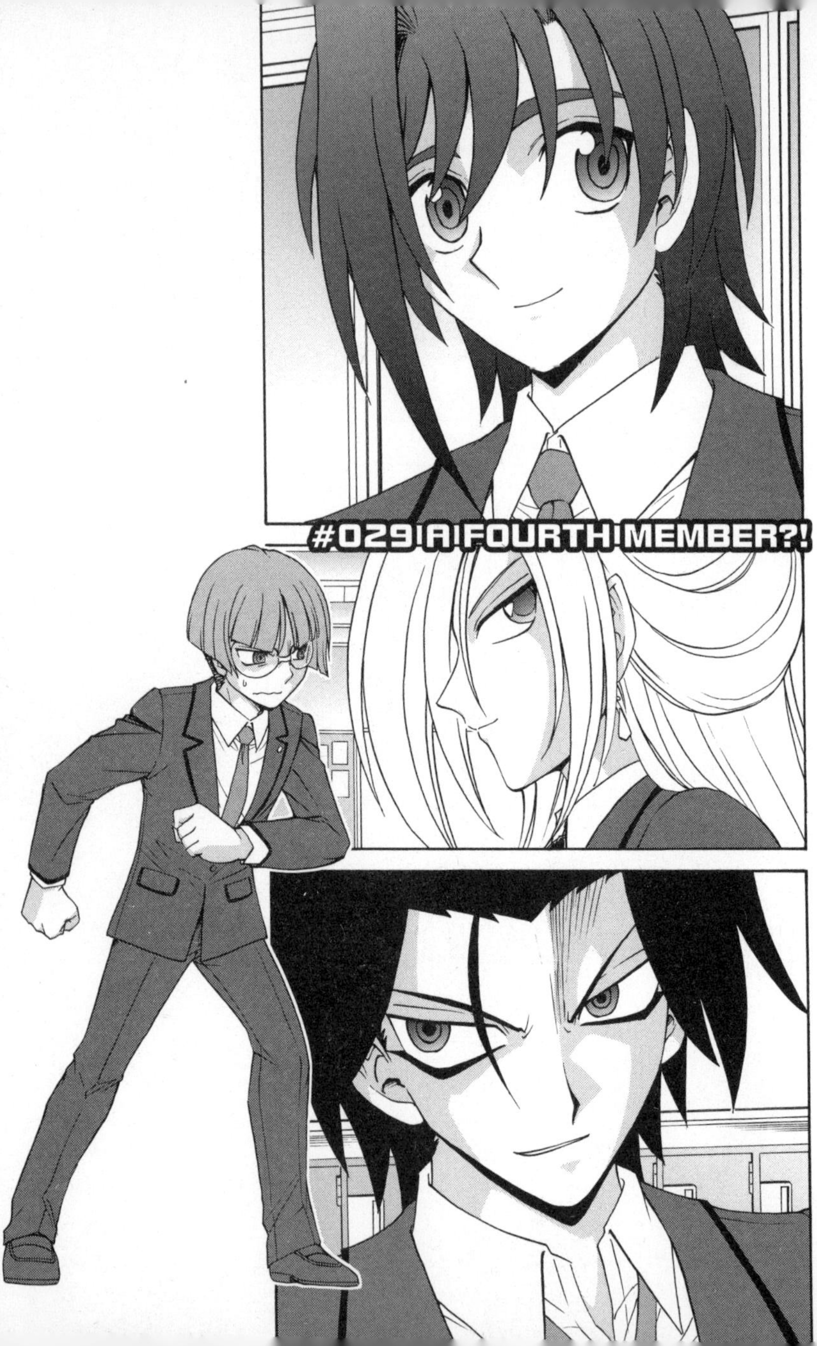
#029 A FOURTH MEMBER?!

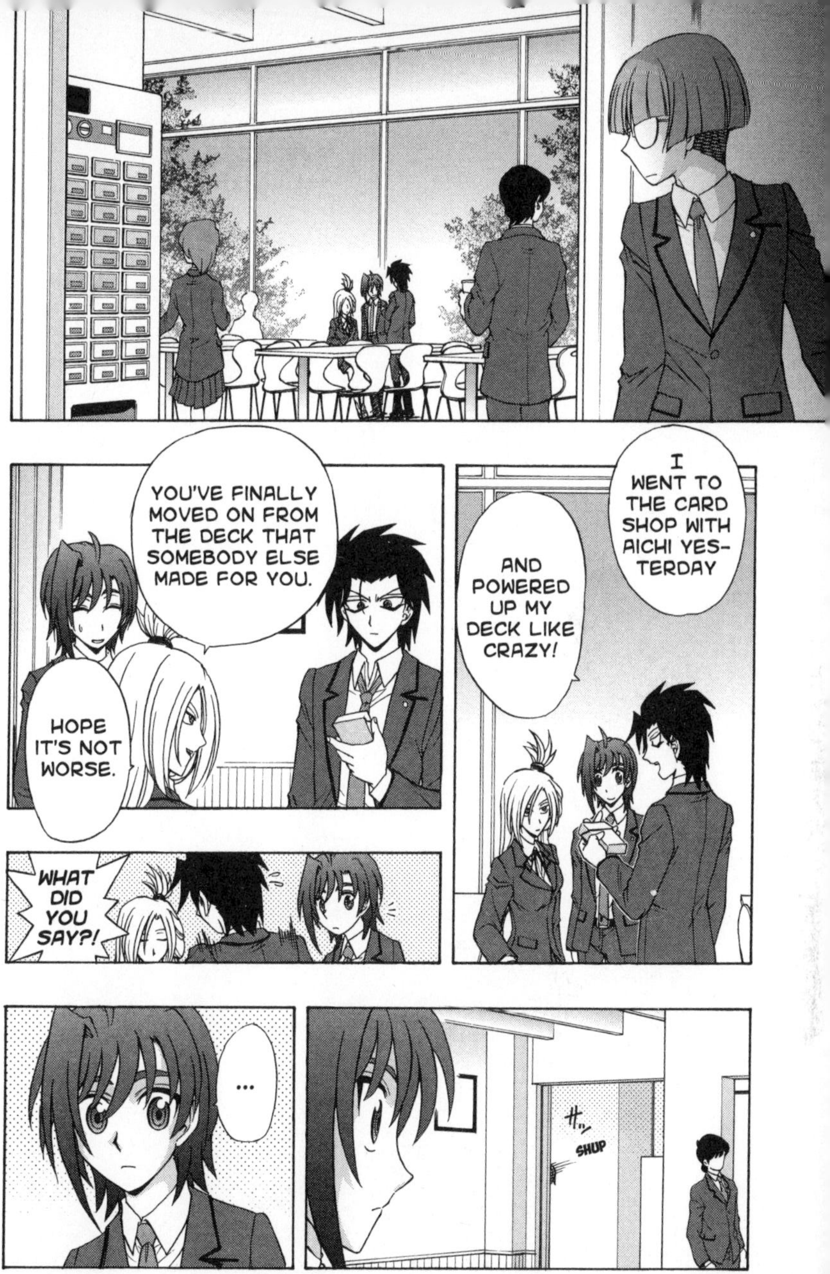
I WENT TO THE CARD SHOP WITH AICHI YES-TERDAY
AND POWERED UP MY DECK LIKE CRAZY!
YOU'VE FINALLY MOVED ON FROM THE DECK THAT SOMEBODY ELSE MADE FOR YOU.
HOPE IT'S NOT WORSE.
WHAT DID YOU SAY?!
SHUP
...

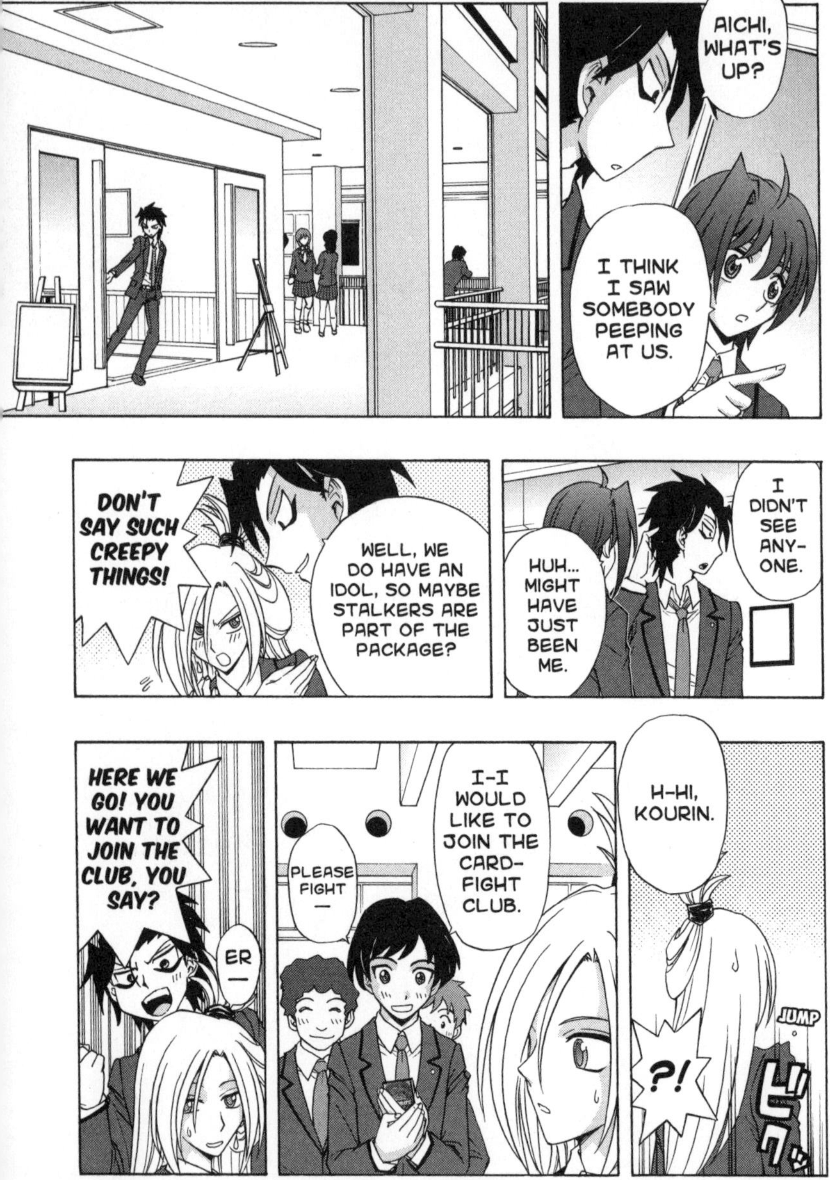
AICHI, WHAT'S UP?
I THINK I SAW SOMEBODY PEEPING AT US.
I DIDN'T SEE ANY-ONE.
HUH... MIGHT HAVE JUST BEEN ME.
WELL, WE DO HAVE AN IDOL, SO MAYBE STALKERS ARE PART OF THE PACKAGE?
DON'T SAY SUCH CREEPY THINGS!
H-HI, KOURIN.
JUMP
?!
ビクッ
I-I WOULD LIKE TO JOIN THE CARD-FIGHT CLUB.
PLEASE FIGHT —
HERE WE GO! YOU WANT TO JOIN THE CLUB, YOU SAY?
ER —

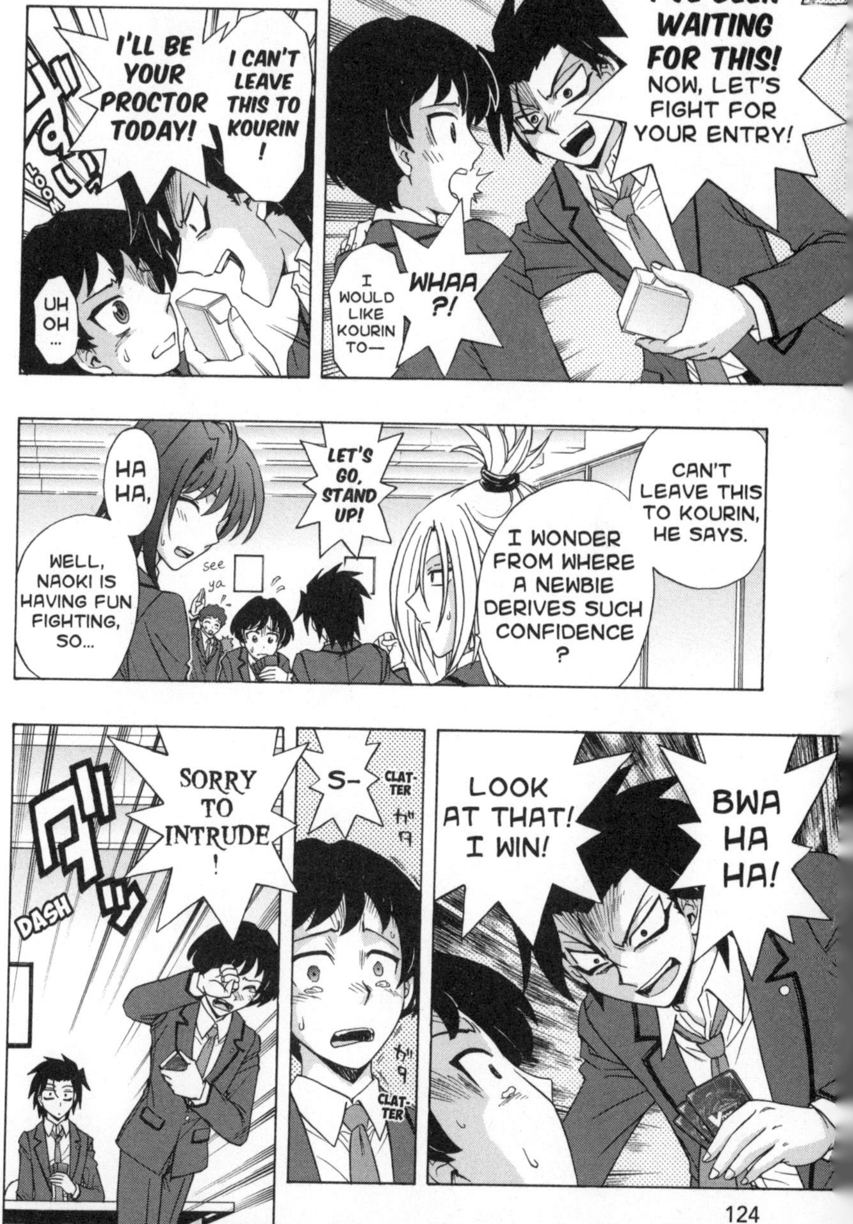
I'VE BEEN WAITING FOR THIS! NOW, LET'S FIGHT FOR YOUR ENTRY!
WHAA ?!
I WOULD LIKE KOURIN TO—
I CAN'T LEAVE THIS TO KOURIN !
I'LL BE YOUR PROCTOR TODAY!
UH OH ...
CAN'T LEAVE THIS TO KOURIN, HE SAYS.
I WONDER FROM WHERE A NEWBIE DERIVES SUCH CONFIDENCE ?
LET'S GO, STAND UP!
see ya
HA HA,
WELL, NAOKI IS HAVING FUN FIGHTING, SO...
BWA HA HA!
LOOK AT THAT! I WIN!
S-
CLATTER
CLATTER
SORRY TO INTRUDE !
DASH

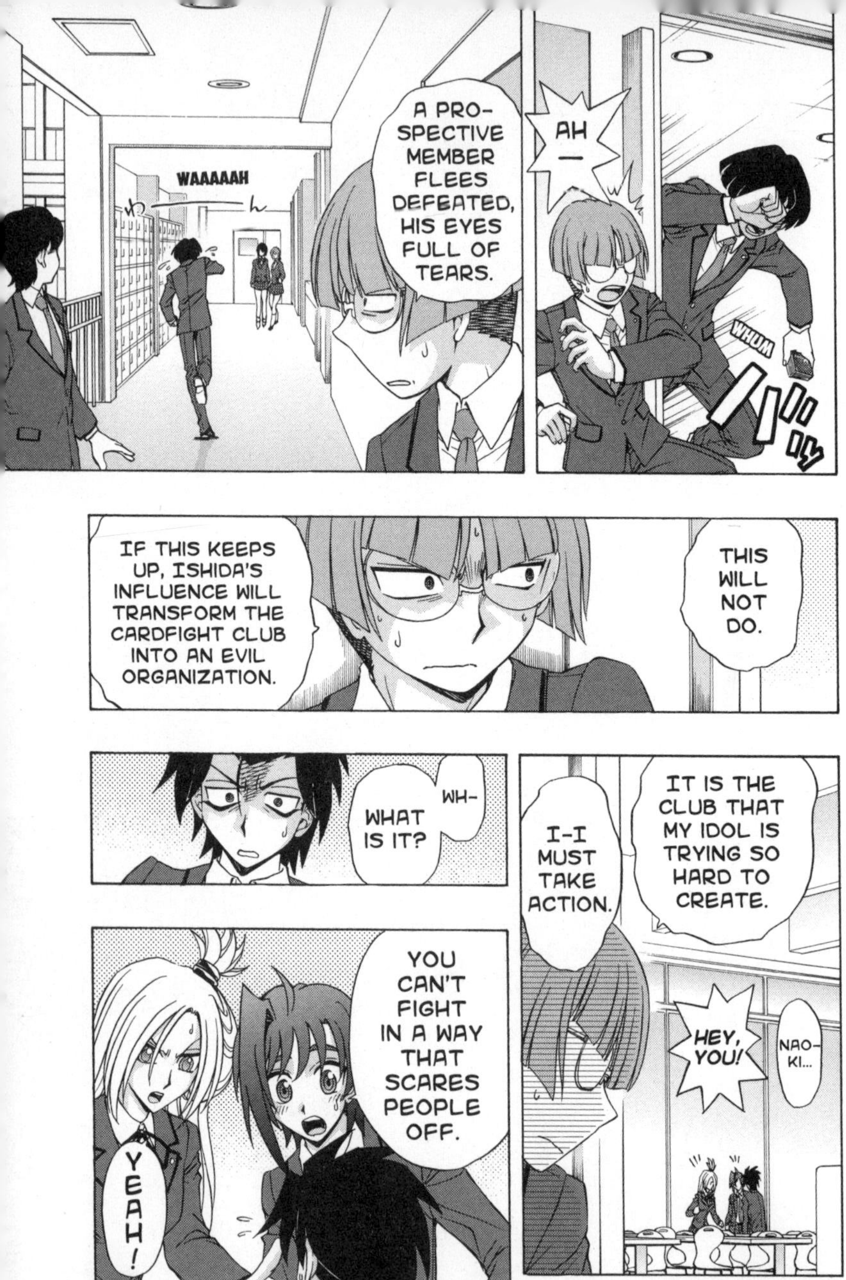
AH—
WHUM
A PRO-SPECTIVE MEMBER FLEES DEFEATED, HIS EYES FULL OF TEARS.
WAAAAAH
THIS WILL NOT DO.
IF THIS KEEPS UP, ISHIDA'S INFLUENCE WILL TRANSFORM THE CARDFIGHT CLUB INTO AN EVIL ORGANIZATION.
IT IS THE CLUB THAT MY IDOL IS TRYING SO HARD TO CREATE.
I-I MUST TAKE ACTION.
NAO-KI...
HEY, YOU!
WH-
WHAT IS IT?
YOU CAN'T FIGHT IN A WAY THAT SCARES PEOPLE OFF.
YEAH!

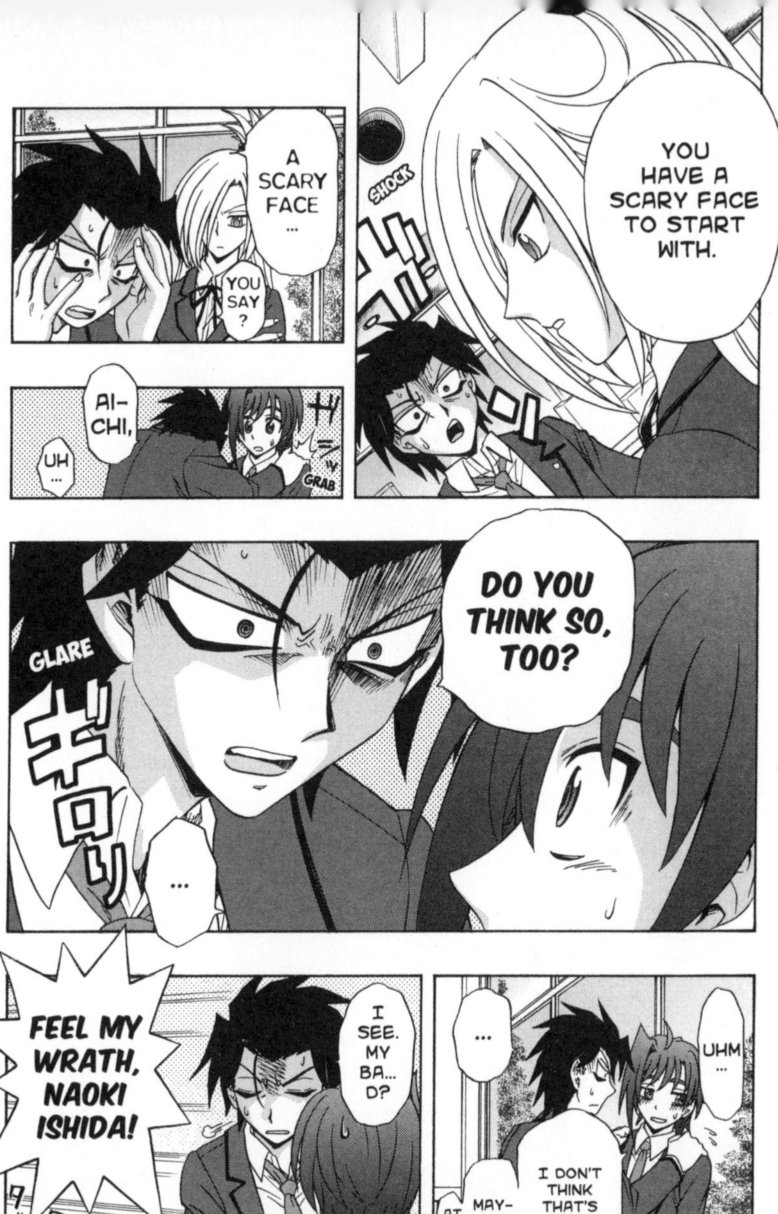
YOU HAVE A SCARY FACE TO START WITH.
SHOCK
A SCARY FACE ...
YOU SAY?
AI-CHI,
UH ...
GRAB
DO YOU THINK SO, TOO?
GLARE
...
UHM ...
...
I DON'T THINK THAT'S TRUE,
MAY-BE?
AT ALL?
I SEE. MY BA... D?
FEEL MY WRATH, NAOKI ISHIDA!
TUP
TUP

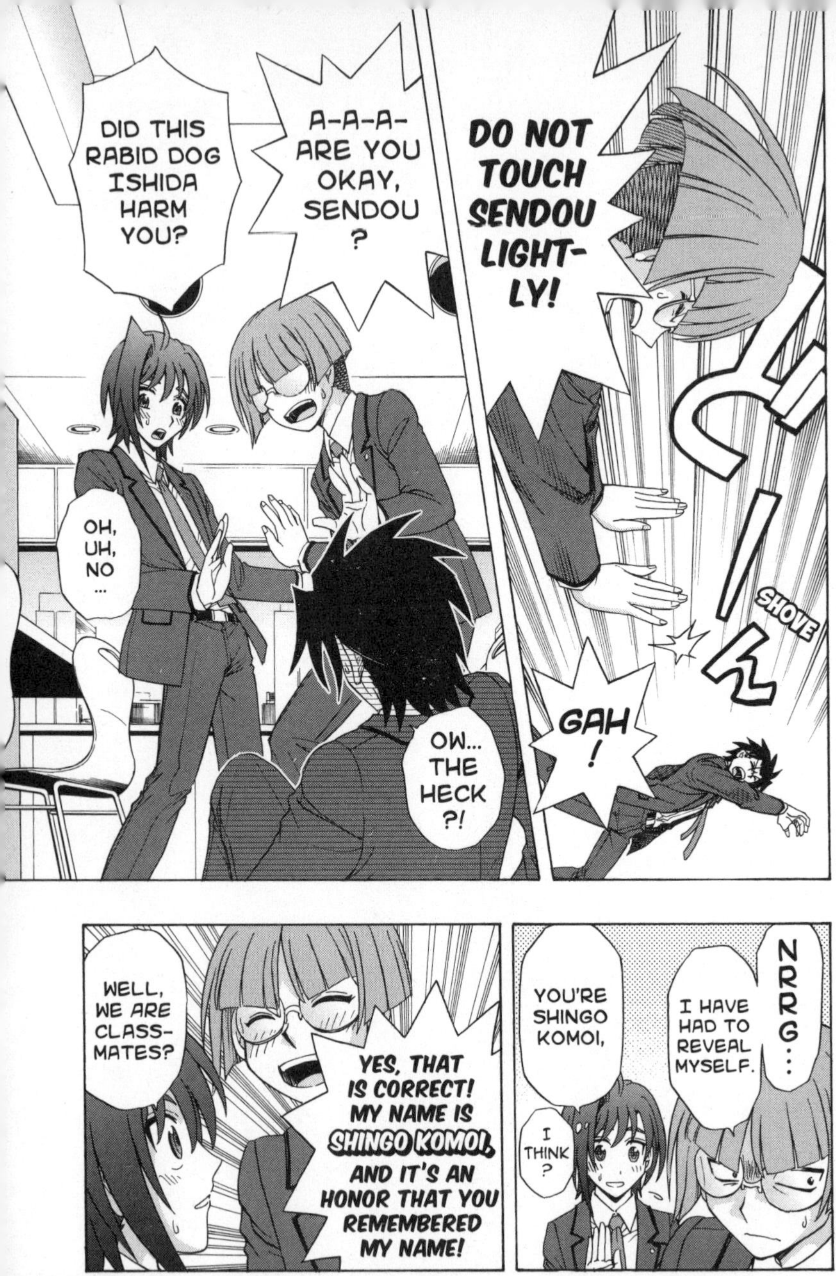
DO NOT TOUCH SENDOU LIGHTLY!
SHOVE
GAH!
A-A-A-ARE YOU OKAY, SENDOU?
DID THIS RABID DOG ISHIDA HARM YOU?
OH, UH, NO ...
OW... THE HECK?!
NRRG...
I HAVE HAD TO REVEAL MYSELF.
YOU'RE SHINGO KOMOI,
I THINK?
WELL, WE ARE CLASSMATES?
YES, THAT IS CORRECT! MY NAME IS SHINGO KOMOI, AND IT'S AN HONOR THAT YOU REMEMBERED MY NAME!

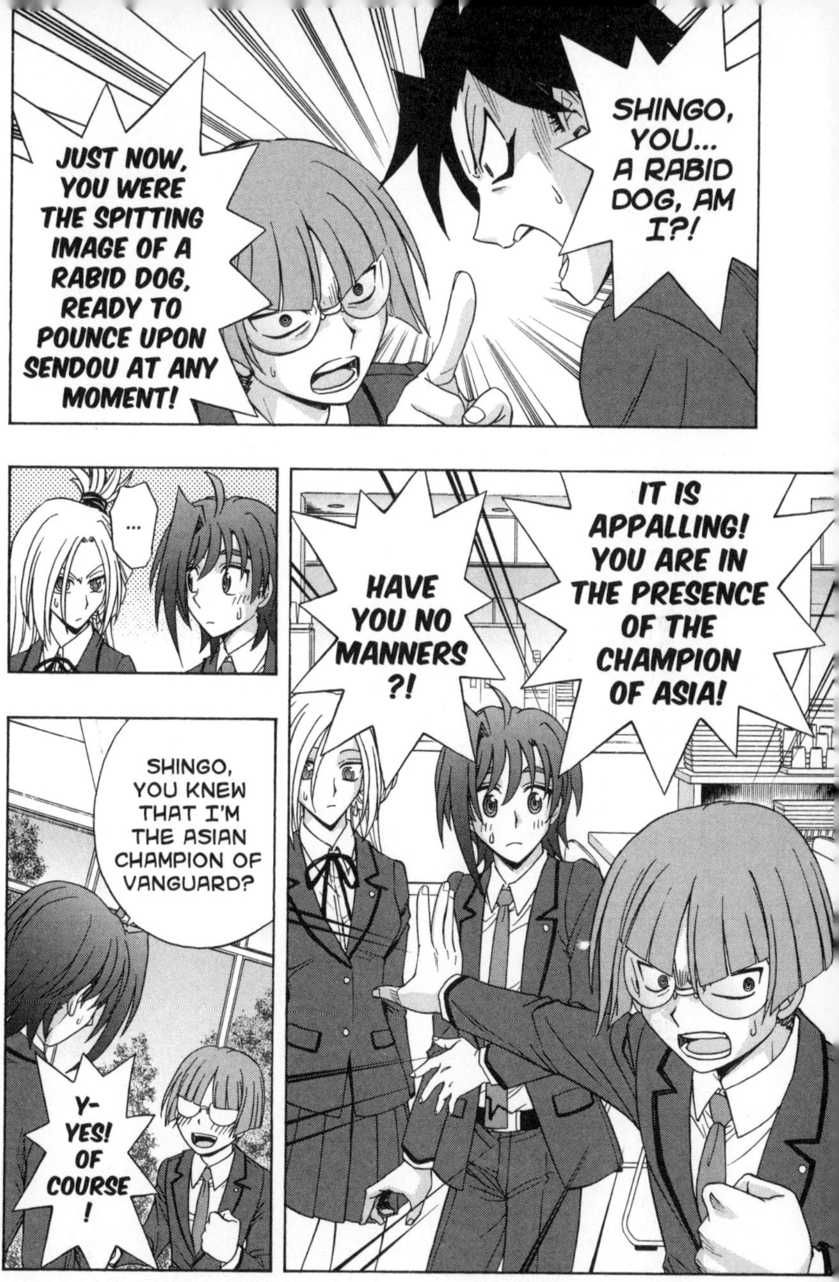
SHINGO, YOU... A RABID DOG, AM I?!
JUST NOW, YOU WERE THE SPITTING IMAGE OF A RABID DOG, READY TO POUNCE UPON SENDOU AT ANY MOMENT!
IT IS APPALLING! YOU ARE IN THE PRESENCE OF THE CHAMPION OF ASIA!
HAVE YOU NO MANNERS?!
...
SHINGO, YOU KNEW THAT I'M THE ASIAN CHAMPION OF VANGUARD?
Y-YES! OF COURSE!

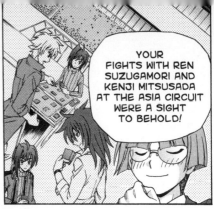

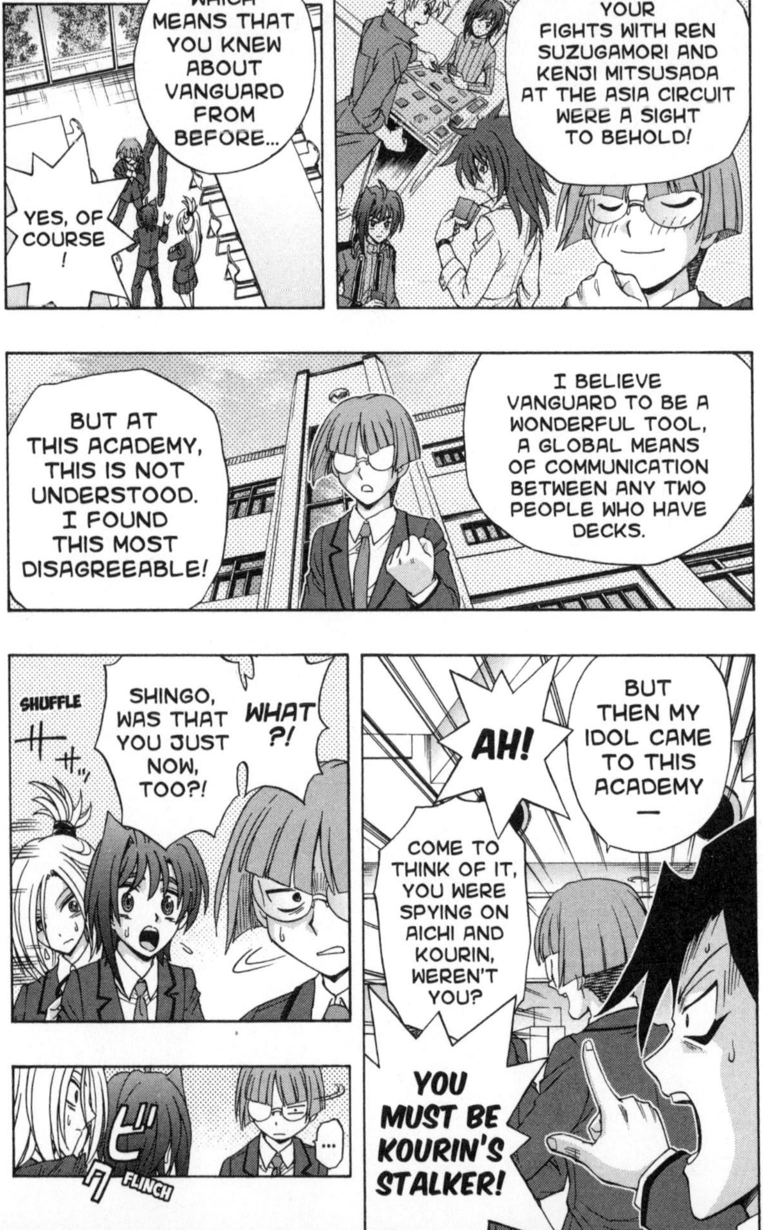
YOUR FIGHTS WITH REN SUZUGAMORI AND KENJI MITSUSADA AT THE ASIA CIRCUIT WERE A SIGHT TO BEHOLD!
WHICH MEANS THAT YOU KNEW ABOUT VANGUARD FROM BEFORE...
YES, OF COURSE!
I BELIEVE VANGUARD TO BE A WONDERFUL TOOL, A GLOBAL MEANS OF COMMUNICATION BETWEEN ANY TWO PEOPLE WHO HAVE DECKS.
BUT AT THIS ACADEMY, THIS IS NOT UNDERSTOOD. I FOUND THIS MOST DISAGREEABLE!
BUT THEN MY IDOL CAME TO THIS ACADEMY —
AH!
COME TO THINK OF IT, YOU WERE SPYING ON AICHI AND KOURIN, WEREN'T YOU?
YOU MUST BE KOURIN'S STALKER!
WHAT?!
SHINGO, WAS THAT YOU JUST NOW, TOO?!
SHUFFLE
...
ビク
FLINCH

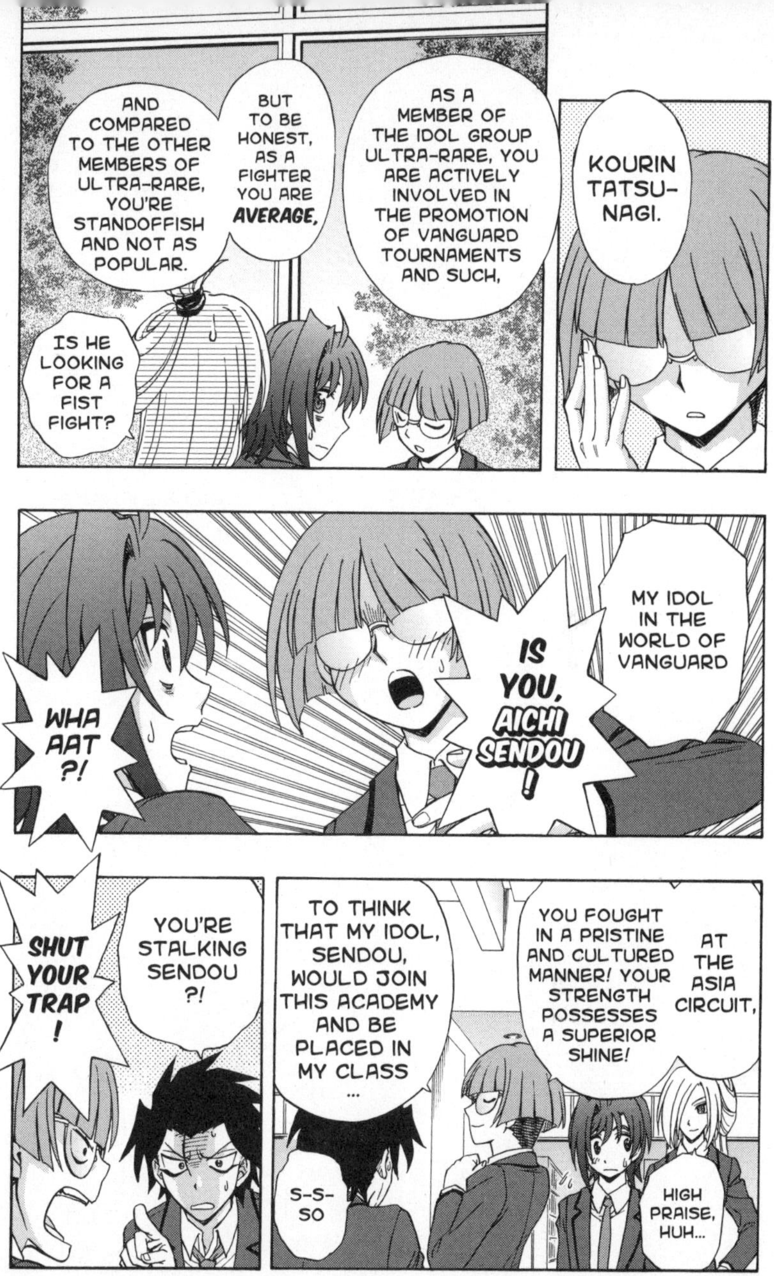
KOURIN TATSUNAGI.
AS A MEMBER OF THE IDOL GROUP ULTRA-RARE, YOU ARE ACTIVELY INVOLVED IN THE PROMOTION OF VANGUARD TOURNAMENTS AND SUCH,
BUT TO BE HONEST, AS A FIGHTER YOU ARE **AVERAGE,**
AND COMPARED TO THE OTHER MEMBERS OF ULTRA-RARE, YOU'RE STANDOFFISH AND NOT AS POPULAR.
IS HE LOOKING FOR A FIST FIGHT?
MY IDOL IN THE WORLD OF VANGUARD
IS YOU, AICHI SENDOU!
WHAAAT?!
AT THE ASIA CIRCUIT,
YOU FOUGHT IN A PRISTINE AND CULTURED MANNER! YOUR STRENGTH POSSESSES A SUPERIOR SHINE!
TO THINK THAT MY IDOL, SENDOU, WOULD JOIN THIS ACADEMY AND BE PLACED IN MY CLASS ...
HIGH PRAISE, HUH...
S-S-SO
YOU'RE STALKING SENDOU ?!
SHUT YOUR TRAP!

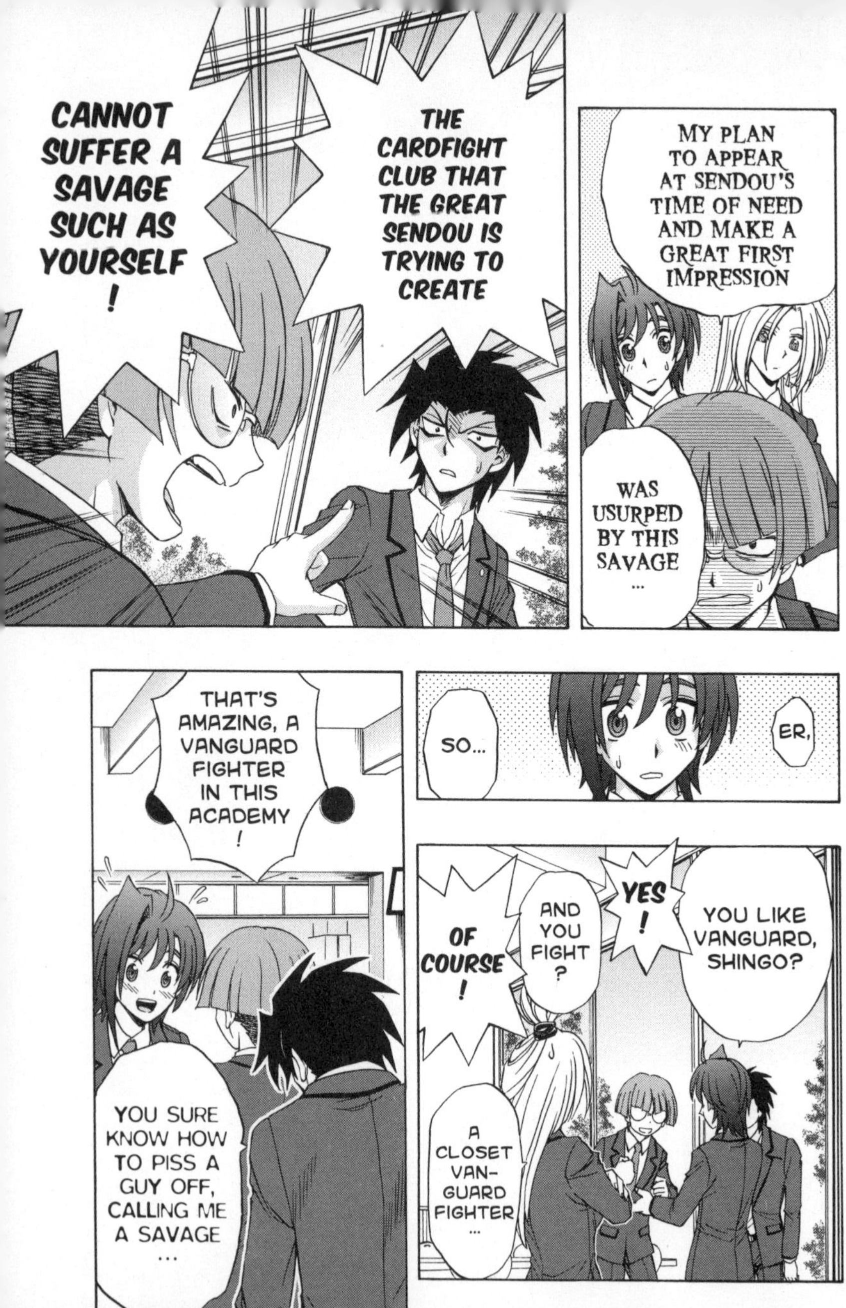
MY PLAN TO APPEAR AT SENDOU'S TIME OF NEED AND MAKE A GREAT FIRST IMPRESSION
WAS USURPED BY THIS SAVAGE...
THE CARDFIGHT CLUB THAT THE GREAT SENDOU IS TRYING TO CREATE
CANNOT SUFFER A SAVAGE SUCH AS YOURSELF!
ER,
SO...
YOU LIKE VANGUARD, SHINGO?
YES!
AND YOU FIGHT?
OF COURSE!
A CLOSET VAN-GUARD FIGHTER...
THAT'S AMAZING, A VANGUARD FIGHTER IN THIS ACADEMY!
YOU SURE KNOW HOW TO PISS A GUY OFF, CALLING ME A SAVAGE...

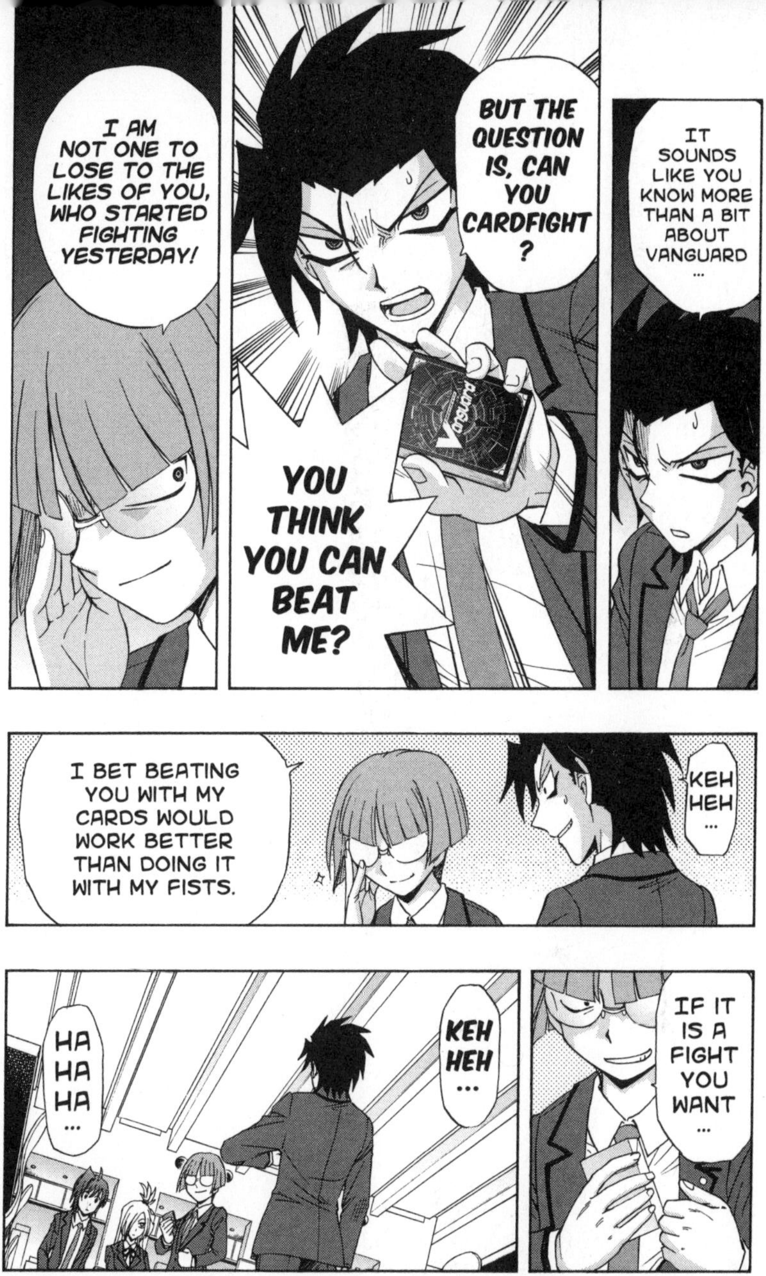
IT SOUNDS LIKE YOU KNOW MORE THAN A BIT ABOUT VANGUARD ...
BUT THE QUESTION IS, CAN YOU CARDFIGHT ?
YOU THINK YOU CAN BEAT ME?
I AM NOT ONE TO LOSE TO THE LIKES OF YOU, WHO STARTED FIGHTING YESTERDAY!
KEH HEH ...
I BET BEATING YOU WITH MY CARDS WOULD WORK BETTER THAN DOING IT WITH MY FISTS.
IF IT IS A FIGHT YOU WANT ...
KEH HEH ...
HA HA HA ...

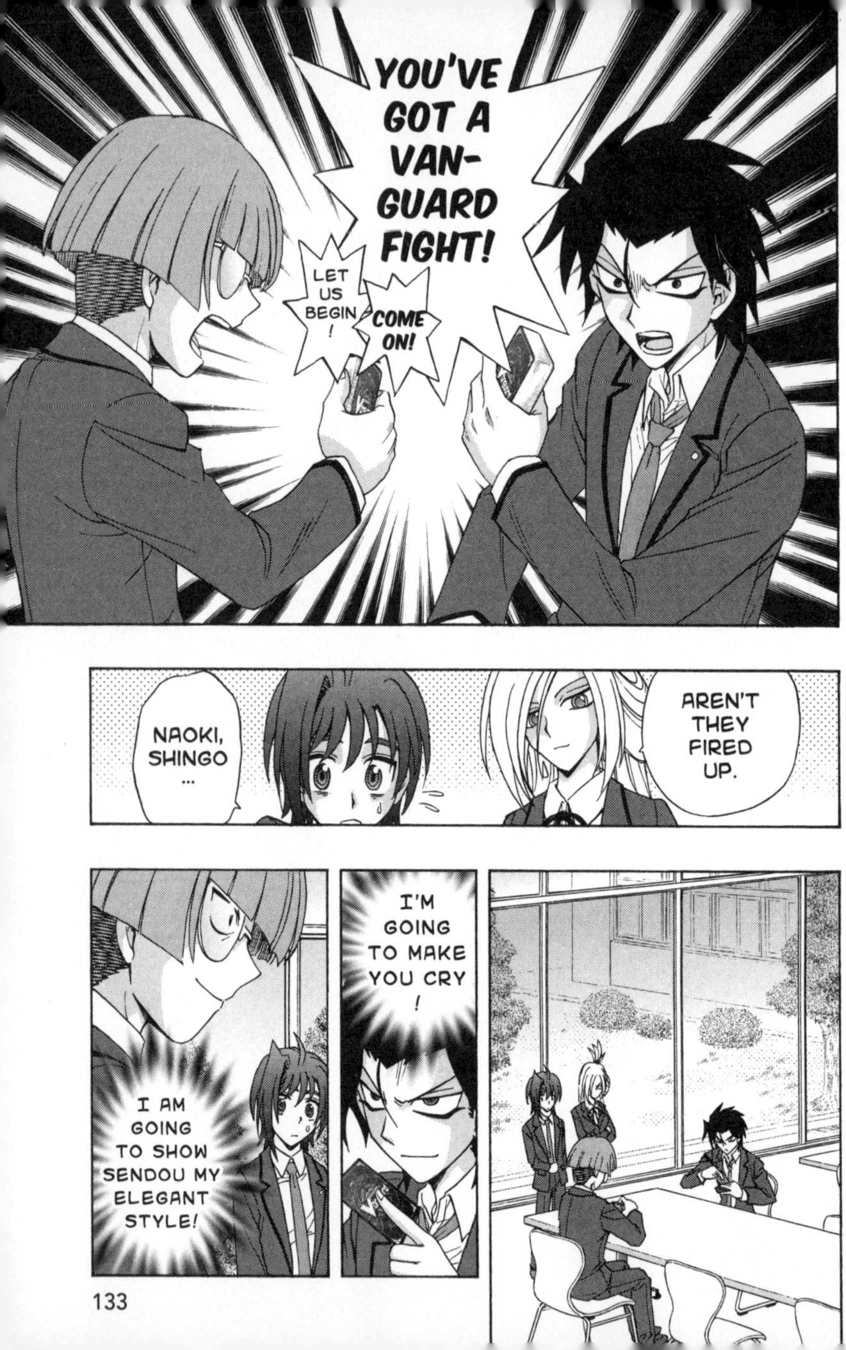
YOU'VE GOT A VAN-GUARD FIGHT!
COME ON!
LET US BEGIN!
AREN'T THEY FIRED UP.
NAOKI, SHINGO...
I'M GOING TO MAKE YOU CRY!
I AM GOING TO SHOW SENDOU MY ELEGANT STYLE!

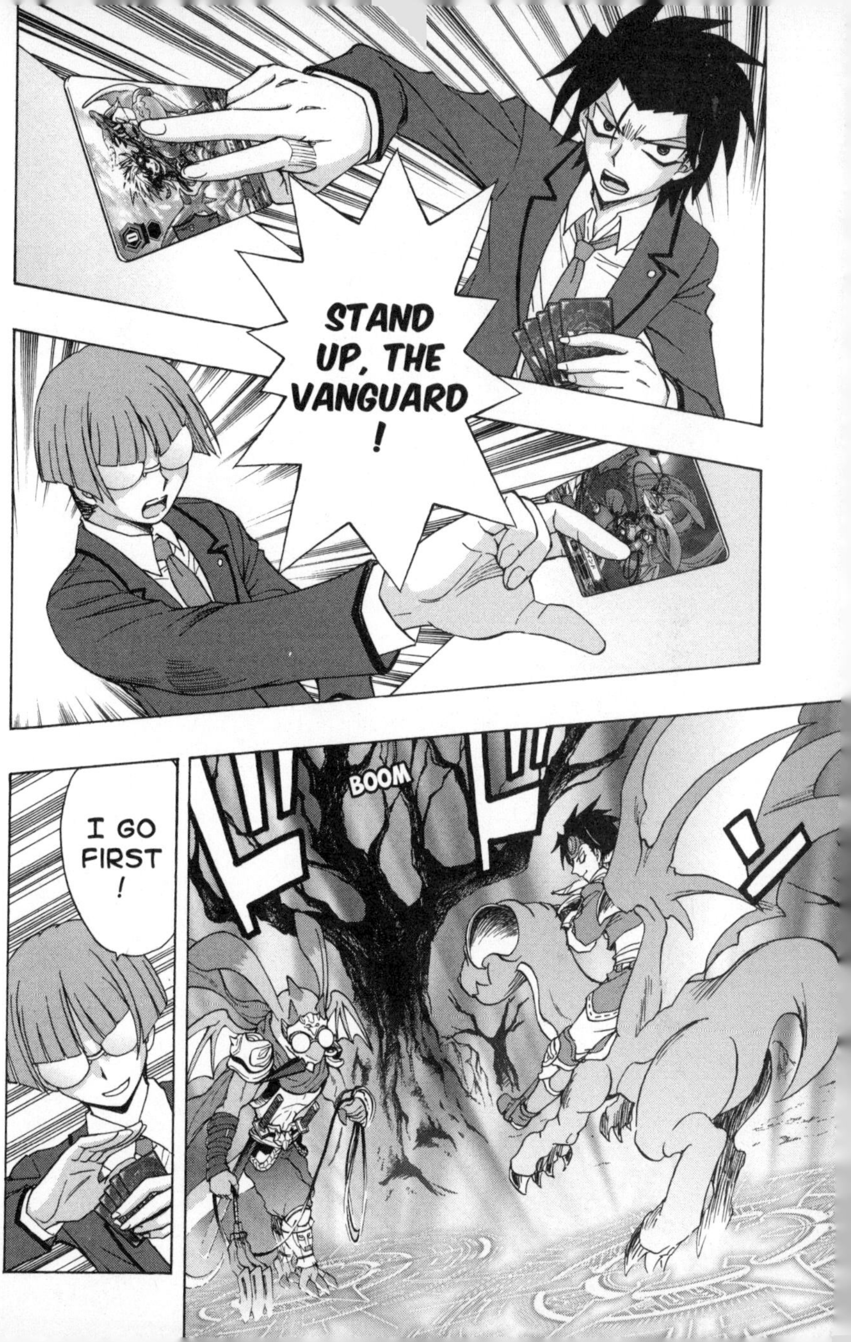
STAND UP, THE VANGUARD!
BOOM
I GO FIRST!

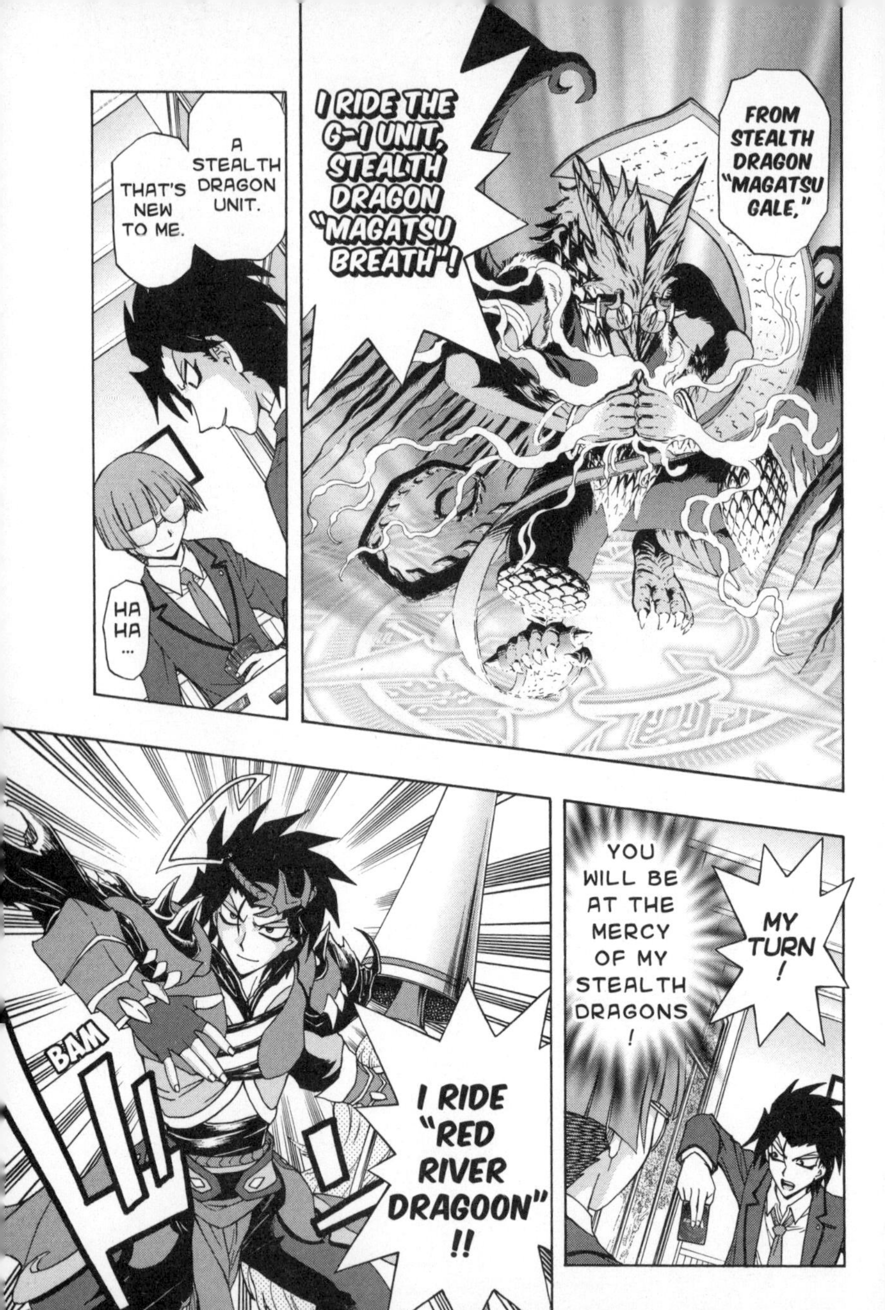
FROM STEALTH DRAGON "MAGATSU GALE,"
I RIDE THE G-1 UNIT, STEALTH DRAGON "MAGATSU BREATH"!
A STEALTH DRAGON UNIT.
THAT'S NEW TO ME.
HA HA ...
MY TURN!
YOU WILL BE AT THE MERCY OF MY STEALTH DRAGONS!
I RIDE "RED RIVER DRAGOON"!!
BAM

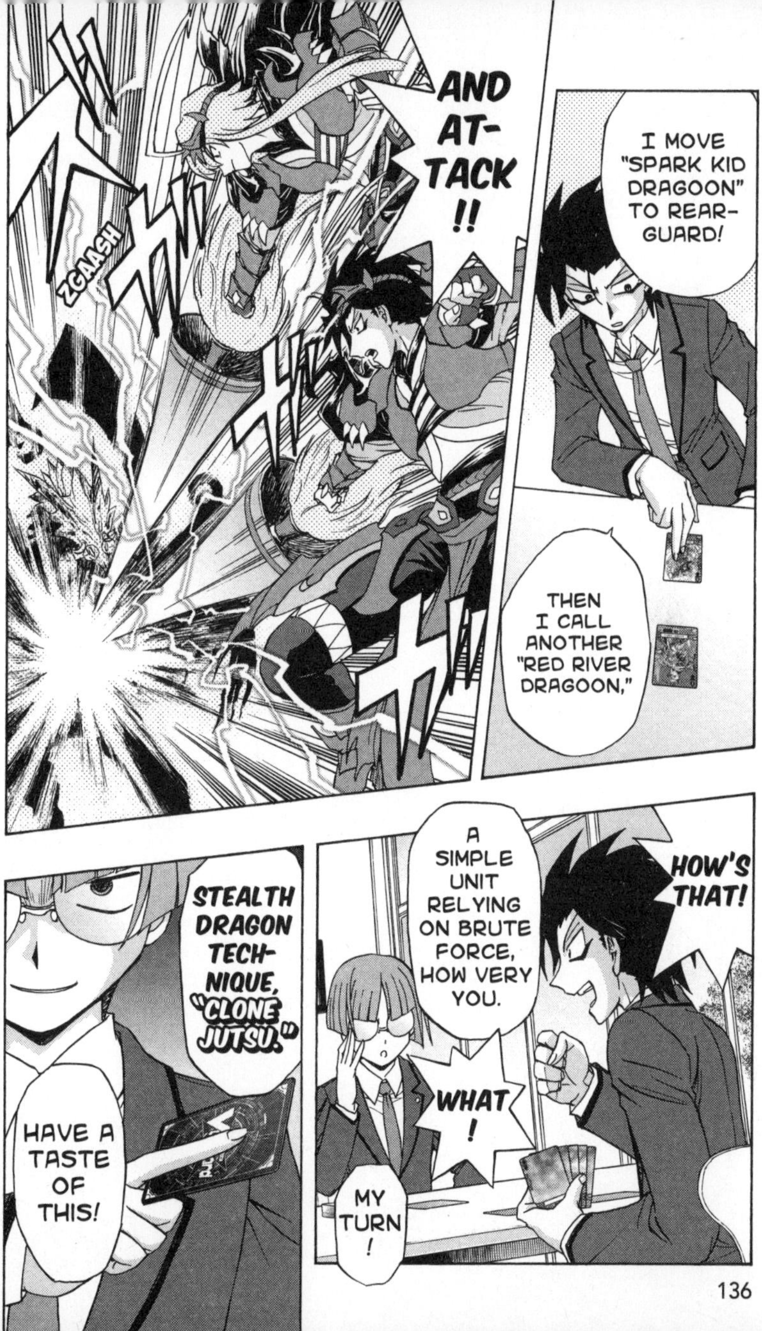
I MOVE "SPARK KID DRAGOON" TO REAR-GUARD!
THEN I CALL ANOTHER "RED RIVER DRAGOON,"
AND AT-TACK!!
ZGAASH
HOW'S THAT!
A SIMPLE UNIT RELYING ON BRUTE FORCE, HOW VERY YOU.
WHAT!
MY TURN!
STEALTH DRAGON TECH-NIQUE, "CLONE JUTSU."
HAVE A TASTE OF THIS!

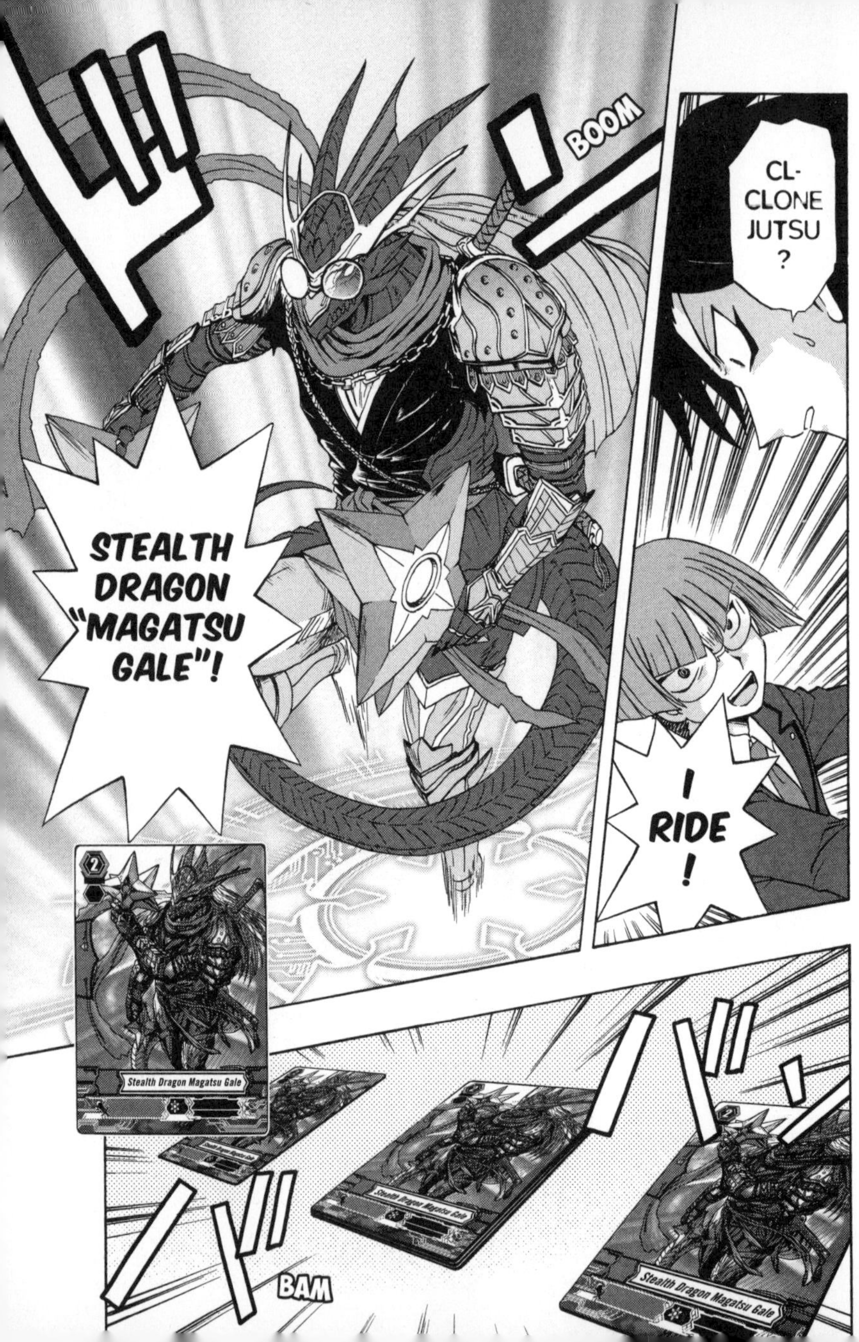

CL-
CLONE
JUTSU
?
I
RIDE
!
BOOM
STEALTH
DRAGON
"MAGATSU
GALE"!
Stealth Dragon Magatsu Gale
Stealth Dragon Magatsu Gale
Stealth Dragon Magatsu Gale
BAM

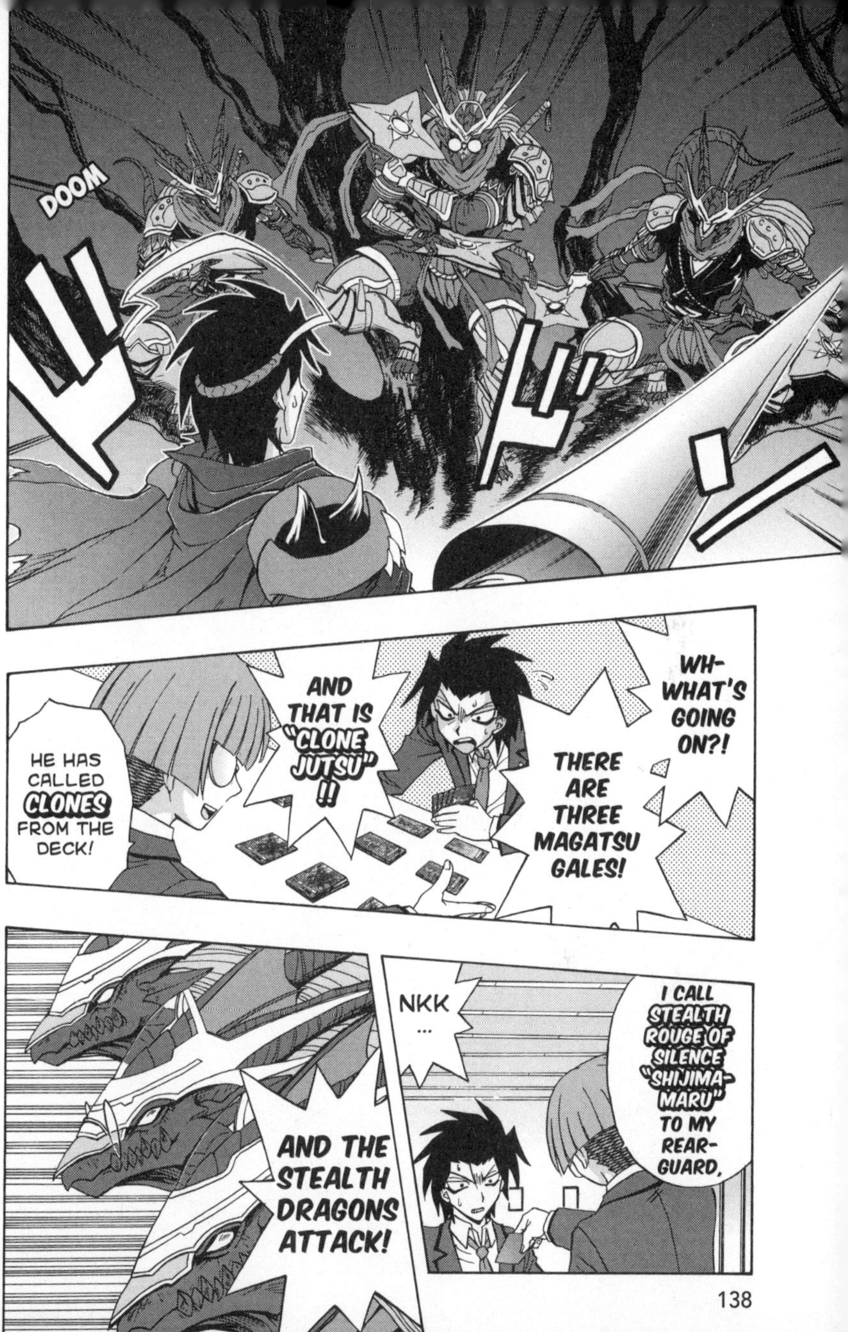
DOOM
WH- WHAT'S GOING ON?!
THERE ARE THREE MAGATSU GALES!
AND THAT IS "CLONE JUTSU"!!
HE HAS CALLED CLONES FROM THE DECK!
I CALL STEALTH ROUGE OF SILENCE "SHIJIMA-MARU" TO MY REAR-GUARD,
NKK ...
AND THE STEALTH DRAGONS ATTACK!

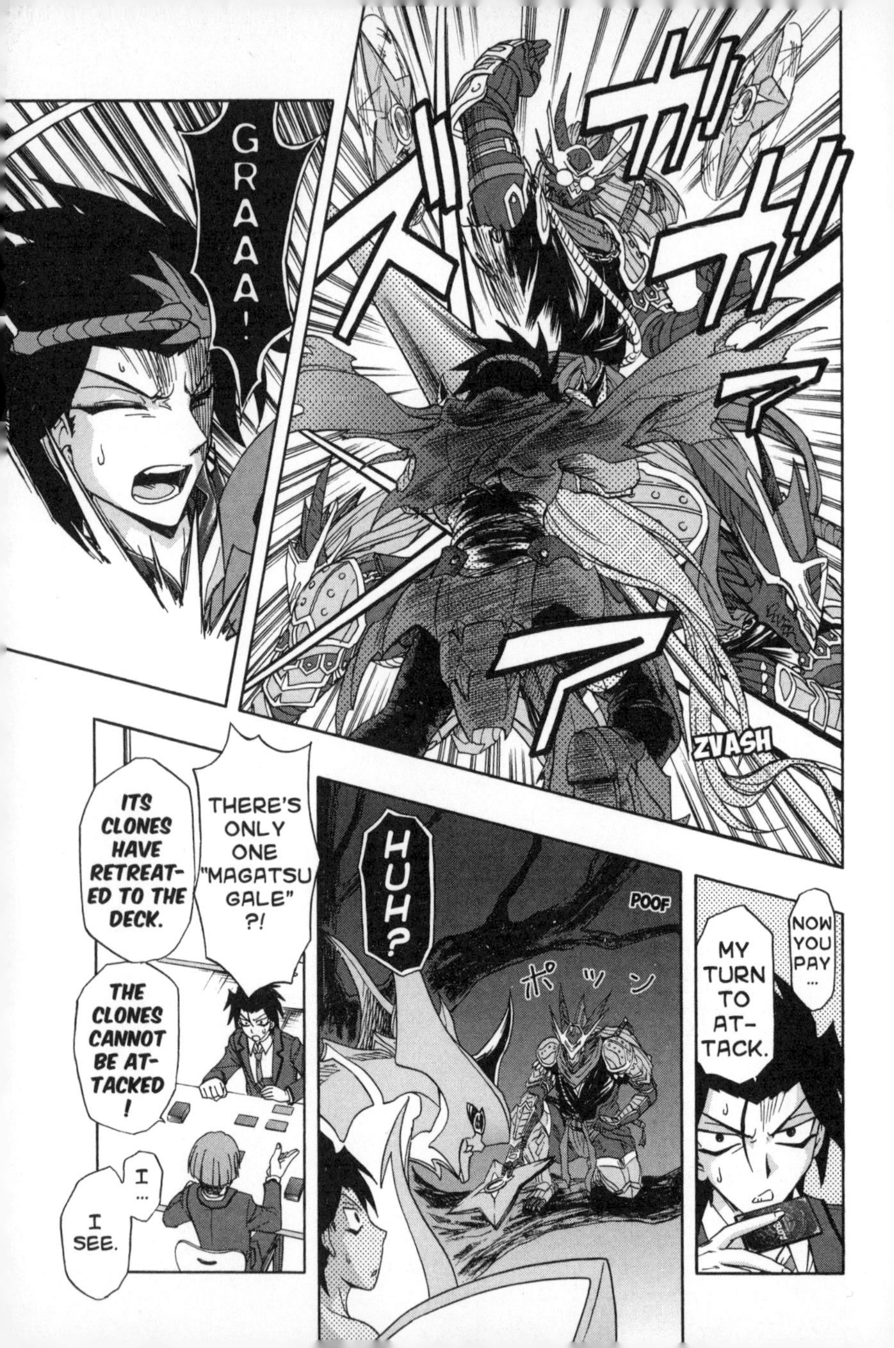
ZVASH
GRAAAA!
NOW YOU PAY...
MY TURN TO AT-TACK.
HUH?
POOF
ポッン
THERE'S ONLY ONE "MAGATSU GALE" ?!
ITS CLONES HAVE RETREAT-ED TO THE DECK.
THE CLONES CANNOT BE AT-TACKED!
I... I SEE.

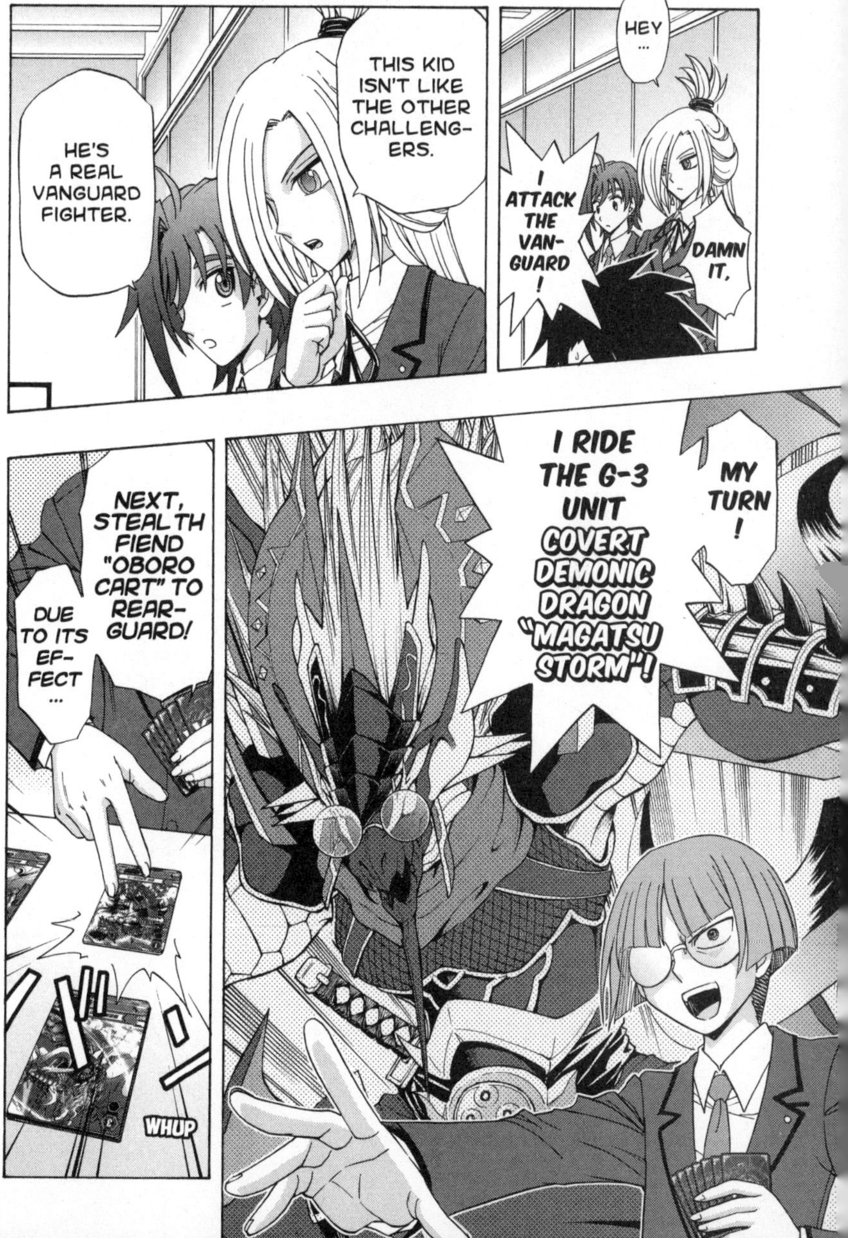
HEY ...
DAMN IT,
I ATTACK THE VAN-GUARD!
THIS KID ISN'T LIKE THE OTHER CHALLENG-ERS.
HE'S A REAL VANGUARD FIGHTER.
MY TURN!
I RIDE THE G-3 UNIT COVERT DEMONIC DRAGON "MAGATSU STORM"!
NEXT, STEALTH FIEND "OBORO CART" TO REAR-GUARD!
DUE TO ITS EF-FECT ...
WHUP

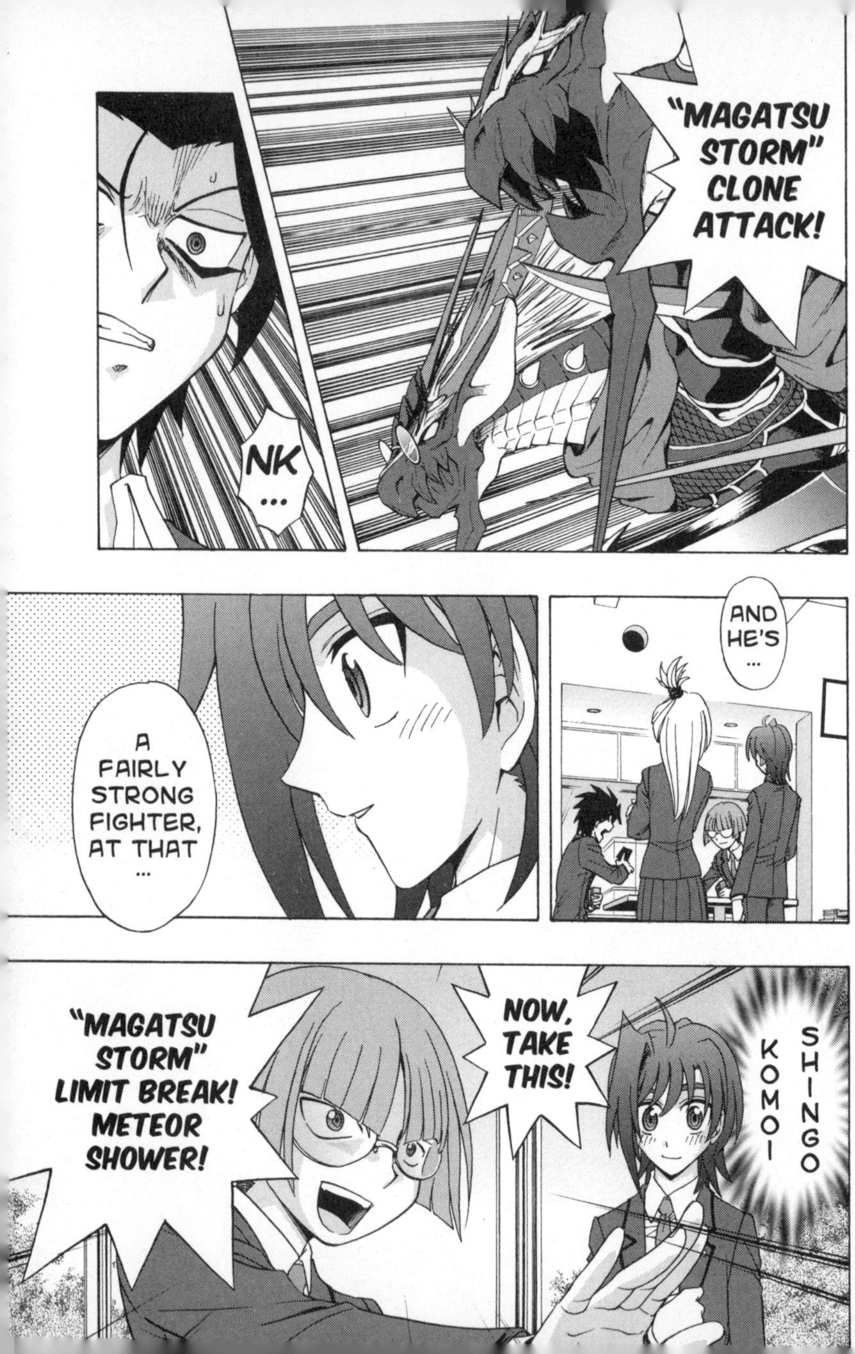
"MAGATSU STORM" CLONE ATTACK!
NK ...
AND HE'S ...
A FAIRLY STRONG FIGHTER, AT THAT ...
SHINGO KOMOI
NOW, TAKE THIS!
"MAGATSU STORM" LIMIT BREAK! METEOR SHOWER!

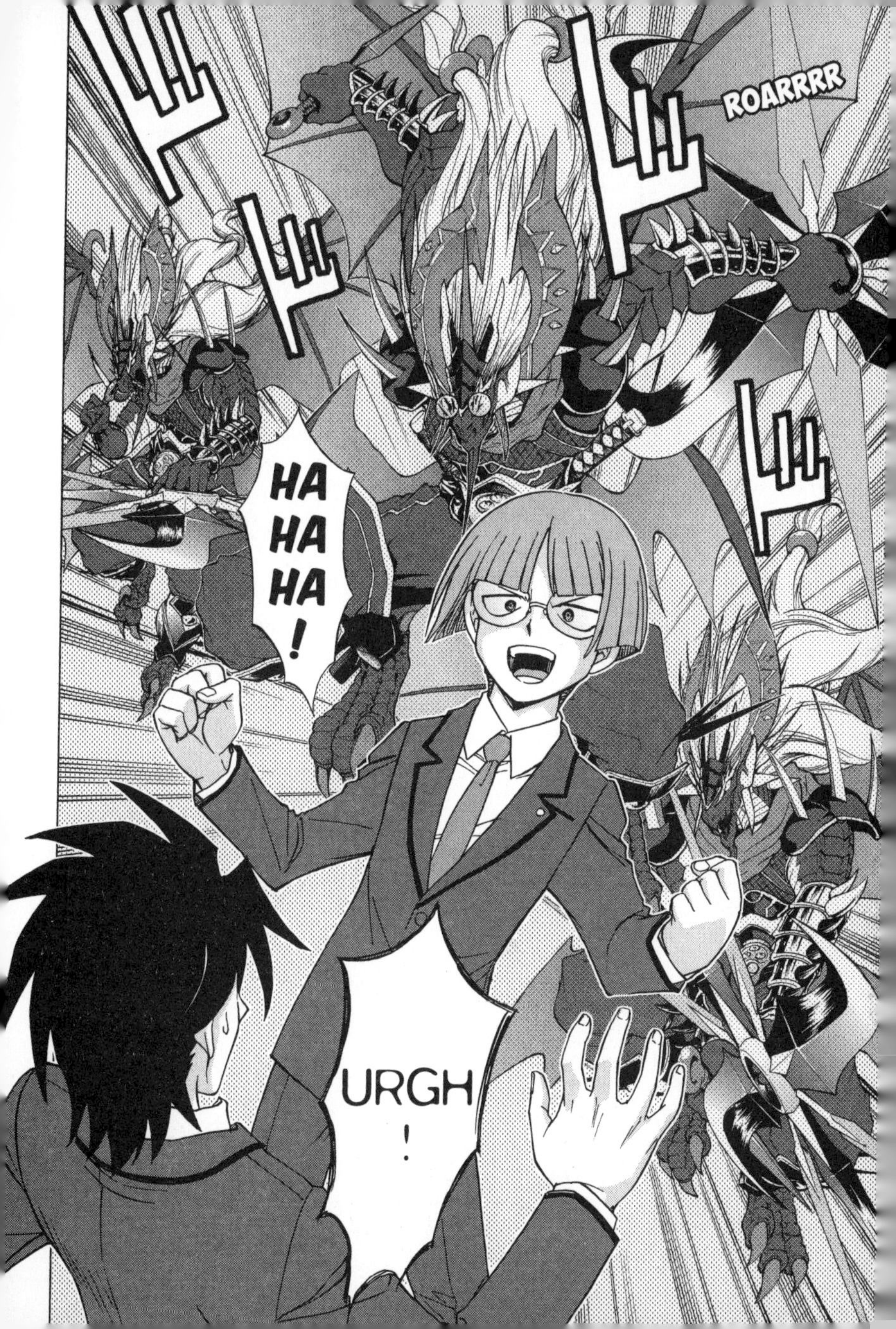
ROARRRR
ドドドド
HA HA HA HA !
URGH !

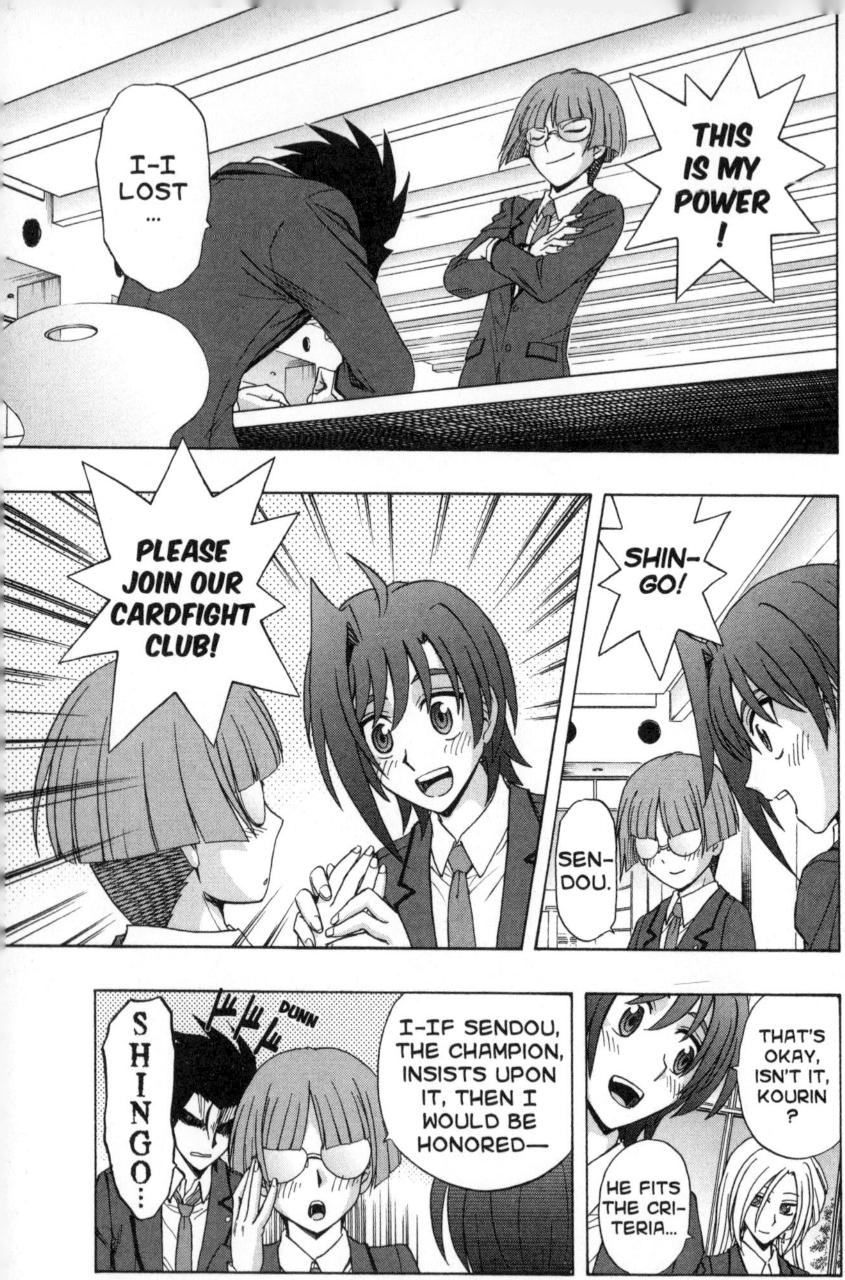
THIS IS MY POWER!
I-I LOST...
SHIN-GO!
SEN-DOU.
PLEASE JOIN OUR CARDFIGHT CLUB!
THAT'S OKAY, ISN'T IT, KOURIN?
HE FITS THE CRITERIA...
I-IF SENDOU, THE CHAMPION, INSISTS UPON IT, THEN I WOULD BE HONORED—
DUNN
SHINGO...

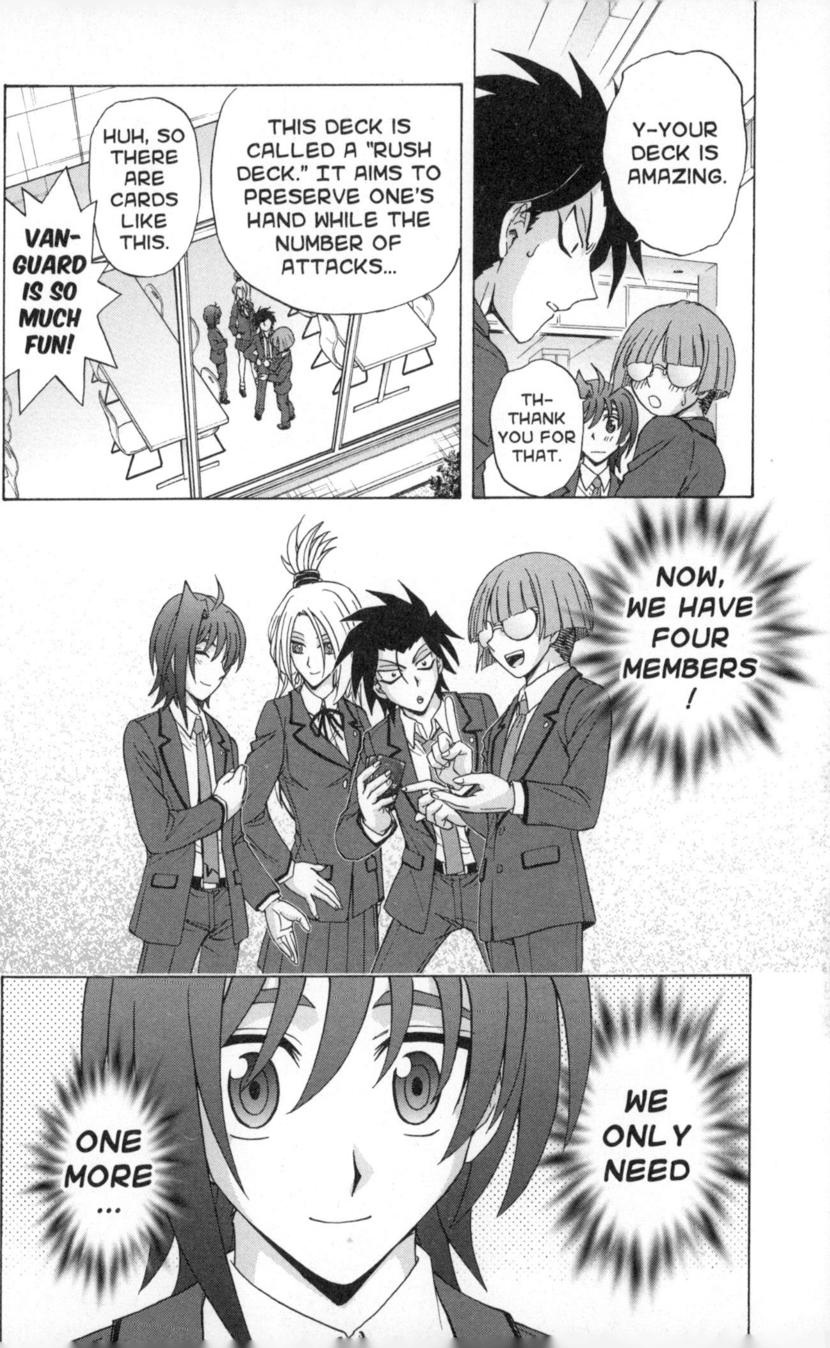

Y-YOUR DECK IS AMAZING.
TH-THANK YOU FOR THAT.
THIS DECK IS CALLED A "RUSH DECK." IT AIMS TO PRESERVE ONE'S HAND WHILE THE NUMBER OF ATTACKS...
HUH, SO THERE ARE CARDS LIKE THIS.
VAN-GUARD IS SO MUCH FUN!
NOW, WE HAVE FOUR MEMBERS!
WE ONLY NEED
ONE MORE...

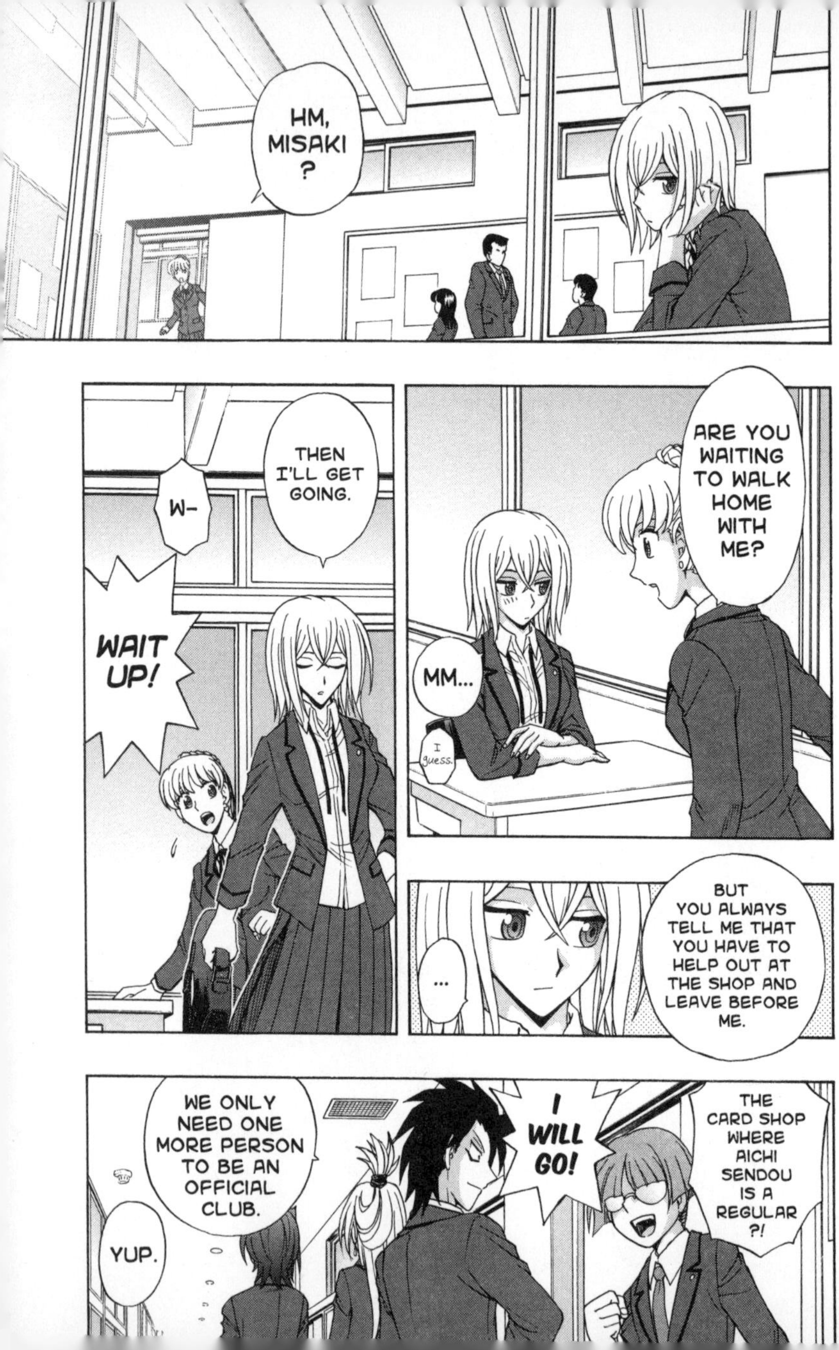
HM, MISAKI ?
ARE YOU WAITING TO WALK HOME WITH ME?
MM...
I guess.
BUT YOU ALWAYS TELL ME THAT YOU HAVE TO HELP OUT AT THE SHOP AND LEAVE BEFORE ME.
...
THEN I'LL GET GOING.
W-
WAIT UP!
THE CARD SHOP WHERE AICHI SENDOU IS A REGULAR ?!
I WILL GO!
WE ONLY NEED ONE MORE PERSON TO BE AN OFFICIAL CLUB.
YUP.

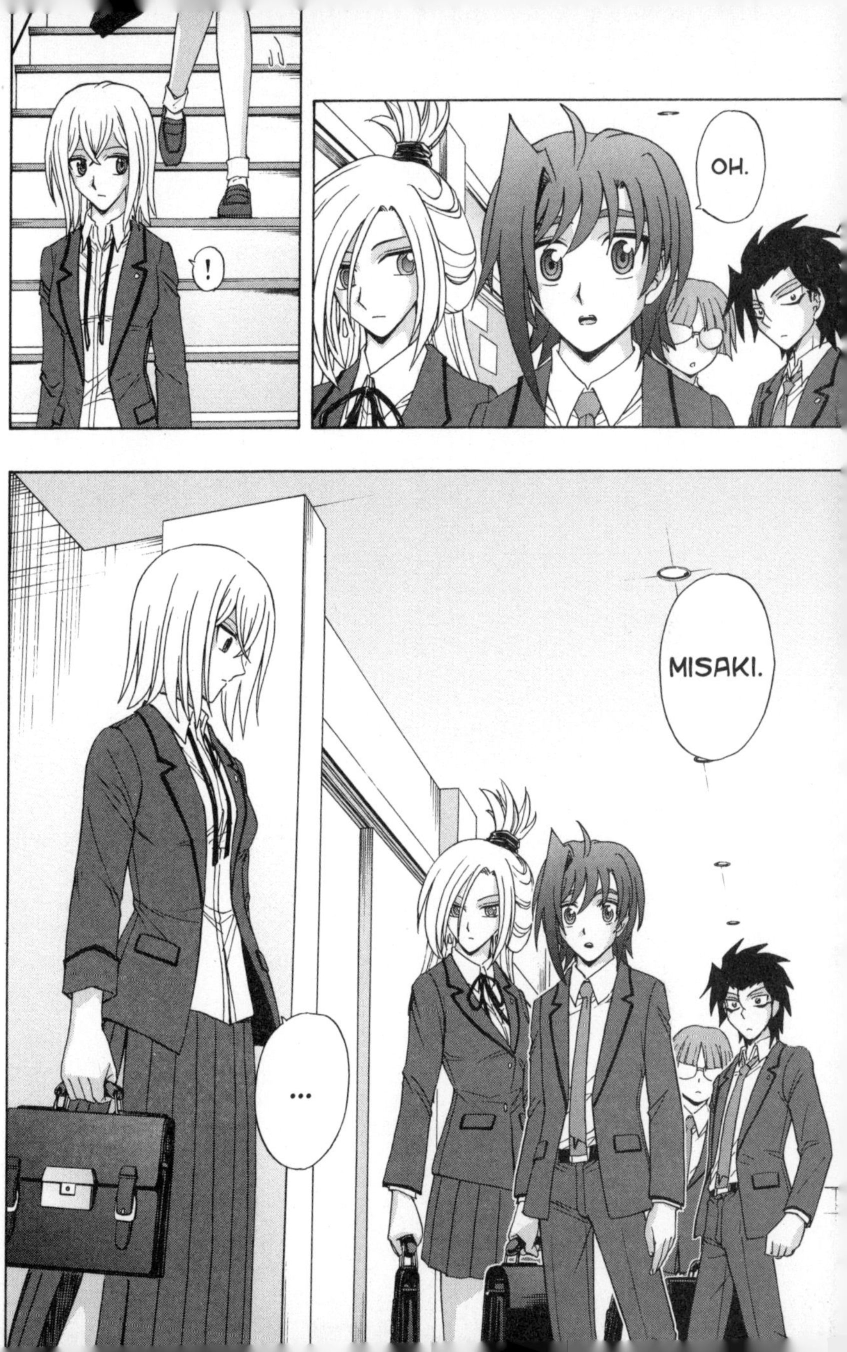
OH.
!
MISAKI.
...

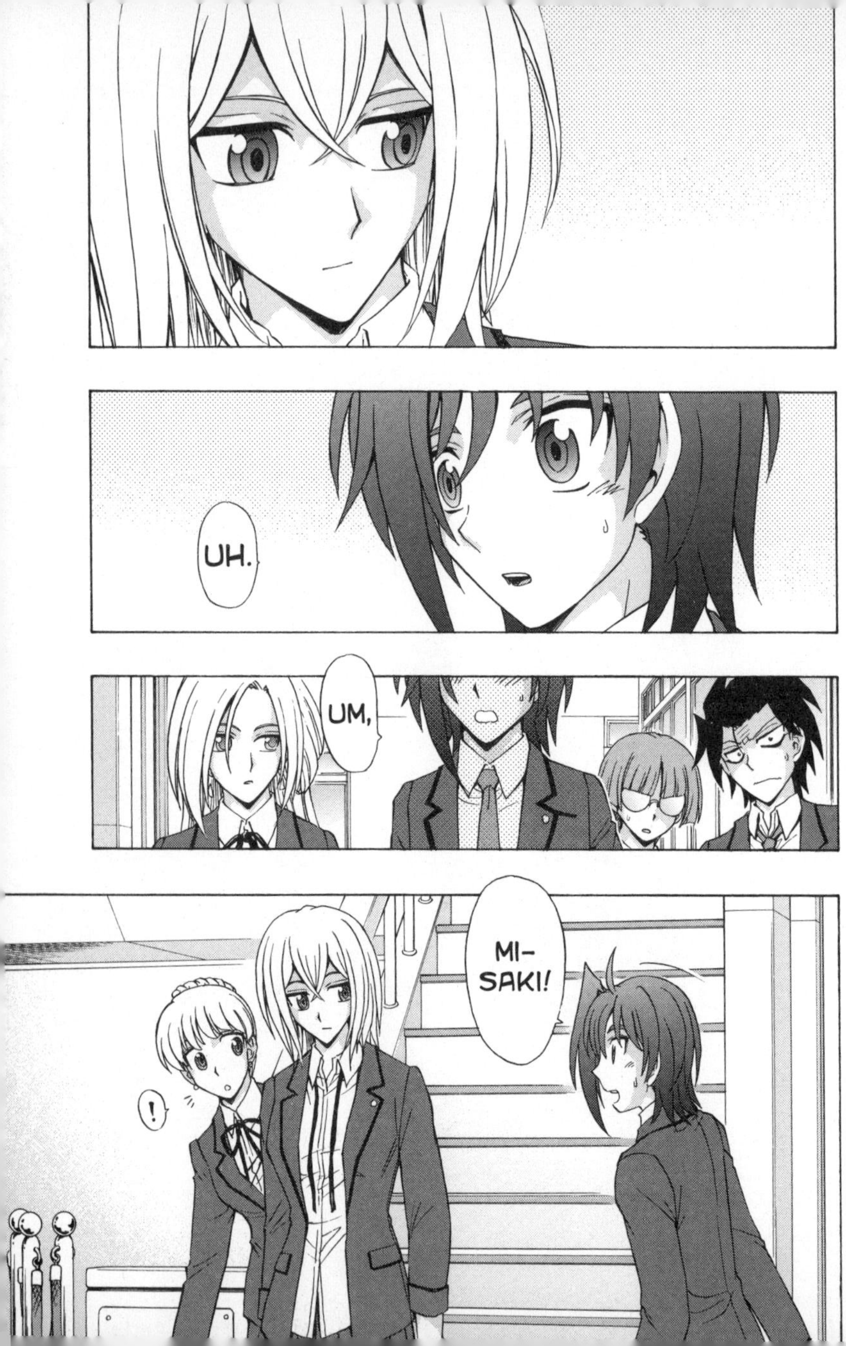
UH.
UM,
MI-SAKI!
!

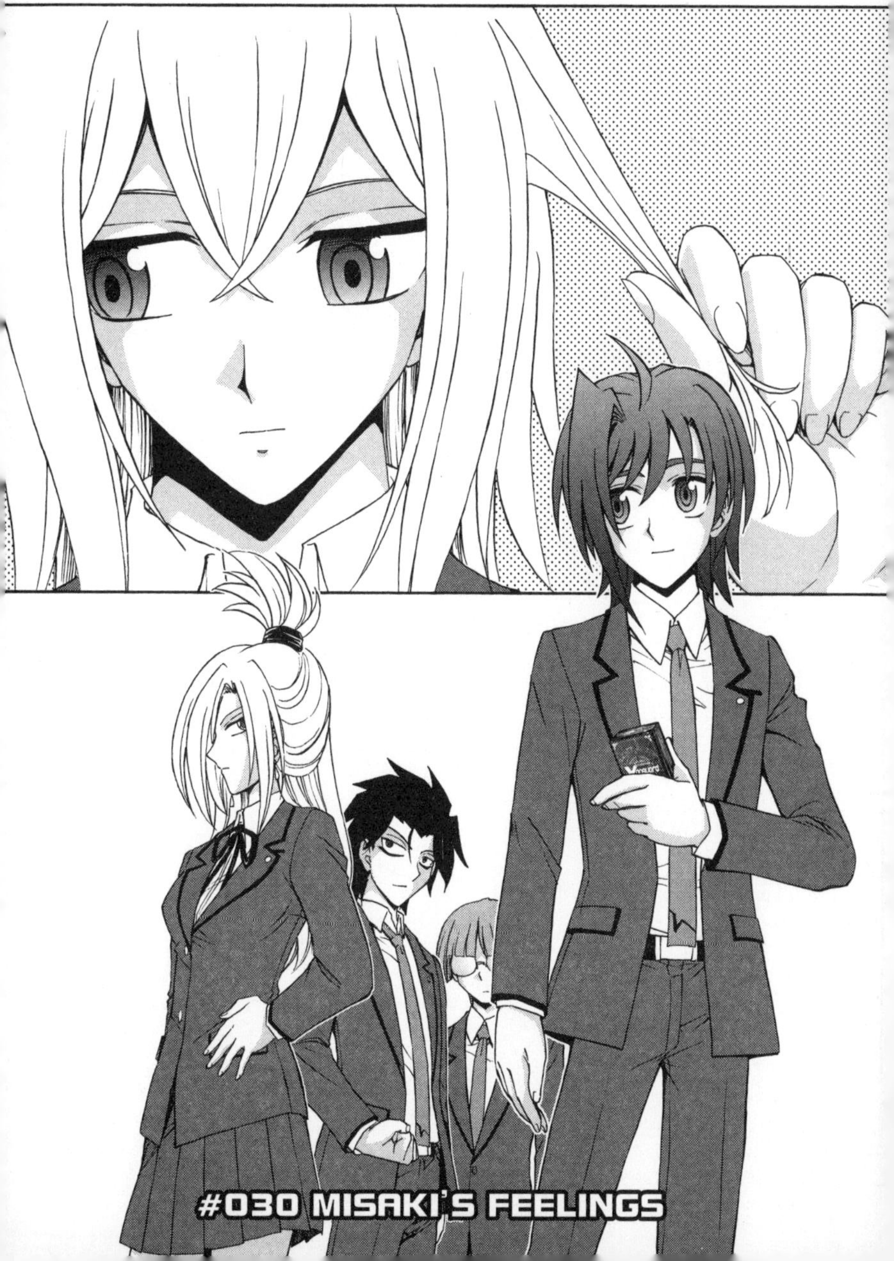
#030 MISAKI'S FEELINGS

WE NOW NEED ONLY ONE MORE PERSON TO BECOME A PROPER CLUB!

AS OF TODAY, OUR CARDFIGHT CLUB HAS GROWN TO FOUR MEMBERS!

I SEE.

HUH ?

I HAVE PLANS WITH THIS GIRL TODAY, SO I CAN'T HELP OUT AT THE SHOP.

I'M SORRY.

A- AND,

WE WERE ALL PLANNING TO HEAD TO CARD CAPITAL.

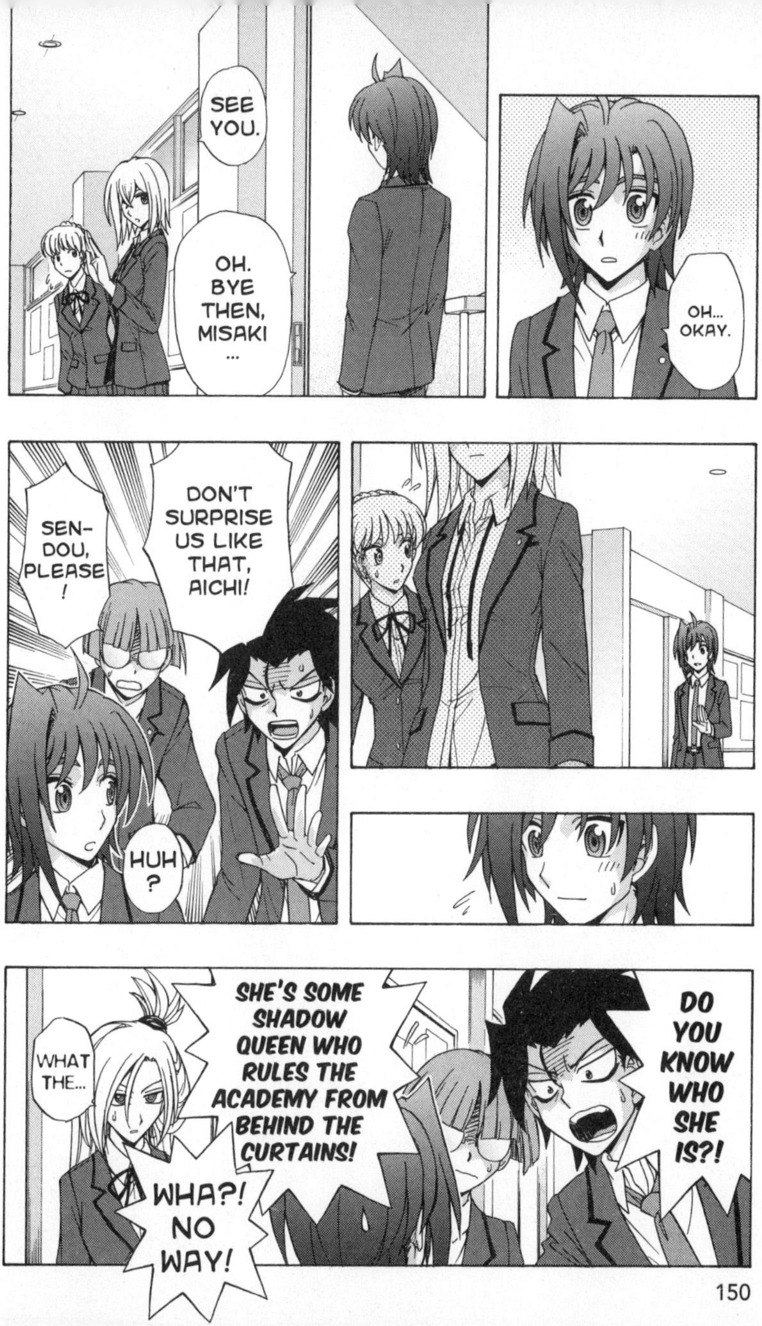
OH... OKAY.
SEE YOU.
OH. BYE THEN, MISAKI ...
DON'T SURPRISE US LIKE THAT, AICHI!
SEN-DOU, PLEASE!
HUH?
DO YOU KNOW WHO SHE IS?!
SHE'S SOME SHADOW QUEEN WHO RULES THE ACADEMY FROM BEHIND THE CURTAINS!
WHAT THE...
WHA?! NO WAY!

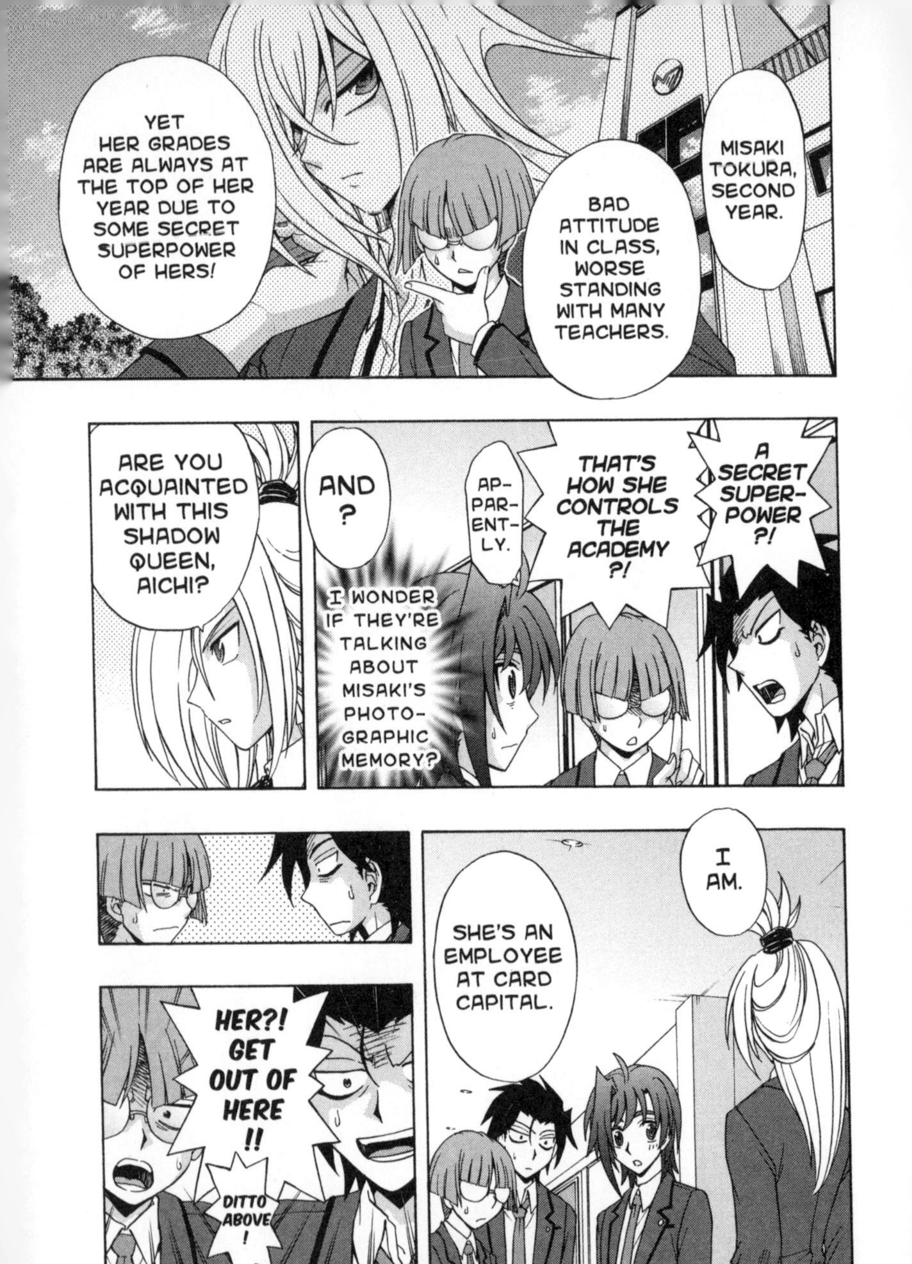
MISAKI TOKURA, SECOND YEAR.
BAD ATTITUDE IN CLASS, WORSE STANDING WITH MANY TEACHERS.
YET HER GRADES ARE ALWAYS AT THE TOP OF HER YEAR DUE TO SOME SECRET SUPERPOWER OF HERS!
A SECRET SUPER-POWER?!
THAT'S HOW SHE CONTROLS THE ACADEMY?!
AP-PAR-ENT-LY.
AND?
I WONDER IF THEY'RE TALKING ABOUT MISAKI'S PHOTO-GRAPHIC MEMORY?
ARE YOU ACQUAINTED WITH THIS SHADOW QUEEN, AICHI?
I AM.
SHE'S AN EMPLOYEE AT CARD CAPITAL.
HER?! GET OUT OF HERE !!
DITTO ABOVE !

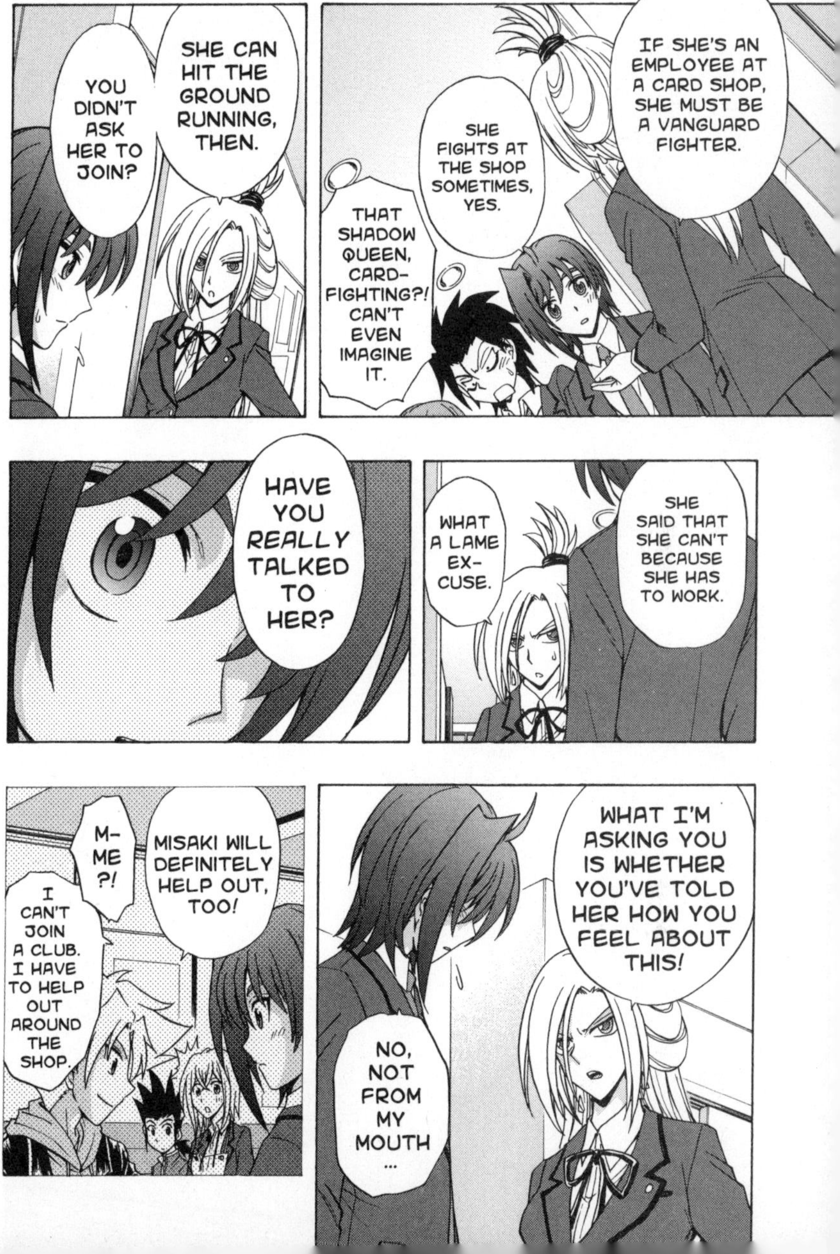
IF SHE'S AN EMPLOYEE AT A CARD SHOP, SHE MUST BE A VANGUARD FIGHTER.
SHE FIGHTS AT THE SHOP SOMETIMES, YES.
THAT SHADOW QUEEN, CARD-FIGHTING?! CAN'T EVEN IMAGINE IT.
SHE CAN HIT THE GROUND RUNNING, THEN.
YOU DIDN'T ASK HER TO JOIN?
SHE SAID THAT SHE CAN'T BECAUSE SHE HAS TO WORK.
WHAT A LAME EX-CUSE.
HAVE YOU REALLY TALKED TO HER?
WHAT I'M ASKING YOU IS WHETHER YOU'VE TOLD HER HOW YOU FEEL ABOUT THIS!
NO, NOT FROM MY MOUTH...
MISAKI WILL DEFINITELY HELP OUT, TOO!
M-ME?!
I CAN'T JOIN A CLUB. I HAVE TO HELP OUT AROUND THE SHOP.

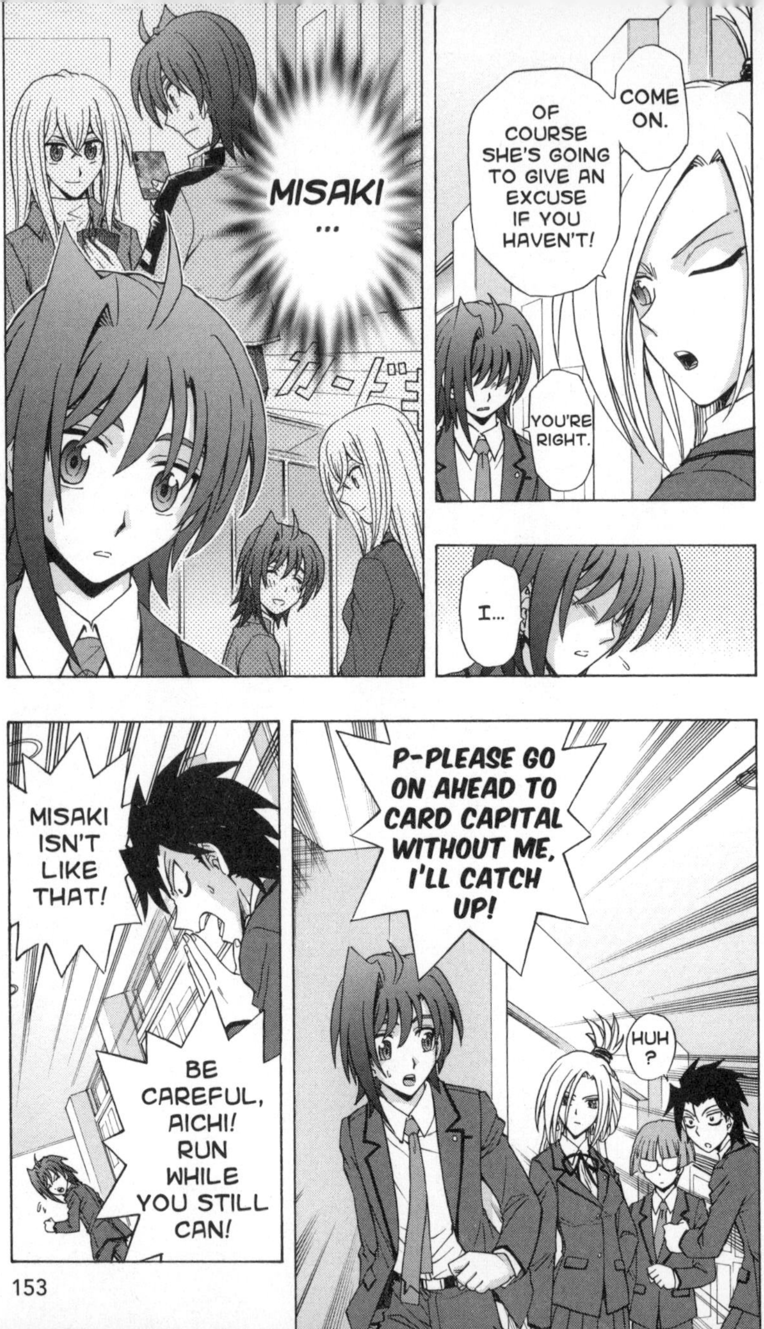
COME ON.
OF COURSE SHE'S GOING TO GIVE AN EXCUSE IF YOU HAVEN'T!
YOU'RE RIGHT.
I...
MISAKI ...
P-PLEASE GO ON AHEAD TO CARD CAPITAL WITHOUT ME, I'LL CATCH UP!
HUH ?
MISAKI ISN'T LIKE THAT!
BE CAREFUL, AICHI! RUN WHILE YOU STILL CAN!

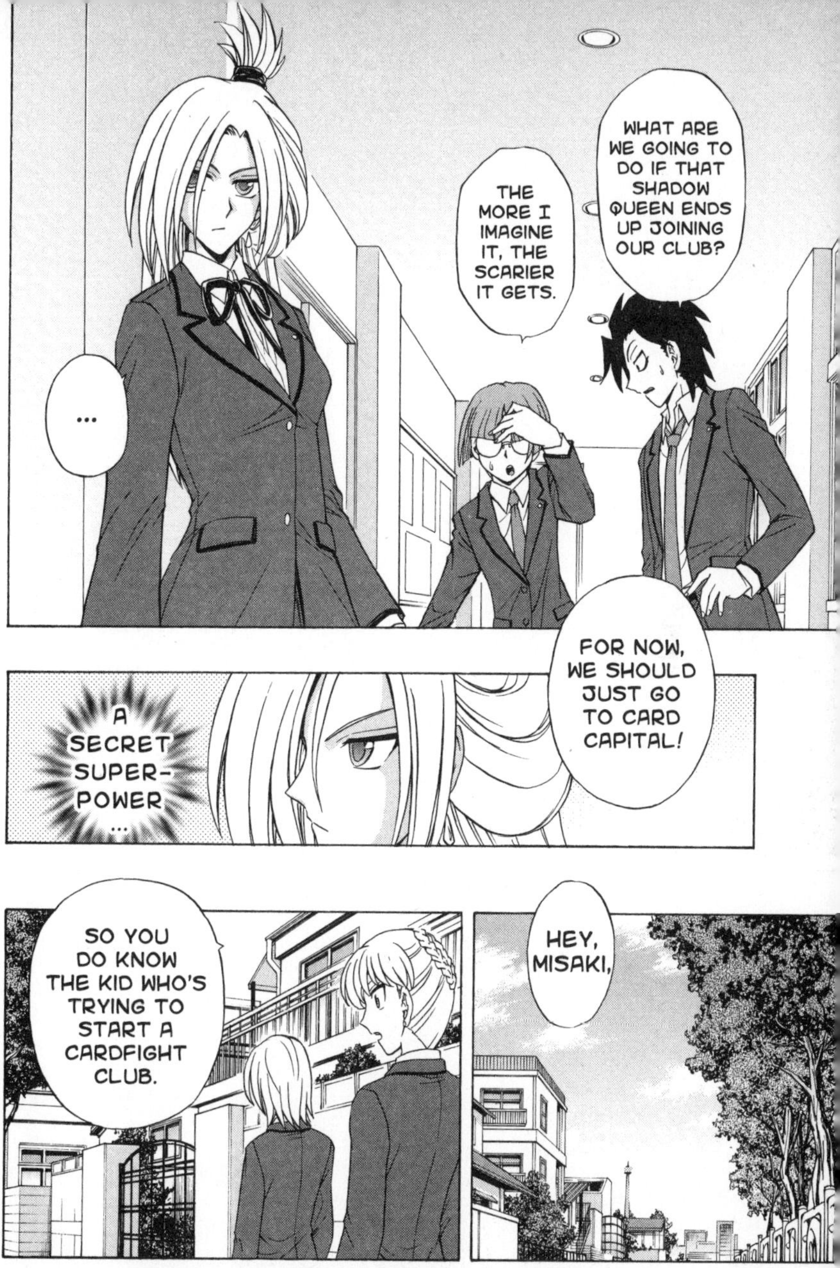
WHAT ARE WE GOING TO DO IF THAT SHADOW QUEEN ENDS UP JOINING OUR CLUB?
THE MORE I IMAGINE IT, THE SCARIER IT GETS.
...
FOR NOW, WE SHOULD JUST GO TO CARD CAPITAL!
A SECRET SUPER-POWER ...
HEY, MISAKI,
SO YOU DO KNOW THE KID WHO'S TRYING TO START A CARDFIGHT CLUB.

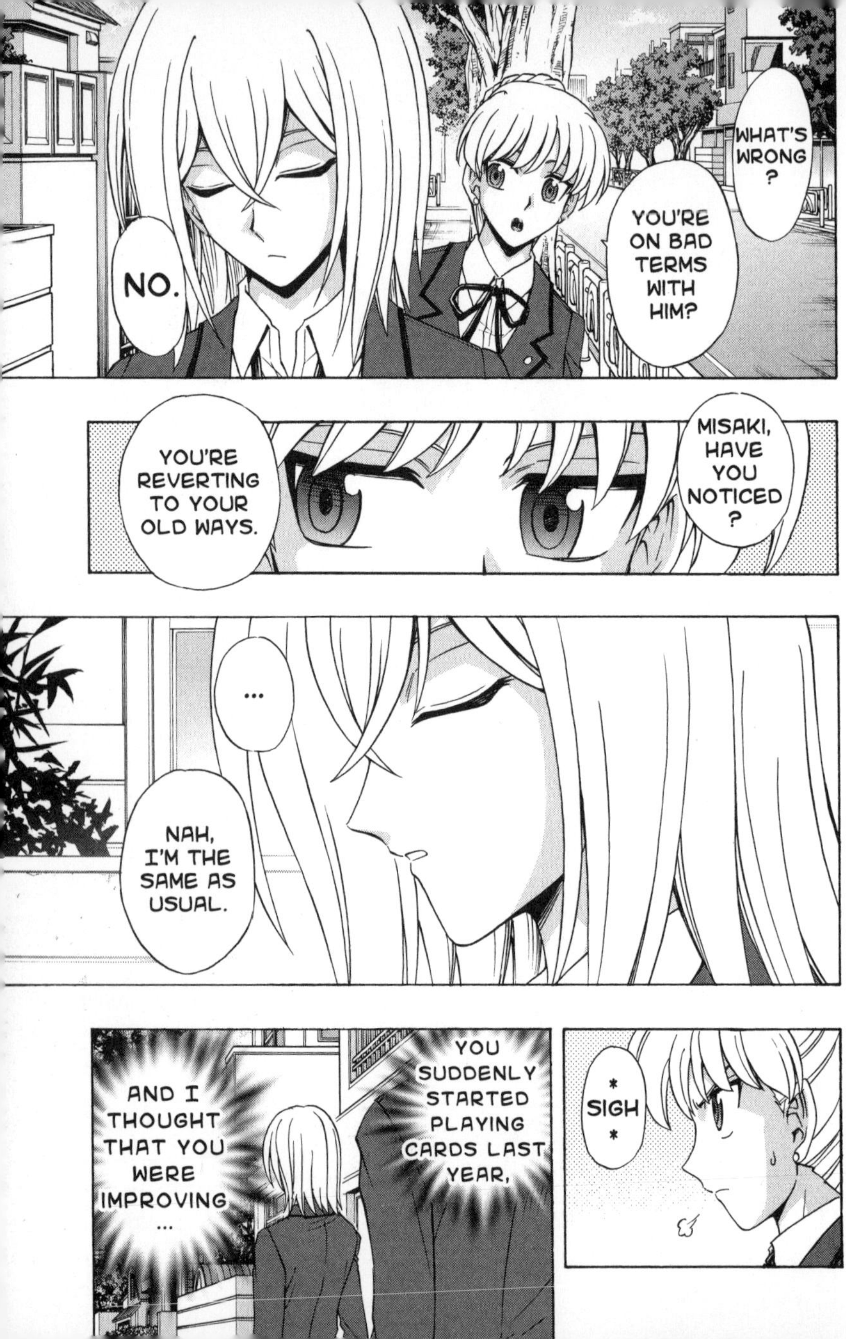
WHAT'S WRONG?
YOU'RE ON BAD TERMS WITH HIM?
NO.
MISAKI, HAVE YOU NOTICED?
YOU'RE REVERTING TO YOUR OLD WAYS.
...
NAH, I'M THE SAME AS USUAL.
SIGH
YOU SUDDENLY STARTED PLAYING CARDS LAST YEAR,
AND I THOUGHT THAT YOU WERE IMPROVING...

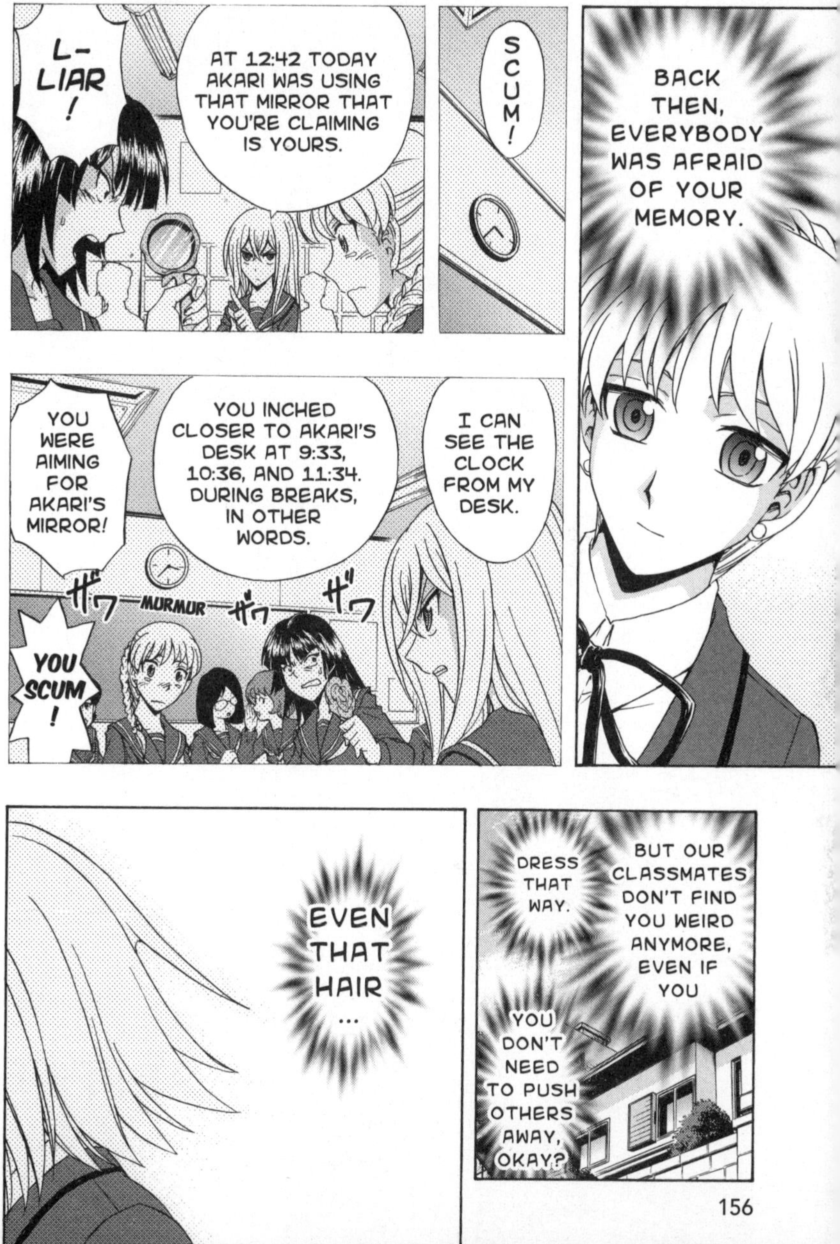

BACK THEN, EVERYBODY WAS AFRAID OF YOUR MEMORY.
SCUM!
AT 12:42 TODAY AKARI WAS USING THAT MIRROR THAT YOU'RE CLAIMING IS YOURS.
L-LIAR!
I CAN SEE THE CLOCK FROM MY DESK.
YOU INCHED CLOSER TO AKARI'S DESK AT 9:33, 10:36, AND 11:34. DURING BREAKS, IN OTHER WORDS.
YOU WERE AIMING FOR AKARI'S MIRROR!
ザワ MURMUR ザワ ザワ
YOU SCUM!
BUT OUR CLASSMATES DON'T FIND YOU WEIRD ANYMORE, EVEN IF YOU
DRESS THAT WAY.
YOU DON'T NEED TO PUSH OTHERS AWAY, OKAY?
EVEN THAT HAIR ...

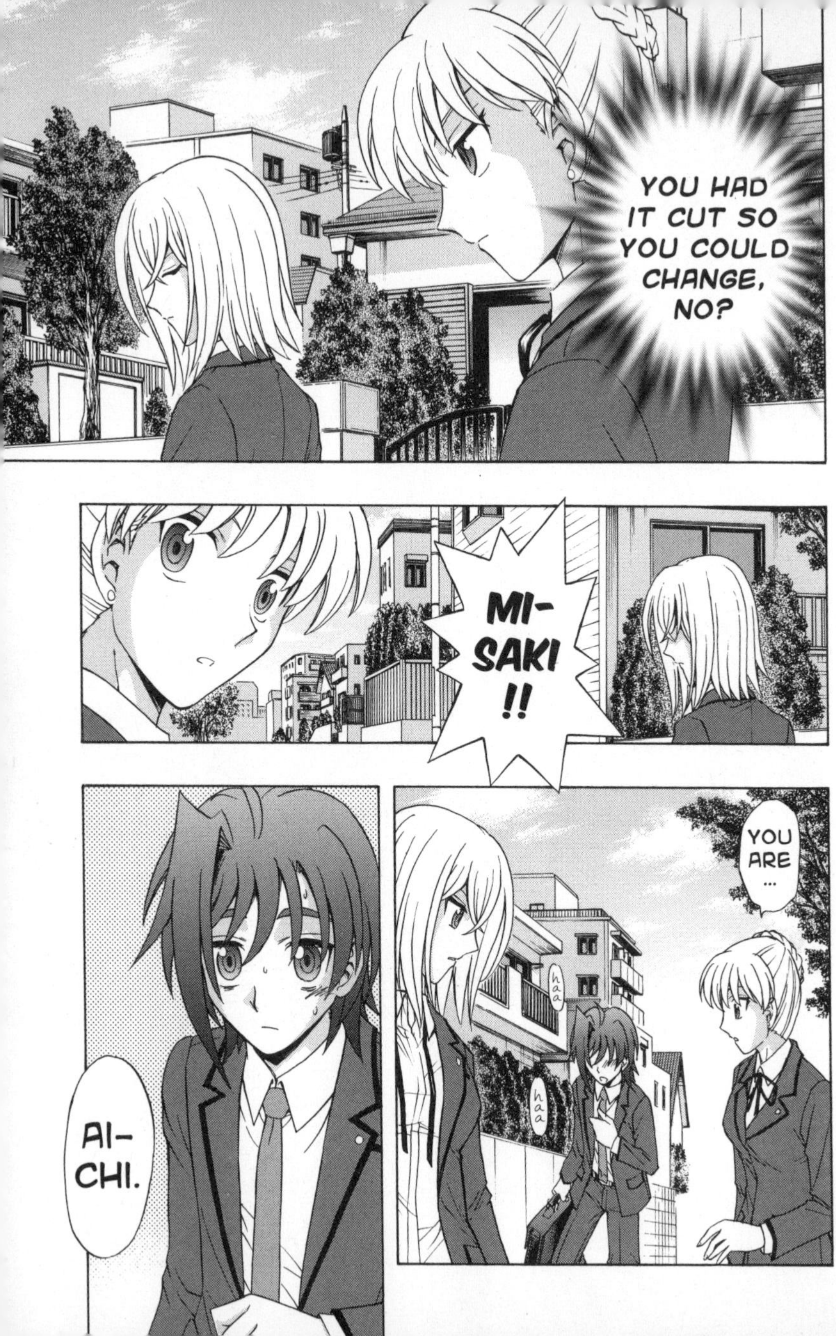
YOU HAD IT CUT SO YOU COULD CHANGE, NO?
MI-SAKI!!
YOU ARE ...
haa
haa
AI-CHI.

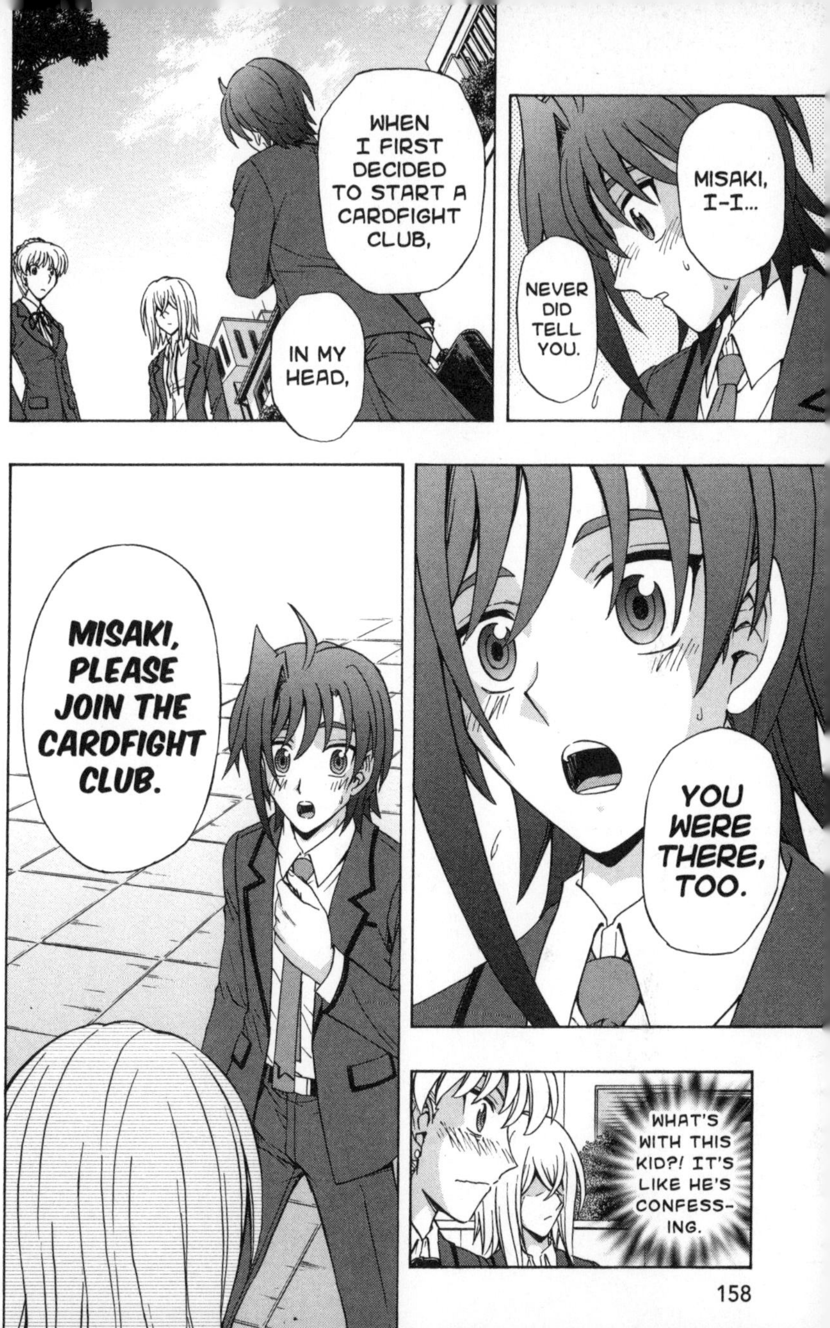
MISAKI, I-I...
NEVER DID TELL YOU.
WHEN I FIRST DECIDED TO START A CARDFIGHT CLUB,
IN MY HEAD,
YOU WERE THERE, TOO.
WHAT'S WITH THIS KID?! IT'S LIKE HE'S CONFESSING.
MISAKI, PLEASE JOIN THE CARDFIGHT CLUB.

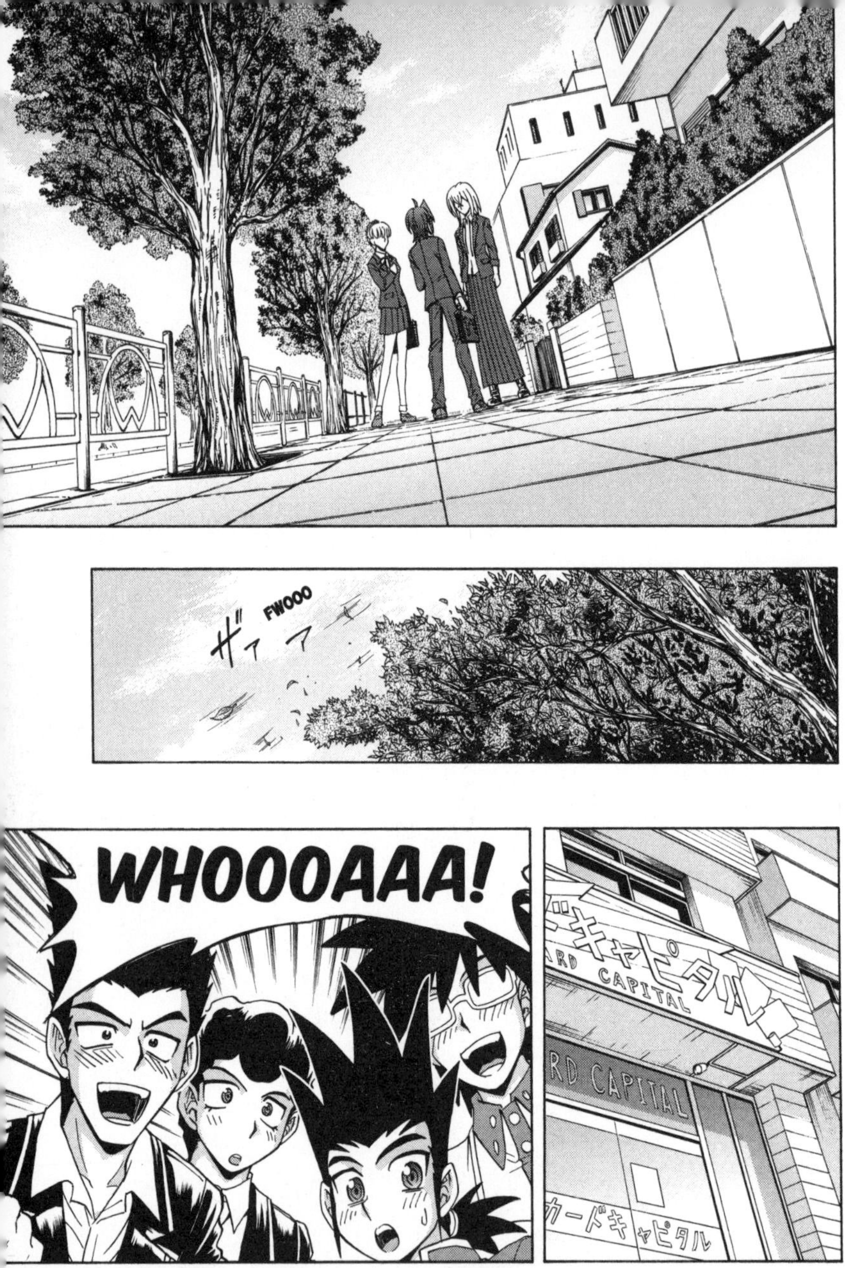
FWOOO
ザァァ
RD CAPITAL
キャピタル
RD CAPITAL
カードキャピタル
WHOOOAAA!

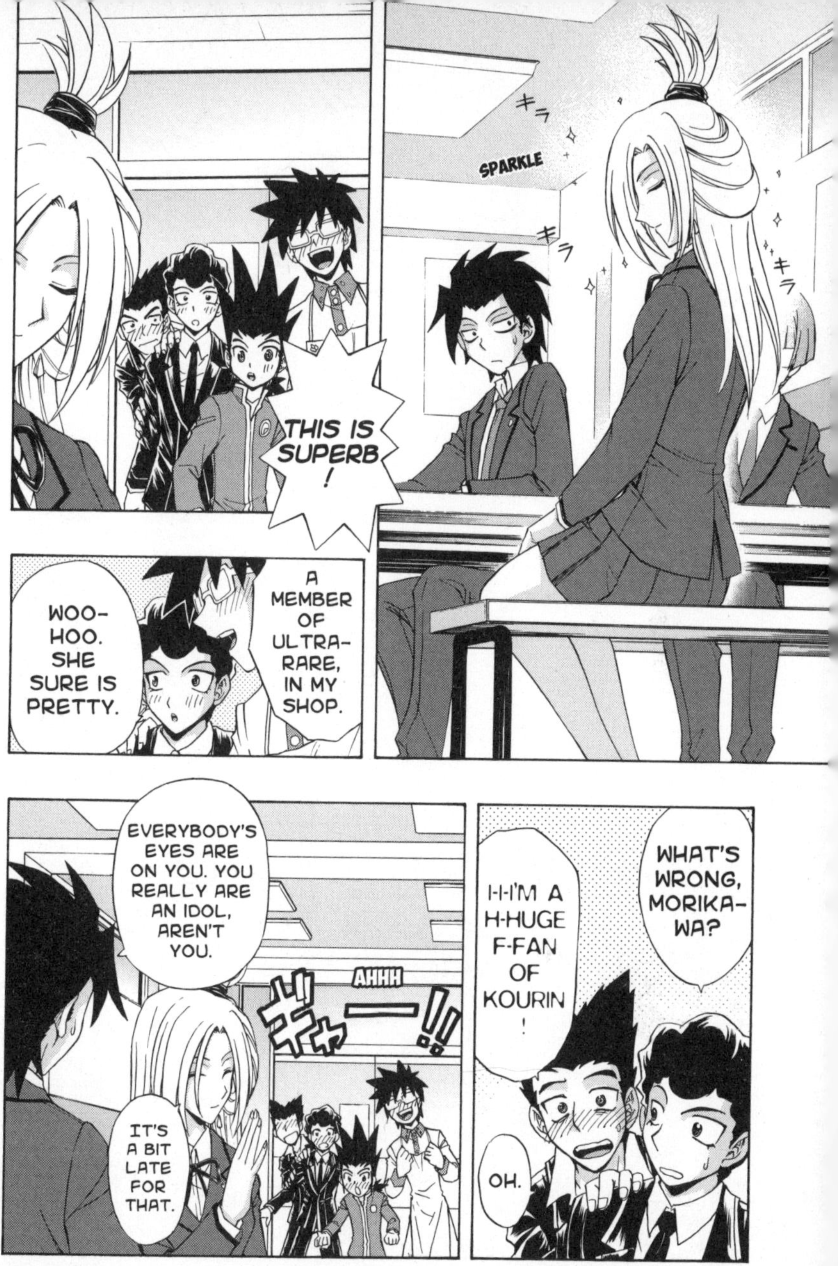
キラ
SPARKLE
キラ
キラ
THIS IS SUPERB!
A MEMBER OF ULTRA-RARE, IN MY SHOP.
WOO-HOO. SHE SURE IS PRETTY.
WHAT'S WRONG, MORIKAWA?
I-I-I'M A H-HUGE F-FAN OF KOURIN!
OH.
EVERYBODY'S EYES ARE ON YOU. YOU REALLY ARE AN IDOL, AREN'T YOU.
ギャー!!
AHHH
IT'S A BIT LATE FOR THAT.

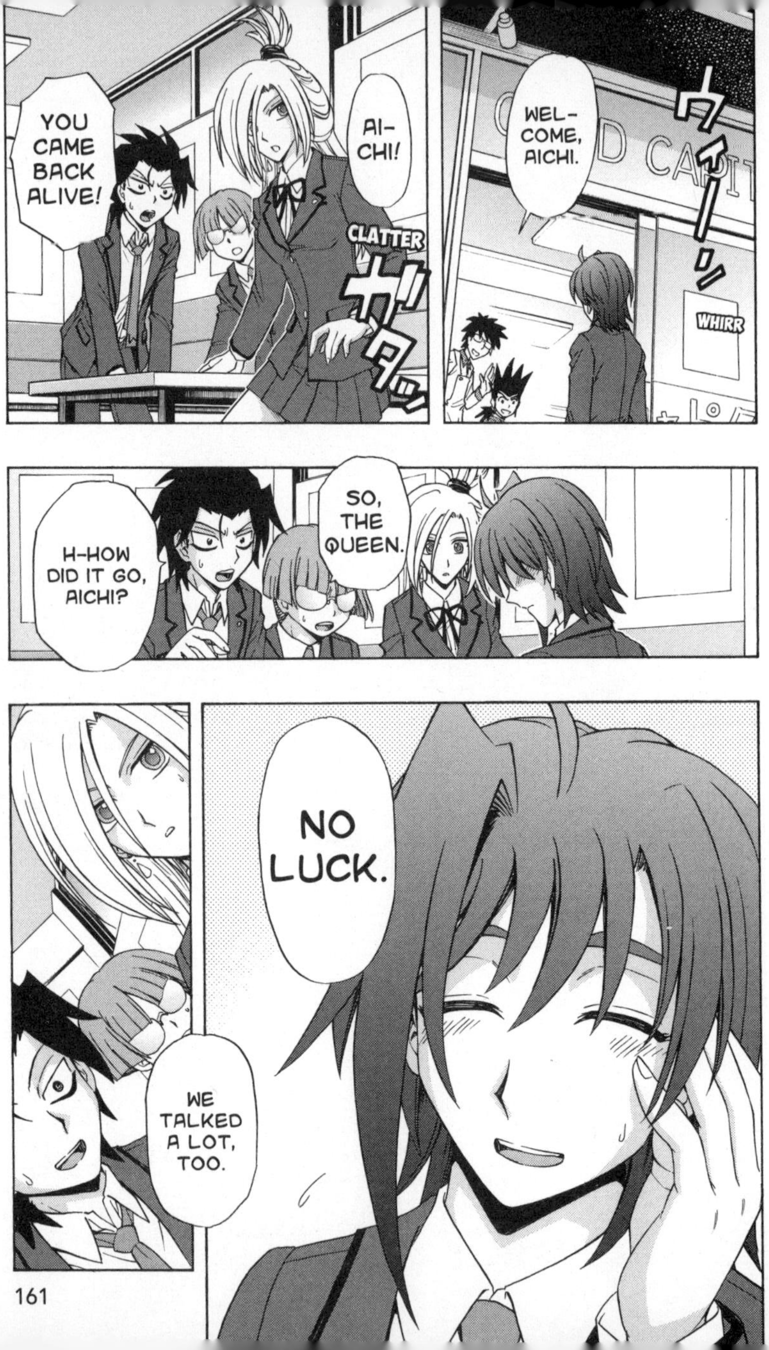
WEL-
COME,
AICHI.
ウィーン
WHIRR
AI-
CHI!
CLATTER
ガタッ
YOU
CAME
BACK
ALIVE!
SO,
THE
QUEEN.
H-HOW
DID IT GO,
AICHI?
NO
LUCK.
WE
TALKED
A LOT,
TOO.

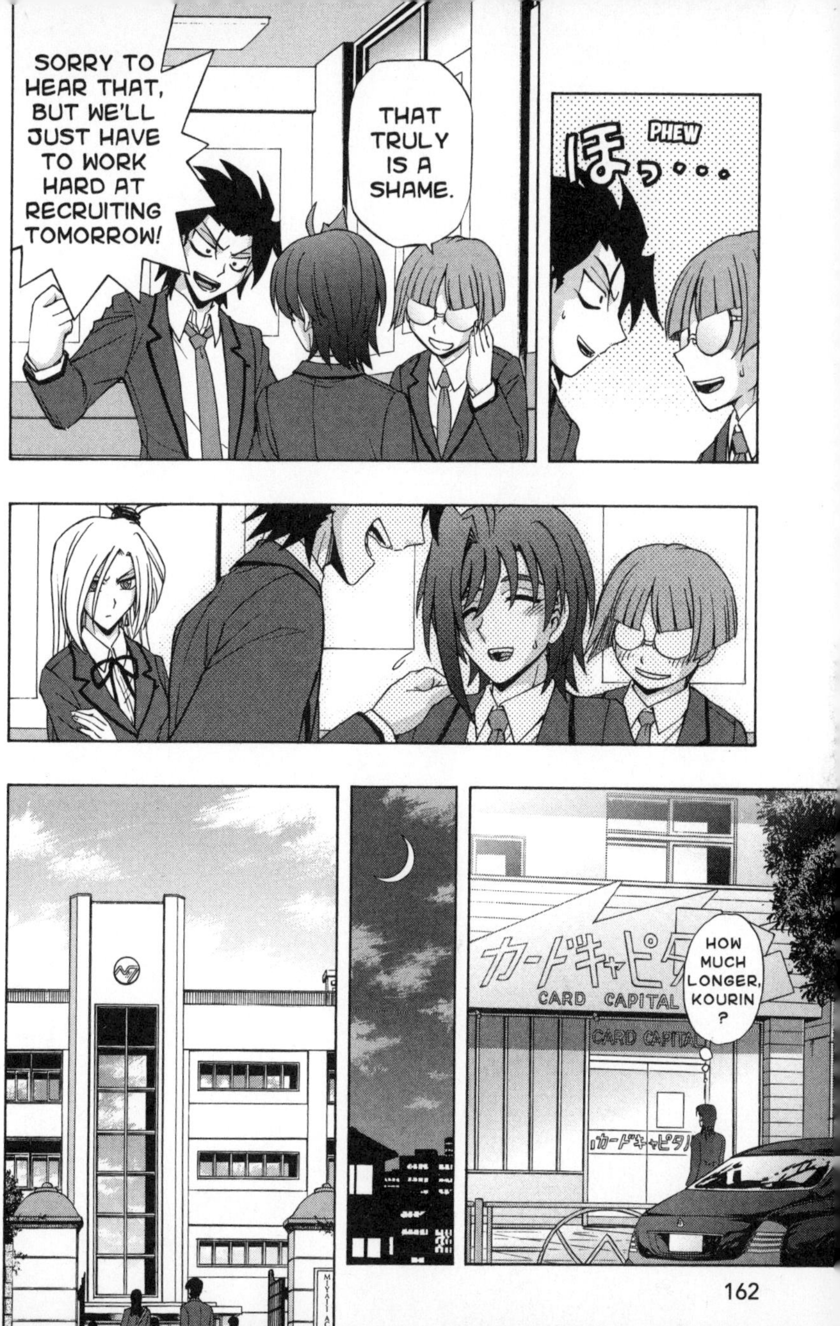
PHEW
ほっ・・・・
THAT TRULY IS A SHAME.
SORRY TO HEAR THAT, BUT WE'LL JUST HAVE TO WORK HARD AT RECRUITING TOMORROW!
CARD CAPITAL
CARD CAPITAL
HOW MUCH LONGER, KOURIN?

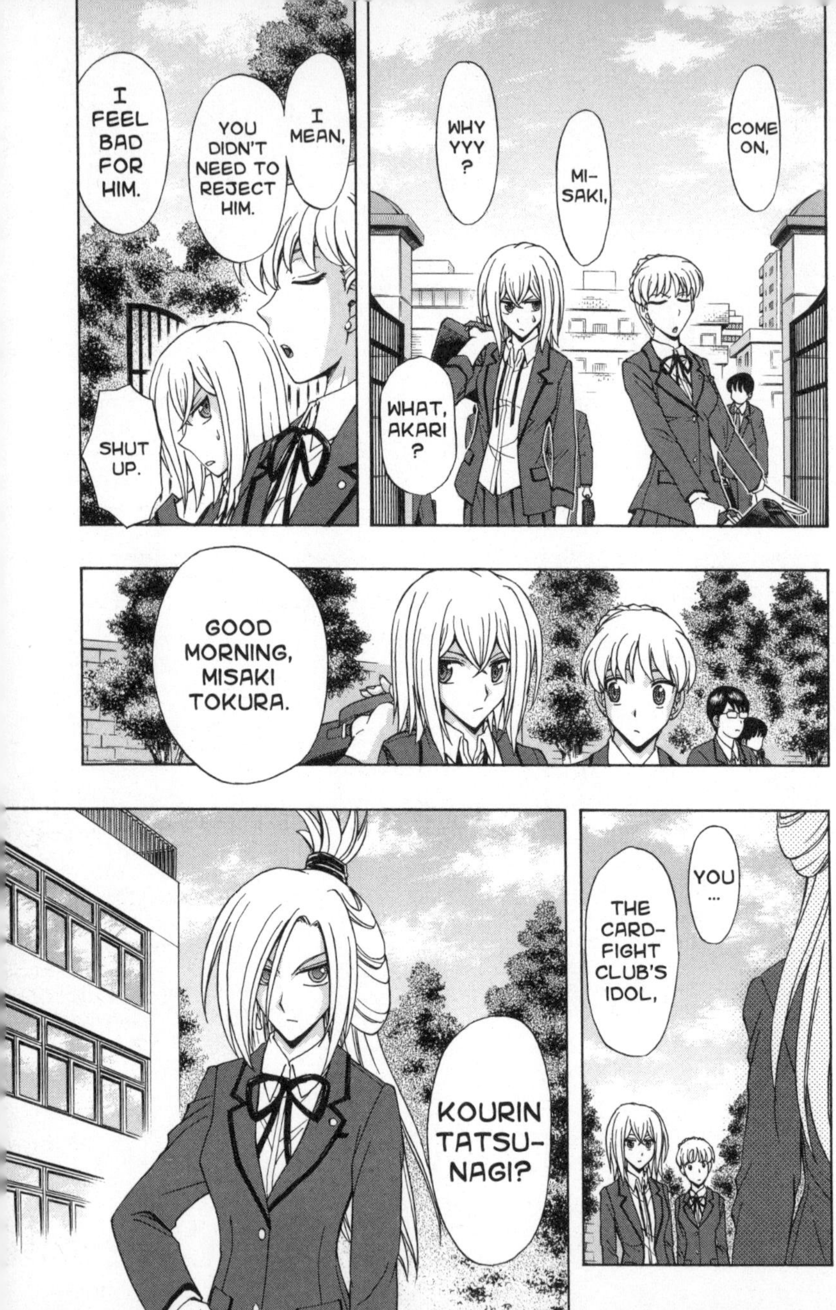
COME ON,
MI-SAKI,
WHY YYY?
WHAT, AKARI?
I MEAN,
YOU DIDN'T NEED TO REJECT HIM.
I FEEL BAD FOR HIM.
SHUT UP.
GOOD MORNING, MISAKI TOKURA.
YOU...
THE CARD-FIGHT CLUB'S IDOL,
KOURIN TATSU-NAGI?

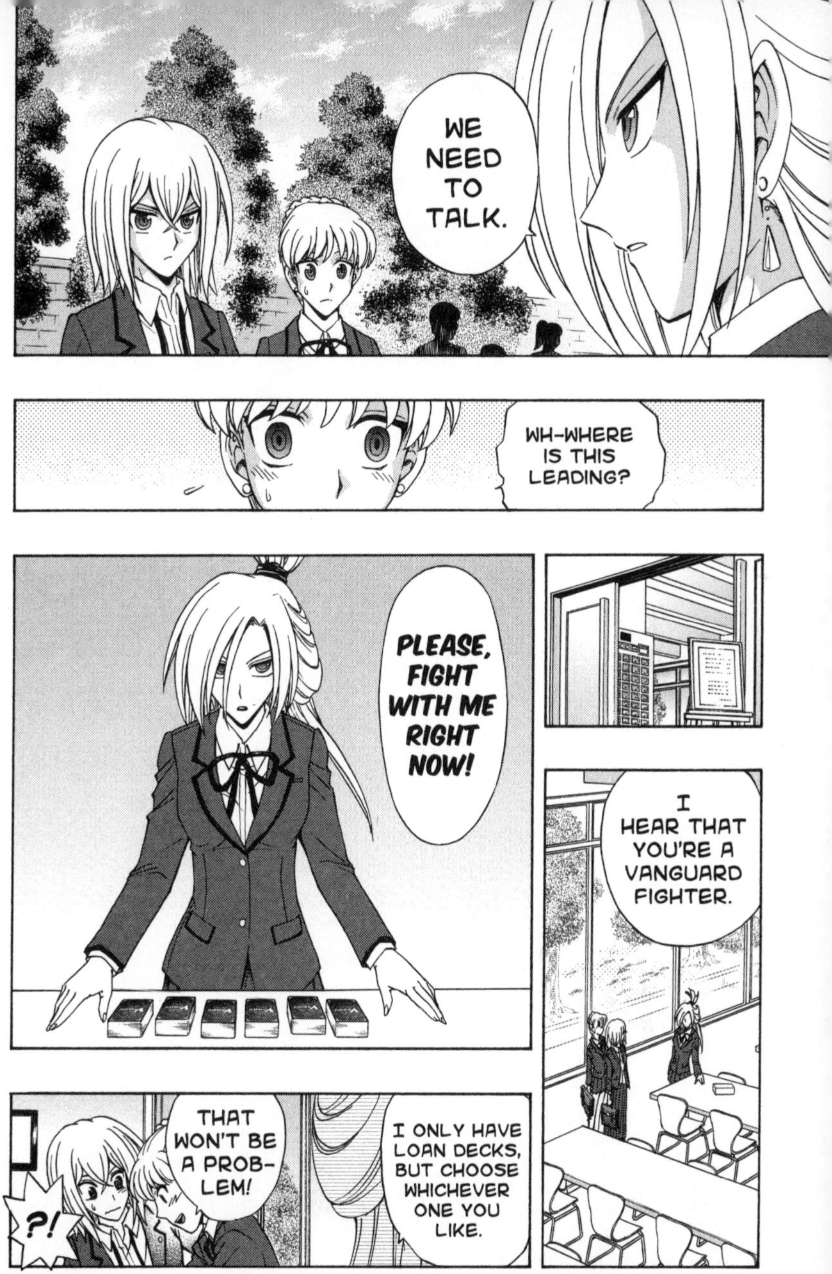
WE NEED TO TALK.
WH-WHERE IS THIS LEADING?
I HEAR THAT YOU'RE A VANGUARD FIGHTER.
PLEASE, FIGHT WITH ME RIGHT NOW!
I ONLY HAVE LOAN DECKS, BUT CHOOSE WHICHEVER ONE YOU LIKE.
THAT WON'T BE A PROB-LEM!
?!

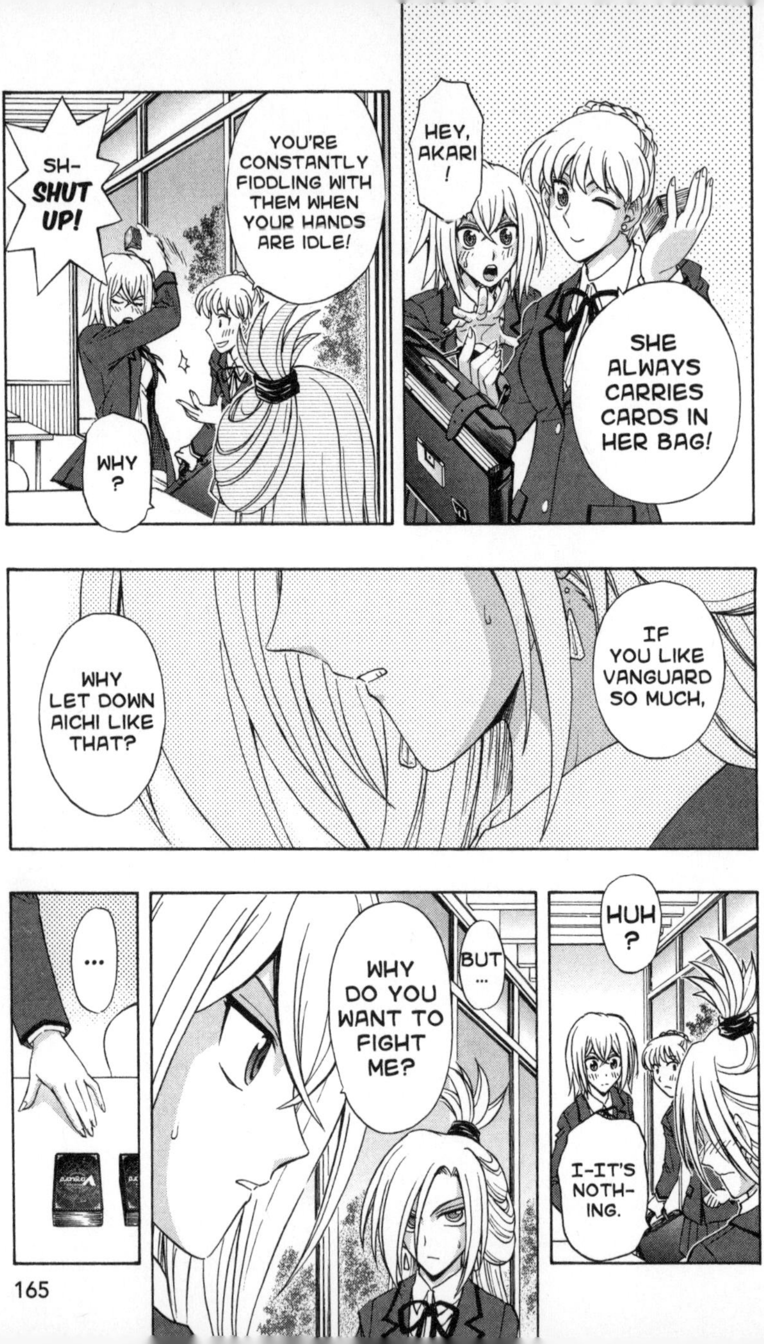
HEY, AKARI!
SHE ALWAYS CARRIES CARDS IN HER BAG!
YOU'RE CONSTANTLY FIDDLING WITH THEM WHEN YOUR HANDS ARE IDLE!
SH- SHUT UP!
WHY?
IF YOU LIKE VANGUARD SO MUCH,
WHY LET DOWN AICHI LIKE THAT?
HUH?
I-IT'S NOTHING.
BUT...
WHY DO YOU WANT TO FIGHT ME?
...

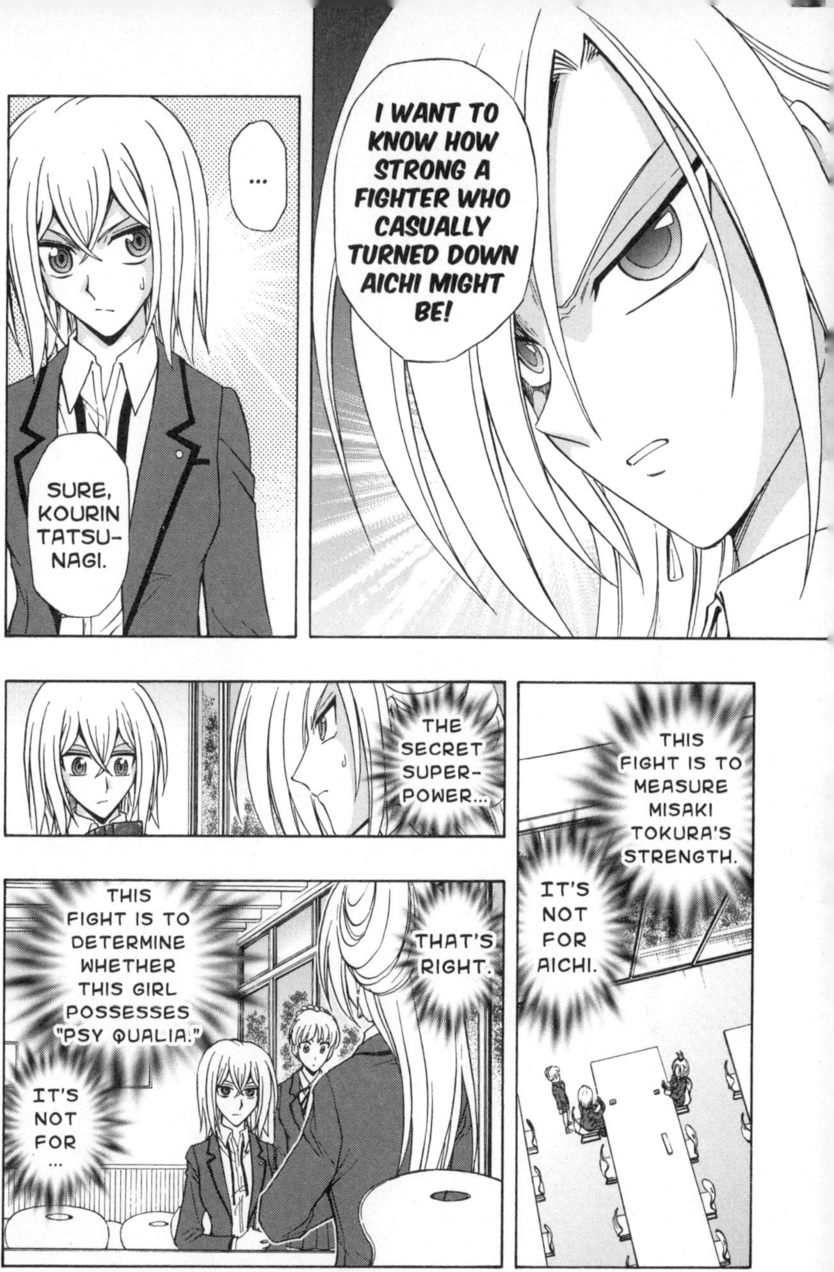
I WANT TO KNOW HOW STRONG A FIGHTER WHO CASUALLY TURNED DOWN AICHI MIGHT BE!
...
SURE, KOURIN TATSU-NAGI.
THIS FIGHT IS TO MEASURE MISAKI TOKURA'S STRENGTH.
IT'S NOT FOR AICHI.
THE SECRET SUPER-POWER...
THAT'S RIGHT.
THIS FIGHT IS TO DETERMINE WHETHER THIS GIRL POSSESSES "PSY QUALIA."
IT'S NOT FOR ...

STAND UP, THE VANGUARD!

BADUM

I GO FIRST.

I RIDE "CIRCLE MAGUS" AND END MY TURN.

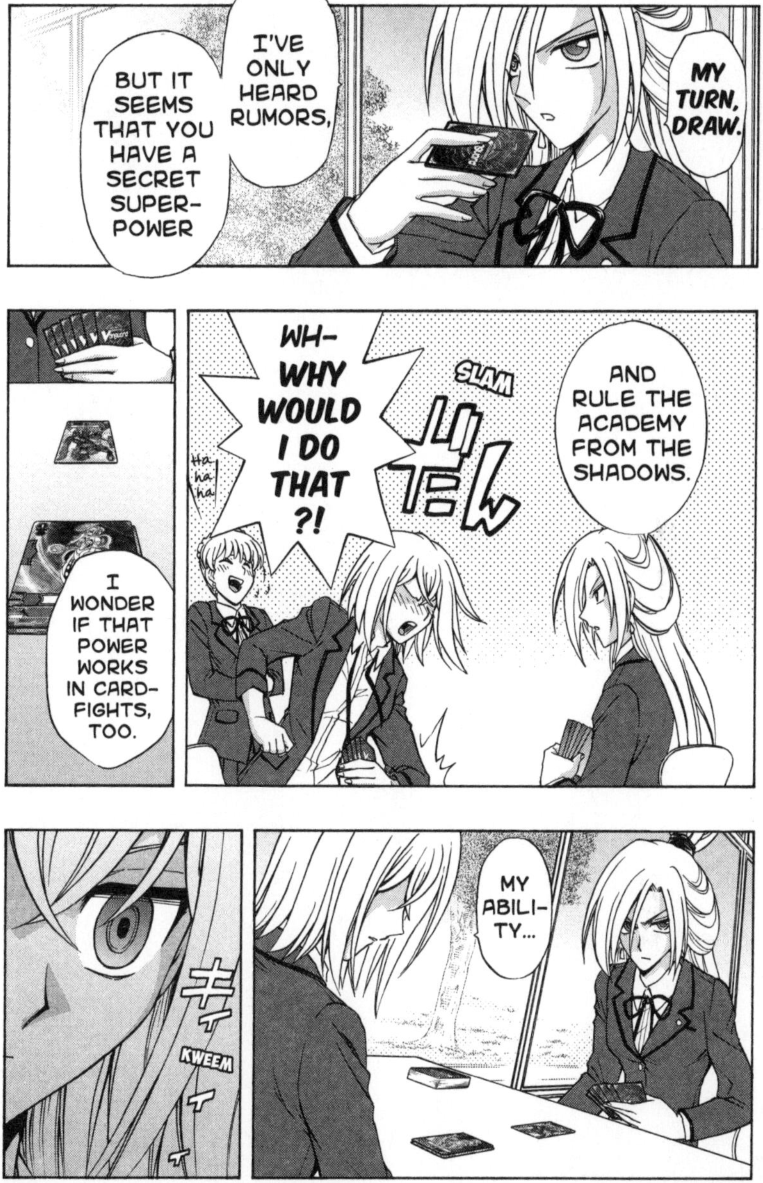
MY TURN, DRAW.
I'VE ONLY HEARD RUMORS,
BUT IT SEEMS THAT YOU HAVE A SECRET SUPER-POWER
AND RULE THE ACADEMY FROM THE SHADOWS.
SLAM
WH- WHY WOULD I DO THAT?!
Ha ha ha
I WONDER IF THAT POWER WORKS IN CARD-FIGHTS, TOO.
MY ABILI-TY...
KWEEM

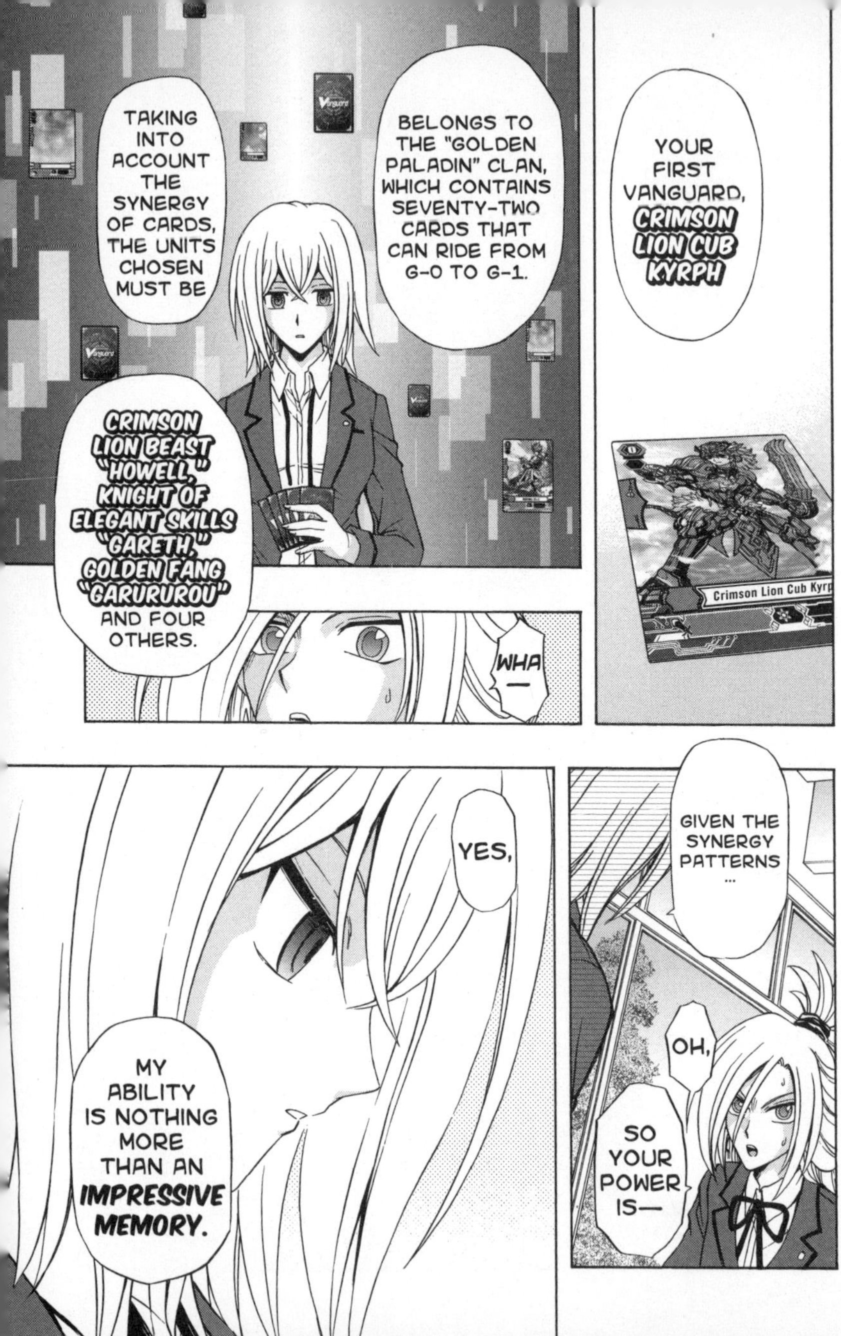
YOUR FIRST VANGUARD, CRIMSON LION CUB KYRPH
Crimson Lion Cub Kyrp
BELONGS TO THE "GOLDEN PALADIN" CLAN, WHICH CONTAINS SEVENTY-TWO CARDS THAT CAN RIDE FROM G-0 TO G-1.
TAKING INTO ACCOUNT THE SYNERGY OF CARDS, THE UNITS CHOSEN MUST BE
CRIMSON LION BEAST "HOWELL," KNIGHT OF ELEGANT SKILLS "GARETH," GOLDEN FANG "GARURUROU" AND FOUR OTHERS.
WHA—
GIVEN THE SYNERGY PATTERNS ...
OH,
SO YOUR POWER IS—
YES,
MY ABILITY IS NOTHING MORE THAN AN IMPRESSIVE MEMORY.

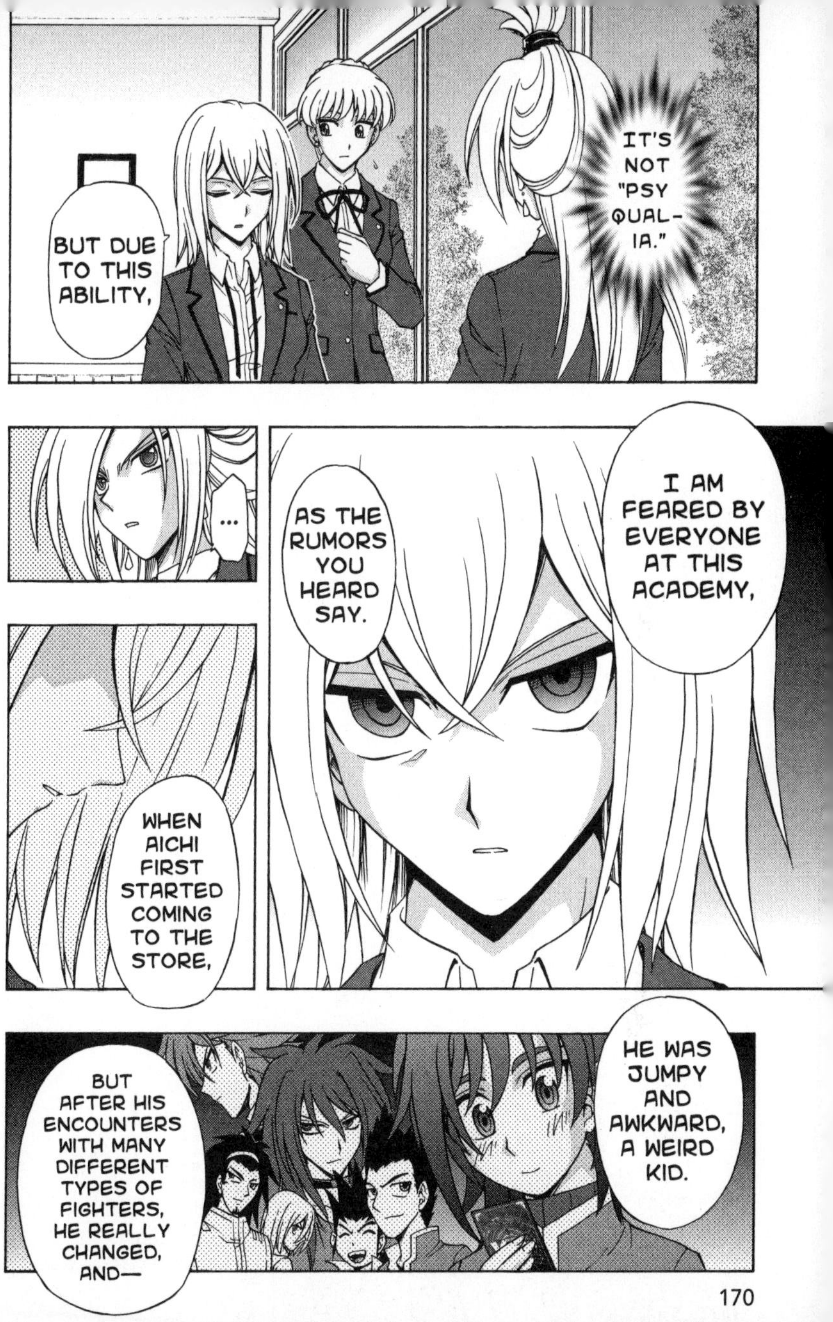
IT'S NOT "PSY QUALIA."
BUT DUE TO THIS ABILITY,
I AM FEARED BY EVERYONE AT THIS ACADEMY,
AS THE RUMORS YOU HEARD SAY.
...
WHEN AICHI FIRST STARTED COMING TO THE STORE,
HE WAS JUMPY AND AWKWARD, A WEIRD KID.
BUT AFTER HIS ENCOUNTERS WITH MANY DIFFERENT TYPES OF FIGHTERS, HE REALLY CHANGED, AND—

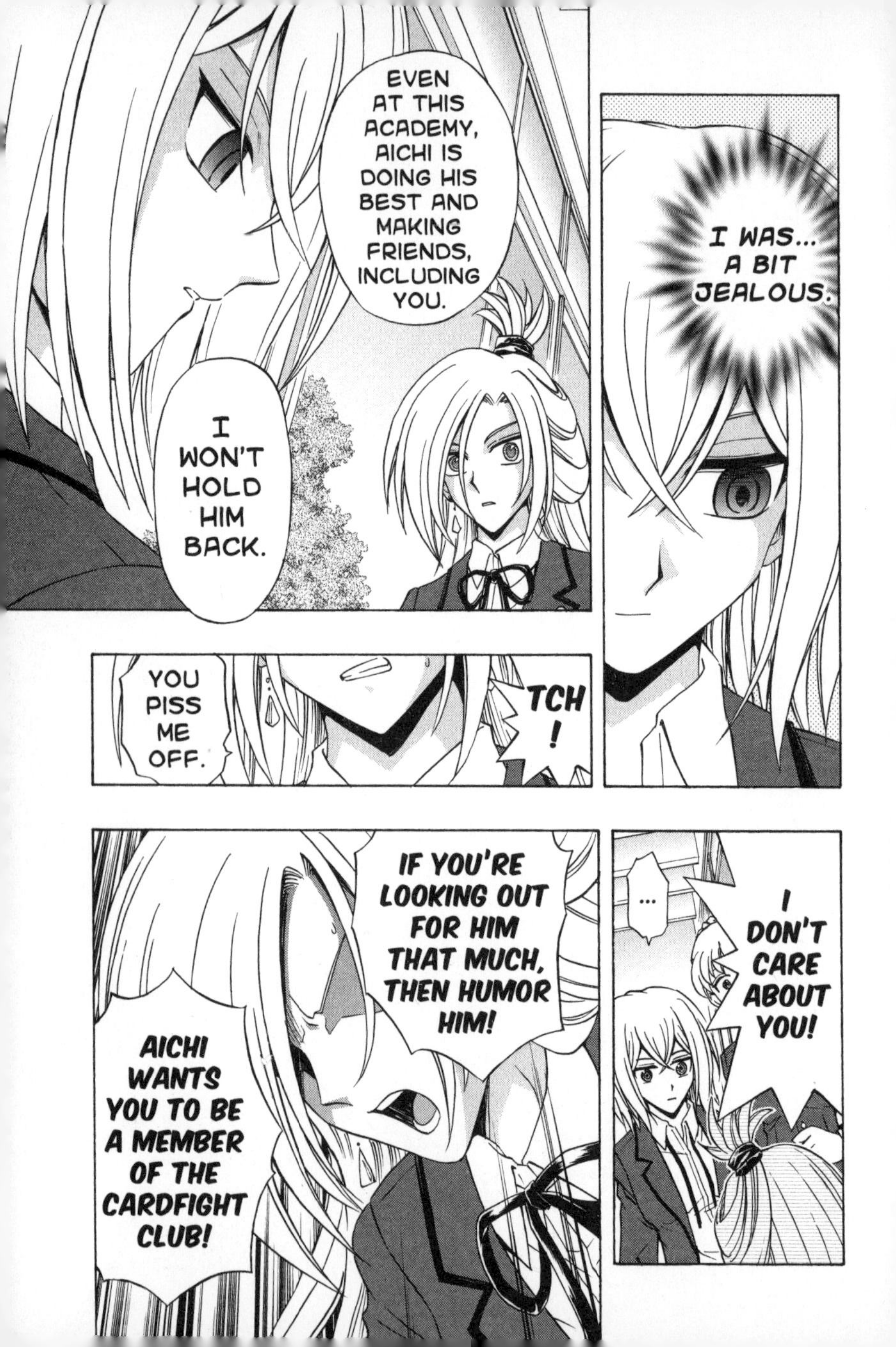
I WAS... A BIT JEALOUS.
EVEN AT THIS ACADEMY, AICHI IS DOING HIS BEST AND MAKING FRIENDS, INCLUDING YOU.
I WON'T HOLD HIM BACK.
TCH!
YOU PISS ME OFF.
...
I DON'T CARE ABOUT YOU!
IF YOU'RE LOOKING OUT FOR HIM THAT MUCH, THEN HUMOR HIM!
AICHI WANTS YOU TO BE A MEMBER OF THE CARDFIGHT CLUB!

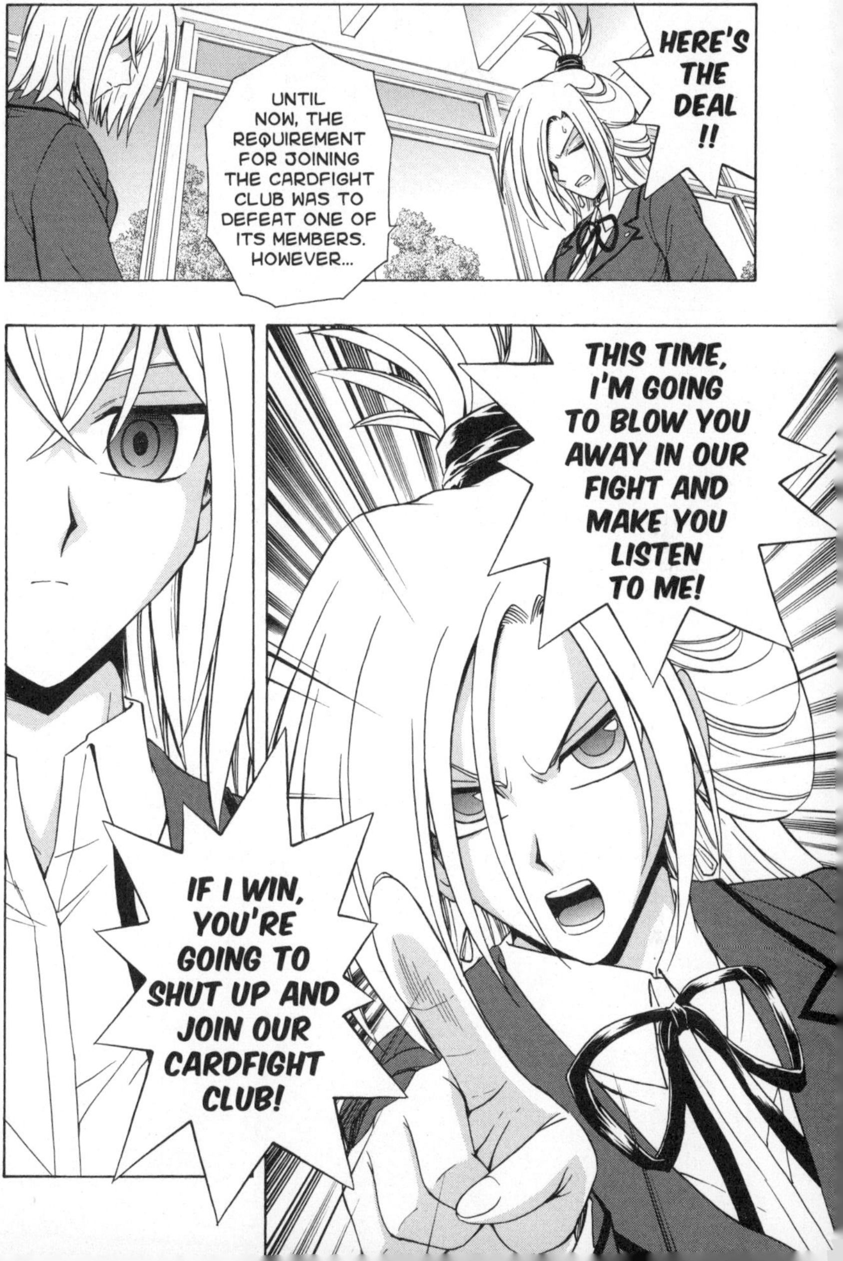
HERE'S THE DEAL !!
UNTIL NOW, THE REQUIREMENT FOR JOINING THE CARDFIGHT CLUB WAS TO DEFEAT ONE OF ITS MEMBERS. HOWEVER...
THIS TIME, I'M GOING TO BLOW YOU AWAY IN OUR FIGHT AND MAKE YOU LISTEN TO ME!
IF I WIN, YOU'RE GOING TO SHUT UP AND JOIN OUR CARDFIGHT CLUB!

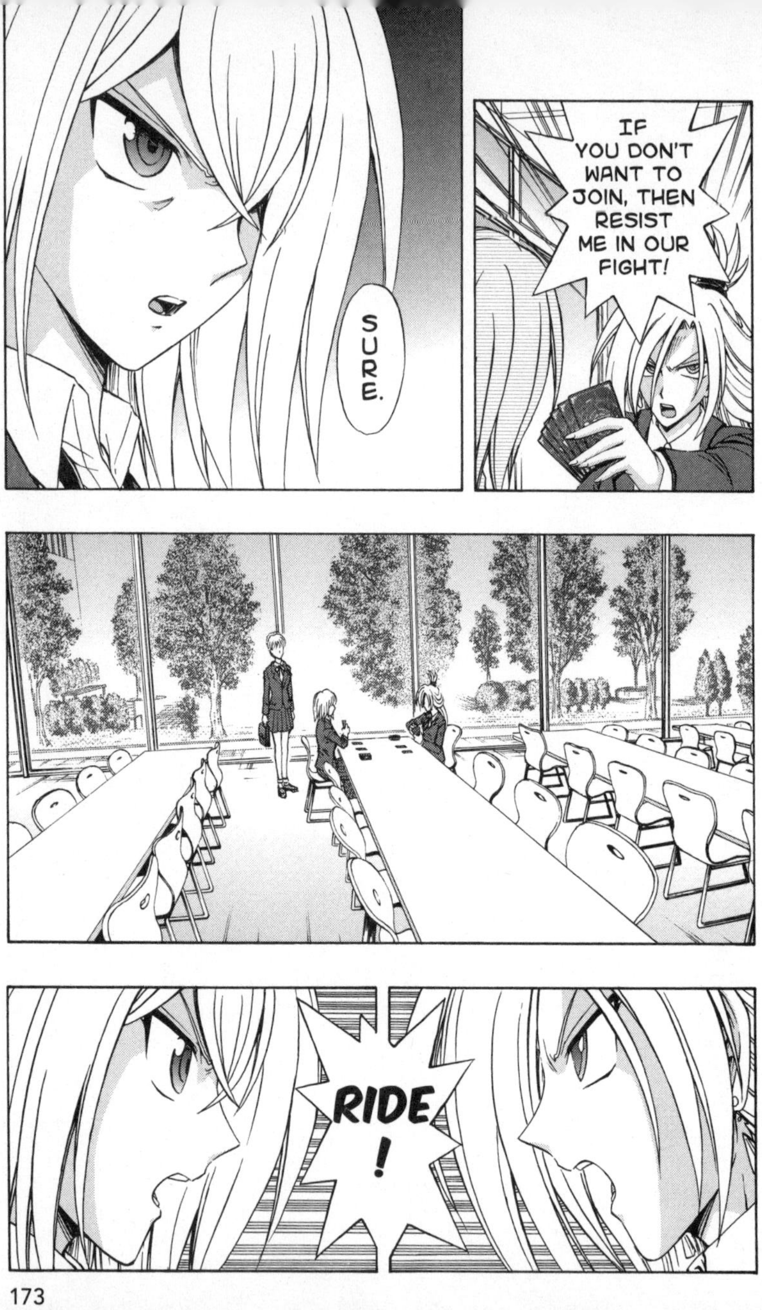
IF YOU DON'T WANT TO JOIN, THEN RESIST ME IN OUR FIGHT!
SURE.
RIDE!

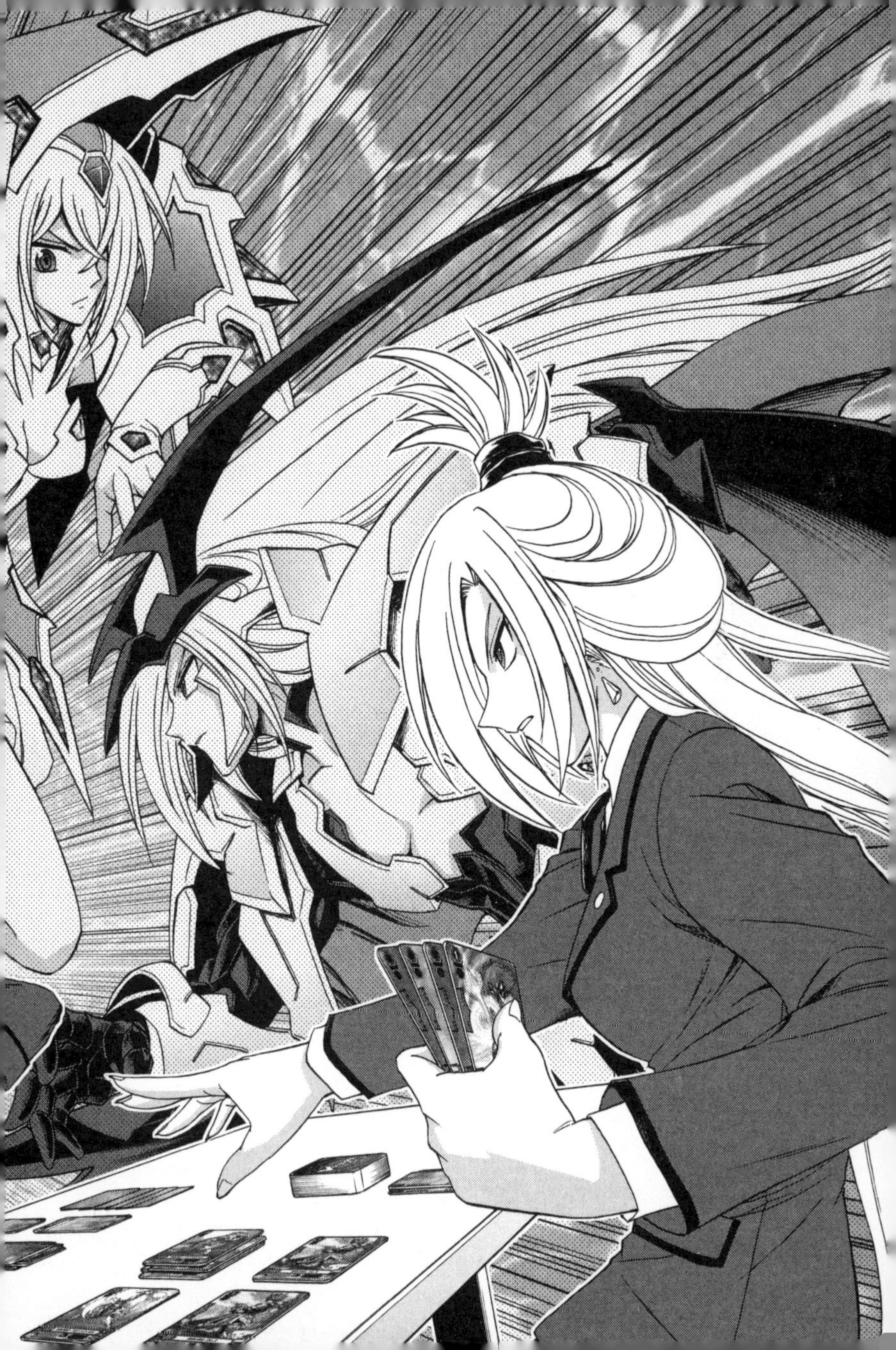

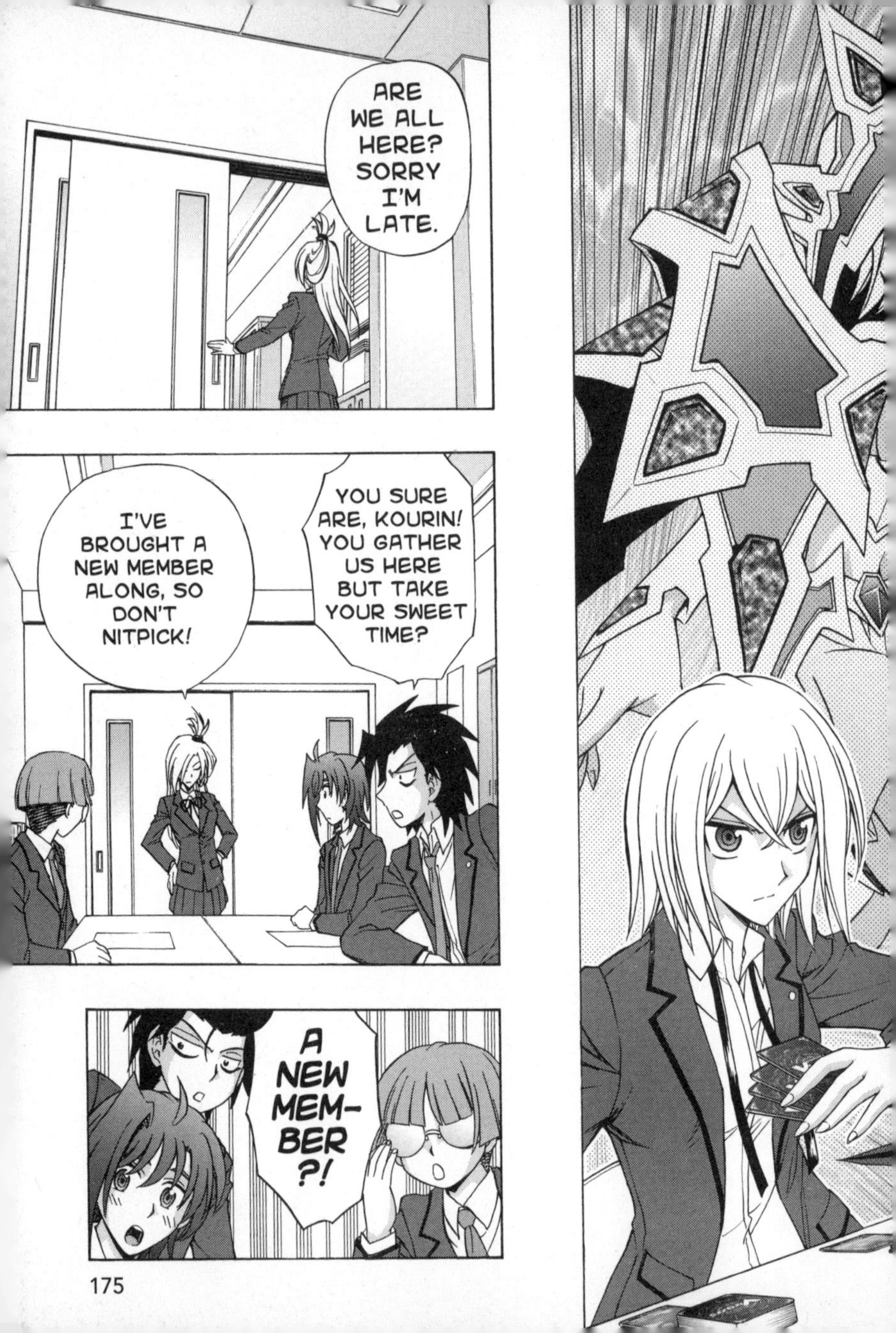
ARE WE ALL HERE? SORRY I'M LATE.
YOU SURE ARE, KOURIN! YOU GATHER US HERE BUT TAKE YOUR SWEET TIME?
I'VE BROUGHT A NEW MEMBER ALONG, SO DON'T NITPICK!
A NEW MEM-BER?!

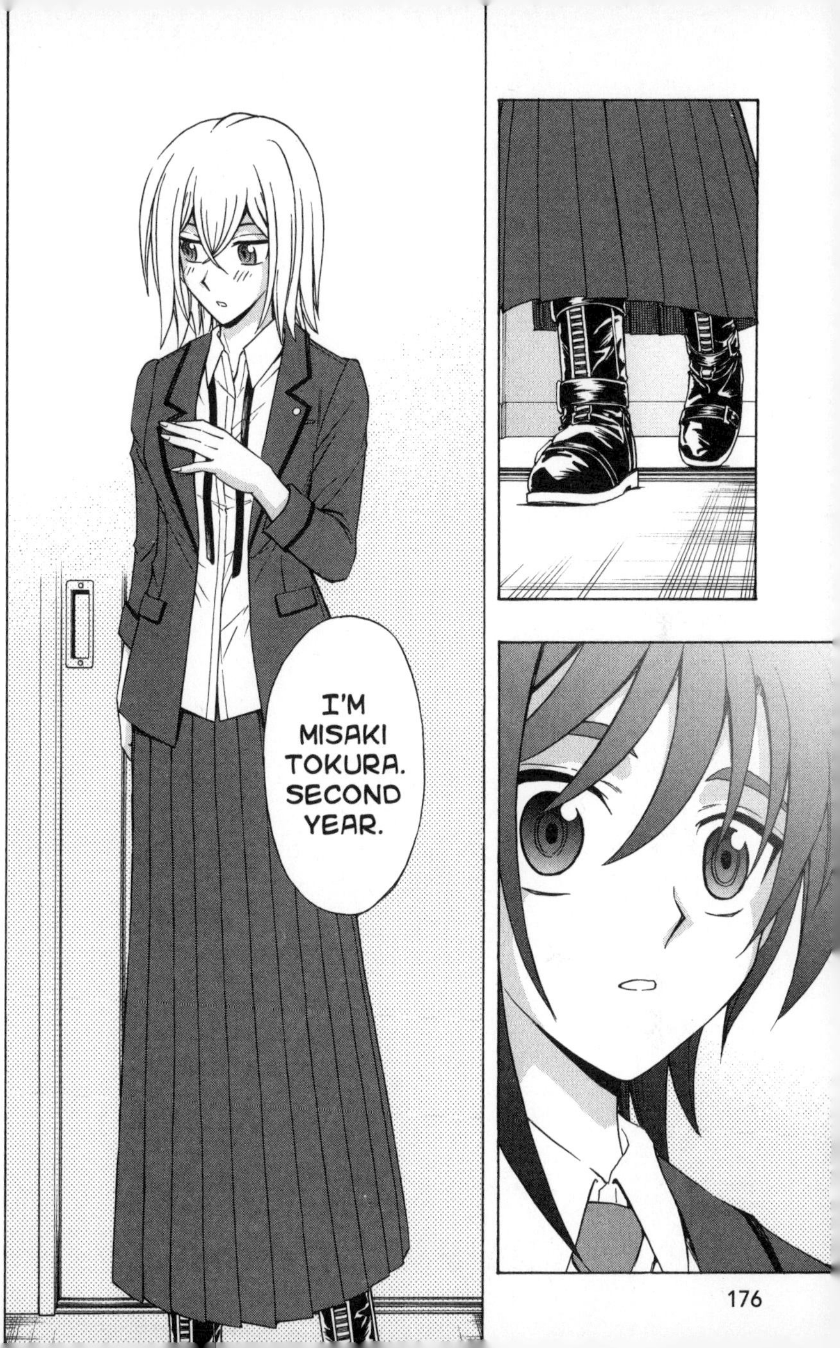
I'M MISAKI TOKURA. SECOND YEAR.

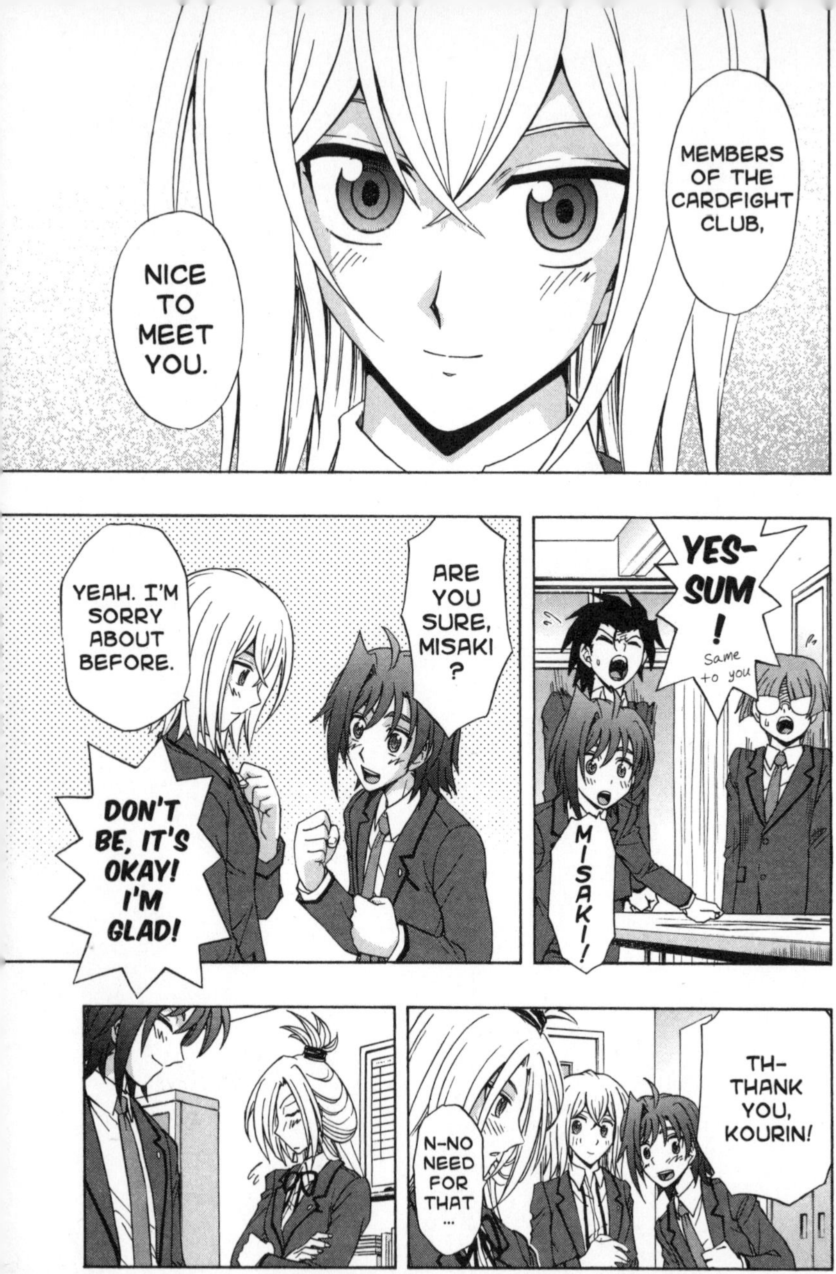
MEMBERS OF THE CARDFIGHT CLUB,
NICE TO MEET YOU.
YES-SUM!
Same to you
MISAKI!
ARE YOU SURE, MISAKI?
YEAH. I'M SORRY ABOUT BEFORE.
DON'T BE, IT'S OKAY! I'M GLAD!
TH-THANK YOU, KOURIN!
N-NO NEED FOR THAT...

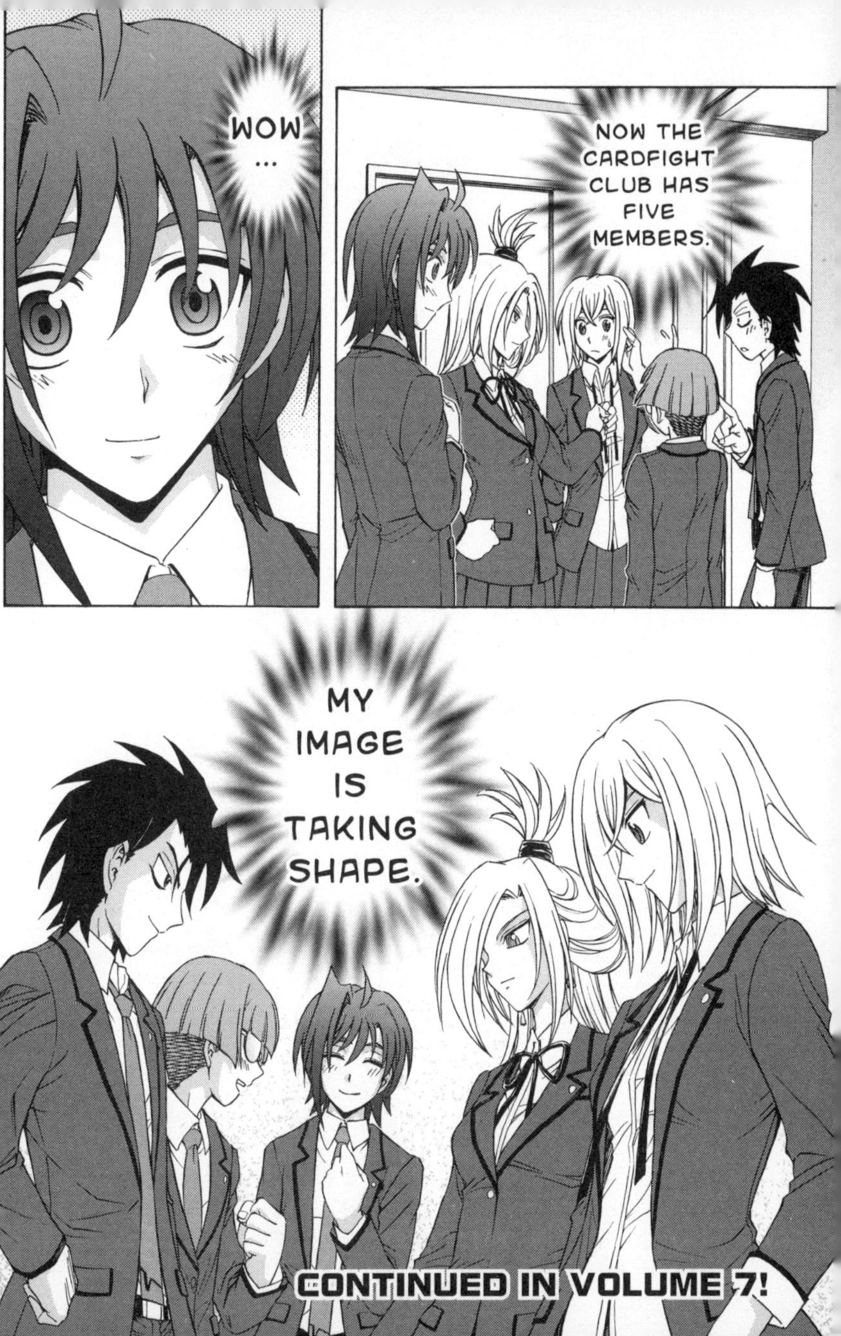
NOW THE CARDFIGHT CLUB HAS FIVE MEMBERS.
WOW ...
MY IMAGE IS TAKING SHAPE.
CONTINUED IN VOLUME 7!

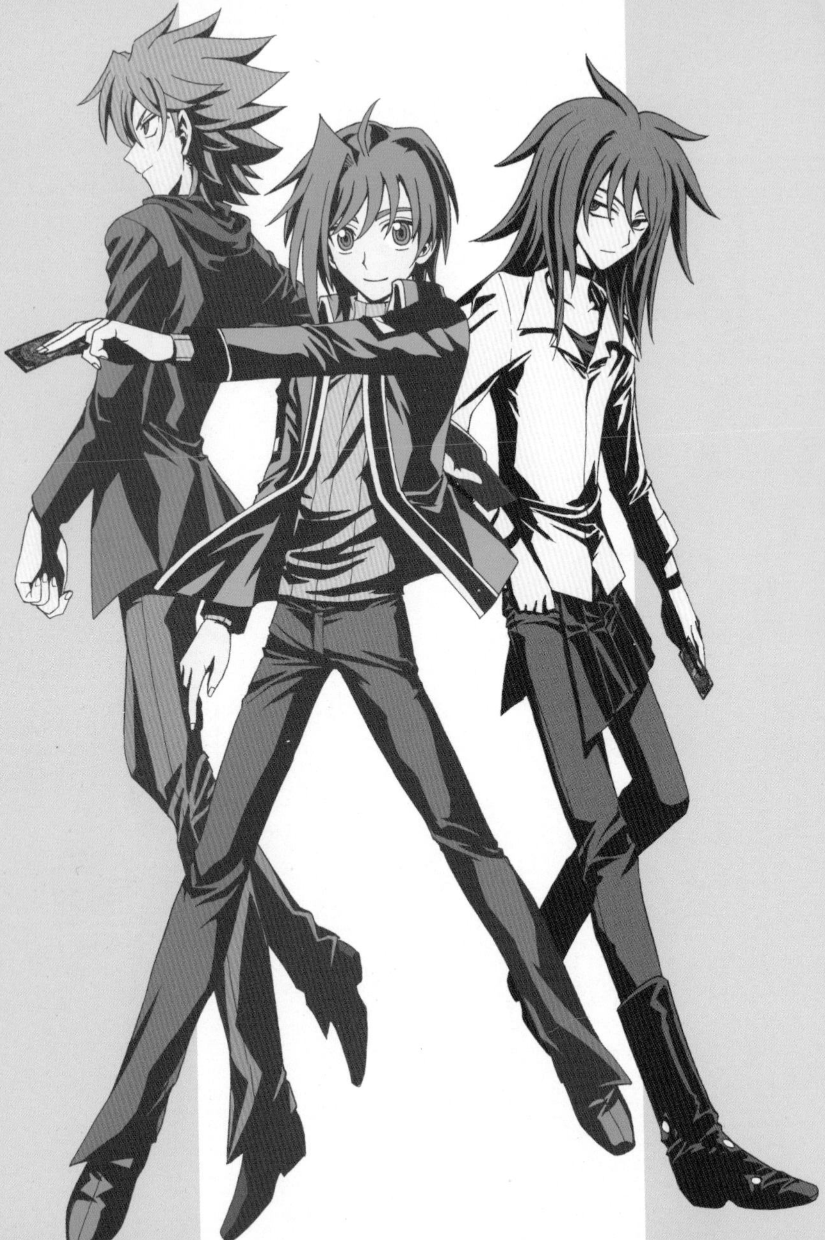

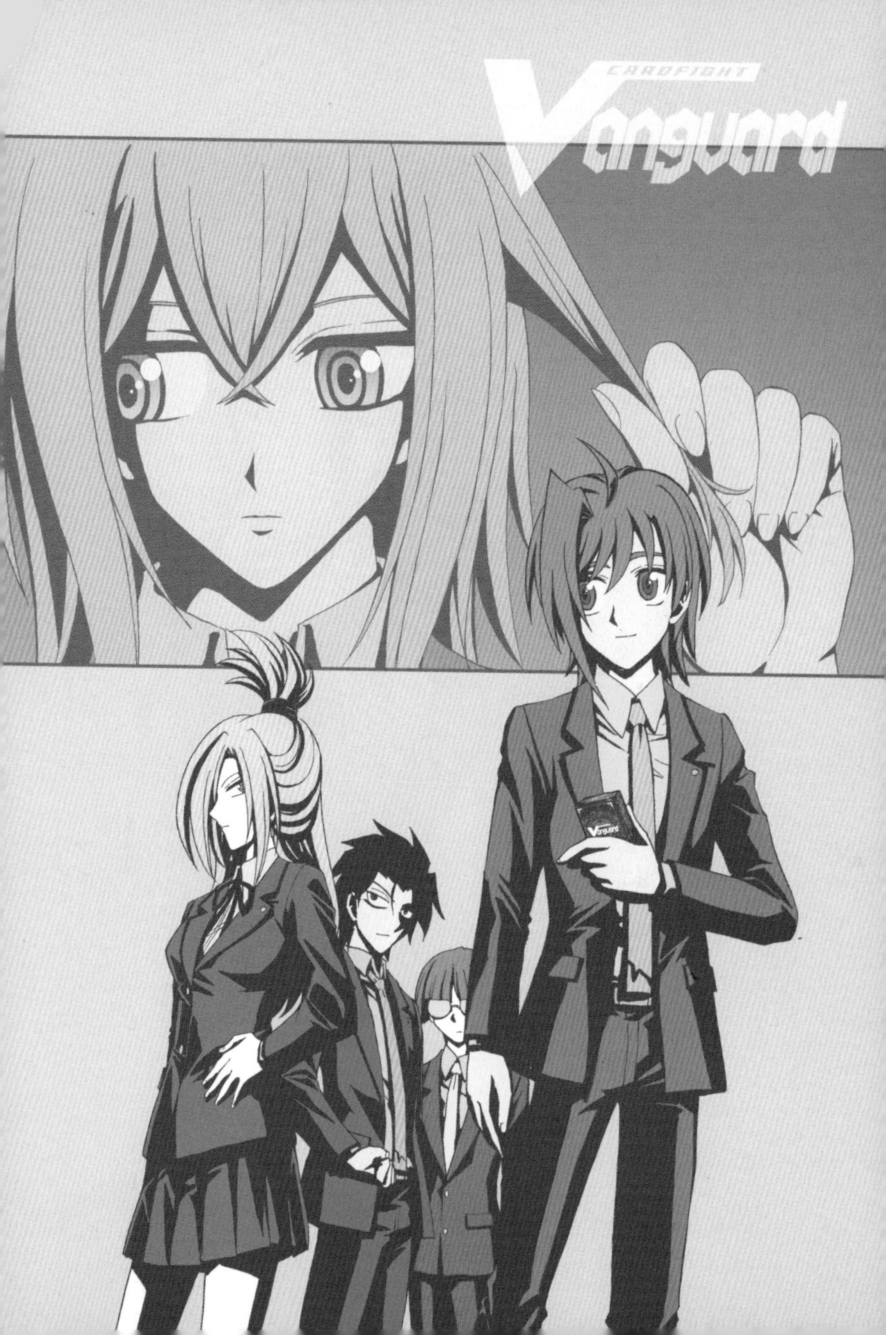
CARDFIGHT
Vanguard

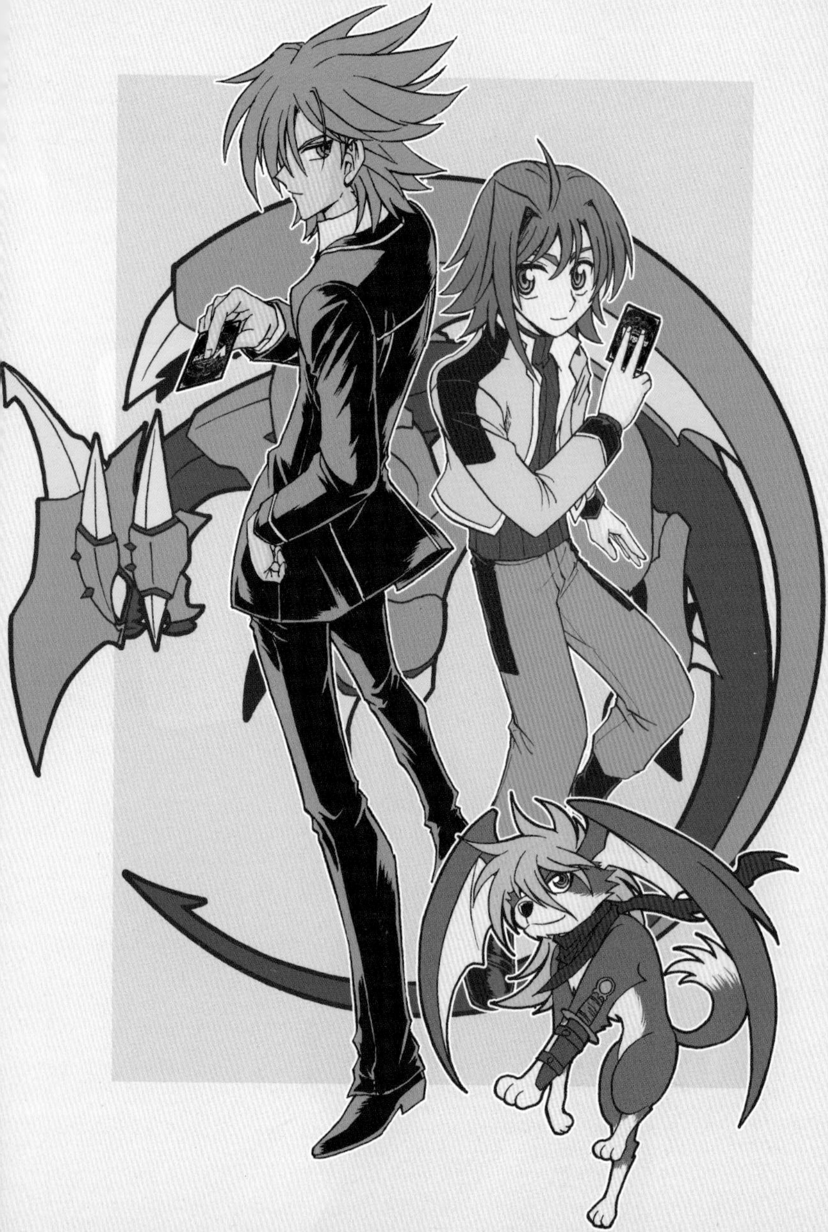

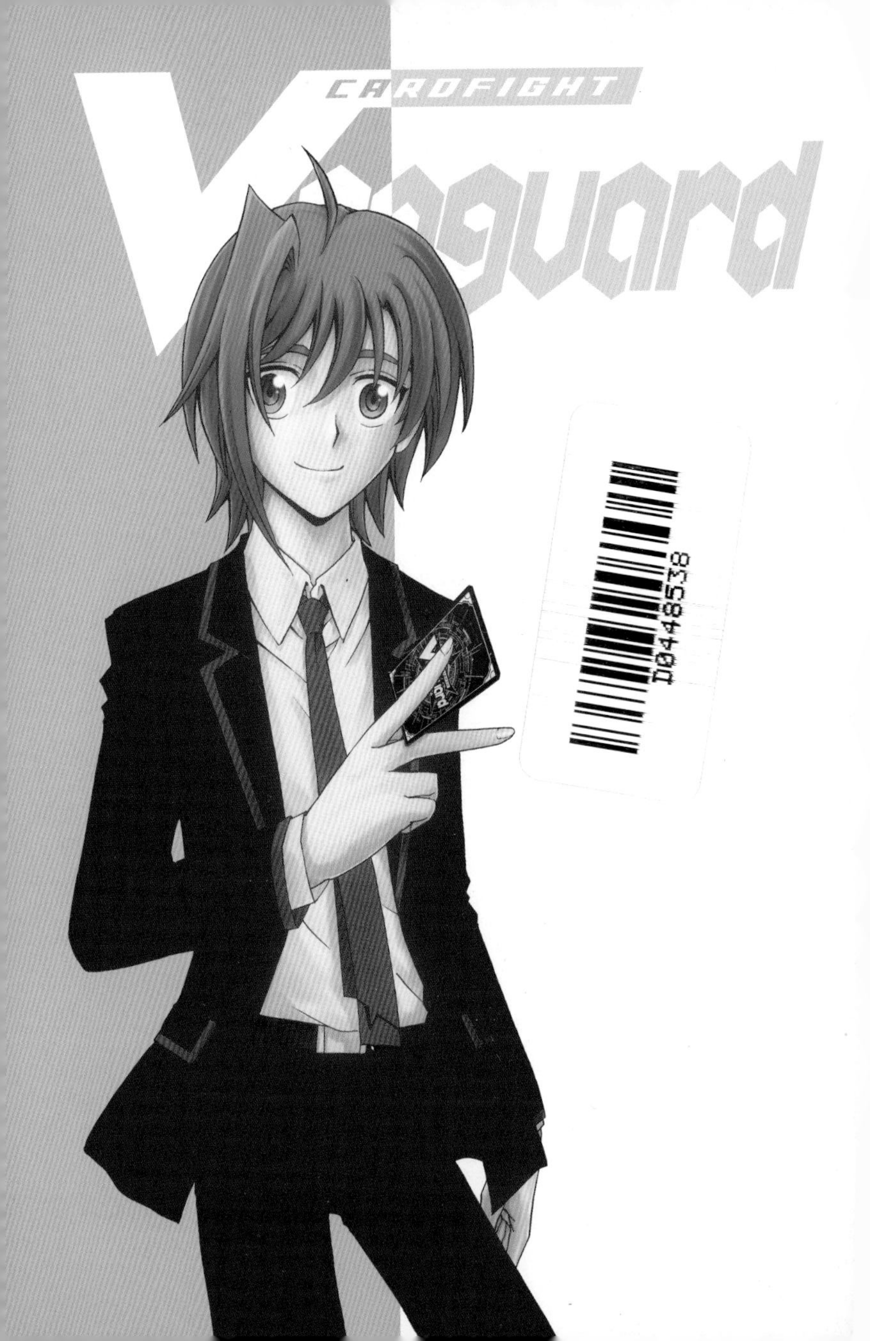
CARDFIGHT